Thank You, St. Jude

This is to certify that

_____

is a Subscriber to The Voice of St. Jude
and Participates in the Masses, Prayers and
good works offered for Subscribers.

Joachin De Rada C.M.F.

CLARETIAN MISSIONARY FATHERS

ROBERT A. ORSI

Thank You, St. Jude

WOMEN'S DEVOTION TO THE PATRON SAINT OF HOPELESS CAUSES

Yale University Press / New Haven & London

Frontispiece: certificate of subscription to the *Voice of St. Jude*, ca. 1945.

Some of the material in Chapter 6 appeared in a substantially different form in " 'Mildred, Is It Fun To Be a Cripple?': The Culture of Suffering in Mid-Twentieth-Century American Catholicism," *The South Atlantic Quarterly* 93 (1994): 547-590.

Published with assistance from the foundation established in memory of Amasa Stone Mather of the Class of 1907, Yale College.

Designed by Nancy Ovedovitz and set in Minion type by Keystone Typesetting, Inc. Printed in the United States of America by Vail-Ballou Press, Binghamton, New York.

Library of Congress Cataloging-in-Publication Data

Orsi, Robert A.
Thank you, St. Jude : women's devotion to the patron saint of hopeless causes / Robert A. Orsi.
p. cm.
Includes bibliographical references and index.
ISBN 0-300-06476-4 (cloth)
0-300-07659-2 (pbk.)
1. Jude, Saint—Cult—United States. 2. Catholic women—United States—Religious life. 3. United States—Religious life and customs. I. Title.
BT693.O77 1996
282'.092—dc20   95-26017
CIP
A catalogue record for this book is available from the British Library.

The paper in this book meets the guidelines for permanence and durability of the Committee on Production Guidelines for Book Longevity of the Council on Library Resources.

10   9   8   7   6   5

For my daughter, Claire

Contents

Preface

This is a study of the prayers that American Catholic women in circumstances they identify as "hopeless" have made to Jude Thaddeus, Saint of Hopeless Causes, since 1929, when his devotion was founded in South Chicago. It explores how Jude, who was all but completely unknown in this country at the time, came to be one of the most popular saints in the United States—the most popular in times of dire need—at first alongside, then in place of more familiar holy helpers like Saints Anthony, Bridget, or Anne. It is about the circumstances that made for "hopelessness" among the women who prayed to Jude, the daughters and granddaughters of immigrants from southern and eastern Europe and Ireland, growing up in tumultuous times for themselves and their church. Finally, it is a study of what these women did to the world—and to themselves—by praying to St. Jude.

My decision to focus on the prayers and practices of female devout and on the relationships they formed with Jude requires some introductory comment here, because men were certainly involved in the history of the National Shrine of St. Jude and practice of the devotion. The saint included among his many titles that of patron and protector of the Chicago police; each year, during the fall novena in his honor, thousands of officers in dress uniform processed around the Shrine, certainly the most visible and dramatic sign of Jude's presence in the city—and of Catholic prominence in Chicago civic life, too. The cult—a technical term for Catholic devotions to the Virgin Mary and saints, with none of the connotations of abuse, deviance, and irrationality that the word has taken on in popular usage—has always been in the care and under the authority of men, the Claretian Missionaries, and donations to the Shrine underwrite the order's seminary in Chicago and its various works around the world. Photographs of Shrine directors, visiting priests and prelates, and handsome, boyish seminarians appeared regularly in the Shrine's promotional magazine, the *Voice of St. Jude;* the boys in particular were meant to illustrate the real benefit of devotion to St. Jude: support for vocations to the priesthood. Jude is inevitably associated in many people's minds, furthermore, with the nightclub and television entertainer Danny Thomas, whose promotions of the cult in thanksgiving for the saint's timely intervention in his foundering career were a favorite topic of Catholic family magazines in the 1950s. All of the letters that go out from the Shrine, finally, in response to petitions, requests, and thanksgivings sent in by Jude's devout around the country, are signed by the Shrine director, "Father Robert," who is thus probably the most visible, widely known representative of the devotion.

But Father Robert doesn't exist. The name was made up a few years ago to establish continuity in the public's experience and perception of the devotion amid frequent behind-the-scenes changes in clerical personnel. Letters to the Shrine are actually handled by a small staff of women working together in a downtown office, under the watchful and somewhat mournful gaze of an enormous statue of St. Jude.[1]

I was given a tour of the Shrine's postal operations by Bea,[2] who has been answering the saint's mail for forty years. Bea says she replies to correspondents' queries or problems by consulting either a small library of Catholic reference books near her desk or her own life experience; only the most complicated problems get referred to the Shrine director. The postman calls Bea "Ann Landers," a reference to the newspaper advice columnist, and she herself says, "Sometimes I feel like I should be called Reverend Bea." But not even Bea's longtime correspondents—her pets, as she calls them—know that they are being counseled and comforted by a woman. When one phones asking for Father Robert, Bea tells the caller that the priest is out of the office and answers the query herself.

This gendered discrepancy between "front and back regions," as social theorist Anthony Giddens has called culture's necessary structuring of the world, is generally characteristic of devotion to St. Jude, and of most Catholic popular piety.[3] Just as behind the public front of Father Robert are women working for the saint, so it has been women's support, love, and loyalty—again behind the onstage prominence of male celebrities, marching policemen, and clerical authorities—that has sustained and spread devotion to St. Jude over the years. Bea told me that most letters—and most donations, including the really big ones—come from women, and her estimate was seconded by her co-workers in the mail room.

Women have special roles in the practice of the devotion. They express what is needed from the saint, even when the object of their prayers is someone else. They undertake the necessary negotiations with Jude, making and keeping the bargains that bind heaven and earth together, quite often bartering their own pain and distress for someone else's happy ending. They especially assumed the duty of praying for men, whereas there are very few instances in the published correspondence of the Shrine of a man praying to Jude on behalf of a woman. Mothers, wives, sisters, daughters, and girlfriends establish the bond with Jude in bad times for themselves and others, and then they work to maintain this association with the powerful saint over the years, making sure that he is appropriately thanked for his ongoing help. Some women were so identified with Jude—indeed, understood by family and friends to be so intimately related to him—that they were regularly called on to serve as go-betweens, intercessors to the intercessor, and some of them expected to be personally thanked if Jude answered their prayers for others.

Men acknowledged and relied on women's distinct devotional capacities—or, depending on how one interprets Catholic popular piety, exploited their culturally mandated devotional responsibilities. One man described his ex-wife as a "better pray-er" than he and admitted that it was only after they divorced that he began calling on St. Jude for himself. Jude's male devout usually identify the saint with a specific woman in their lives, referring to him as "my mother's saint," for example, or pointing out that they were communicating with the Shrine at the insistence of their wives or mothers. As one man told me, "My mother gave me the material about St. Jude. She had quite a strong devotion to him, and I picked up some literature at her house on

Ashland Avenue [in Chicago]. . . . My mother lived on Ashland Avenue for forty-five years. She called on St. Jude whenever she had a problem, and I have followed in her footsteps."[4]

Women enjoyed more vivid and compelling relationships with Jude. There is a real difference in affective tone between men's and women's descriptions of their encounters with Jude, according to the evidence of the few men I spoke with and of the handful of letters published over the years at the Shrine that are clearly from men. The saint's male devout approach him more formally, seemingly content to use the Shrine's written prayers in their petitions, and they do not imagine Jude with the passionate detail that women devout do. American Catholic men have characteristically participated in such organizations as the Holy Name and St. Vincent de Paul societies, which were akin in spirit to fraternal orders, combining social service, male camaraderie, and religious devotions, and offering ambitious men the opportunity to make useful connections in the local neighborhoods. This was the ethos, too, of the St. Jude's Police League, which was primarily dedicated to raising funds for the Claretian seminary in Momence, Illinois.

Bea told me that the letters women write to the Shrine are about evenly divided between matters of health and love. When correspondents seek advice about Catholic teachings on divorce, a painfully vexed issued in a community that does not permit remarriage, or what to do with abusive spouses, Bea's sympathies are clear: "I want to say, 'Why don't you just leave him!'" She advises the women to get assistance and to keep praying to Jude, although she is careful never to say "St. Jude *will* help you" because "we never know what the Lord will do" (and perhaps because she wants the women to help themselves, too). God sometimes answers our prayers in unexpected ways, Bea says, but she always reassures Jude's female clients that the Shrine will keep on praying with them. Bea's identification of the two main areas of primary concern to Jude's female devout holds as well for the thousands of pieces of correspondence published since 1935 in the Shrine's magazines, the *Voice of St. Jude* and its successor, *St. Jude's Journal,* as does her estimate of the predominance of women among the cult's letter writers. The gender of about 1,700 correspondents published in the *Voice of St. Jude* could be determined (out of some 2,500 letters printed overall), and of these all but about fifty were women.[5]

Women predominated in my fieldwork, too, although I never indicated that I was working on a study of women's devotions—at the time I was doing fieldwork this had not yet become my focus. Only a few men ever contacted me. Priests embarrassed by the overrepresentation of women in their churches or at the devotions they sponsored in the 1940s and 1950s argued that women had more time on their hands, which made it *seem* as if they were more devout than men. But all of the women I spoke with had full-time work, so this explanation for their prominence among my sources is inadequate (and it fails to account for their presence in church, too). Likewise, no one ever told me a story at the Shrine or elsewhere about a policeman calling on St. Jude, though I did hear about a policewoman's prayers, from her mother.

Given all of this evidence, historical and contemporary, not only of women's numerical predominance in the practice of this devotion but of their special place and roles in it and their centrality to the cult's narrative practices, it would have been odd—indeed, methodologically perverse—for me to have continued thinking of this devotion as I had at the very beginning, without reference to gender or to women's history and experience. I will leave it to others to discover that beneath the already obscured level of women's devotional practice is another even more deeply buried world of men's intimate engagement with Jude—not a few men, but many. I could see no sign of this, however, and this is not my subject.

I base my understanding of the devotion on three levels of primary sources. The first is the correspondence published in the *Voice of St. Jude* between 1935 and 1958 and in *St. Jude's Journal* after 1963; this was the foundation and touchstone of my research. I put copies of each letter (or letter fragment) on separate filing cards and then extensively cross-referenced them by subject. Published letters are identified in the notes just as they are in the Shrine's periodicals: by the correspondent's initials (occasionally by name), location, and the date the letter appeared.

Clearly there are problems with this source. The published letters were culled from hundreds of thousands of pieces of correspondence received at the Shrine annually and were then further edited by the staff of the magazines. This process of selection makes it extremely unlikely that really hateful letters would be published, for example, or that requests for favors disapproved by the church—for a successful divorce and remarriage, say—would appear, and none do. But beyond these obvious cases, the Shrine had little reason to censor the texts and sufficient respect for the devout to treat them carefully. Studied in the aggregate, the letters are revealing enough: anger and disappointment with Jude finds expression; deeply felt needs are voiced; the full range of devotional practices are described (including some that would be eventually discouraged by the Shrine); and the many ways in which women thought of Jude are apparent.

I supplemented the published correspondence with other sources. I distributed a very general list of questions to devout attending novenas at the Shrine in 1987 and 1988, asking them to describe their devotion to Jude—when they first heard of him, what sorts of petitions they have addressed to him over the years, what they imagine he looks like (if they do), and so on. This was not a questionnaire, a research methodology I am neither trained to do nor interested in, but simply a way of initiating conversations about Jude. I invited the devout either to write their responses out on the document itself or to get in touch with me while I was still at the Shrine or by phone or letter after I returned home. About seventy women (and five men) chose to write on the document, most of them at considerable length. These are identified in the notes by the prefix *Per.comm.* (personal communication) and by the initials of the devout (fictitious, but consistent throughout), gender, age, place of residence, and marital status.[6]

I also had conversations of varying length with thirty-five women, at the Shrine in 1987 and 1988, on other visits to Chicago afterward, or by telephone. These women appear in the text under pseudonyms, as I promised them, and I have changed some details of their stories to make them further anonymous.

Jude's is a national devotion, and in order to reach at least some of his far-flung devout, I established a toll-free 800 telephone number that the Shrine graciously distributed to a portion of its mailing list. These sources are identified in the notes with the prefix *800,* followed by the same information listed above; again, the vast majority of the callers were women. I also received some forty letters from devout from all over the United States, in response either to my 800 mailing or to the document distributed at the Shrine, which had come into their hands somehow, typically from a friend who had visited the Shrine. These are identified as *Per.corr.* (personal correspondence), again followed by information about gender, age, location, and marital status.

Finally, although I learned a great deal from all of the women and men who generously took the time to share their experiences of and reflections on St. Jude with me, my talks with a few women in particular proved to be especially rich and instructive, and I want to set them apart here from my other sources. I find it almost impossible to say why this happened, beyond noting some simple interpersonal details—we got along well, trusted each other, enjoyed each other's company for the short time we were together. Clara, Judy, and Isabel (none of these are their real names, of course) are all married with grown children and live in or around Chicago; all were in their early fifties when we met.[7] Kathy is younger, in her mid-thirties, and single. Pat, who was in her mid-fifties, lived in Detroit. Clara and Kathy had their own businesses; the others worked at jobs they liked and valued. Pat was employed in the public schools for many years, Isabel worked for an oncologist. Our conversations lasted from three to five hours, and all gave me their telephone numbers for follow-up questions. Their individual stories will emerge as the book proceeds.

There was a real intensity and immediacy to women's storytelling about Jude, understandable given his special province. Because I am committed, by personal inclination and research ethics, never to hide my own intentions and purposes, I told all the people I spoke with about St. Jude what I was thinking about what they said, and I asked for their comments on my initial, tentative interpretations of the cult. Needless to say, I did not always agree with them, and the reading of the devotion presented here is mine, not theirs—although I hope that they will recognize themselves in it.

I was especially careful to discuss with them my impressions of Jude's place in their own lives. These conversations were not modeled on psychoanalysis, and so I was never the invisible other. My intention in doing fieldwork was to have a series of wide-ranging, unstructured dialogues about St. Jude with longtime devout, and that is what transpired.

Such a structure of interlocking sources was necessary because of the insufficiency of any one of the sources taken by itself. It was my commitment throughout the study not to assert anything about the devotion or make any interpretation based on the testimony of only one or two devout. This is the reason for the long lists of citations in the notes, and for the long labor of cross-referencing. I moved back and forth between my conversations and the published sources, using each as a lens for thinking about the other.

I have not edited any woman's reflections, condensed long sections of conversation, or drawn together remarks from different points in our meetings; I have indicated any elisions I have made in their comments. I changed only enough detail to protect individuals' privacy, and I have made nothing up. There are no composite portraits in the book. Finally, all of the women and men I spoke with understood that I was writing a book and would probably cite them. All were enthusiastic about the project, eager to contribute to making Jude still better known, perhaps among a new clientele (as they conceived one of the advantages of the work), and happy to participate. All gave permission to quote them. With one conspicuous exception, most were unconcerned about protecting their anonymity. Clara said she'd rip off my nose if I revealed her identity. I hope I have hidden it adequately.

In addition to these primary sources, my reading of American Catholic culture and ideology—what might be called a worldview, as long as this is understood as a dynamic, ongoing creation, politically inflected and immensely consequential for everyday life, not a static reality that people live inside of—is based on scores of articles, book condensations, fiction, poems, and jokes, from the many different Catholic magazines available to the community in the years under consideration. Some of these magazines, like the *Voice of St. Jude,* were published by shrines and cults; others, like *Catholic World, Ave Maria,* and *America,* were the work of specific religious orders; still others were more or less trade journals for clergy, *Homiletic and Pastoral Review* and *American Ecclesiastical Review. Hospital Progress* was published for Catholic hospital professionals. Taken altogether, this was the everyday literary culture of American Catholicism.

By the late 1920s, Catholic magazines were in the process of being transformed by college-educated editors sophisticated in the ways of American popular journalism into attractive, accessible, upbeat periodicals in a self-consciously American voice, offering articles and fiction on subjects of interest to the middle-class children of immigrants. (A popular feature was the evocation of "Old World" customs for increasingly assimilated Catholics.) Catholic magazines and newspapers together sustained the community's sense of its own distinctiveness in American culture as they detailed the aesthetics of assimilation and articulated the moral ideals and uneasiness of an emerging middle class, tentative about its place in a once hostile culture. They served as the training ground for Catholic intellectuals, supported a host of Catholic entrepreneurs, gave a Catholic gloss to every aspect of American culture from highways and kitchen design to foreign policy, and thus became visible expressions of the integration and unity of American Catholic culture—a coherence that did not really exist outside of these magazines and newspapers.

Catholics had other sources for their theology, of course: the pastors and prelates of the airwaves like Fulton Sheen, Catholic fiction, catechisms, sermons, religious education classes, book clubs, moral handbooks, and so on. All of these other idioms converged in the magazines, however, which regularly printed excerpts from popular theological books, condensations of Catholic novels, articles by or about Catholic television, radio, and film personalities, and the sermons of famous Catholic preachers, along with the usual fare of American family magazines.

Catholic magazines could be found everywhere. Salesmen sold subscriptions door to door in cities, suburbs, and rural areas, often traveling in big cars with the name of their magazine painted on the side doors. Subscriptions and individual issues were offered as promotions in local parish fund-raising drives, stocked in the libraries of Catholic hospitals, schools, convents, and rectories, and given as gifts, prizes, and incentives. By 1959, at the end of the most intense period of devotional creativity in American Catholic history (a spiritual explosion considered in the first chapter), the Catholic Press Association reported that there were 24,273,972 subscribers to 580 periodicals in the country.[8] Devotionalism supported and was in turn supported by this literary culture.

The magazines have until recently been overlooked as sources for the history of American Catholic culture, but in that medium popular theology was practiced with considerable fervor and verve, literally in response to current events as they unfolded. Clergy read the periodicals and talked about them in their sermons, and issues of particular magazines were discussed in Catholic schools. Ample space was allotted for readers' comments, and their letters were generally lively and provocative—and sometimes at odds with editorial positions. This was a thriving and important idiom, in which modern American Catholics not only discovered who they were but constituted themselves as well, and where voices of alarm and authority sought to direct, educate, and discipline the tastes and hopes of new generations of Catholic men and women.

In the middle of our conversation, Isabel took out a much-handled and beat-up novena booklet, the collection of nine days' prayers in honor of St. Jude published by the Shrine and illustrated with images of the saint. She had mentioned that for some years she had been writing her prayer intentions right into the margins of her prayer books, and I wondered what this looked like. Isabel pointed to a page on which tiny script in several inks wound like a vine around the Shrine's prayers. I asked Isabel if she would choose a name and tell me something about that person. "OK," she said:

That's my grandson, my great nephew, my godchild now, J.G., he was in my CCD [Confraternity of Christian Doctrine] class, he would make a fine priest. T.M., right now he's going through a crisis, and I'd love to have him get my daughter out of his system, and then he can go and be a priest. There was a boy here, he was a server [altar boy], would have made an excellent priest, but something happened—he reached puberty and got crazy about girls, and he really got to be obnoxious up there [on the altar], but I'm still praying for him. If God wants you, he'll get you. You can't get away from him.

This is for my sister to quit drinking, and J. wants to have a baby, R. had her surgery yesterday, Joe's son needs a job, A.J.'s got a lot of problems, sick parents and all that. J.B. is half dead, she's my friend, my very good friend. H.P., she just had surgery again yesterday, she's got cancer. . . . G., she is a fantastic older woman, and her husband; she had her breast removed under a local, and she's got recurrent cancer here and there. And my mother-in-law, and my great-nephew.

These are the sick ones up here [pointing to the top of the page], and J.T., and my husband, my daughters, and my sister and her daughters, and M.S., that's a girl I used to work with, she had a baby. A.C. had another cancer—I work for a cancer doctor, [and these are] the cancer patients I promised to pray for. This is a poor lady.

This is my group of friends. I have a group of crazy friends, [we all] go on vacation together. And my relatives, for their health and everything else. And the doctors I work for, and the principal of St. F. School, my friends I haven't seen in a long time, my niece, M., she had her eyes shot—there was a kid playing with a B.B. gun down the street and hit her in the right eye, and it gushed out blood and she lost her eye and everything else.

Our pastor is really obnoxious, so I'm praying for him.

And this section is for "eternal rest to our departed relatives and friends": E. and M., my mother and father. And I. and S. and Father P., who was our last pastor, I. and F., that's J.'s mother and father, and then my grandmother and grandfather, and my father's mother and father. And then different friends that I got to know, benefactors, patients, all I promised them. And my girlfriend's daughter that left home.

And my daughter, she's going to school and she's—I wanted her to be a physical therapist, but she's into being a radiology tech, so maybe that's it. So that they all marry good guys that will pray with them, that they are God's friends. OK, and then the intentions of my special friends. And help me to lose weight, as if I ever do, right? And for my daughter the cop, don't let her get hurt, and let God use me in all the little things he wants, to give me strength, and the courage, and all this other junk. My sister to get a nice home.

I divided this up into paragraphs and sentences, following the intonations of Isabel's voice: for her, it was one long interlocking story. She had gathered her world on the pages of the prayer book, lovingly inscribing each person and his or her grave and trivial needs (as she discerned them or they told her), nosily assuming a stake in everyone's life, showing her affection, assuming authority, caring and intruding at once.

My questions to the devout about praying always opened out like this to lives within lives, stories within stories, all organized around and oriented toward St. Jude.

Acknowledgments

I have worked on this study for many years in several different settings—perhaps this is why it is so often preoccupied with questions of space and time—and I have been helped along the way by many people and institutions. Without them, the book would not have come into being.

The National Endowment for the Humanities provided me a year off from teaching, which allowed me to write a first draft of the book. Fordham University initially and then Indiana University also gave me essential research support at key moments.

I have always been fortunate in having the company of critical but sympathetic colleagues, especially so here at Indiana; I have benefited from my conversations with all of them, in particular with Rob Campany, David Haberman, Jan Nattier, Steve Stein, and Sam Preus. Sarah Pike managed to provide me with invaluable help in the final preparations of the manuscript as she was finishing her own dissertation. Versions of this work in progress were presented at several universities, and I want to thank most heartily all the faculty and graduate students who met and talked with me, fed me and drank with me, and questioned everything I said about St. Jude. I must mention in particular my friends at Harvard and Duke who have had most of this book read to them in parts over the years, especially David Hall at Harvard and Liz Clark at Duke.

During the long evolution of this project I stumbled several times, losing heart and direction. At these points, my own patron saints appeared to offer support and encouragement: Susan Klebanoff, Ann Braude, Temma Kaplan, Patrick Olivelle, Bill Reese, Jeff Isaac, Maria Laurino, Greg Shopen, Colleen McDannell, Karen McCarthy Brown, Kevin Norton, Ray and Ivona Hedin, Tad Meyer, Michael Jackson and Francine Lorimer, and, as always, Jeff Keller. My parents have generously come to understand the trip from New York City to Bloomington as a short commute, and they have been on hand with practical assistance whenever I needed them; my brother, Francis Jude Thaddeus Orsi, and his wife, Cathy, have been faithful companions too. Chuck Grench at Yale University Press has taken too many anxious phone calls from me, providing a sympathetic ear in discussions that inevitably segued from matters of publishing to those of the heart. Yale further blessed me by assigning Dan Heaton as my editor. Dan gave the manuscript the benefit of his skilled eye and me the benefit of his wit. The Thursday Night Seminar in Bloomington was another point of stability. I owe a special debt of gratitude to Martha Cooley, with whom I spoke every week across the continent to review issues and problems of the writer's craft; with her husband, Jonathan Halperin, she also offered food and shelter on my trips to the Library of Congress.

The Claretians and the lay staff of *U.S. Catholic* could not have been more generous in allowing me to research the devotion that they have so sensitively tended these many years. Thanks in particular to Kevin Axe, Mark Brummel, Ralph Scorpio, Cathy O'Connell-Cahill, and especially Tom McGrath.

I have met with many of St. Jude's devout over the years, corresponded with others, talked with some on the telephone, and read the letters hundreds of them have sent to Chicago since 1935. Many will be encountered in the text. I found the devout I met to be an extraordinarily impressive group of women, articulate about their faith, funny, and strong. The hours I spent with them on either very cold or unbearably hot Chicago days were helpful to me in more ways than I understood at the time, although this will not surprise them. To all of you, my sincerest thanks.

Acknowledgments

xx

The circumstances of my life changed dramatically while I was working on the book: in its earliest days I was encouraged, supported, accompanied by Jane Harlan, in its latter period by Joanne Gumo.

Through all of it I have had the gracious and zany company of a girl who always seemed to grow much faster than the book did. When it started she could barely talk; by the end she'd casually ask when I picked her up at school, "So, how'd Jude go today?" It is dedicated to her.

I was flying to New York several years ago for a meeting I was very apprehensive about; this project was well under way by the time, and I had already spoken to many of Jude's devout and read the Shrine's correspondence. The plane approached LaGuardia and then, to my great dismay, began circling and circling and circling. This went on for about forty-five minutes. Finally the pilot came on the loudspeaker. He apologized for the delay, announced that landing in New York was now out of the question, and assured us that the airline would provide buses for us—from Philadelphia, no less!—back to the city.

I was desperate. This meant I would miss my appointment. Without premeditation I said quietly, "St. Jude, I really need to land in New York—please, do something." I had barely finished this little prayer when the pilot came back on, with a bemused tone in his voice. "Well, folks," he said, "I've never seen anything like this, but apparently something's changed down there and we've been told to land. We'll be on the ground in five minutes. Flight attendants, prepare the cabin for landing."

I am not a devout, but I promised to tell this story at the time, and here it is. I would still say to the women who asked me that I do not believe in St. Jude.

But what's belief got to do with it?

Thank You, St. Jude

1

"From South Chicago to Heaven"
The Making of the National Shrine of St. Jude

Older residents say that in the good times South Chicago's skies were black by midmorning from the soot cleaned out of the chimneys of the steel mills along Lake Michigan. Things were good in South Chicago when the mills were going strong. Railroad cars clanked through the yards to the high sound of warning whistles, barges moved along the shore, and the noise of trip-hammers reverberated all day in the neighborhoods. Women say it was impossible to keep their families' clothes clean because of the cinders in the air, and professional men brought extra white shirts with them to their offices so they could change when the soot got too thick on their sleeves.

But the skies were clearer and the neighborhood quiet in the spring of 1929, a sign of the economic crisis that was already upon the people of South Chicago, whose lives were so immediately and intimately linked to steel, and a portent as well, for those who could read it, of the bad times coming. It was under this clear and threatening sky that young women from the area's Catholic ethnic neighborhoods first began gathering at the base of an unknown saint's statue in a Mexican church situated amid the mills.

NUESTRA SEÑORA DE GUADALUPE

South Chicago grew out of the old Ainsworth Station of the Lake Shore and Michigan Railroad in the early 1870s, after the Calumet and Chicago Canal and Dock Company had begun to improve the conditions of the lake shore there for industry.[1] Irish and Swedish laborers settled in the area first, followed by southern and eastern Europeans. By the 1920s, South Chicago was a mixed neighborhood of Polish, Irish, and Croatian families mainly, with smaller pockets of Swedes, Germans, Slovaks, and Italians scattered throughout. People lived in single-family frame houses or in double-deckers known as "mother-daughters"—an architectural expression of family mores and expectations— and each community had its own churches, social clubs, mutual aid societies, and stores.

There was also a small number of Mexican migrants living in the area. Some Mexican workers came to the city at the end of the sugar beet season each year in Wisconsin, Minnesota, and Michigan; others traveled up from the South along the rail lines, supporting themselves by odd jobs in the train yards as they went. The core of the Mexican community in South Chicago had been recruited by mill agents, first during the strikes of 1919 and again in the early 1920s when federal legislation halted the flow of cheap labor from southern and eastern Europe. A large number of Mexican workers was brought to the neighborhood from Fort Worth, Texas, in 1923, by the largest mill in South Chicago, Illinois Steel (which later became U.S. Steel, still later U.S.X.).

By 1926 approximately thirty-five thousand Mexicans were settled in three Chicago neighborhoods—Back of the Yards, the Near West Side, and South Chicago. The Mexican settlement in the latter neighborhood, which numbered some four thousand workers and their families, was bounded by Illinois Steel on the east, the wide expanse of Commercial Avenue on the west, the railroad tracks just below 87th Street on the north, and 92nd Street on the south. Of the three Mexican enclaves in the city, the one in South Chicago was the most densely populated—and the most isolated from its neighbors.

The southern and eastern European and Irish immigrants who had battled their way into the city's industries and politics in the first two decades of the century resented the Mexican workers, who competed with them and their children for jobs and housing. Most galling of all, as the older residents saw it, Mexicans had been admitted into the country in place of family and friends from the old countries. It would be a while before these workers understood their mutual interests, and in the meantime their children fought in the neighborhood's streets and alleys while the adults made the migrants feel unwanted in their churches, as they had themselves been made to feel a generation or so before by longer-established Catholics.

Chicago's progressive Protestants were the first to take an interest in the welfare of Mexicans in the city. Migrants were welcomed into the settlement houses operating in the three neighborhoods—Hull House on the Near West Side, University of Chicago Settlement House in the Back of the Yards, and Bird Memorial Center, run by the Congregational Church, in South Chicago— and Protestant missionaries were soon appearing among the camps of Mexican workers in the railroad yards and at the doors of their homes. South Chicago's Catholics took note of this activity and brought it to the attention of Auxiliary Bishop Edward Hoban in the summer of 1923, coincidentally the same time that two Jesuit missionaries were finishing a report for the city's formidable cardinal-elect, George Mundelein, on the spiritual and temporal conditions among Mexican Catholics in Chicago.[2]

The archbishop, who is said to have had special concern for the Mexican community, assigned an older, highly respected university professor, Jesuit Father William T. Kane, to work among South Chicago's migrant families.[3] Using money donated by the president of Illinois Steel, Kane bought an old house at 9024 South Mackinaw Avenue, at the eastern edge of the area's Mexican community, and made it into a chapel, which he called the Mission of Our Lady of Guadalupe. Kane spoke Spanish fluently and seems to have been popular, but poor health forced his retirement after several months at the new mission. He was replaced first by another Jesuit and then by a secular priest— that is, one not associated with a religious order—from Mexico, Michael Garcia. Although Father Garcia was also well-liked, some of the local Anglos who had been recruited by Kane to support the mission's work were distressed by his appointment. They felt that his broken English was a liability for a pastor in the United States, and they complained about it to the archbishop. Mundelein himself firmly believed (to the dismay of at least some members of the various ethnic groups under his care) that the church had a responsibility to "Americanize" newcomers and their children, and so, listening sympathetically to the complaints from South Chicago, he decided to take another course there.

The archbishop traveled to Rome in the spring of 1924 to receive his red hat.

Father Tort, surrounded by Mexican families and local benefactors, in front of the Claretians' boxcar chapel, sometime between 1924 and 1928.

During his stay he met with members of the Missionary Sons of the Immaculate Heart of Mary, a Spanish order of priests better known as the Claretian Missionaries, after their founder, St. Anthony Claret. The Claretians had raised the idea of a mission among Chicago's Mexicans with the diocese some years before, although nothing had come of the proposal at the time. Now the cardinal asked them to come to Chicago. The order formally assumed responsibility for the mission at Our Lady of Guadalupe on All Saints Day, November 1, 1924.

Mundelein had assigned the Claretians care of all the Mexican neighborhoods in Chicago, and the first thing they did in the city was survey the extent of their task. They compiled a census of the city's Mexican population, opened several chapels (including at least one in an abandoned boxcar), and established ten "catechetical centers" for the instruction of migrant families.[4] This was a tremendous undertaking for a small group of men and must have seemed daunting at times, but the community in South Chicago included an experienced priest of great energy and enthusiasm, James Tort, who had arrived in the city in the summer of 1925 and soon established himself as leader of the mission.

Later chroniclers of the Shrine of St. Jude claimed that Padrecito Jaime Tort, as his parishioners called him, was the scion of Catalonian nobility, but this is a reflection of the esteem of his friends and confreres rather than historical fact. A more sober story was recorded in the official necrology written for the order at Father Tort's death in 1955. The founder of the American devotion to St. Jude was born in a small, prosperous town in the province of Barcelona on April 21, 1880, to modestly comfortable and deeply pious parents. Jaime entered the Claretian seminary at Barbastro when he was fifteen years old and was ordained in 1906. He was subsequently assigned first to the Canary Islands, where by his own account he developed a respect for the varieties of Catholic popular religion, and then to Mexico City, from which he fled during the Carranza purges of 1914 (in a hail of bullets, according to Shrine legend). After some years in Texas and Arizona, he moved to Chicago, where he became pastor of the mission at Guadalupe in 1927.[5]

Tort is warmly remembered by his fellow priests as a "little high-pressure" man for whom "resting was moving and moving, resting," in the words of his obituary. He was a shrewd businessman and an accomplished fund raiser by the time he got to Chicago. Tort quickly realized that the financial resources of the Mexican community were limited, and he must also have known that Cardinal Mundelein, who encouraged him to proceed with plans to build a church in South Chicago, demanded that the priests of his diocese pay their own debts. So early on the new pastor of Guadalupe evolved a strategy that would serve him well through the years, forging ties with middle-class Catholics outside the Mexican community and involving them—at least in spirit—in the life and work of the mission as he secured their financial backing for his plans.[6]

In the summer of 1927, Father Tort founded a "Mexican Aid Society" under the patronage of the Immaculate Heart of Mary and St. Thérèse of the Child Jesus and dedicated "to support[ing] financially or personally" the priest's numerous initiatives among the migrant families. He assembled a building committee of prominent local Anglo Catholics—which in Chicago Mexican American usage means anyone who is not Mexican—and courted patrons among the city's powerful Catholic businessmen, lawyers, real estate developers, and politicians, many of whom were members of lay Catholic fraternal orders, like the Knights of Columbus, or service-oriented devotional associations, like the Holy Name Society. Tort was able to purchase three lots at the northeastern corner of Brandon Avenue and 91st Street with their help, and with the further assistance of Frederick J. Lewis, an east-side roofer, real estate developer, and Knight of St. Gregory, he added two more lots and a small house by early fall 1927. Altogether this property cost $30,000. It is not surprising, given Tort's extramural fund-raising strategies, that only one speech at the groundbreaking ceremonies for the new church on February 5, 1928, was given in what a newspaper reporter called "the Mexican language," an impassioned lament for the persecuted church in Mexico delivered by an exiled prelate. On Palm Sunday later that spring, some ten thousand people "of all nationalities," according to another newspaper story, "Polish, Irish, Germans, [and] Croatians," along with representatives of the Knights of Columbus, the Catholic Order of Foresters, the Catholic Knights of America, and the Knights of St. Gregory, all in colorful ceremonial garb, gathered on the broken ground to observe the placement of the church's cornerstone. This was a remarkable congregation of people who otherwise kept away from each other in the neighborhoods, and their coming together at the future site of Guadalupe was a sign both of Tort's considerable diplomatic skills and, as we will see, of changes in the social life of American Catholicism.[7]

Exalting in the realization of his dreams, Tort exclaimed (in English), "Now when I will see this great enterprise completed according to my wishes, then may I say, 'from South Chicago to Heaven.'"[8] Four months later, on September 30, 1928, only a year after Tort's appointment as pastor of the mission, the church of Our Lady of Guadalupe was formally dedicated by Cardinal Mundelein.

Nuestra Señora de Guadalupe, who had first appeared to a poor Mexican Indian, was presiding now over a poor community along Lake Michigan. The church and rectory cost $150,000. The Chicago Claretians had about $10,000 in the bank at the time of the dedication ceremonies. The archdiocese had lent the order between $80,000 and $90,000, and Mundelein had verbally promised to assume $5,000 of this annually, expecting the priests and parishioners to pay off the rest. But the steel industry was already registering the first shocks of the Depression, and unemployment was rising in the neighborhood. To make matters worse, it soon developed that the Claretians had apparently misunderstood the precise terms of the cardinal's assistance. The archdiocese was willing to pay the interest on the loan for two years, but after that, the Claretians were on their own.[9]

This must have seemed a hopeless situation, even to Guadalupe's indefatigable pastor. But in addition to debts and worries, and besides his own prodigious energy and skills, Padrecito Tort also had a personal devotion to an obscure saint named Jude. This turned out to be all the help he needed.

"It all started" in 1923, as the Shrine tells its story, when Tort, who was stationed at the time in the mining town of Prescott, Arizona, found an image of St. Jude in a pew. The saint was the object of a small cult in Central and South America, and the holy card Tort came upon may have been carried north by a traveler or migrating miner. There was a shrine to St. Jude in a Claretian church in Santiago, Chile, where he was venerated as the Patron Saint of Hopeless Causes; he was also the object of a special devotion among the city's prostitutes. This latter association is a further indication of Jude's obscurity at the time, because marginal holy figures often serve as the protectors or guardians of socially marginal or outcast groups.[10] Tort began praying to this saint, and when he moved to Chicago two years later he brought Jude with him.

Just after the completion of Guadalupe, a woman named Rose McDonald, perhaps knowing of Tort's devotion, offered to donate a statue of St. Jude to the church. The saint was so unfamiliar to North American Catholics that Father Tort could not find a statue of him among Chicago's many retailers of religious objects and was finally compelled to commission one based on a Spanish image (possibly the holy card) in his possession. Tort specifically insisted, the Shrine's chroniclers say, that the artist render Jude's eyes "loving and tender" and his hands "strong but gentle."

THE STORY OF THE SWITCHED STATUES

The legend of the founding of the National Shrine of St. Jude takes over now. There were several statues in the church of Our Lady of Guadalupe during the bleak spring of 1929. The Little Flower of Jesus, St. Thérèse of Lisieux, occupied a prominent position, perhaps above the right side altar, as befitted such a well-known and popular figure. According to some accounts (though not the earliest) Jude stood beneath her in a much less important place; at least two published descriptions of the origins of the devotion locate him to the side of the right altar. A former Shrine director remembered that there were also statues of Mother Cabrini and St. Joseph in the church. All accounts agree, however, that Tort imagined Jude and Thérèse competing with one another over who would be the subject of a new devotion.[11]

"I need help," Tort is said to have told the two figures in February, 1929. "The one of you two who would help me the most will be put up there in the shrine; the other one, on that pedestal."

The choice of the Little Flower as the patroness of the Mexican Aid Society, as well as the central place initially accorded her in the church, may indicate the pastor's earliest ambitions. Thérèse was a very popular figure among American

Catholics and a more likely candidate for a successful devotion than the unknown Jude. But there was already a cult of the Little Flower at a nearby Carmelite parish in Chicago—indeed, this had inspired Tort's plans in the first place—and a thriving national devotion based in Oklahoma City. Catholic devotions were jealously guarded by their founders and promoters. The Claretians themselves attempted in 1961 to copyright materials associated with Jude's Shrine after another religious order began appropriating them for its own fund-raising efforts. A second devotion to the Little Flower in the same city would have represented unseemly, impolitic, and possibly unsuccessful competition, and would have certainly led to conflict with the more powerful Carmelites.[12] So it was all for the best that something else began happening in South Chicago.

As the plight of the area worsened, women from the Catholic neighborhoods around Guadalupe—not Mexican women, but the daughters and granddaughters of Irish and southern and eastern European immigrants—began visiting the church in ever-increasing numbers to bring their petitions not to *Nuestra Señora* over the main altar, or to the Little Flower, or to Mother Cabrini, but to the least known male holy figure in the church. During Holy Week 1929, according to the Shrine's chroniclers, the clergy at Guadalupe, acknowledging the evident intentions of the supernatural as these were expressed through the preferences of the devout, switched the two statues. St. Jude had won the competition "hands down," and Thérèse ceded the place of prominence to her "holy rival." Jude himself had chosen Chicago, the modest, unassuming, but powerful industrial city of the heartland, where meat was slaughtered and steel refined and where the nation's railroads converged, as the site of the modern emergence of his cult.[13]

Many new heroes were fashioned by the complex and ambivalent hopes and needs, resentments and fears, of the Depression, and in this troubled time devotion to St. Jude flourished. More than a thousand people stood in the street outside the packed church during the celebration of the first novena in the saint's honor on October 28, 1929.[14] The saint in turn promptly rewarded his new home with a miracle. Sarah Muldowney of 7941 South Manestee Avenue was close to death after an attack of meningitis; her doctors had given up all hope for her. Summoned by the dying woman's sister, Father Tort rushed to the hospital with a relic of St. Jude and touched it to Sarah's body while her relatives called on the saint. "Suddenly," Tort's necrologist reports, "the sick [woman] recovered her health, [her family and the attending medical professionals] all claiming it as a miracle of the Patron of hopeless cases."

"From then on," this writer continues, "thousands upon thousands of favors credited to Saint Jude's powerful intercession have been reported year after year at the Saint Jude's National Shrine, 3208 E 91st St., Chicago 17, Ill, or at his [sic] down town Office, 221 W Madison St., Chicago 6, Illinois." Even allowing for the exaggerations of the Shrine clergy, the devotion grew at an astonishing pace. By 1935, when regular reports on the cult began appearing in the Shrine's new periodical, the *Voice of St. Jude*, "thousands" of letters were arriving in Chicago yearly from around the country to request favors of the saint or to thank him for favors received. By 1937, as the economy plunged into recession and unemployment rose again, the tally had become thousands of letters *daily*. Four thousand people tried to get into each service of the spring novena that grim year to hear Father James Keane, founder of the enormously popular Chicago devotion to Our Lady of Sorrows, preach against communism and birth control.[15]

Jude was just the link that Tort had been looking for between the needs of Guadalupe and the piety and generosity of Anglos, and he set out now skillfully and tirelessly to promote the new devotion. With Mundelein's blessing and a granting of special indulgences from Rome, Tort founded the League of St. Jude in November 1929. Membership cost one dollar a year or twenty-five dollars for an individual perpetual membership, one hundred dollars for a family. In February 1932, Tort organized the Police Branch of the League of St. Jude and dedicated it both to meeting the spiritual needs of the police and to "building and maintaining" a seminary for Claretian students in the Midwest.[16] Finally, in January 1935, the Shrine began publishing the *Voice of St. Jude*, an ambitious, nationally distributed, illustrated devotional magazine that reported on events at the National Shrine as well as offering readers short fiction, medical and household advice, humor, and social and political commentary. By 1936 subscriptions to the *Voice* numbered in the "thousands," according to a Shrine report, and the clergy in Chicago were already referring to it as a "world famous" Catholic publication.[17]

By the middle of the Depression decade, then, the structure of the national devotion to St. Jude was in place and working—how well, Tort would soon see.

THE BREAKUP OF THE IMMIGRANT HOUSEHOLD

The hope of Guadalupe's pastor that a saint would rescue him from the financial precipice was widely shared by other debt-burdened priests in the years after the First World War, as they struggled with the consequences of the

The Shrine's original statue of St. Jude, modeled on the holy card found by Father Tort in Prescott, Arizona.

changing demography and geography of American Catholicism. Historians of the various Catholic immigrant communities have observed that inner-city ethnic enclaves began to dissolve in the years between 1924, when Congress closed American ports to further immigration from southern and eastern Europe, and 1941, when war ended the Great Depression. Social, economic, and demographic forces converged to undermine the powerful immigrant households that had ruled over the lives of individuals and dominated the culture of urban Catholicism since the late nineteenth century. By the end of the period, Catholic families in this country looked very different from their counterparts in 1890 or 1910.

The men and women who came to the United States from southern and eastern Europe at the end of the nineteenth and the beginning of the twentieth centuries had traveled along well-established and carefully maintained networks of family and friends. They had left the Old World for family reasons, and although they did not often keep the promises made on the eve of their departures that they would return, once the immigrants established themselves in this country they faithfully supported the relatives they had left behind. In the industrial cities of the Northeast and Midwest the newcomers settled in among friends and relatives who helped them find their way into the industrial economy and survive its harsh and recurrent bad times.[18]

Grounded in these economic realities and sanctioned by cultural traditions, the immigrant family became a mighty force. Its elders demanded submission and obedience from individual members, particularly in matters of work, love, and home. The first children born and raised on these shores dutifully handed their earnings over to their parents, muted their own ambitions and desires, married according to the traditions of their families and cultures, and afterward stayed close by in the old neighborhoods, just as was expected of them. The success of the immigrant family has been well documented in recent years, although its historians, eager to revise the earlier image of sorrowful and uprooted urban masses, have generally overlooked the degree of coercion that sustained this domestic authority and solidarity.

All of this began to break down, however, in the years after the First World War.[19] The disruptions of international conflict, followed by restrictive legislation and political changes in southern and eastern Europe and in Ireland, stopped the flow of newcomers. There would be no more greenhorns to give fresh life to the old ways. The older immigrants, many of whom had originally planned to stay only as long as it took to make enough money to live comfortably back home, found themselves still here thirty years later, with family, work, and property all on this side of the Atlantic. When the immigrants failed to return to Europe after deeply cherished political aspirations for their homelands had been realized after the war, time's passing began to look more and more like decision.[20]

At the same time, the immigrants' sons and daughters—who spoke English as their native language, claimed American citizenship as their birthright, and were more comfortable with the ways of American society than their parents had ever been—were demanding to make their own choices about where to work, whom to marry, and where to live, precisely those domains over which the immigrant family had exercised its most jealous authority. Adolescence as a distinct stage of life was not known to the immigrant generations. One was either a child, who stayed at home and played with other members of the family, or an adult, who went out and worked for the family. But now for the first time in twentieth-century American Catholic history, the immigrants' children, abetted by progressive educational legislation and a pervasive popular culture addressed specifically to them, were taking on the lineaments of something like adolescence.[21]

The years between the wars were marked in all the ethnic communities of American Catholicism by bitter intergenerational tensions that had many sources, not simply the rejection of the old ways by the young as many claimed, at the time and since, and this familial acrimony was sharpened by economic anxiety. The immigrants knew that their economic control of their children was slipping. Better educated and more ambitious than their parents, the immigrants' children were beginning to make their way into the professions, urban bureaucracies, service industries, and white-collar positions—sectors of the industrial or emergent postindustrial economy that were beyond the reach of kinship connections or family authority. The immigrants raged bitterly against their children not only because young people had abandoned the old ways but because the choices they were now demanding to make for themselves threatened the economic order of the immigrant household. The family economy, which had worked so well in the hard years after the immigrants arrived, was breaking up.

More changes followed. The immigrants' children were marrying in increasing numbers outside the borders of their parents' world. A significant exogamous trend became evident in the Polish American community for the first time in the 1920s, for example, and two decades later, a survey of a large Polish national parish in Pennsylvania revealed that more than half of its young people were selecting their mates from outside the community. Similar patterns emerged in other American Catholic communities. Increasing numbers of the second generation were even marrying outside the church altogether—more than thirty percent of all Catholic marriages nationwide in the 1940s, according to one survey.[22]

Young Catholics often moved away from their parents' neighborhoods after their marriages if they could afford to, either to better areas of the cities or to the suburbs that had begun to appear around the great industrial centers of the Northeast and Midwest. By 1921, "Irish-Americans were dispersing throughout the typical industrial metropolis, their residential patterns determined more by economic than by ethnic considerations," and within the decade, the children of other immigrants would do the same. Writing about Italian Americans in Providence, Rhode Island, Judith Smith says that "by the late 1920s and 1930s the decision to live near family was made in the context of an expanded array of alternatives facing the children's generation" so that "networks of proximity and support could no longer be assumed." Jay Dolan refers to this as the time of the "suburbanization" of American Catholicism.[23] The gathering of ethnically mixed crowds at events at the National Shrine, then, reflected a deeper reorientation of the American Catholic social world: in schools, Catholic youth organizations, at workplaces around the city, younger Catholics were meeting across ethnic lines.

These changes came at a certain cost for the second and third generations, though. The immigrant neighborhood, because it was such a closely guarded world of strong authority, offered its residents a safe, recognizable, and protected environment. People who left the enclaves in these years still talk about the open doors, attentive neighbors, and commonly supervised streets of their childhoods, as if the uncertainty of what they were doing by leaving these streets seared an image of lost security into their memories forever. But now they were discovering new risks and responsibilities and experiencing unfamiliar anxieties as they searched for ways to live and define themselves beyond the confines of the old neighborhood.[24]

The American Catholic family had shrunk down to the nuclear core of parents (who were usually very young) and children, and the immigrants' sons and daughters had to rely more on their own resources in meeting responsibilities and taking care of troubles that had once been shared by the extended family living in close proximity. Younger Catholic couples, in and outside the enclaves, had greater ambitions for their children's success in American society than their parents had had for them, which meant that they had to worry more about their offsprings' performances on the various stages of the nation's meritocracy. And at the same time, the old neighborhood continued to make its demands on them, just like the old countries had on their parents at the start of their married lives. The immigrants' children had to negotiate with their spouses and their scattered siblings for the care of aging parents who insisted on remaining in crumbling tenements. The tensions this provoked were registered in church marriage tribunals during this era: conflict between traditional ways—as expressed by foreign-born in-laws—and modern values has been one of the major sources of marital discord among young American Catholic couples in this century, especially in Polish and Italian communities.[25]

The immigrants' children found themselves, in the middle years of this century, in a situation that was oddly analogous to their parents' during the years of immigration. They had made their way from one world to another, where they believed that they could make better lives for themselves and their children. They had left behind (even if this was true only in terms of social values and orientations, not actual location) angry, hurt, confused relatives to whom they were still bound by ties of affection, duty, and fear. They had to find new ways of honoring the family ties they had been raised to respect because the old ways had become impossible or irrelevant to them. The immigrants in their time had turned to the familiar saints of childhood to help them understand and endure the distress of being caught between worlds and to negotiate their way across the intervening space. Their children, particularly their daughters, would do the same now, and in this case, their needs nicely complemented those of the clergy who had their own sources of distress in these years.

THE HEYDAY OF AMERICAN CATHOLIC DEVOTIONALISM

All of this growth and movement among younger Catholics meant new churches, rectories, schools, and convents, as well as salaries (however meager) for the men and women, lay and religious, who lived and worked in them. Communities seemed to be forever gathering to celebrate brick and mortar, and the festival of the cornerstone became this generation's characteristic public ritual. Glossy booklets printed to commemorate these events listed the grocery stores, funeral parlors, law firms, and trucking companies that had made the dream of a new temple possible, but always at the head of the procession on such days, surrounded by prominent Catholic men in plumes and swords, was a priest, smiling and waving, and wondering how he was going to pay for it all.

There were times when it seemed to the laity that all their priests thought and talked about was money. Ambitious and career-minded young clergy knew that what mattered to their superiors was not how well they cured souls but how carefully they shepherded the bottom line. Historian James O'Toole refers to this as "the great age of Catholic monumentalism," when a "this-worldly morality" governed the thinking of prelates and pastors measured their success as priests by the size of their physical plants. Many serious pastoral duties, such as visiting the sick, were assigned to men who had proven to be inept at raising funds and buildings, the "real work" of the clergy, according to the angry complaint of a part-time hospital chaplain in the late 1930s who had encountered the scorn of parish priests firsthand.[26]

Popular devotions have always been a dependable source of revenue in Catholic societies, and needy clergy turned to them now with redoubled fervor, displaying an inexhaustible ingenuity in dreaming up novel practices that they promoted with anxious enthusiasm. A priest in Ohio, for example, began printing "tickets to heaven" in 1946 "in [the] form of . . . Prayer card[s] with the essential acts necessary for salvation" outlined on them, available in "20 different languages and Braille." A convent in New York distributed, for a small donation, unconsecrated hosts as "Perpetual Help Wafers." New devotional leagues were regularly constituted. "Join the League of Saint Dymphna," a group of Ohio Franciscans urged the readers of *St. Anthony's Messenger* in July 1940, promising "to care for the spiritual needs of mentally sick patients, . . . living or deceased." Shrines mushroomed across the landscape. The clergy of St. Elizabeth's in Altadena, California, built a full-scale replica of the Lourdes grotto on the church's grounds in 1939, attracting three hundred thousand visitors from around the country between October of that year and the following June. Across the continent, in Oceanside, New York, Father Robert Barrett, pastor of St. Anthony's, constructed an underground shrine with many altars to his church's patron saint, including one with "a marble figure of the dead [St. Anthony] lying on a moss and wild flower bed in a vine-draped bower with birds, his only mourners." Father Barrett claimed fifty thousand visitors during his first Christmas season in 1940.[27]

Longer-established cults competed with these newer rivals for the purses of the faithful by generating innovative items and services. The Carmelite Shrine of the Little Flower in Oklahoma City offered annuity bonds and a bedroom night-light image of Thérèse—specially manufactured by Corning Glass—in addition to the usual novena prayers, vigil lights, holy water fonts, and perpetual associations. The Franciscan Shrine of St. Anthony in Cincinnati published booklets on health, diet ("Easy Exercise Routine Re-Makes Your Figure") and better secretarial skills for the saint's prospective clients, while continuing to promote "St. Anthony's Lilies," which were said to provide "relief in illness" and aid in "overcom[ing] temptations against purity." The suggested donation for the lilies was twenty-five cents apiece.[28]

In 1922 the Diocese of Albany, New York, was negotiating to buy property belonging to the Jesuit Shrine of the North American Martyrs in Auriesville. When Francis A. Breen, director of the shrine, warned his superiors against the sale because, as Breen promised, once the shrine's debts were paid it would become a "gold mine" for the order, he was simply making explicit what all smart priests knew: the saints were a good investment. So important indeed had this kind of fund raising become in American Catholicism by the 1940s that even a prominent defender of devotional culture, Father Joseph P. Donovan, a regular contributor to the *Homiletic and Pastoral Review,* conceded that "if Catholics were at a public devotion without giving to a collection they might ask in wonderment . . . 'Is this a Catholic novena?'"[29]

There was a striking convergence in these years between novel forms and methods of devotional promotion and the new American advertising industry. Both were using ever more extravagant language to sell their products to a new national market that they were simultaneously constituting and exploiting, and both were directed mainly at women. Devotional pitches were as direct and outrageous as the infamous ads for Listerine: "Have you any difficult case to be solved quickly," St. Jude's shrine asked in 1939, "any trouble for which help is needed, or anything that seems impossible to become a reality? . . . If you wish his visible and speedy help, join and be a fervent promoter of St. Jude's League." Another notice in the *Voice of St. Jude,* soliciting membership in the Shrine's Purgatorial Society, claimed: "God, in applying to the souls the fruits of the Masses, takes many things into consideration; now, all other things being equal, evidently one who is enrolled more times will have a larger share in the fruits of the Masses and prayers of this Pious Union." American Catholic shrine clergy in the nineteenth century tended to deemphasize the miraculous when they described their devotions.[30] In the twentieth century, though, the miraculous became the central appeal, both in advertising and devotionalism, to a new national constituency. Through novel devices and strategies, such as postal advertisements and the placements of ads in newspapers around the country, and with the aid of new print and broadcast technologies, devotional promoters like those in Chicago shaped and reached a population beyond parochial borders.

Modern advertisers, wielding sophisticated methods and techniques taken from the new discipline of psychology, cunningly exacerbated and then capitalized on fear and vulnerability in marketing consumer goods, and so did their clerical counterparts, although here the clergy had an obvious advantage: what was bad breath compared to the lingering torments of a loved one in purgatory, dirty laundry compared to a sick child? Devotional promoters and salesmen were adept at working distress for gain. A full-page advertisement for statues of the Infant of Prague appeared in the October 1951 issue of the *Voice of St. Jude* with this pitch: "Perhaps *you* are troubled, worried, sick at heart . . . perhaps you are seeking aid to some pressing problem . . . perhaps you need consolation, confidence, guidance, comfort or courage. If so, you too may be blessed if you introduce into your home the devotion to the Infant Jesus of Prague." Suffering was the best market for devotional goods and services, and advertisements like this were everywhere in the Catholic press. "You owe it to yourself," another notice, this one for a "Home Shrine of St. Christopher," proclaimed in 1944, obviously targeting the unhappiness of wartime separations, "to establish this devotion for the protection of your family and friends." Although they were not unique among American clergy in this, Tort and his assistants and successors were accomplished practitioners of this art. At one point, for example, the Shrine suggested that petitions to Jude about desperate matters could be given added "force" if they were accompanied by subscriptions to the *Voice of St. Jude,* clearly one way of making hopelessness pay.[31]

Many clergy were not comfortable with all of this promotional activity, and voices of dissent were heard long before the 1950s and 1960s. In the fastness of their rectories or in the pages of periodicals published solely for them, priests wondered whether their financial dependence on popular devotions was not encouraging "slot machine" religion among the laity or fostering a culture of "credulity . . . for anything and everything that savors of the supernatural." "Many a chary churchman," Joseph Donovan observed in 1946, "suspects that novenas have their appeal to pastors" as "an easy way of getting necessary or useful parish support" from "persons of shallow and whimsical devotional tendencies, tendencies which may be left uncultivated without any noticeable loss in the spiritual riches of the parish, and, if cultivated, produce no appreciable gain." Others fretted that this extravagant panoply of devotions would draw the faithful away from the "essence of Catholicism," as one critic lamented, as it attracted the ridicule and contempt of outsiders. (The latter concern at least was not misplaced: even though the middle years of the century also witnessed a proliferation of Protestant popular religious practices, the cult of saints became one of the marks, and surely the most provocative and exotic one, of

Catholic difference in modern American culture.) Some priests in their most bitter moments went as far as to suggest that they and their fellow clergy had become holy racketeers, and sometimes their congregations shared the suspicion.[32]

But clerical support for devotionalism was not always cynical—or it was rarely only cynical. Priests and nuns not only promoted popular devotions, they also participated in them, and Jude numbered hundreds of religious among his devout, including Father Tort. The clergy encouraged the many different forms of popular piety for pastoral reasons, as a way for people to cultivate and enjoy greater intimacy with the sacred, at the same time that they exploited these devotions for their own ambitions and financial needs. Lay people tolerated this ethos because they genuinely wanted to support the work of the church and because they had needs that could be satisfied only with religious objects and devotional practices. Joseph Donovan urged other priests, especially the most critical, toward a more sympathetic understanding of devotionalism. In a meditation on popular religion that appeared in the *Homiletic and Pastoral Review* in the summer of 1943, Donovan asked himself whether any theological justification could be found for the devotional practice, recently brought to his attention by some outraged colleagues, of eating holy cards. "We cannot be too quick to find fault," he reflects, "for Saint Bernadette did and was told to do things that we American Catholics antecedently would have called ridiculous," and the Virgin herself "deigned to stoop to the tastes of her clients, raw as those clients might have been in mere human refinement." Pointing to the similarities in the preaching styles of Bernardino da Siena and Billy Sunday, Donovan concluded that while "devotional life, like other phases of life, can become exuberant," it was still through practices associated with devotionalism that heaven and earth very often communicated with each other. The theology of Donovan's argument was widely shared in Catholic culture.[33] Devotions were not imposed from the top down, and they were not simply improvised independently by the laity in times of need; rather, devotionalism was one of the ways that priests, nuns, and lay people shaped and shared a common Catholic culture together.

A BRIEF SOCIAL HISTORY OF THE PRAYERS MADE TO ST. JUDE

There were no more exuberant devotional promoters than Father Tort and his successors at the National Shrine of St. Jude. Over the years these men and their lay associates evolved a full repertoire of devices to attract and sustain the loyalty and generosity of the cult's national clientele, including a Purgatorial Society (with a "renewable" perpetual membership), the St. Jude's Burse (to encourage small donations to the seminary), and a perpetual mass league that promised ten thousand yearly masses to its members. At various times the Shrine marketed wall plaques of St. Jude, St. Jude car medallions, blessed oil, calendars, rosary rings and small personal shrines for soldiers overseas during the Second World War, and different sorts of rosaries (including one filled with soil taken from the Roman catacombs), along with prayer books, statues, medals, scapulars, and vigil lights that burned for various intervals of times.

Jude in turn accomplished what was asked of him by the Claretians. With the help of the small (and occasional large) donations sent in by the devout, subscriptions to the *Voice of St. Jude,* and the fund-raising work of the police, the order was able to build a seminary in Momence, Illinois, on beautifully landscaped grounds; purchase and maintain valuable real estate in Chicago's downtown business district; support a bilingual parochial school under the care of a Mexican order of teaching sisters; fund a full range of traditional parish activities at Guadalupe; and remodel both Shrine and church several times. The League of St. Jude, according to an understated assessment by the historian of the Claretians in the United States, "has proved to be one of the most profitable ventures for the Province and the Congregation," so profitable, in fact, that the steady flow of donations made possible the restructuring and settlement of the parish's debt in 1944. The devout were so reliable in their commitment to the Shrine that in June 1949, to cite just one example of the Claretians' confidence, the director could propose raising funds for a completely new marble altar for the saint—by October of that year.[34]

Devotion to St. Jude grew steadily. Participation in popular devotions sometimes declines in hard times, when money is needed for other things. But Jude's cult thrived during the Depression, perhaps because, as evidence from the letters to the Shrine suggest, the saint's devout were not drawn from the completely destitute but from the class that was just holding onto, precariously, the small gains of the earlier decade. One man told me that his mother sent a monthly donation to Chicago right through the Depression in gratitude for something Jude had done for her, even though the family had little enough money to spare.[35] Faithfulness to heavenly obligations was one of the ways that hardworking Catholic families, distressed like other Americans by what they perceived as their own personal failures during the Depression, continued to show their worth and quality.

Unemployed men made novenas to St. Jude with their families; children prayed that their fathers would keep their jobs; families looked to Jude to help them find stability, calm, and courage in a terrifying time. Disoriented by the severity of the crisis and often unable to imagine an end to it, Americans generally seem to have been gripped by an urgent desire to communicate their anxieties and frustrations directly to some single powerful figure who would attend to them personally, acknowledge the depth of their fear, and offer them some hope that they could not attain by themselves. This is evident in the way that millions of poor Americans imagined and reached out to Franklin and Eleanor Roosevelt: the White House received an unprecedented volume of mail during the Depression, some five to eight thousand letters *daily*. The form letters that were sent out in response to these, over the president's signature, were viewed lovingly as signs of the president's concern for each of the correspondents individually, and they were treated with something like the devotion accorded by Catholics to the relics of the saints. Changing technology served as a powerful conduit for this fantasy of an intimate bond with the president. Needy people huddled close to their radios listening to Roosevelt's voice coming to them along the recently organized national broadcasting networks and felt that he was "talking with each of them personally," as Lorena Hickok reported from New Orleans. Government under FDR was "extraordinarily personal," according to historian Robert McElvaine. Roosevelt was not alone in inspiring this kind of devotion or exploiting technology like this in these years. Father Coughlin, for example, also created a national community through the warmth and charismatic power of his radio voice, and by addressing people's fear; at the height of his popularity, the Radio Priest was receiving more than ten thousand letters a day.[36] Scores of devotional promoters were using the same technologies and techniques to reach the same needy audiences in the same years.

Jude's popularity increased still more when economic distress gave way to war. The families of just-mustered G.I.'s gathered in improvised rituals around their men to ask for the saint's protection and his assurances of a safe return for their loved ones. Hundreds of thousands of American Catholic soldiers went to war (this and later ones) with medals of Jude around their necks or his image in their pockets, the gifts of worried mothers, wives, sweethearts. Then, through the long years of separation, these women came together in rituals of endurance on the home front. They met together in churches around the country to pray to Jude, then afterward went back to each other's kitchens for coffee and to talk about how hard it was to make ends meet with their men

away or to find good babysitting when they went to work. The Shrine organized special novenas in the war years for peace and victory and offered the
saint's clientele devotional objects specially designed for battlefield conditions,
like plastic-coated prayer cards printed on heavy-duty cardboard and bibles
encased in steel to be worn over soldiers' hearts.[37]

Some American Catholic historians have seen the powers of the saints wane
in the immediate postwar years, when American Catholics became more secure and prosperous and so less dependent on heavenly support.[38] But this was
not the fate of the Patron Saint of Hopeless Cases, and it was not simply so
elsewhere in American Catholic popular culture either. Particular devotions
declined. The once-powerful cult of Our Lady of Sorrows in Chicago, for
example, which had provided so much consolation during the sad years of the
Depression, lost most of its following after the war. A process of attrition began
to undermine some local cults, as the population of Catholic neighborhoods
changed (although even this was not irrevocable, and many of these old world
cults were revived in the 1970s during the period of rediscovered ethnic pride
among the third and fourth generations).[39] Criticism of devotionalism within
the American church intensified in the postwar period as the movement for
liturgical reform gathered momentum here and in Europe, and this had some
impact on American practice.

But there was even more brick and mortar to be paid for as the pace at
which American Catholic families grew and moved quickened in the postwar
years, and priests continued to create and promote devotions while lay people
found new needs in a changing environment to bring to the saints. The trajec-
tory of American Catholic economic history from the thirties to the early
sixties was solidly upward; most scholars use the designation "middle class" to
describe what Catholics had become or were becoming in the postwar years.[40]
But the hold of the immigrants' children and grandchildren on this achievement was tenuous, and they were exposed to all the vulnerabilities of their new
status: recently achieved comfort and security could be quickly enough undermined by sickness, temporary unemployment, or other family crises. Jude did
not lack for clients in the postwar world.

By 1954, the membership of "St. Jude's League" numbered in the "hundreds
of thousands." The Shrine was no longer under Tort's direction by this time.
Worn out by his many responsibilities and plans, the priest begged his supe-
riors in 1936 to relieve him of his post. The Claretians knew just how important
Jude's cult was to other projects, and Tort was replaced by a young priest,
Anthony Catalina, who proved to be a capable administrator. The respon-

sibilities of the director of Jude's shrine included supervision of the publication of the *Voice of St. Jude* and presiding over the activities of the publicly prominent Police Branch. Even in the 1960s and 1970s, when the prestige, if not the popularity, of shrines declined in American Catholicism, the directors of Jude's shrine and the various editors of *Voice of St. Jude*, clerical and lay, have been skilled and competent men.[41]

And Jude was no longer the obscure saint. By the middle years of the century, as a result of the promotional skills of the clergy and the dedication of the saint's devout to spreading the word about him, Jude was intimately and inevitably associated with disaster in the imaginations of American Catholics. This was the holy figure they now automatically thought of when something went really wrong in their lives. Even women who had never prayed to the saint before found themselves calling out his name, spontaneously and unexpectedly, in desperate situations. This was a remarkable achievement for a saint who did not even have a statue in this country until 1929.

ANOMALIES OF PLACE IN THE MAKING OF THE SHRINE

Claretian gratitude to St. Jude did not prevent the regular eruption of tensions between the directors of the Shrine and the pastors of the church that housed it. Parish priests often resented the competition of shrines, which generally have been the province of religious orders in Catholic history, not of the regular diocesan clergy. During the years of furious devotional promotion in the United States, the secular clergy constantly accused religious at nearby shrines of invading their territories to take money that really belonged to them.[42] But in the case of the South Chicago shrine, competition erupted not with rival priests outside the Order but among the Claretians themselves, specifically between the pastor of Our Lady of Guadalupe and the director of the National Shrine of St. Jude. An examination of this tension takes us deeper into the meanings of Jude's shrine on the American Catholic landscape in this time.

The Church of Our Lady of Guadalupe and the League of St. Jude were both under the jurisdiction of the Claretian Order, of course. The League had the "right" (*derecho*), in the language of the norms governing its relations to the church, to use the facilities at Guadalupe for its various devotions, in consultation with the pastor; in return, the League would make a contribution for the upkeep of the church. These guidelines left a great deal unspecified, though, and in this silence resentments festered. Guadalupe's pastor requested clarifica-

Our Lady of Guadalupe Church, South Chicago, ca. late 1940s.

tion in 1947. Who was responsible, he wanted to know, for cleaning the walls of the church, blackened by the smoke of hundreds of vigil lights, or for scraping the melted wax off the floors—a church employee or someone paid for by the League? Were the sisters who lived next door to the church "bound to do clerical work for the League"? Was there some way of reducing the competition between the regular liturgical rites of the parish church and the special weekly devotions to St. Jude?[43]

This tension was grounded in a curious spatial anomaly that characterized Jude's Shrine from its founding. The National Shrine of St. Jude, to restate the obvious, is located *inside* a Mexican American parish; the Claretians referred to this as the "site" of the devotion. But until very recently the Mexicans at Guadalupe did not participate with any particular fervor in the devotion to the saint who towers over the right side of their church, preferring to bring their prayers instead to Nuestra Señora de Guadalupe. People in the neighborhood, familiar with the sight of outsiders pulling up to the church (occasionally in limousines) to make their prayers, sometimes referred to Jude as "el santo blanco," an indication of how great a distance the Spanish Jude had traveled from Prescott, Arizona. Spanish-language devotions to Jude were not held at the Shrine until the mid-1970s.[44] The Shrine provided work for some neighborhood people: the saint's correspondence, for example, has long been answered by a small group of women, many of them Mexican Americans from Guadalupe, first in the South Chicago rectory and later in the order's downtown headquarters, who have passed the job on through the years to their daughters and nieces. Jude was an unavoidable fact of parish life; Mexican Americans in the neighborhood participated in the Shrine's annual novenas and in other Shrine events that were necessarily also parish occasions. But Jude was not a local hero.

The saint's Anglo devout, meanwhile, even those who grew up in South Chicago, refer to the church as St. Jude's. Confusing, even misleading, promotions in the early years of the devotion encouraged the misnomer; pictures in the *Voice of St. Jude* of the parish baseball team in the 1930s, for example, showed boys wearing uniforms emblazoned with *St. Jude's*, not *Nuestra Señora de Guadalupe*. The Claretians never denied that Our Lady of Guadalupe was a Mexican American parish, but by identifying pictures of the church as the National Shrine of St. Jude and generally talking about the Shrine as if it were distinct from the church, they managed to distance the two. Judy, who grew up in one of the Polish sections of South Chicago, insisted that Our Lady of Guadalupe was actually once officially called St. Jude's (it was not, of course) and that it was renamed only after the surrounding neighborhood had become Mexican, although she could not remember when this renaming took place. Another woman informed me confidently, while we were actually sitting together in front of the image of Guadalupe over the main altar, that the name of the parish was St. Jude's.[45] It is hardly surprising, then, that many of the devout I have spoken to outside of Chicago have no idea that the Shrine is actually located inside a Mexican American parish.

The paradox of this place is evident in the way the Shrine clergy themselves have imagined, described, and administered the location over the years. Tort often used the familiar tropes of the Catholic pilgrimage tradition to describe what he called the Chicago "throne of [St. Jude's] mercy and compassion," as in this message, written in 1935: "The sick, the afflicted, the lame and the blind, the suffering, the erring, all find solace here. An incessant stream of pilgrims has always come to visit the Shrine, proving the great and powerful influence St. Jude has in the presence of his relatives, Jesus and Mary." At the same time, the first pastor of Guadalupe and his successors continually emphasized to

Jude's far-flung clients that they need never come to Chicago to participate fully in the cult. According to a recent director, the order has never "put a lot of emphasis on visiting a place," and he estimated that about 95 percent of Jude's devout would never make a pilgrimage to Chicago.[46]

In the 1950s, to compound this confusion, the Claretians, thinking of Jude's shrine more traditionally as a place to be visited, considered moving it to another location in central Illinois where they could provide better parking facilities and amenities for visitors—whom they were not encouraging and who were not coming in any case. Writers at the Shrine had been imaginatively speculating for years about why Jude chose Chicago, of all American cities, as the site of the international revival of his devotion. They had come to see a meaningful resemblance between the long-forgotten, unassumingly modest but extraordinarily powerful saint and Carl Sandburg's "city of the big shoulders," the unassuming but powerful industrial center of the heartland. Yet these same men made plans for moving the saint out of his "hometown," as Danny Thomas called Jude's Chicago.

The devout have also imagined the Shrine in conflicting ways. They believed that the saint was present in a special way in Chicago and that prayers said *at* the Shrine were particularly efficacious. They requested that their petitions be placed beside his relics on the altar.[47] People from South Chicago and immediately surrounding neighborhoods drop in to rest and pray before the soothing rose-colored marble of the saint's altar, which they experience as a place of peace. The annual novenas in honor of the saint continue to be well-attended. But at the same time, the devout have always understood that it was not necessary to come to Chicago to experience the saint's presence (however real they believed it to be there) and rarely expressed any interest in making the trip. Many Chicago-area devout have never been to the Shrine, some do not even know where it is, and others exaggerate the dangers of the neighborhood around the Shrine to account for their keeping away.

This curious confusion about the meaning of place reflected developments in European and American Catholic devotionalism under way since the eighteenth century. Premodern European popular piety, especially among the peoples of the Mediterranean and Ireland, had been resolutely local. Saints presided over specific locales, and their power did not customarily extend beyond definite borders whose significance was usually political or cultural as well as sacred. A shrine or healing site might mark the break between two rival communities or two competing ways of life—between settled and nomadic social worlds, for example, or rural and urban. In cultures of Celtic origin, particular features of the local landscape—springs, rocks, grottoes, and so on—were themselves thought to be places of supernatural power.[48] To encounter the saint, a person in need went to that saint's special place, the one spot on the landscape where his or her power was situated or focused.

This is not to say that popular devotionalism was a phenomenon of complete immobility, however. The saints sometimes migrated from one locale to another. A popular figure and cult might be copied in other locations far removed from the original site of the saint's presence. Furthermore, because the materials of devotionalism—bones, candles, oils, waters, and similar objects—have always been liable to removal, a latent tension between the stationary and the motile has always run through devotionalism. As a result of this ambivalence, changing social conditions, such as shifts in local political power or the waning of some way of life, have not uncommonly been articulated through the media of the cult of saints, by the removal of relics from one location to another, for example, or the abandonment of a once-popular shrine.[49] But even objects that had been moved in such circumstances were eventually reconnected to new places, and there were specific *local* reasons why St. James and not someone else was venerated in Compostella, Spain, and not someplace else. Place and power were connected or successively reconnected.

The localism of popular devotions was undermined by a number of different factors in the emergence of modern Europe. The processes of industrialization and urbanization remapped the continent, and revolutions in transportation and communication slowly redirected the focus of life outward from village and town to region and nation. At the same time, the papacy, reformed and revitalized after the Council of Trent, was demanding—and gradually securing—a Rome-centered piety.[50] Local devotions were difficult to control: rooted in ancient customs and popular prerogatives, European piety was frequently anticlerical and anti-institutional. In Tridentine Catholicism, however, priests educated in schools under Roman supervision and loyal to the central authorities sought to establish ecclesiastical supervision over the unruly impulses of popular piety; at the same time Rome encouraged the diffusion of universal devotions, especially to Mary, avatar of the church in its corporate unity, and extended its authority in general over piety.

This history did not proceed in a straight line. The new regulations and orientations of Trent spread slowly over the Continent, in uneven patterns, sometimes meeting open defiance, more often encountering inertia and apathy. Individual priests were themselves deeply attached to local ways for many reasons and were more or less enthusiastic in promoting the newer cults and uprooting the old. Furthermore, people could still take little vials of healing water, bits of stone, or other souvenirs away from even the most universal and Roman devotions, like that to Our Lady of Lourdes, and so they could still improvise their own worlds of meaning and practice around the officially sanctioned idioms when they got back home.[51] The universal cults had different, even discrepant, meanings on various levels—personal, parish, national, and international—and in different places; most often they coexisted with resilient local customs. Nevertheless, the church was officially set on a new course.

This ambivalent movement away from the sacred-in-place was recapitulated in the history of American Catholic popular devotionalism. Immigrants with roots in premodern Europe initially re-created a place-oriented devotionalism in the late nineteenth and early twentieth centuries.[52] Their popular devotions were usually connected to the history and geography of southern and eastern Europe, and they addressed their prayers to holy figures who were intimately associated with their histories and cultures (such as the Polish Black Madonna of Czestochowa) or with particular features of the landscape of the old countries (like the devotion to the Madonna of Montevergine among Italian Americans) or with the orders of the priests and nuns who had accompanied the immigrants to the New World. These devotions, like most others in the modern church, were poised between two orientations: linked to the ancient ways of Celtic and Mediterranean cultures, as modern cults they were also required to have Rome's approval and to be situated under the authority of clergy. But there was often tension between clergy and people around the practices of popular cults, and in some immigrant communities, shrines established outside ecclesiastical control persisted.

The holy figures who made the journey over with the immigrants soon became associated with specific places in the New World, too. American Catholics have characteristically identified where they lived by the names of the saints who presided over their parishes, rezoning the nation's cities into a distinctly Catholic atlas of neighborhoods called St. Brendan's, St. Stan's, Our Lady of Mercy, the Immaculate Conception. The immigrants' saints were neighborhood spirits, as locally identified as their bakers, funeral directors, and ward heelers, and the celebrations of the feast days of these saints were times when the whole neighborhood came together to acknowledge the power of the local holy figure.

Yankee Catholic and middle-class Irish and German popular piety before the period of the new immigration had also been oriented to place, though the impress of the new universalism was apparent in nineteenth-century American

Catholicism, and there were early signs of a nationalizing impulse. American Catholic devotions in the nineteenth century were mostly derived from and connected to European sites and practices. Father Joseph Baker, for example, modeled his enormously successful Shrine of Our Lady of Victory in Lackawanna, New York, after the Parisian shrine of the same name, which he had visited on the first American Catholic tour of holy places in 1874. Life-size dioramas of the Virgin appearing to Bernadette in the grotto at Lourdes (often complete with a trickling spring, an ancient Celtic touch in modern America) or to the children on the hillside at Fatima were reproduced around the United States, literally bringing the topography of the European countryside into American Catholic churches and neighborhoods, as well as to the grounds of the University of Notre Dame, where one of the first American reproductions of Lourdes was constructed in 1877.[53]

But place did not matter much to Jude's devout or to the promoters of his cult. Jude was an oddly unencumbered, even disassociated, figure when he made his first appearance in American Catholic culture. He was of no particular significance to the Claretians, unlike their founder, whose cult the order was never able to promote successfully in the United States, however much it tried. European devotions to St. Jude appeared for the most part only after the American revival of his cult. Although he was the object of a very modest devotion in Central and South America, St. Jude was not adopted by Spanish speakers in the United States, as we have seen. He had no specific tie to South Chicago, and none was ever elaborated; the vague homology between modest Jude and humble Chicago seems to have been important mainly to the more literary seminarians at Momence. The saint's feast day was not a neighborhood celebration.

So St. Jude was not only an unknown saint, but a placeless one, too.

A NATIONAL SHRINE

It is more accurate, however, to say that *local* place was of no special significance to the saint's devout; there was, in fact, a way that place mattered to them a great deal. The Claretians called the Shrine the National Shrine of St. Jude. Tort emphasized that the cult existed "to make St. Jude Thaddeus . . . better known in every city, town and hamlet of this Country," clearly a nationalizing ambition, and his successors have consistently repeated this commitment. The devout shared it, too. From the earliest days of the devotion, Jude's clients, who came from all of the older ethnic groups (as Tort intended) and from all parts of the country, imagined themselves a nationally dispersed and broadly inclusive association. "I am sending you a small offering," a client from Buffalo, New York, wrote in 1949, "to be used in helping you spread more and more literature about dear Saint Jude all over the Country." Jude was identified on the Shrine's petition forms as "saint of the whole world, Catholic or non-Catholic," and the devout seemed particularly proud that some Protestants prayed to the saint, too, which seemed to confirm his status as a uniquely American intercessor.[54]

This national focus was new in American Catholic popular piety. The promoters of the very popular Shrine of St. Anthony of Padua in Cincinnati, for example, which was founded in the late nineteenth century, never referred to it as a "national shrine" but as "Saint Anthony's favorite shrine." The furthest that the Carmelite Fathers at the Little Flower Shrine in Oklahoma would go was to proclaim theirs the "first shrine in the world dedicated to Saint Thérèse." Both orders could just as easily have made claims to national stature, of course.[55] The work of the priests at Notre Dame to promulgate Marian devotions throughout the United States in the mid-nineteenth century was a reflection not of an incipient national consciousness primarily but of the universalism of modern, Rome-centered, Marian devotions. The supralocal impulse here was to bring the United States into the universal church, not to Americanize devotionalism. Notre Dame's founder, Edward Sorin, C.S.C., an enthusiastic advocate of popular devotions, imagined the many shrines he built at the university serving as the focus for regional, not national, pilgrimages. Whatever sense of an emergent American identity can be glimpsed in Notre Dame's devotional efforts, moreover—which were contemporary with Isaac Hecker's ambition to develop a distinctly American Catholicism—was soon overwhelmed by the combined forces of the new immigration from Europe and the Papal denunciations of "Americanism." Since the 1920s, on the other hand, there have been many "national" shrines, with a greater self-consciousness of and pride in their American presence.

Warren Susman has argued that Americans in the 1920s and 1930s were becoming newly aware of themselves as a national community and were searching for the appropriate myths and models to experience, confirm, and express this new feeling. National radio networks first appeared in 1927 and played an important role in shaping heightened national self-consciousness, as did the many crazes that swept the country, the movies that everyone was seeing, and the products they were all either buying or desiring in the big department stores that were threatening local markets. All of this, says Susman, "created a special community of all Americans . . . unthinkable previously."[56]

The same awareness was evident across American Catholic culture. National societies of American Catholic poets, librarians, philosophers, and anthropologists, among others, proliferated in the second and third decades of this century. Jay Dolan has interpreted these developments as evidence of the community's efforts in this period after immigration to shape "something approaching an American Catholicism" and "to make Catholicism recognized in America." This was a strong but ambivalent impulse in the community, a very tentative rapprochement of an emerging middle class with American culture, which at the same time retained much of the unease and defensiveness more characteristic of American Catholicism.[57]

These trends reflected broader centrifugal forces in American Catholic social life, as they had in early modern Europe. There was a diminishing sense of local community throughout American Catholicism as the second and third generations abandoned the inner city ethnic enclaves their parents had built for outlying urban areas and the suburbs. Ethnic politics soon registered this reorientation. Irish Americans first came to national prominence in this period, moving beyond the parochial politics of the years of the postfamine immigration, and newer ethnic politicians, like New York's Fiorello LaGuardia, were attaining citywide and sometimes even national reputations. Powerful prelates, like Boston's William Cardinal O'Connell and later New York's Francis Cardinal Spellman, achieved a level of national recognition that was unheard of a generation before.[58] This movement among American Catholics from the local to the national constituted a revolution in the social geography of the community.

One of the consequences of these developments, in addition to the many uncertainties presented by the unfamiliar environments, was that the immigrants' children were confronted now with the challenge of integrating their local and ethnic identities with their emergent sense of being Americans. A recent historian of Polish America notes that there was a powerful yearning in that community in the 1920s for Pulaski Day parades, Polish street names, and public monuments honoring Polish heroes, and this impulse was reproduced in other communities as well. The point was not to celebrate being Polish but to evoke Polish cultural symbols as a way of claiming space on the American landscape and the American calendar. Ethnic pride was reconceived as access to national participation, and this in turn, transformed the meaning of ethnicity itself. The designations *Polish American* or *Italian American* were losing their local coordinates; instead, to be Polish American in the community's changing social circumstances now meant that one felt affinities with others of similar heritage living all over the United States, and more generally with other second- and third-generation Catholics from southern and eastern European homes.[59]

This was precisely the space that mattered to Jude's devout and precisely the space in which the saint was situated. To borrow a term from William Christian Jr., Jude's "territory of grace"—that area over which a saint extends his or her "benevolent power"—was not South Chicago but the entire nation. One woman told me that she feels as close to St. Jude in Colorado as she did when she was living in Chicago. This shrine was not situated in an ethnic enclave like other devotional idioms the devout would have been (all-too) familiar with, but out there, in a vague—but not ethnic—national, "American," space. Jude's clients treated the Shrine as a point of reference on the emergent national map of American Catholicism. So the Shrine is best thought of not in traditional terms, as a place to be visited, a site of power to which people traveled in pilgrimage, but as a kind of radio transmitter: just as the national radio networks shaped constituencies of the dispersed through signals sent and received, so the Shrine constituted its clientele across great distances through petitions sent, donations received, subscriptions, membership dues, and all of Tort's other promotional devices.[60]

Historians of American Catholicism have tended to interpret popular religious practices in the period under consideration here as isolating, atavistic, and regressive; saints' cults and all that went with them were, in this understanding, the inassimilable core of preconciliar American Catholicism, the way that Catholics marked out and maintained their own ghetto.[61] But this perspective does not recognize that a new devotional culture was taking shape alongside the immigrants' piety. The middle years of this century were an extraordinarily creative period in the history of Roman Catholic popular piety, as clergy and laity both—often for different reasons and sometimes at odds with each other—experimented with the familiar forms of piety that they had inherited in their tradition, within the broader context of tremendous social change. Modern Catholic devotionalism took as easily to the airwaves and highways as it did to the ways of Madison Avenue.[62] American Catholics huddled around their shrinelike receivers to recite rosaries led by someone half a continent away and to participate in novenas in other cities. This modern, indigenous, postimmigration devotionalism reflected and addressed the different experiences of the immigrants' children. It did not simply replace the older devotional forms, but extended, supplemented, and (in some cases) reimagined them, as the immigrants' children struggled to make sense of the changing and unfamiliar circumstances of their lives through the familiar idioms of popular Catholicism. The cult of the Patron Saint of Hopeless Cases and Things Despaired Of was one of the most important (and lasting) expressions of this new devotional culture.

CHANGE AND CONTINUITY IN THE 1960S AND BEYOND

The devotion to St. Jude still exists. According to the present manager of the correspondence staff, the shrine in Chicago still receives about three thousand pieces of mail a day, still from all over the United States. The saint's clients are getting older, but some young people find their way into the devotion, too, usually through their mothers and grandmothers. The local Mexican community in South Chicago participates more actively in the cult, bringing new perspectives and enthusiasm. "Thank you, St. Jude" notices appear in the classified sections of newspapers around the country.

It is generally thought that the liturgical reforms inspired by the Second Vatican Council of 1962–1965, which came just as the American Catholic community was, in this view of it, maturing intellectually and economically, brought an end to the great era of popular piety. As journalist Paul Hendrickson has written in his evocative memoir of seminary life in these years, it seemed as if one day in the mid-1960s the saints suddenly disappeared from the churches, replaced by huge and colorful banners with words of moral exhortation, like PEACE and AGAPE, stitched on them in big felt letters.[63] The era of exuberant improvisation in the idioms of the saints was over. But that is not quite what happened.

First of all, the saints did not go quietly from their niches in America's neo-Gothic cathedrals—which had been built with funds that those saints had been largely responsible for raising. The effort to change the inner lives of American Catholics, to reconfigure the way they engaged the sacred, practiced their faith, and indeed, the way they faced the everyday challenges of their lives, unfolded as a tense and complex process that met with resistance, ambivalence, and uncertainty at all levels, as such efforts to "reform" popular piety always do. A bitter internecine conflict erupted over the continued appropriateness of some of the most beloved practices associated with American Catholic popular piety and the cult of saints. The many devotional forms that had been developed in the preceding decades were criticized as regressive and irrelevant expressions of an infantile faith no longer acceptable in a spiritually sophisticated community. Popular piety was said to detract from the central act of worship in the

Catholic community, the shared celebration of the liturgy. These devotions would persist "as long as there are masses of people with low levels of religious instruction and formal education," Gary MacEoin, a prominent Catholic layman, wrote in 1966, but for better-educated and successful Catholics (who were increasing steadily in numbers) spirituality would "evolve into a variety of more scriptural, more personal and liturgical forms."[64]

The spirit of the time is evident in a mocking article published in 1965 in *Ave Maria,* once a bastion of popular devotionalism, by an irate and impassioned laywoman: "We must do away with superstition and quaint old-world folklore emanating from the ghetto. Down with nine-hour storm novenas, nine First Fridays so you can die happy, sewing sequins on the Infant of Prague's nightie, and dressing little Mary Hermoine in blue the first year of her life. Thank goodness we've outgrown all that nonsense, and now, with the help of authentic sources, we can really get down to the roots of liturgical living." In another article, a young mother superior taunts her aging father by telling him that she is taking his beloved statue of the Sacred Heart "to the dump." When the old man asks why, his daughter says, "It would break your heart to know, but for too long you have nursed your piety on this sickening, saccharine symbol of impiety." She comes back the next day for her father's statue of the Infant of Prague, dressed in a gown hand-sewn by her mother, long-since dead, and later tells the old man that now "it too lies smashed among the egg crates of the city dumping ground." When her father turns to the pastor of his parish for consolation and understanding, all the priest can do is warn him not be "an old fogey" and "to keep up with the rest of us." Other young American Catholics treated popular devotions as if they were exotic imports from European Catholicism, utterly strange to the American ethos, ignoring or denying their own roots in the same culture, or the origins of these practices on American shores.[65]

Some reformers attempted to recast popular devotionalism in what they considered a new, more spiritually mature idiom. At a conference he convened at Notre Dame in 1966 to determine what could be salvaged of his once enormously popular Family Rosary Crusade in the new spiritual environment, Father Patrick Peyton was told by a panel of distinguished theologians to break from "magical mathematics and mechanical indulgences" (in the words of Bernhard Häring), to incorporate a concern for social justice in his promotions of the rosary by studying and addressing the material conditions of the people in areas designated for rosary crusades, and to allow greater time for Scripture study and interior prayer. In postconciliar culture, the saints and the

Virgin Mary were to be reimagined in the languages of friendship, morality, or mythology, deemphasizing what the reformers considered an inappropriate and extravagant emphasis on the miraculous and the material. The old alliance between clergy and laity in the practice of popular devotions was broken.[66]

The reformers insisted that if popular devotions were to remain a feature of Catholic life, they would have to be surrounded by *words*. One way of understanding the transitions of the early 1960s, as Paul Hendrickson's recollection of the banners suggests, is as a shift from a culture of intimacy with many different holy figures, vividly imagined as real persons with foibles and idiosyncracies, who entered into complex relations with their devout in a domain relatively unmediated by official authorities, to a culture in which religious practice was to be bounded and authorized by words. Devotions now had to be accompanied by some sort of discursive practice, either explanatory sermons, clerical reflections on the meaning of particular expressions of piety, or readings of scripture, as if by hedging popular practices with the written and spoken word, their improvisatory and disruptive potential could be controlled or diminished.[67]

Words were not absent from preconciliar culture, of course, with all its prayer cards, novena booklets, and pious ejaculations—short utterances of praise, thanksgiving, or petition. The difference is that the words of the old devotionalism were efficacious in relation to specific cultic practices and disciplines, such as vows and novenas, and only as they expressed and realized relationships with particular holy figures. The new words belonged to a highly educated, professionalized class of specialists in church life—teachers, liturgists, educators, administrators—whose emergence at this time reflected the confident entry of American Catholics into the middle class; the words on the banners derived their power and legitimacy from the authority of this class in the ecclesiastical institution, not from their association with a beloved saint.

The National Shrine of St. Jude had begun to feel the sting of this criticism as early as 1954. The director at the time, Joachim DePrada, published a series of apologetic meditations that attempted to present Jude as a model of the moral life and not only as the intercessory figure of extraordinary power his devout believed him to be—and as he had long been promoted by the Shrine. DePrada deemphasized the place of petitionary prayer in the practice of the cult—the words that put people and all their needs and desires in direct relation with the saint—and affirmed instead the necessity of disinterested love of the saint, a love unrelated to any material request and certainly unsullied by the sorts of coercive strategies Jude's devout were adept at wielding. DePrada also assured his unnamed detractors that the church's official teaching on the cult of saints was carefully explained at the beginning of each celebration of Jude at the Shrine "so those making the novena for the first time may not be confused and forget that Saint Jude is just our intercessor and that ultimately all power comes from God." By 1963 the Shrine, clearly on the defensive, was charging that "ignorant persons tend to scoff at novenas, disdaining them as a 'short cut' and an attempted substitute for a full and rigorous spiritual life."[68] St. Jude was clearly not going to escape the conflicts of the times.

One of DePrada's successors, Father James Maloney, a sophisticated and diplomatic young man, a Chicago native, and a student of Tort's, set out to bring the devotion in line with the ethos of the Second Vatican Council. Father Maloney was dedicated both to the spirit of the reforms and to the preservation and promotion of Jude's cult, which had now become his official responsibility; his hope was to use the idioms and practices of the cult as the media for bringing the devout into the church's new era. A scripturally oriented novena booklet was issued in January 1967, and the devout were encouraged to incorporate Bible study in their devotions. Novena prayers were structured antiphonally as a dialogue between priest and people. Sunday devotions to St. Jude were discontinued: the day was reserved for the celebration of the Eucharist, "in conformity with the liturgical spirit." The devout were continually reminded, as part of an ongoing and insistent effort to subordinate the devotion to the Eucharist, that their prayers to the saints had to be "united with the official prayer or liturgy of the church, the Sacrifice of the Mass."[69]

The interior of Guadalupe was also remodeled in conformity with postconciliar theology and aesthetics. Father Maloney was determined to deemphasize the prominence of Jude's shrine in the church, but he was obviously constrained by the enormity of the rose-marble construction. His solution was to color the whole nave a soft red so that the right altar, to which Jude had ascended some forty years before in victory over the Little Flower, would blend in less conspicuously with the rest of the church. A garishly colored bas relief of souls writhing in the flames of purgatory, a last vestige of Tort's remunerative Purgatorial Society, was taken down, and the smoky room off the back of the church that was filled with vigil lights requested by Jude's many devout was replaced by a smaller alcove of tiered electric candles. A plaque that Father Maloney fixed to the wall of this clean, well-lit, and smoke-free room explained that the lights were symbols of—and much stress was put now on the *symbolic* nature of the candles—the corporate prayers of the devout and their "inward faith," not markers of favors desired or received.[70]

The plaque in the alcove of electric candles, in the style of post–Vatican II church art.

Finally, the devotion was more generally reimagined by Shrine theologians as an expression of social responsibility. The devout were warned not to scatter holy cards of St. Jude in the backs of churches, as they had been doing for years, but instead to undertake "missions" for the saint in their neighborhoods. The cult of saints is rooted in concern for others, Father Maloney told the devout, and in the belief in the unity of the church, living and dead; the actions of these holy figures for us must inspire and reflect our own solicitude for each other. Jude should serve as a moral witness, and the most appropriate response to him was imitation: the devout were urged to emulate his evangelical zeal and ecumenical reach, his courage, prudence, patience, kindness, and generosity. We do not pray *to* Jude, Father Maloney emphasized, but with him, for others and for ourselves, in a "Family of Prayer."[71]

Maloney and his staff were attempting in these various ways to diminish what they saw as the magical elements of the devotion, its materialistic concern for small, specific favors (as petitionary prayer was often understood now). The space allotted to the devout's accounts of these favors in the Shrine's magazine gradually shrank in the late 1950s, and Jude's face was replaced on the correspondence pages with an image of a man pointing to a postage stamp. In 1960 the letters of thanksgiving and petition were completely eliminated from the periodical, which was refigured in 1963 as *U.S. Catholic*, a family magazine more in tune with the changing ethos. Brief selections from the devout's letters were printed now in the small, four-page pamphlet, *St. Jude's Journal*, an exclusively devotional periodical that replaced the *Voice* as the Shrine's link with the devout.[72]

The Shrine was especially worried about how the devout were using one of the most popular devotional items, St. Jude's Holy Oil. The Shrine had long promoted the oil as a healing medium; the potent substance was mailed out in small black, octagonally shaped vials. Jude's most desperately ill clients requested it, usually those suffering from painful or embarrassing illnesses or tending dying relatives. But by the time of Maloney's tenure, rumors were circulating at the Shrine that the oil was being used in obscure, coercive "black magic" rituals. In their most forceful effort to reorient the devotion, the Shrine clergy eliminated St. Jude's Holy Oil sometime in the early to mid-1960s.[73] This was the sharpest indication of a disjuncture between the clergy's new understanding of the devotion and the devout's customary practices.

But today when devout write in asking for the oil, as many do, the correspondence staff diligently informs them that it is no longer available in Chicago—and provides the address of another shrine at which it can still be obtained. This contradiction reminds us that clergy can only go so far in their efforts to remake popular devotional practices, even in period of apparent excitement and enthusiasm for such change. The National Shrine of St. Jude took shape between the ambitions of the clergy in Chicago and the needs of the devout around the country, and it would survive this way, too.

Father Maloney acknowledged and respected the limits imposed on his ambitions by the desires and long-established practices of the devout. He continually reassured Jude's clients that "despite the outward changes in our form of worship, this personal relationship with Our Lord—and with Our Patron—becomes a most important part of our Novena services." The message was clear: people could still call on Jude for help with specific, everyday problems. The intensity and complexity of the director's struggle to accommodate the devout, sustain the financially necessary devotion for the Claretian Order, and respond to the Council's spirit sometimes found public expression in *St.*

Jude's Journal in his tense, ambivalent announcements about the changes under way. In May 1968, for example, commenting on the new room of electric vigil lights, Father Maloney confessed that "we have always felt . . . vigil lights are not needed by St. Jude, but they fulfill those who write in to us. Certainly, the vigil lights are not needed by S. Jude, but they fulfill a human need to express the constancy of our faith."[74] These sentences literally move in opposite directions.

Many of the old ways persisted, furthermore, in the public life of the cult. When a relic of St. Jude obtained earlier from Rome was moved to a special reliquary in 1961, for instance, it was heralded with the Shrine's customary promotional enthusiasm as "one of the largest single relics of St. Jude in the world." Medals and statues of the saint were still promoted, the devout were still encouraged to erect their own St. Jude lawn shrines, and articles continued to appear (in *St. Jude's Journal*) that described the saint's "family tree," a decidedly unscriptural orientation.[75] Vigil lights were still available in Chicago, although they were electric now and clean.

When the Vatican announced in 1969 that scores of saints were historically unverifiable figures and withdrew them from the official calendar, the Shrine received "a great deal of mail from people who have been aroused and even alarmed by this action." Father Maloney hastened to assure the devout of Jude's safety. "[T]he Church lacks the power," he wrote, "to make anyone a saint," and so, obviously, "she certainly lacks the power to unmake any saint whom God has made." Father Maloney's point is theologically orthodox—he is simply affirming the traditional doctrine that only God makes saints—but his article underscores the limits of the church's authority over popular devotions. The church, he is telling the devout, can never take Jude away from you; this assurance is an admission of the qualified but genuine autonomy of popular religion. It is hardly surprising then that devotion to Jude has retained a place on the contemporary American Catholic landscape when St. Christopher, who was not only one of the most popular of the saints unmade by Rome but also one of the ones against whom the historical argument was strongest, is still venerated in Europe alone at eleven separate shrines, where cars are blessed and journeys protected in his name.[76]

St. Jude was—and remains—the Patron Saint of Hopeless Cases. His devout have always said that they turned to him, at least initially, when they felt most lost and bereft and abandoned by other figures, human and divine, whom they had otherwise counted on for assistance and consolation. Once they had established a connection to the saint in such a time of desperate need, they often held him in reserve for that moment of subsequent crises when things slipped finally out of control. Isabel told me that even though she deeply disliked the man her daughter was planning to marry, she had not brought the situation to Jude's attention because she still felt there was something she could do about it herself. Her circumstances had not become hopeless yet.

But what did the generations of American Catholic women who came of age in the middle years of this century experience as hopeless?

Before we can ask what they wanted from the saint, we need to see what was so deeply troubling to the immigrants' daughters specifically, amid all the other changes that characterized these years of American Catholic history, that they declared their circumstances beyond hope.

2

Hopeless Causes and Things Despaired Of

Although the lives of the immigrants' sons and daughters alike were changing in the years between the wars, the difficulties of young women were distinct and in many ways more intense than those of their male kin. They found themselves at the center of family conflict, contending with sharply divergent pressures, demands, and responsibilities. They led the way in most of the social changes described in the previous chapter, especially in the most fiercely contested domains of work and love, but at the same time they were held responsible for looking after the kin left behind in the old neighborhoods. This meant that they were exposed more than their husbands and brothers to the older generation's anger and resentment, which were directed mainly at them anyway for wanting to take such steps out toward their own desires. The differences between the experiences of the immigrants' daughters and sons began at school and in the workplace and extended to all the other areas of their lives. It was this generation of American Catholic women, caught between cultures, between competing expectations and needs, and between newly separated geographical locations, that first imagined Jude into being.

THE IMMIGRANTS' DAUGHTERS BETWEEN WORLDS

In working-class communities, opportunities in the postindustrial economy opened up first to young women who found positions as secretaries, clerks, stenographers, and typists in various sectors of the white-collar world long before most of their male counterparts had the necessary skills to follow them. The immigrants' daughters had been educated for this kind of work in commercial and secretarial courses in high school. Parents who demanded that their sons take the work waiting for them in industry alongside their male relatives as soon as they legally could were often willing to let their daughters stay longer in school to prepare themselves for these office jobs. By 1930, according to a historian of women's work in the United States, the "female-intensive clerical and service sectors of the economy accounted for more than one-half of the female nonagricultural labor force and employed the majority of urban working-class women, both black and white."[1] American Catholic men, on the other hand, of all ethnic cultures, remained blue-collar into the 1960s.

A better education, more accomplished social skills, more sophisticated wardrobes, and a particular kind of poise and self-presentation was required of young women in banks, law offices, and insurance companies than was asked of their brothers and boyfriends in the factories and union halls, and the appearance and speech of young women began to distinguish them from the men in their communities. This had consequences for women's relationships. Because they were staying longer in school, girls often had an even more extended sojourn between childhood and adulthood than their brothers did, which meant more time for conflict to erupt with their parents. Young women had always been carefully guarded in ethnic communities, where their obedience and submission were regarded as emblems of the integrity and authority of the immigrant households. Now as they became more "American" and independent, a development their parents had more or less permitted on behalf of the family economy, they also became, in their parents' view, more difficult to control.[2] They began to dress in ways the older generations could not approve, they were making friends at school and work who came from other neighborhoods and ethnic groups, and with these new friends they were going to the movies, where their new hopes for themselves found confirmation in the era's Hollywood romances and melodramas.

When it came time to get married, the immigrants' daughters looked beyond the borders of their neighborhoods and families. Jesuit sociologist John L. Thomas found that the interethnic and mixed marriages he studied from these years were initiated by the women involved.[3] Women's marital choices did not have to extend beyond their ethnic group or church to be the occasion of domestic conflict, though: in most Catholic enclaves, marrying someone not from the town in the old country or from the local circle of relatives and friends was reason enough for bitterness and recrimination. Once they had married men unlike their fathers and uncles, furthermore, these women attempted to build new kinds of marriages with them. They wanted more equal and mutually supportive relations with their husbands than their own parents had known (or had been willing to disclose in public). Father Thomas noted a "drive for increased companionship of husband and wife, greater equality in the status of women, and diminishing expressions of parental authority" among newlywed Catholics in these years, and again his research suggested that the impetus for this change was coming mainly from the immigrants' daughters, whom he found to be generally "less tolerant and less long-suffering than [Catholic women had been] formerly."[4] They were also more likely to become dissatisfied with their marriages. According to the records of the Archdiocese of Chicago's marriage court in the 1940s, more and more Catholic women of all backgrounds were seeking annulments on grounds of cruelty and abuse, which Thomas attributed to the fact that the sons of immigrants were less modern in their marital values than their wives.[5]

At the same time, it was harder for the immigrants' daughters, despite their American ways, to separate themselves from the Old World than it was for their brothers and husbands. Young wives, even those who had successfully married out of their enclaves and moved away, were responsible for maintaining the networks of kinship support and obligation now scattered across the city. They were expected to keep some connection to the old ways—to provide the familiar foods for the holidays, for example, and to remember the traditional courtesies that the folks back in the neighborhoods looked for. Young married women frequently found themselves shuttling back and forth between their new homes and neighborhoods and the old, struggling to balance the responsibilities they bore in both locations.[6] Perhaps this is why so many of Jude's devout told me stories of praying to the saint in their cars.

Social and economic circumstances further conspired against women in this regard. The Depression gave many of the old neighborhoods their children back, and young women found themselves contending with the renewed authority of mothers and mothers-in-law. Many women also returned to their childhood homes during the war years, when they were finding it difficult to manage without their husbands' help, and then again during the housing shortage of the postwar years, which forced many of them to take temporary shelter under the roofs of their mothers or their husbands' mothers, a situation, one woman recalled, "I was not really comfortable with . . . and prayed to Saint Jude for improvement."[7]

While their domestic responsibilities were becoming more intricate and geographically demanding, the immigrants' daughters also found themselves deprived of the circles of female support that had been so important to their mothers and grandmothers. The areas of second and third settlement did not provide the same kind of dependable society of female neighbors and kin ready to come across the hall to help out in a crisis. The collapse of these ties left many of the immigrants' daughters feeling helpless, isolated, and vulnerable. It is against this background that we should understand one woman's comment to me that "the problems today are enormous and overwhelming," especially for women, upon whom the "stress of modern living" falls most heavily.[8]

If the story of these tumultuous years of change in American Catholic family history is organized around a series of dichotomies—the immigrant family survived or perished; the old ways were honored or betrayed; ethnic loyalties and identifications persisted or were denied; the suburbs supplanted the inner-city enclaves—the special dilemmas of young women, and the reasons why they turned to St. Jude, will be obscured. Instead, the immigrants' daughters found themselves in the tense space between the poles of these dichotomies and between these locations on the social landscape. The immigrant family and its customs did indeed persist for a long time, even when the social and economic conditions that had made it necessary and (to its children) inescapable had begun to change, because the young women of these households worked and sacrificed for them; the old ways were honored by the people—and especially the young women—moving fastest away from them; and the suburbs were connected to the inner cities by women's ties of responsibility.

The women who turned to Jude in these years did so in socially defined roles, identifying themselves in their petitions as daughters, mothers, and wives praying for husbands, parents, and children. But in the circumstances of the American Catholic family in this century these were not fixed positions with determinate meanings. Jude's devout, from the 1930s to the 1960s, first as young women just setting out and then as older ones dealing with the dilemmas of aging, were compelled by circumstance and inclined by their values, hopes, and experience to improvise at the important transitional moments of their biographies—when they went from being single to married women, for example, or became grandmothers—unlike their own mothers and aunts, who could follow the dictates of the family and tradition. They shared this existential responsibility with other American women of their generations.[9]

The immigrants' daughters and granddaughters had to negotiate between the image of what they should be and desire as dictated by their families and culture and their own hopes of what they might become. As they struggled to find the language to make and justify their choices, those in charge of the old ways redoubled their efforts to impose the traditional disciplines and constraints. These were not always hopeless times, but they were fraught with conflict, anger, and loneliness, as well as with exciting possibilities.

JUDE AND THE TIMES OF WOMEN'S LIVES

It was as a companion in such moments that Sylvia, a fifty-eight-year-old woman I spoke to in Chicago one morning, thought of St. Jude. Sylvia had first turned to the saint for help getting a date for the high school prom. St. Jude answered her prayer; the boy who asked her to the dance "turned out to be my first love," and Sylvia has been praying to St. Jude ever since. She carries a "first-class relic" of the saint—skin, bone, clothing, or a special object associated with the saint's life—with her wherever she goes and keeps his statue in her bedroom. Sylvia says that Jude accompanied her the first time she went "solo" in her car and helped her become a "good driver," which she needed to be in order to meet the various demands of work and family. She and her sister prayed together to meet good Catholic husbands. Her sister did—her boyfriend proposed to her on St. Jude's feast day—but Sylvia did not, and she lived at home taking care of her parents, who are both dead now. Her neighborhood has become dangerous; she is uneasy when she goes out and frightened when she stays in, and she wants to retire to a better place soon. Again she is counting on St. Jude. An inspector was coming from the Federal Housing Authority on the evening of the day we met to see whether her property qualified for a housing subsidy program, which would make it easier for her to sell it. Sylvia had stopped by the Shrine specifically to pray to St. Jude that this would go well.

Many of Jude's devout first turned to him as Sylvia did in late adolescence, at the suggestion of a girlfriend or sympathetic female relative, when they were dealing with problems of dating and courtship that were taking them beyond the counsel available in their traditions and beyond their parents' approval and their mothers' experience.[10] Their mothers' courtships had proceeded under the watchful gaze of mistrustful chaperons and jealous menfolk, and their suitors had often been chosen by their families from a local circle of available and familiar men. The marriage of Sylvia's parents, for example, had been arranged by their families. Not so for Jude's devout. Young women called on the saint to authorize their choices of husbands in the face of family disapproval and to mute the conflict that seemed to erupt inevitably between immigrant fathers and their daughters' prospective husbands (particularly when the latter came from outside the older men's social and cultural worlds), or between themselves and their boyfriends' mothers.

Young women also asked Jude to assist them in their encounter with the newly uncertain boundaries of sexual behavior outside the codes of the enclaves. There were new risks and new complications for young single women, especially in the years during and after the Second World War, when the enclaves began to dissolve at a quickened pace; the first thanksgiving for Jude's "protection" of a daughter was published by the Shrine in 1941. A girl reported to the Shrine in 1954 that her boyfriend "had some warped ideas about purity," which she apparently shared to some extent because she went on to say that "we were finding it extremely difficult to overcome the temptations that beset a young engaged couple." Family members implored Jude to watch out for daughters and sisters living by themselves near their work in the cities. "My oldest sister was living alone in an apartment," a correspondent told the Shrine in 1952. "She went with so many different men, it worried our family. I began praying to Saint Jude and within two weeks she became engaged to a fine young man with whom she had been corresponding." Young Catholic women were themselves particularly aware of the saint's usefulness in such exciting but anxious times. "I have found," a girl wrote the Shrine in 1967, "that I can always rely on Saint Jude to help me through all the frustrations and problems of being a teenager."[11]

Once married life began, Jude's help was sought in dealing with the stresses and disappointments that often accompanied it, especially in these years of rising romantic and economic expectations. New brides had to contend with the well-established authority of their husbands' female relatives, a situation that is always difficult but particularly so when the couple married across ethnic (or religious) boundaries and the young women involved were not familiar with the rules. Jude was called on during the various housing short-ages, inflations, and military drafts of the middle years of the century, when it seemed to new couples that anything could go wrong. "Here is my story," a woman began her letter to the Shrine in 1953. Six months after her marriage she discovered she was pregnant and "because of complications the doctor said I must get in bed and stay there until I was better." This was not good news: like other young couples in these years, she and her husband had wanted and acquired things after their marriage—"a new apartment . . . new furniture . . . a new car"—and they were carrying a heavy monthly debt. With her out of work now, they were not sure they were going to make it. Then "while I was confined to bed, my husband received a draft notice to report for a physical." Still reeling from this, he went out one morning and discovered that neighborhood toughs had slashed the tires on his car. "It was now," the Shrine's correspondent wrote, "that I prayed to Saint Jude." She concluded her letter, "It may seem like small matters, but to us newlyweds they looked like mountains."[12]

Sometimes women could not continue in the promises or the marriages they had made.[13] It was difficult to break off marriage engagements: treading warily between families, attempting to assert themselves without giving so much offense that their families would boycott their weddings, young women often felt that they had only one chance to make their own decisions before their families intervened and imposed their wills on them. They had risked so much to claim these relationships that they now wanted to extricate themselves from. It was even more difficult, of course, to end a marriage. "Hopeless" meant (and still means) precise things to a Catholic woman in a bad marriage: she was up against her church's absolute prohibition on divorce and the diffi-culties and embarrassments of obtaining an annulment, in addition to the more universal problems of finding love again and contending with feelings of loneliness, failure, and shame. American Catholic women in these especially painful circumstances have taken their stories to Jude.

Mothers looked to Jude for guidance and support in raising their children amid the changing mores and styles of the 1950s and 1960s. One woman told me that when her daughter became addicted to drugs in the early 1970s, the family's doctor, to whom she had turned for counsel, told her to give up on the child and let her go to her own destruction. "I told [the doctor] no, I couldn't," and he kept telling me, she's over eighteen, and we have no control. And so I prayed to Saint Jude again."[14] Jude's help was regularly sought, finally, amid the transitions of later life, when the devout found themselves first caring for elderly parents and then experiencing the onset of their own aging and the decline of their husbands and kin. They prayed to him for troubled grand-children who lived far away; they described to the saint their disappointments and confusions about the directions their families had taken.[15] Jude was there as they nursed their husbands through the many debilitating illnesses of older men, and when the men were too sick to live at home anymore, the devout took Jude with them as they went about the sad task of finding suitable residential care for them.

A woman named Rae described her feelings about this time in her life in a long letter to me. Her devotion to St. Jude went back to the mid-1940s, when she and her young husband were evicted from their apartment immediately after the birth of their first child. She has prayed to him every day of her life since, usually addressing a statue of the saint she kept on the bureau in her bedroom. She particularly needed Jude in the middle years of her marriage, when her husband's drinking threatened to destroy their family. Then five years before he died, Rae's husband suffered a stroke. Rae carried an image of St. Jude with her on every visit to the hospital and propped one up on the table beside her husband's bed for him to look at when she was not there. "I also prayed," she went on, "that he would go into a nursing home, which he had to, and that [also] came about as a result of prayers." Again Rae visited her husband every day, and "he always had the Saint Jude with him." She asked Jude to make her husband comfortable and to keep him from becoming more limited physically and mentally than he (and perhaps she, too) could bear. "I always prayed that if he was in a wheelchair, he would be able to walk, at least for his own gratification, and he did, for six months, before his death. He was able to walk," she concluded, "not by himself, but with a nurse; but he did, on his own, lift his legs, and walk."

Widows of all ages have looked to Jude for support. From the way they told their stories it is clear that these women in particular recognized that they had been assigned a role largely defined against them when their husbands died: like women who did not marry, widowed women were in danger of being isolated on the edges of social worlds organized around marriage and family. The months just after their husbands' deaths were particularly difficult, as women accustomed to male company and assistance first began making their way alone in unfamiliar circumstances. "Five years ago, my husband passed away after many years of illness," a woman told the Shrine, "leaving me with two small boys, two and four. I was on the verge of a nervous breakdown and I don't know how I would have lived that first year if my mother hadn't given me a Saint Jude Prayer Card." Widows writing to Chicago reported anxious confrontations with bureaucracies, lawyers, and insurance companies as they tried to settle business affairs in the immediate wake of their husbands' deaths; they turned to Jude when difficulties in these encounters made them sad, angry, or frightened. Finally, the saint accompanied these women into the later, longer loneliness of widowhood, after their children had grown up and moved out of their homes. "I lost my husband seven years ago," a woman from Massachusetts told the Shrine in 1943. "Practically alone, I am fifty four years old. My daughter lives outside of Philadelphia and is married. I feel as though I can't expect any help from her now. But dear Saint Jude looks after me and helps me when I need his assistance."[16]

Older women petitioned Jude for many different favors. They readied themselves for dying with his help. They asked him to ensure the care of handicapped children after they were gone. They prayed that he would bring family members, especially their own children, and friends back to the church if they had strayed, as if they were trying to set the spiritual lives of their loved ones in order, one final expression of the responsibility they had been assuming over their lifetimes for the spiritual and temporal welfare of their families and friends.[17]

"IT'S NOT ONLY THE ECONOMY THAT GETS DEPRESSED ..."

There would seem to be nothing historically specific about the sorts of life-course prayers women brought to Jude: the experience of aging was not unique to the first generations of Jude's devout, nor was loneliness, fear, or disappointment in love. To turn to Jude on such occasions of perennial human distress seems itself almost a natural response, an instinctual desire for solace and support channeled in these cases by Catholic idiom toward the saints, but widely shared by all humans at all times.

Yet there were specific social-historical reasons why the immigrants' daughters should feel romantic disappointment with sharper intensity and more acute self-awareness than their mothers did, having to do with the organization and culture of the modern family in capitalist society, the dissolution of the enclaves, the advent of advertising and movies, and the history of public education, among other factors. "It's not only the economy that gets depressed," Judy told me, describing the long time in the early 1980s when her husband had entered a cycle of periodic unemployment in South Chicago's steel mills after many decades of steady work in them; "people get depressed, too"—and the depression of the economy is often the trigger for the anger and despair of people, as in Judy's own experience. Jude certainly helped in times of personal transition, sickness, and sorrow, but these were not "private" as opposed to "public" occasions, perennial as opposed to social-historical matters. Family historian Rayna Rapp has written that "as a social (and not a natural) construction, the family's boundaries are always decomposing and recomposing in continuous interaction with larger domains."[18] However one understands the interplay of the "natural" and the historical in the history of families, between the biological or physiological, on the one hand, and the impress of cultural formations on the other, it is clear that family life—the experience of love, the sorts of bonds that form between parents and children and among siblings, the responsibilities that individuals feel and acknowledge for each other—is shaped at its most intimate levels by broader social circumstance. The history of the Depression inescapably includes its impact on the intimate relations between men and women, for example, on how they understood and imagined each other, and the story of depression inescapably includes its broader cultural, social, and economic situation.

It is especially difficult to draw a clear line between the historically contingent and the perennially human in the context of the social history of praying. Women's prayers to Jude were situated precisely at the point where personal, intimate experience intersected with the greater impersonal forces of history under way outside the door. Jude was called on at those moments when the effects and implications of changing historical circumstances, like economic distress, new technologies, and war—to name just three of the recurring situations that appear in the devout's letters to Chicago—were directly and unavoidably experienced within the self and the family, in women's relationships and responsibilities, and in their bodies.

I will turn now to four such intersections in order to enter more deeply into the social history of hopelessness: the convergence of the private with the public during the Depression, during the Second World War, in the period of sharply increased birth rates following the war, and as more and more young married women with children entered the workforce in the same years. The narrative line of this history is drawn from the petitions themselves: in their letters to the Shrine women identified for themselves and others the most troubling and vexing dimensions of the times as they experienced them and as they went on to live them in the company of St. Jude. The petitionary record does not seem to demand a radical rearrangement of the periods of contemporary American history, as some historians have suggested women's documents

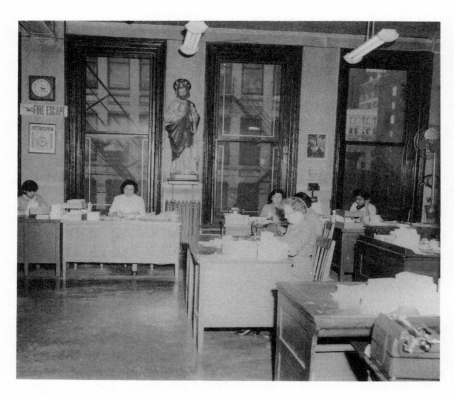

The Shrine's correspondence staff in Jude's downtown Chicago office, ca. 1950.

necessarily do. What generally mattered to women was generally mattering to men, too. But the prayers women made to Jude do disclose differences in the way they and the men around them experienced their times—and each other. In the twentieth century, at least, American women have not so much had a different history as a particular—and often discrepant—experience of the same history as men. The documents of the cult of lost causes and things despaired of—the letters written to the Shrine in Chicago, the stories women tell about themselves in relation to St. Jude, and the prayers they addressed to him— make possible an inner history of women's lives in these times.

JUDE AND THE GREAT DEPRESSION

By the choices they had begun to make in the late 1920s about work and residence, the immigrants' children had left themselves exposed to "the vagaries of the market economy," in Robert McElvaine's phrase.[19] Outside the secure (if confining) bounds of the family economy, second- and third-generation American Catholic workers had become increasingly dependent on their wages, secured in an unprotected labor market, for survival, rather than the many informal support mechanisms in the social worlds of the enclaves, based on reciprocity, duty, and cultural tradition. In the 1930s they felt the sting of this change. The economic crisis of the thirties presented the immigrants' sons and daughters with different challenges that demanded different responses and expressions of courage from them.

The immigrants' older sons struggled to hold on to what they had accomplished and attained; their younger brothers and cousins wanted to get on with what they had been brought up to do and what they knew was expected of them—and what was expected of them was work.[20] Instead, they lost their jobs or could not find any, or they were forced to work under the daily threat of being laid off or of having their earnings reduced. When they failed to do what they knew their communities required of them, as men often did in these hard times, they suffered awful shame and guilt; even though they knew that everyone was in trouble and the economy was a mess, they still blamed themselves for their failures, as American workers have usually done. Their initial response to the crisis was "bewilderment, defeat, and self-blame."[21] These men had to find the resources to keep going, to get out in the mornings and look for whatever work they could find, so that they could begin to regain what they had lost.

While the immigrants' sons were fighting to stay in place, however, the Depression crisis called for new and flexible strategies from women and opened for them new areas of opportunity, as well as responsibility. The first response of most American families to the hard times was to increase the amount of work women had to do: by the middle years of the crisis, women who were already used to working very hard were working harder than ever. The Depression increased the everyday demands on women of all ages. Younger women, just beginning to define their own goals, were expected to forgo school, marriage, and childbearing in order to help their families survive. Older married women were compelled to enter the workforce for the first time, while remaining responsible for the domestic management of their households—and often enough of their parents' and in-laws' households—as well.[22]

But these harder- and longer-working women were also discovering their own competence, authority, and agency. Because workers in white-collar situations held onto their jobs longer than those in industry, women often became their families' most dependable wage earners. They could see themselves assuming greater responsibilities for the support of their families, and despite the considerable fears of the period—which had mainly to do with male failure and vulnerability—women also experienced a new confidence grounded in the essential economic contribution they were making to their families' survival. Single and married women alike worked out new roles in the broader context of changing family patterns under extraordinary social and economic pressures.

But this confidence did not come quickly or easily. Male unemployment at first provoked deep panic in women, who discovered just how dependent they were on their men's earnings at the same time as they found out how vulnerable those earnings were. The inability of their fathers or husbands to hold onto their jobs raised the specter of a permanently unstable future. Once this awful thing had occurred—indeed, once it had even been recognized as possible or likely—women were gripped by the dreadful apprehension that further terrible things could happen at any moment and go on happening. Perhaps they would have to move out of their homes; their children might get sick; their husbands would desert them. The future became completely vulnerable. These were not unreasonable fears, of course: desertions and separations multiplied during the Depression, as husbands ran out on the families they could no longer face; the families of the unemployed did in fact sicken more often and more persistently than those of working people; and many people did lose their homes. But even when these dreaded things did not happen, feelings of vulnerability and unease persisted. Mrs. N.G. conveyed a sense of spiraling disaster to the Shrine in 1938. Her son, who seems to have been the family's primary support, had been looking for work for months without success. Then the health of her younger daughter, who had long needed a serious operation the family could not afford, deteriorated suddenly. Mrs. N.G.'s brother was out of work. There seemed to be nowhere to turn, and just before she addressed herself to Jude, Mrs. N.G. said, "I was desperate."[23]

Women had learned the fragility of their own security. "I prayed to Saint Jude," another woman confided to the Shrine, "that my husband would not gain the habit of drinking and would have his cut in salary restored or at least in part." But what would happen if this man did start drinking, as many did, or if his bosses decided to fire him, or refused to raise his pay? Women whose men were fired from jobs they had held for many years, which had given them a false but deep sense of security, seem to have been beset by special feelings of terror, as betrayal and rejection compounded economic distress. Again, it was not a question of either terror or confidence: the (necessary) dynamic of these years for women was the uneasy and delicate movement from terror and dread to authority and strength, from fear to the confidence that they could make the contribution necessary—that they could find work, find the doctors their children needed (as Mrs. N.G. eventually did for her daughter), that they could go out and earn their families' daily bread.[24]

Women also had to undertake what one historian has called the "emotional work" of keeping up the spirits of their fathers, brothers, husbands, and boyfriends during long periods of unemployment or inadequate or unsatisfactory employment, in many ways the most grueling of their assignments in these years. A kind of grim faith was necessary to survive, and men often looked to women to provide this when they could not do it themselves, just at the time that women were discovering the illusory nature of their own security and the extent of their vulnerability. Men were stunned and surprised by their sudden reversals and failures, women reported to the Shrine, and they became anxious and discouraged. "Please publish my thanksgiving to Saint Jude," a woman wrote in 1937, "for the recovery of my brother to his normal condition," explaining that the man had been "on the verge of a nervous breakdown owing to very heavy losses" in his business. Persistent unemployment in a culture that held the unemployed responsible for what was happening to them had pernicious consequences for relations between men and women. Men heard the disappointment, fear and, often enough, recrimination in the voices of the women who were depending on them and shared their anxiety that they would never find work again. "I think Roosevelt's program saved the self-respect and the sanity of a lot of men," a steelworker told oral historians many years after the crisis; more pungently, a woman told another group of researchers at the time, "They're not men anymore, if you know what I mean."[25]

Family life became a delicate set of exchanges as humiliated men raged against the women on whom they were now dependent as never before, while women strove to give men the encouragement and support they needed even as they held them, consciously and not, responsible for what had befallen them. The results were often petty family tyrannies and anger, which must have been particularly vexing to the immigrants' daughters hoping for better things in their marriages. Historians have debated whether the economic crisis undermined home life and eroded relations between men and women or whether the shared struggle for survival brought families closer together, but this way of framing the question again threatens to obscure the precise strains on women (and men), because in fact both were true. Men and women alike struggled with the intimate implications of ideology for self-esteem and mutual respect.[26]

Outside their homes as well women were caught in the ideological contradiction between the world as it was said to be and the world as they had to inhabit it. Married women compelled by need to enter the workforce found themselves vilified by religious and secular authorities.[27] Proposals regularly appeared in state legislatures to solve the economic crisis by prohibiting women from working at a time when families would have starved if they did not. Women were expected to maintain their families' self-respect and self-worth and their own courage and confidence in an ideological context that made unemployment a mark of a family's lack of competence and worth.

But the immigrants' daughters also discovered the limits of their own abilities to make things better and struggled with their own feelings of inadequacy and failure. Women often simply could do nothing to help when their men sank into terrible and frightening despair after months (or even years) of looking for work, nothing to console them when they found work they considered humiliating. The depth of these tensions may be gauged by the intensity of the relief women expressed to the Shrine when their men's circumstances improved. "I am so thankful to Saint Jude," wrote an older woman whose husband had been having special trouble competing with younger workers, "that I feel like shouting from the housetops." The devout are thrilled and breathless with relief for their men (and for themselves), so excited that they are afraid they will not be able to put the full range of their emotions into suitable words of thanksgiving. Letters of thanksgiving for Jude's help during the Depression continued to arrive in Chicago for years afterward, as women recalled with relief the saint's assistance in this desperate time.[28]

Economic distress did not end in 1941, of course. Intermittent unemployment and periodic downturns in the industrial economy continued to make things difficult for American Catholic workers even as the nation entered more fully into the postindustrial world after the war. The belief persisted that anyone can find work who really wants to, along with the corollary that the unemployed must be responsible for their own distress; unemployed men continued to blame themselves and women continued to struggle with feelings of powerlessness, vulnerability, and abandonment. Authoritative voices continued to speak out against women working outside their homes. Jude, at least, if not the devout themselves and their husbands, sons, and brothers, would always find work in the United States.[29]

HOME FRONT PRAYERS

The economic crisis of the 1930s ended in war, and "homefront heroines," as the Shrine referred to them in its pitches for wartime contributions, were soon bringing Jude new stories of distress. The war took sixteen million American men away from their families, leaving wives, mothers, and sisters behind to fend for themselves. The immigrants' daughters experienced the war as separation and hard work, according to the letters they wrote the National Shrine. What they wanted most of all from Jude was to keep their men out of service; failing that, they wanted them back as soon as possible. Women prayed openly that something unexpected would happen (with Jude's help) to prevent their men from being sent overseas. They sent in notes of thanksgiving when their men were spared assignment through silly bureaucratic mishaps. They did not scruple to celebrate when Jude kept their husbands, sons, or brothers from being sent to a combat zone, alone of all the members of a fighting unit, or when their husbands were declared physically unfit for service (a circumstance Jude's male devout seemed to have found humiliating). Women especially missed having their men around on important family occasions like baptisms and first communions and called on Jude to make it possible for them to come home for these events, regardless of military requirements or the exigencies of war. Those wives and mothers compelled to resign themselves to the departure of their men begged Jude for a last furlough before their soldiers and sailors left for overseas.[30]

These prayers contrasted with the editorial position of the *Voice of St. Jude.* The Shrine clergy, holding out the Virgin Mary as the "homefront heroine of all time," called on women to do wartime service of sacrifice, support, and encouragement. In "The Army Gets a Mother," a short story published in the magazine in 1942, a woman surrenders her son to the army despite her initial reluctance, then goes on to enlist herself. But no letter was ever published at the Shrine during this war or any other from a woman thanking Jude for a man's enlistment nor any asking the saint to make the men overseas valorous, ready to sacrifice their lives. The Shrine openly supported the war effort in the 1940s, so it seems reasonable to assume that if such letters had been received, they would have found their way into print. There has not been a lot of patriotic ardor on the letters pages of the *Voice of St. Jude.* Whatever anxieties and needs Jude's male devout may have been confiding to the saint privately, their few published prayers were concerned with making it into the services, staying safe in combat, being promoted, and dealing more effectively with the military bureaucracies.[31] But the women in their lives were praying against these petitions: Jude heard competing requests from men and women during the war.

Women on the home front once again found themselves caught between the world as it was said to be and as it appeared to them in their everyday experience. One familiar contradiction centered on their working outside their homes both for the war effort and for their own survival. The distress of separation was not only romantic, although this was certainly part of it. G.I. salaries were not sufficient for women to live on, and they were forced to come up with strategies for economic survival, like living doubled-up with relatives. Women's war work was widely recognized as necessary and just as widely condemned, as it had been in the Depression.[32] The wartime icons of the latchkey kid or the child locked for hours in a car in the parking lot of a defense plant are less revealing of the lowered standards of mothering in the period— which is how they were intended to be read—than of the shortsighted mistreatment of working women and their children during the war. Women found themselves trying to balance the competing responsibilities of home and work in a hostile environment. The United States was alone among the Allies in not making safe, affordable child care available to women working in the war industries, and shopkeepers resisted requests that they keep their stores open in the evenings so that working women could shop after work.

A second contradiction concerned the nature of women's ties with their men overseas. Social commentators, including the clergy at the Shrine, held women responsible for the protection and safeguarding of their men abroad, for sharing their distress and watching over them in sickness; their peacetime responsibilities were not to be abridged by war, even though there was nothing these women could do for their men so far away. So women were called on to surrender their men willingly, patriotically, to violence, while still somehow nurturing and caring for them; this was their wartime bind. But how could they fulfill their duties across the great distances opened by war? "A few months ago when war was declared," Mrs. J. Konrad wrote the Shrine from Long Island, New York, "I prayed to St. Jude for protection for my nephew. He is on the U.S.S. Langley which had been sunk a few months ago and [he] was taken on the tanker Pecor and that was sunk." Mrs. Konrad—like many other wives, mothers, and sisters—prayed her nephew through the war. Women on the home front were particularly upset when they were unable to communicate with their men in the services, especially when the latter were facing some difficulty or challenge, or when the silence from overseas became unbearably long. The most hopeless of these times was when someone they loved was listed as missing in action.[33]

Women encountered a last, but perduring, contradiction at the end of the war. Americans were told by familiar voices on the radio that the war was over; the soldiers' return from the fields of violence into the healing embrace of their wives and sweethearts was captured in photographs. Violence had been left behind like materiel in another world, and men who just months before had witnessed and wreaked destruction were expected now to resume their every-day lives. Jude's devout have understood, however, that wars do not end like this; they could see that the battles were not over in their men's imaginations and memories, and they knew firsthand what society seemed determined to deny. "Coming home after his discharge," a woman wrote the Shrine in 1949 about her son who had served overseas, "it was not hard to see that he was a changed boy—given to gambling and to drink. He absolutely refused to receive the sacraments, said he was an atheist, had no conscience, etc. I was just desperate." Another devout described a similar postwar situation in 1951: "My son, after the war, was an alcoholic and got to the point he could not keep away from it."[34] Prolonged separation and daily stress (on the home front and in the trenches) took their toll on marriages: although the marriage rate soared in the war years as young people acted quickly before the war took one or both of them away, wartime marriages were notoriously unstable, adding to the strains of the postwar years.

Wars never end and neither do women's responsibilities. A long letter from a woman living in Illinois appeared in *St. Jude's Journal* in October 1967 about her son's tour of duty in Vietnam and its aftermath. Father Maloney, who was presiding over the Shrine at the time, was a critic of the war, and the occasional prayers for peace published in the *Journal* in these years may have communicated to Mrs. V.S.S., as the correspondent is identified, that this was a safe space for her to tell her complicated story. I will quote the story she tells almost in its entirety here, even though it is long, because it reveals so starkly many of the dilemmas, contradictions, and binds that have characterized women's experience of their men at war:

> In November, 1965, my son was sent to Vietnam. This was a terrible blow to me, and out of desperation I enlisted the aid of St. Jude to guard and protect my boy and bring him home again safely. I made the Novena every Wednesday during the 1½ years that he was there.
>
> St. Jude was certainly guarding him and did not fail me, and I wish to publicly acknowledge my deepest gratitude and complete faith.
>
> My son was wounded in September, 1966 when a sniper hi[t] him in the right cheek, and the bullet blew out ten of his teeth and one side of his tongue. An emergency tracheotomy had to be performed, as he was choking on his own blood.
>
> I shall always believe that it was St. Jude who nudged the Viet Cong's elbow

and spoiled his aim. I shudder when I think what might or could have happened if it had not been for St. Jude's help. My boy came home in April and the scar on his cheek is barely noticeable.

I hope St. Jude has not tired of my pleas, for once again I have to enlist his help. While my son was in Vietnam he fell in love with a very pretty Vietnamese girl. He has decided to go back and marry her, and is leaving for Vietnam this evening. This is what he wants, and if it makes him happy, then I too will be happy. Evidently this is God's will.

My son came home first to his own environment, before he came to this decision, so who am I to question what will be? All I ask and pray for is that he has a wonderful trip and that St. Jude will once again protect him and guide him home again safe and well.[35]

Perhaps we must redraw the periods of modern American history after all. The Depression did not end in 1941, as women's recollections (still resonant with relief) years later indicate. The Second World War did not end in 1945 or Korea in 1953 or Vietnam in 1975. Women struggled for years afterward with depressed or alcoholic husbands and sons, with men angry and confused about their memories and experiences or so profoundly changed by them as to be almost unrecognizable, and with physically disabled men. The history of hopelessness is not completely contiguous with official chronologies, and Jude was called on to heal troubled memories long after the voices on the radio and the pictures in the paper proclaimed that the crises were past.

THE DISTRESS OF THE CHILDBEARING YEARS

American Catholic women came out of World War II like others of their generation, ready to have all the things that had been denied them for so long. Although the immediate postwar years were beset by housing shortages and high inflation, the economy had begun to climb by the mid-1950s, and the standard of living among Catholics improved as well. The community's newfound prosperity was reflected in the prayers that began to appear on the letters pages of the *Voice of St. Jude* for new homes in the ever widening suburbs and for safe automobile vacations on the nation's burgeoning, federally subsidized highways. Things had begun to go so well indeed for American Catholics that in the summer of 1953 a young woman turned to Jude for help in acquiring "more acumen in handling money."[36]

Women's prayers to St. Jude in the late 1940s and throughout the 1950s centered largely on two domains of distress, childbearing and work. Both were areas of conflict and (again) of contradiction in women's experience. In one, conflict emerged out of the deeply internalized discrepancy between women's desire for children and their fear of childbirth, both impulses operating in the broader context of their culture's identification of them with childbearing. In the other, conflict arose from the disjuncture between mandated social roles and economic realities. Women's own desires and possibilities were overshadowed in both, and often overwhelmed, by social expectations, demands, and ambivalence.

Although women had prayed to St. Jude for help having children before the postwar period (there is, after all, a perennial dimension to the desire for children and the fear of birth's pains), it was in these years that the letters about birth become more numerous—and more frantic. American Catholic women certainly seemed to want babies: national fertility rates doubled between 1940 and 1957, and Catholic families kept pace with this trend. The immigrants' younger daughters and granddaughters were marrying earlier than their older sisters and mothers had before them, and they were having more children sooner after their marriages than the older women had.[37] But the evidence of the letters is that these young Catholic brides were terrified of what was in store for them before it all happened, that they felt threatened and vulnerable during the experience, and that they were uncertain of what to make of it all afterward. These were the three acts of the narratives crafted for the National Shrine by Jude's devout during these years.

The immigrants' daughters were giving birth in a changed medical and social environment. The mothers and grandmothers of Jude's devout had delivered their children at home, where they were attended to and surrounded by female relatives, friends, and neighbors, who encouraged and cheered them on, offered advice, and commented freely and not always kindly on the decisions and actions of male medical practitioners, if one happened to have been called. By 1943, however, 72 percent of American babies were born in hospitals, compared with 35 percent in 1933; the figure for hospital births in 1955 was 95 percent of the total. Women found the experience of bearing children in this environment "sterile both in the antiseptic sense and in the human dimension," according to Judith Walzer Leavitt, a historian of American childbirth practices. Furthermore, the chorus of support and caustic comment was gone. American obstetricians were finally successful in these years in eliminating everyone else from the labor room besides themselves, obstetrical nurses who had been securely organized under their authority, and the birthing mother herself. According to Leavitt: "In hospital deliveries women left their family and friends at the door of the labor room and faced their birthings alone . . . separated from the people [they] loved . . . in an unfamiliar environment controlled by others."[38]

The birthing mother was not completely present, either. Technological innovation, the tendency toward ever greater medical intervention in the birthing process, and the expanding use of tranquilizing and painkilling drugs all contributed to making women the spectators at the births of their children (while not only not making childbirth safer but actually adding to its risks). Just how superfluous the birthing mother had become was indicated in a "landmark article" published in the *Transactions of the American Gynecological Society* by a prominent obstetrician, Joseph DeLee, who mused that it might be better for all concerned if all babies were delivered by cesarean section. The distress occasioned by these circumstances emerged in a famous forum held in the pages of the *Ladies Home Journal* in 1958. Responding to the editors' invitation to describe their recent childbirths, women openly lamented what had happened to them. One woman, writing from Elkhart, Indiana, recalled the "brutal inconsiderate treatment" she had received in the hospital, while another, from Columbus, Ohio, said that she had been "foiled in every attempt to follow" her own wishes. "The cruelest part of [hospital] childbirth," a third woman complained, "is being alone among strangers." Commenting on this last woman's distress, Leavitt writes, "She found nothing familiar to comfort her through the difficult hours, only the routine of hospital life that she and others described as an assembly line."[39]

By 1950, then, ever younger Catholic women in ever greater numbers were having more and more babies in circumstances that were increasingly out of their control, at the same time that their cultures—American and Catholic—were telling them with increasing stridency that this was not only the central experience of their lives but the event that defined their meaning and purpose as human beings. The rush to marry and have children after the war was not simply the result of the attractive charms of domesticity to a war-weary world. The frantic baby boom of the 1950s is an example of the way that personal desire—in this case to have babies and raise families—becomes a conduit of cultural and social imposition generally, and the site of the construction of gender specifically. Women without children were considered "sick, damaged, perverted" in the 1950s, and they were treated by popular psychologists, clerical commentators on the contemporary scene, and (often, sadly enough) by their neighbors and friends as unfulfilled and unfortunate persons.[40]

The terrible power of this compulsion still resonates most poignantly in the stories that those women who could not fulfill the assigned role, for whatever reason, tell about themselves. The culture was cruelest to them: by denying that they could ever be happy without husbands and children, it sought to make them into object lessons for everyone else. "I don't ask Jude to get married anymore," one of his devout, a sixty-year-old high-school teacher in Detroit named Patricia told me as we drove around the city discussing her devotion to the saint on a winter evening. (A small statue of St. Jude rode on the dashboard.) Once upon a time, Pat said, "all I ever wanted to do was get married and have lots of babies." It was not that she was unhappy as a young single woman, but "I was beginning to feel that my friends were getting married and I wasn't and maybe I should be." Her first prayer to Jude, in the 1950s, was to send her a boyfriend, and a week later, a man in a class she was taking asked her out (her first date in years, Pat added as an aside). He came by to get her at her mother's house, and when he opened the car door for her a medal of St. Jude on a gold chain slipped out from his unbuttoned collar, which Pat took as a sign that this was the man Jude intended for her to wed. But they saw each other only a few more times. Pat says she realizes now that marriage was probably never God's will for her, and St. Jude has helped her accept this.

Pat is not alone in remembering the distress of this intimate cultural imposition. Even women who managed to conform look back on the time uneasily. Judy told me that her first prayer to St. Jude in the 1960s, like Pat's, was "to get a husband." She was twenty-seven years old and "starting to panic. . . . My mom was twenty-five when she got married, but it took her three years to be able to get pregnant, and then she was never able to get pregnant again. She went through her changes when she was thirty-five. [So] I thought, Oh my God, if I'm not going to get married until I'm whatever years [old], and have to wait three years . . ." Judy broke off the story here for a moment; perhaps she was remembering the dismay this arithmetic had caused her decades before. Then she began again: "All of my friends—friends I went to high school with, friends I went to college with—almost everyone was married. So panic set in. I did not want to be just a career person, I wanted to have kids. I love kids. I always wanted to have children, so I got a little frantic at that point." Judy finally did have children, the first one just a year after her marriage, and her lingering pride in her own fertility emphasizes the old terror. "Well, I was nothing like my mother," she ended this part of her story, "because we were married in June of 1965, Jeannie was born in June of 1966, Johnnie was born in May of 1967. So I was nothing at all like my mom in that respect."

Because women's desire to have "lots of babies" was shaped at least in part by coercion and compulsion, it was inevitably accompanied by panic and uncertainty. "I became obsessed with fear," a woman wrote the Shrine from St. Louis in the summer of 1950, "about two weeks before delivery [and] I found I could not find solace even in prayer." Another discovered just how terrified she was when, confined to bed during her fourth pregnancy (which had followed immediately upon the birth of her third child), she suddenly began sobbing hysterically after hearing Danny Thomas describe in a television interview the comfort he had found in Jude. Still another wrote from Detroit, "During my pregnancy I was quite ill; and I was in such great fear of the pain I would have to endure when the baby would arrive."[41] Then these women went into the hospital to have their babies and found themselves alone just when they most needed support and encouragement.

The immigrants' daughters and granddaughters strove to get pregnant again and again, disregarding their doctors' warnings and families' worries. "Seven different doctors told me I could never have a baby," one new mother proclaimed to the others in the maternity ward, "but I just prayed to my favorite saint—they call him the Saint of the Impossible—and now I have an eight-pound boy!" "I have a friend whose wife always had children who wouldn't live," a woman told the Shrine, adding that she went on trying nonetheless. Another woman was warned by her doctors that she could never carry a fetus past three months but refused to let this stop her. She got pregnant right after her marriage and, just as the doctors had told her, "I had a miscarriage." Undeterred by the dangers to herself or the prospect of an endless series of miscarriages, "a few months later," she reported happily, "I was again pregnant"—and confined to bed. All of this exacted an enormous psychological and physical toll on these young women. They were often as panic-stricken about their later pregnancies as they were about the first, and after giving birth they experienced awful and lingering postpartum depressions. "Last year I had a very sick daughter," a woman wrote from Baton Rouge in 1953, "who had a nervous breakdown after childbirth." "Shortly after the birth of my baby," another woman recounted, "complications set in and I was near despair."[42] But within months they were desperately trying to get pregnant again.

WORKING WOMEN

Troubles did not end after the babies were born, as a woman, writing from Massachusetts, discovered after her prayers for yet another pregnancy were answered. "When I learned that I was to bear a third child, I asked myself,

Where are we going to live? What are we going to do? You see, we too (both ex-G.I.'s) were among the homeless group." As baby followed baby in American Catholic households, young couples found themselves financially strapped. Although American Catholic families were doing better later in the 1950s than these ex-G.I.'s were in 1949, the pressure of high inflation coupled with the manipulated and internalized desires of a consumer society continued to make things difficult for young families. So there was no end to the trend of married women working: their participation in the labor force went from (an already high) 13.8 percent in 1940 to 30.6 percent in 1960, a development that one labor historian has called "one of the most notable economic events in the twentieth century." By 1956, about twenty-two million women, half of them married, were employed outside their homes, a full third of them in clerical work; overall, female employment increased at a rate four times that of men in this period. These realities not only failed to diminish but actually intensified the clamor against married working women in the secular press and, more distressingly for Jude's devout, in Catholic devotional magazines. Celebrations of domestic bliss were everywhere. In magazines, on radio and then television, the home was portrayed as the source of all good in American life, the nation's strongest defense against Communism and the other dire threats of the modern world, the ultimate guarantor of democracy and freedom.[43] How could women leave this sanctuary untended? Their going to work was, according to these accounts, the consequence not of a voracious, consumption-driven economy, beset by periodic inflationary surges, but of their own moral irresponsibility.

Besides living with the very real consequences of this ideological assault, working women were also encountering the ordinary problems and stresses of the work world. Letters expressing anxieties about the periodic unemployment of the correspondents or their ambitious daughters begin to appear in the *Voice* in these years, along with accounts of personality conflicts on the job (which may have been exacerbated by the cultural disapproval of working women), the unfairness of management, and issues of promotion and advancement. Secretaries were required constantly to learn new technologies, from electric typewriters on into the early years of computerization, which contributed additional stress. Because of these changes in office technology, furthermore, clerical work was also becoming more routine and dull; tedium and boredom became real issues, and Jude's devout sought his help in finding promotions to better, more engaging work. After they had moved up, they called on him to strengthen their confidence in these new positions. But often they found their paths blocked: historians of women's work have noted an increasing emphasis in clerical settings on women's age and physical appearance at this time, and letters begin to appear at the Shrine recounting tales of discrimination and expressing fear of obsolescence.[44]

Working women still remained responsible for taking care of things at home, and social failures—from juvenile delinquency to educational problems—were widely attributed to bad mothering in the 1950s. But there had been little improvement in society's willingness to make things any easier for working women. Day care remained an unpopular concept in the United States, and a special problem for women in these years was finding someone trustworthy and dependable to take care of their children when they went out to work. The fact that American Catholic women had to rely on paid child care was another consequence of the breakup of the ethnic enclaves, where neighbors and relatives would have performed this service.

At the height of the baby boom, one of Jude's new devout recounted a horror story that many other readers of the *Voice* would have recognized. Now that their son was ready to start kindergarten, G.H. and her husband decided that she should go back to work "to help our financial standing."[45] She found a position as a secretary and enrolled her son in a local school. But the boy hated kindergarten. Every morning G.H. took her son to school on her way to work, and every morning he screamed and clung to her while she tried to get away. Frustrated and at her wits' end with the situation, G.H. admits that "the teachers and I had given up." Then one morning, after the usual scene, G.H., resigned and in tears, was taking her boy home from school when a woman she did not know approached her and, after listening to her story, urged her to pray to St. Jude.

Several levels of human experience came together in the hopeless moment, as Jude's devout have described them over the years. In hopelessness, the devout encountered the limits of their social world to provide them with comfort, assistance, and solace, and acknowledged the shortcomings of the well-established categories of meaning in helping them understand their experience. They had come to the end of their own abilities to help and protect the people they loved, whom they were supposed to protect and help, and they were at the outer edges of what they could do for themselves. Hopelessness erupted at many sites in women's everyday lives: in their bodies, in their relationships and responsibilities, in their social identities, their sense of agency. It threatened to reconfigure their memories, curtailed their fantasies of what might be possible, constricted their desires. The stakes were very high: Jude's terrain was "matters of terrible importance."[46] Hopelessness was an experience of the whole person as she lived and made meaning in the spaces and circumstances of everyday life, as she was defined by others and as she defined herself.

Just before they called on him, Jude's clients reported that they had lost the context or perspective within which their actions or motivations might make sense; there was no referent point outside the awful present. The future had closed down: the horizon of what is not yet, of what could be expected, anticipated, hoped for, had flattened out. "And withal my soul is enveloped in darkness," read the Shrine's Prayer in Affliction, which was recited over and over by Jude's devout in times of distress, "disquietude, discouragement, mistrust, yes, sometimes even a kind of despair preys upon my soul. . . . I see myself surrounded by a dark cloud."[47] As a result, hopelessness was also an experience of paralysis: how could a woman act if the future into which she would direct her actions had shut down? The devout had come to believe that there was absolutely nothing they could do, for themselves or for their stricken loved ones. To feel hopeless was to be trapped in a constricted space; there was a claustrophobic quality to the devout's panic. Hopelessness felt inescapable: the devout say they had nowhere to turn, no one to call on, could see no alternatives to what was happening. The awful belief that God, too, had abandoned them in the dangerous moment, an oft-repeated sentiment among the Shrine's correspondents, was the most dreadful expression of this sense of a closed future. Not even supernatural intervention was thinkable.

Because it was an encounter with limit, furthermore, the hopeless moment was shocking. The devout reported being stunned or overwhelmed by the unexpected crisis and by the discovery of their inabilities to act or think; they were brought up short against their limitations, by surprise. Nothing in their experience or in what the voices of their social worlds told them had prepared them for this. Perhaps because it was shocking, hopelessness was also transparent: all their defenses breached, the devout found that denial had become more difficult. They were the ones to call a moment hopeless, after all: the turn to Jude always followed on a recognition, an assessment of the true state of things. The devout suggest in their stories that in the hopeless moment they glimpsed dimensions of their experience they had not imagined before. This may be why women so often use the metaphor of darkness in describing their feelings at these times: the dark might have come as a relief from what was revealed in the harsh light of crisis. Darkness was the last reflex of self-protection and denial.

Claustrophobic as the moment was, though, hopelessness was never solely a private experience. There were private aspects of it, but it should be clear by now that even in their most private times—especially in these times, alone with the saint behind the closed doors of their bedrooms—hopeless devout were connected in multiple ways to the social context that had given rise to their experience. Women's prayers to Jude were occasioned by historically situated ruptures in how their roles as mothers, wives, and daughters were experienced and defined, or in times of transition, when they were making the difficult movement from one way of being, from one household or one kind of work, one set of duties, responsibilities, possibilities, and limits to others. Women at prayer have been trying to find ways of living amid the fissures, contradictions, and challenges of their social experience. The isolation the devout report feeling before they called on Jude was caused by and experienced at the center of a fissiparous social world that was proving itself inadequate as a context for meaning or action. The moment called for improvisation, but this kind of flexibility takes courage and confidence, whereas the devout report feeling fear and panic.

Multiple contradictions framed the social experience of American Catholic women in the years when the cult of saints was most popular and widespread, as we have seen. Economic realities forced them to go to work, while the authorities of their cultures, American and Catholic, denounced them for doing so and set up obstacles in their paths to make what was already difficult enough more so. They were told that having children was the most meaningful thing they could do, at the same time that the experience of childbirth was hollowed out by the intrusion of technologies, drugs, and incontrovertible male authority in the birthing space. Protect, nurture, and love your sons, they were told, and sacrifice them willingly in wars. In this way, women were consistently torn between expectation and possibility, between what they were told was right, appropriate, and sacred, and what they had to do to live.

Clara summed up the dilemma of the immigrants' daughters succinctly for me in a written statement that she prepared on her devotion to Jude before our conversation. She was describing the tension between her duties to her son and her responsibilities to her sick mother (whose illnesses, Clara suspected, were a device to get attention and keep her daughter in line). Her obligations clashed sharply one afternoon when her mother and her son expected her to be in two different places, at opposite ends of Chicago, to take care of them. "My circumstances were compound," Clara wrote. "I was torn between staying with my son to give him support and being with my mom to comfort her. I felt helpless."

Hopelessness was experienced when one's community of support collapsed, when no one was able to offer any hope or encouragement or was sufficiently compassionate and understanding to try, when everyone seemed so angry at the women in distress as to be incapable of such kindness. The figures on whom the immigrants' daughters had long counted were not there. This was another way the hopeless moment was transparent: suddenly the devout saw that the people they loved, trusted, and needed could fail or disappoint them, or turn away from them in a moment of vulnerability. The failure of hope is always an event between people; despair is relational, and so it is very difficult, at least at first, to regain hope alone. We look into each other's eyes to ascertain how bad (or good) our situation really is, and we read our friends' and relatives' faces for clues to the relative stability of our world. This is why hopelessness was inevitably experienced by the devout as abandonment.

On the other hand, there is a way in which hopelessness did involve being watched—a way different from the supporting gaze these women say they needed. The devout were well aware that their family and friends were watching and assessing them in their crises. Hopelessness was the experience of exposure and judgment. Everyone could see what was going on, and many people had a stake in what the devout were able, or unable, to do in these circumstances. Ironically and terribly, the hopeless time was also usually an occasion when others' dependence on the women experiencing it was almost total. So the threat of shame, humiliation, and failure was always present.

The feeling of abandonment was gendered, too. The devout called on Jude when the men they trusted and counted on turned away from them or failed them in some essential way, or simply were not there when they were needed; male absence is a consistent theme in the stories women have told to the Shrine, a common component of the broader picture of distress. Sometimes, of course, the men involved were not responsible for the disappointment they caused, and in these cases the devout usually did not blame them; the letters were not (generally) vindictive or mean. At other times, though, the men were responsible, as when immigrant fathers stormed implacably against their daughters' marital choices or when husbands drank their families toward ruin. "My husband was keeping terrible hours," a woman confided to the Shrine in 1954, "gambling, drinking and I believe, unfaithful." Sad and distressing as all this was, though, this was not yet the full extent of this woman's discoveries: she also learned, as many of Jude's devout report of themselves too, how her husband's irresponsibility and meanness entailed serious risks for her and her children. "Our bills were piling up until there was no way in sight of paying them. Our home was on the breaking point. . . . I was losing weight and had no nerves left."[48] Women sought the saint's help when the professional men they had been raised to rely on, especially doctors and priests, proved unable or unwilling to console, advise, or comfort them in grave circumstances—when a doctor, for example, not only told a woman that nothing could be done for a loved one anymore but left her alone in a room, or when a priest refused to sit at her hospital bedside.

The immigrants' daughters recognized how vulnerable they were to male absence, regardless of whether it was occasioned by sickness or emotional abandonment. Male physical debilitation in particular was a disclosure of the precariousness of women's lives. "My husband fell very sick with hemorrhages," a woman wrote the Shrine in 1952, "and he went to the hospital and there was very little income coming in." Another woman, saddened by her husband's chronic pain, experienced another level of distress in the crisis: "Our financial condition was at rock bottom—we had to mortgage our home during my husband's illness in order to support ourselves and two children." Male unemployment, in the Depression and afterward, has provoked in women the terrifying realization of the fragility of their security and the dangers of dependence. One woman reported to the Shrine that when her husband lost his job she "nearly fainted and for a time I cried" before "I told my husband that we had to start praying [to Jude] and praying hard."[49] Judy told me she almost had a "nervous breakdown" when her husband was laid off from the steel mill.

Many letters to the Shrine over the years have been concerned with male alcohol abuse—or rather, more specifically, with the danger that men's drinking posed for the women in their homes. The letters reveal a real dread of drink, a terrible apprehension of the attraction of alcohol (what one woman referred to as her husband's "longing for liquor"), because the correspondents obviously experienced their men's addiction as a risk to themselves. "Excessive drinking by my husband was slowly breaking up our home and bringing all kinds of trouble," wrote one; another confided "my husband is an alcoholic and life had become almost unbearable." A woman from Cleveland told the Shrine, "St. Jude has been my consolation in this cross of mine," her husband's alcoholism. Jude's devout understood their health to be endangered by their husbands' drinking: as one woman reported, "my husband['s] . . . continuous drinking affected my health as well as his."[50]

That American Catholic laymen have not participated in the cult of saints with the passion, dedication, and commitment of their wives, mothers, sisters, and aunts is a reflection in part of the fact that men have not been as socially, economically, or culturally vulnerable as women—or not so in the same ways. Men's vulnerabilities were not fundamentally linked to their relationship with women as women's were to their bonds with men: there has not been a single letter over the years in which a man says that he is afraid that his wife's drinking will ruin their family or that he is uncertain how he will live now that his wife is sick. This is not to say, of course, that men did not suffer; but suffering is always gender specific, emergent out of different sources and holding different meanings for men and for women.

Absence could be more subtle still. Hopelessness could be characterized by the sudden unrecognizability of a loved one. A husband or mother or fiancé has been changed by alcohol, sickness, age, or circumstances and he or she no longer appears the same. Strangeness and unfamiliarity have invaded the home. But perhaps the most distressing strangeness of all was that a woman felt estranged not only from God and other people in the hopeless situation, but from herself as well. The devout sensed that they had come to the end of their capacities for self-healing. It is a simple point but worth recalling here at the end of this anatomy of hopelessness that the experience is the opposite of confidence, courage, and hope. When they turned to Jude, the devout were paralyzed, unable to act for themselves. Reflecting back on the occasion when she first turned to Jude, Kathy described hopelessness as the sense "that you don't have anywhere to turn to—you don't know what to do. You feel powerless, you feel you don't have any control over the situation." Jude's devout recall being exhausted by fear and the threat of shame, claustrophobic, abandoned, estranged, and disoriented, pinned by conflicting demands and expectations.

It was in such times, then, amid feelings like this, that these women turned to a holy figure they had just discovered, who had been imagined into being by other women in circumstances like their own, and asked him to help them.

3

Imagining Women

The prominent devotional magazine *Ave Maria* began a long-running series of stories in 1955 by Anna-Margaret Record about a character named "Marcy Balaird," a married woman with six children who had recently converted with her husband to Catholicism.[1] Up before dawn, Marcy baked bread, dusted, washed and scrubbed, stopping only when her baby needed to nurse. Hard as she worked, Marcy was never done and never satisfied, and she accompanied her labors with a steady drone of self-reproach. Exhausted all the time by this epic battle against domestic disorder, she steadfastly maintained a plucky demeanor for her family, not wanting to burden them with her—ever deepening—distress. Her husband, John, barely noticed her in any case, except when he needed something, never heard what she was saying, never offered to help her. "Glory Be," Marcy occasionally allows herself to mutter at him under her breath, although Record generally rushes in to qualify even Marcy's gentlest protests. Marcy and John, their creator demurs, had few, if any, quarrels "in their ten years of marriage," a happy situation attributable to John's "sweeter disposition." He is "boyish," "lean and handsome"; she is, inevitably, pregnant. "For nine years Marcy had either been pregnant, caring for a small baby, or—as was usual—both." No one was complaining, though: the only thing worse than washing diapers, Marcy considers, is "not having a baby to wash diapers for!" and Record assures her readers that "Marcy would not have traded one of her beloved angel-imps for all the money in the mint; or for that matter, the greater consideration of perfect health." When her non-Catholic doctor warns her that another pregnancy could be fatal, Marcy reflects calmly that "the supernatural must transcend the purely natural."

Having perfect health—which Marcy associates with Protestants—is the least of this woman's worries. Marcy needs to rest, and although Record accuses her of giving in to the "capriciousness of the slightly ill," she permits her character to take to her old bed in her mother's house for a weeklong recuperation. John cannot bear the separation, however, and complains that without his helpmeet "I'm lost and confused and cross with the tykes, poor little souls." With her children under this threat of mistreatment, Marcy hurries home, still too weak to stand without support. She spends her first day back cleaning the huge mess her husband made until at dusk she sets aside her mop, puts on some lipstick so "I'll be beautiful for Daddy," and with graceful timing, just as John walks through the door, "drops the last croquette into the sizzling bacon grease and [takes] a step into his arms." Marcy is happy with this life of hers. She compares herself favorably with John's Protestant sister, Eleanor, a modern American woman who has limited the size of her family so she can pursue a career. Marcy notices that the lines around Eleanor's "carefully accented mouth drooped in a weariness of spirit" that Marcy has never seen in her own mirror (or at least Anna-Margaret Record has never seen, looking over Marcy's shoulder).

Marcy collapses a second time and her doctor insists she have a hysterectomy; after fretting about John's being left "defenseless and lonely," she finally consents to the operation. Marcy contends with fear and pain in the hospital by reciting a little poem over and over—"I do not ask a truce / With Life's incessant pain / But school my lips, Lord / Not to complain"—and when her cheerfulness fails her for a moment she scolds herself, "It's so easy to whine, drat it!" Marcy takes her pain as a spiritual blessing and thinks about "the ways it could be fashioned to one's eternal future . . . as expiation for past sin; as an offering for the souls suffering in Purgatory . . . and as a freely accepted cross."

She wants to share these reflections with John just before her operation, but he turns away from her in anger and disappointment, and Marcy, berating herself for being "senselessly cruel" to her husband, realizes that she "must face death alone." The pain worsens and Marcy prays (silently), "Take it, Lord. For my many sins, take it in expiation." All she asks at the end of her life is that Jesus grant her "the lowest place in heaven."

But Marcy survives, and purged and purified by her ordeal she has learned . . . the real meaning of housework. "The kettle ceased to drag on her patience; she knew satisfaction in its gleaming bottom as the last of the grit and cleanser rinsed away. The ashtrays sparkled as she held them under the hot water tap. The biscuits in the oven sent forth a savory odor." Jesus' life had been "beautified by the services of a housewife like herself," Marcy meditates, and Record closes the series with the message that "women belong in the nursery and kitchen and living room, not riveting in a factory or banging a typewriter, while a day nursery takes care of their children."

More encouraging accounts of women's lives had already begun to appear in American Catholic family magazines by the end of the Second World War, and by the early 1960s Marcy and her sister "saints in aprons" (as they were identified in the title of a popular volume of spiritual advice published by Rose Huesman in 1962) had mostly disappeared. But the long-suffering, self-sacrificing housewife, silent and cheerful in her pain and humiliation and on her way to sanctity (the series about Marcy was called "This Side of Saint-hood") had long been a familiar figure in devotional culture.

Marcy stands at the end of the years of change in American Catholic women's experience; at the beginning there was Anna Maria Taigi, a poor Roman matron who was beatified by Benedict XV in 1920 and quickly adopted by American devotional writers as a model for wives and mothers. Taigi had been a "gay" bride, according to a sketch by Florence Gilmore—likewise published in *Ave Maria*—until "the grace of God touched her soul" (just as Marcy had once been an unthinking Protestant like her sister-in-law with the painted lips). Seeing her "frivolity" in a new light, Taigi took to wearing a hair shirt. She endured a life of terrible sufferings "smilingly and cheerfully," even looking for ways to increase her distress, like going without water on Rome's hottest summer days. She was also, Gilmore writes, "unfailingly patient" with her physically abusive husband, "silent when he was angry, eager to please him in every way."[2]

From Anna Maria Taigi to Marcy Balaird: the immigrants' daughters had grown up with these domestic hagiographies at a time when social and economic circumstances, as well as the extended horizon of their own ambitions and achievements, were making it increasingly unlikely that their lives would (or could) resemble those of the kitchen athletes. Still they were told to emulate women like Marcy Balaird and to undertake a suburban asceticism like hers, and when they failed to do so, they were condemned for their shortcomings in the same magazines that were printing these tales.

DISCIPLINING THE IMMIGRANTS' DAUGHTERS

There was a great deal of anxiety in devotional culture beginning in the 1920s that "in these days of movies, automobiles, trolleys, golf, sensational magazines, woman suffrage and women in business, sport, etc." (as "these days" were described by Martin Scott, S.J., in *Ave Maria*), the immigrants' daughters were not living up to the ideal of "the Catholic woman." The "typical girl of today," Florence Gilmore wrote in 1932, was "unusually pretty, in a rouge and lip-stick way; slangy; gay; sure of herself; in for everything." "The ranks of the Magdalenes will be recruited by numbers all too great," *Ave Maria*'s editors intoned in 1927, because of the atmosphere in "stores and shops and factories and offices." Accusations and denunciations of women were so common that a writer for the *Voice of St. Jude* felt he was doing something very unusual when he offered a few kind words about modern women in 1949.[3]

American Catholic women found themselves attacked precisely for the difficulties they were struggling with in their changing lives and for their new ways of thinking about themselves and the world, attacked for what Clara had called their "compound circumstances." American Catholic writers and moralists imagined young women as voracious creatures, always demanding and desiring something, never satisfied, and willing to work only in order to buy the very luxuries that were eroding the spiritual foundations of their homes and culture.[4] This was a Catholic critique of the American culture of consumption on one level, but it was always gendered: the criticism of consumption was the pivot for an attack against modern Catholic women, not their male counterparts, who seemed to want things like cars and refrigerators only at the instigation of their girlfriends and wives.

Women who wanted marriages that were something other than a spiritual discipline like Anna Maria Taigi's were ridiculed as moral cowards. Modern wives rush off to a psychiatrist or state agency every time there is trouble at home, a writer charged in *The Sign* in 1952, because they fail to understand that a "husband who cannot or will not recognize and control his faults . . . may be, in God's providence, the very means of saving [their] soul[s]." Women's ambitions were "unsexing" them, another writer cautioned, threatening a danger-ous blurring of gender boundaries. Women were warned that their insistence on making choices for themselves was risking the certain destruction of their families and themselves. So dangerous indeed were these women that at times their ambitions were treated as capital offenses. One young woman's murder in a story published in the *Voice of St. Jude* is called "retributive justice" for her having abandoned the "simple shepherd" who loved her since childhood (a story that takes on particular resonance in the context of the efforts of the im-migrants' daughters to choose their own marriage partners in these years).[5] Such denunciations of young women continued in devotional culture well into the 1960s.

But not all women were dangerous, just young women: the immigrants' daughters, not their mothers. Catholic family magazines regularly published short fiction, written by both men and women, lay and religious, about love's tribulations, similar to the popular romance tales of the time, almost invariably depicting young women as wild and uncontrolled and old women (usually immigrants) as calm, confident, and wise. This was the central diptych of popular Catholic fiction—saintly old women/wild young girls. The two tropes were constituted in counterpoint: older women were remembered or portrayed in explicit and inevitable contrast to their younger counterparts, either to the women they had been themselves many years ago or to some younger woman in their households. Rosie, the new bride in Helen Moriarty's 1920 story, "Jim Graney's Wife," is an idle, rebellious, redhead, "intoxicated with life, vain of the beauty which had captivated sober Jim Graney, selfish with youth's supreme and thoughtless egotism." Jim's mother, on the other hand, has attained a quiet beauty through a life of unremitting toil and self-sacrifice for her son. Willful, self-absorbed, and impetuous, young women like Rosie are always luring their "sober" boyfriends into danger. "Let's live on thrills," a teenager named Barbara cries in a story in the *Voice of St. Jude,* taunting her boyfriend to drive fast and recklessly. Young women are defined by their dangerous ambitions, discontent, and unmanageable desires; old women, now at the end of their days—and the proximity of death added a morbid luster to these portraits—looked back contentedly on lives of submission, loyalty, and devotion. "You might seek far," a writer in *Ave Maria* counseled in 1927, "and not find what would comfort you half so well as to look at the pleasant old face, so placid and quietly cheerful, with the young eyes and the white hair drawn smoothly back from the brow."[6] Male writers' own mothers were often used as the standard against which contemporary adolescent girls were judged and found wanting.

This fear of young women drew on ancient reserves of Catholic misogyny and was pervasive in American Catholic culture. Moral education in American seminaries had been dominated since the late nineteenth century by the writings of the seventeenth-century moralist Alphonse Liguori, who taught that great as women's capacity for holiness was (greater even than most men's, he believed), so was their power to tempt and ruin. Seminarians were warned by confessional manuals, ethics textbooks, and the after-hours gossip of older priests to be wary of women's "unscrupulous" wiles, and seminary culture was broadly organized to foster a sensibility of distance and detachment from women. As historian Paula Kane observes about seminary formation in the 1910s and 1920s, "Clerical fears of laywomen were epitomized by the fact that the most frequent warning issued to seminarians about the temptations facing them in the priesthood was that of hearing female confessions." Diocesan seminaries had become clubby, fraternal preserves by this time, which explicitly inculcated an enthusiastic spirit of male camaraderie as a means of securing and maintaining clerical aloofness, authority, and superiority in relation to lay people generally, but especially in relation to lay women.[7]

A posture of aloofness that arises from fear and mistrust can easily become hostility and disdain, however, especially in times when gender roles are changing, and priests regularly had harsh things to say about young women in the devotional press. "If the power of women for good is great," Benedictine Father Walter Stehle wrote in a Liguorian vein in 1954, "their power for evil must be no less so." Allowing that "priests come into much inevitable and necessary contact with women, and depend much on their help and influence in parish affairs," Father Stehle warned his (mainly clerical) readers that the allegedly fairer sex in fact set traps for men, dragging them down "into the mire and misery." When he was a young priest, he admits, still "little conversant with the ways and wiles of women," he did not sufficiently appreciate this threat, but now he knows well that "priests ought to pray humbly and perseveringly and with much intensity for heaven's protection in their official and unavoidable contacts with women." Referring to this as the clergy's "woman problem," Father Stehle recommended some simple (and commonly rehearsed) precautions priests might take to guard against women's ways and then concludes in language that belongs to a well-established tradition of clerical fear of women, "we must . . . be ever watchful and by prayer and self-discipline protect ourselves against the perverting influences of the world and the temptations that are inseparable from our contacts with the world, in particular with women." Detroit's Cardinal Edward Mooney warned his young seminarians in a similar tone about the dangers of women's "gift of sympathy," a real risk for lonely ordained men.[8]

The discomfort and unease—at the least—among priests with the women who filled their pews, took care of the everyday management of their parishes as housekeepers, secretaries, and bookkeepers, and made their dreams of brick and mortar possible, was especially evident among the sponsors and promoters of popular devotions, perhaps because these men knew exactly how dependent they were on women, reminded, as they were, every time they looked out from the altar at their novenas. Some priests tried to deny this embarrassing and frustrating circumstance. We are constantly hearing that women are more pious than men, Benedictine father Francis Grey complained in 1927, on the evidence that "women are more frequently and numerously seen in church than their husbands, brothers, and sons." But how could this claim be true, Grey asks, when the Psalmist and Jesus were both men? Despite the evidence of the pews, he writes, men are in fact more devout, but women have more time on their hands and fewer responsibilities so they can get to church more often. Others tried to do something to change the situation. During the 1930s, the founder of Chicago's enormously popular Sorrowful Mother novena lured men to his services with offers of free cigarettes. Father DePrada chided Jude's faithful in 1958 with the reminder that prayer was not "the practice of pious women and innocent children" alone "but a deadly earnest necessity for all equally." Piety was generally promoted after the Second World War as compatible with masculine identity and authority. One man proudly reported in *Ave Maria* in 1952 his discovery that the rosary, which he had been dismissing as the plaything of "pious women and . . . nuns," was actually a "weapon" of considerable "power," as that most manly saint, Dominic, had shown in his wars against heretics.[9] At least some of the restructuring of popular piety in the United States that followed the Second Vatican Council, like the calls for a new father-centered home prayer life and the elimination of popular devotional practices like sewing costumes for statues, was intended to displace women from the center of everyday religious practice and to make religion acceptable to men.

Surely many individual priests and seminarians were not uneasy with women or mistrustful or resentful of them. But the ethos of American Catholic culture, reflected and reproduced in clerical orientations, was characterized by more suspicious and anxious attitudes toward young women, and this fear generated an attendant impulse to discipline. For their own good, so that they could realize their greater potential for sanctity, and so the men, clerical and lay, who came into contact with them would be safe, these women had to be disciplined. As the lives of the immigrants' daughters changed after the First World War, the theological rationale for discipline was edged with a new social imperative: adolescent females were held accountable by Catholic writers for nothing less than the collapse of Western civilization, from the cultural upheavals of the 1920s, through economic disaster and global war, and on into the years of postwar anxieties. Discipline was explicitly and ubiquitously called for in every medium of Catholic culture—in catechism classes, for example, marriage manuals, moral pedagogy, Catholic etiquette books, romance fiction, Catholic radio and television shows, and devotional tracts. But the most compelling site for the disciplining of young women, given the needs they brought here and the emotional and intellectual power of the images and rituals available, was devotional culture.

During the Depression, for example, to touch down on just one important moment of this history, economic hardship was welcomed by writers in Catholic family magazines as a timely antidote to young women's new aspirations. Mothers who are responsible for "the building of that citadel of the Church and of society—the Christian home," Nellie Ivancovich wrote in *Ave Maria* in 1932, have been threatened of late by their own ambitions in "pagan and materialistic" culture. But there were positive signs that this was changing: "The many reasons that drew a large number of women away from the home—money, pleasure, prosperity—have failed in these days of depression, and people are learning that in the search for these advantages something of much greater value has been lost—the proper care and training of the children."[10] Discipline was also the impulse of the romantic stories published in these periodicals—explicitly the disciplining of a female character, implicitly of the female reader. In the plot typical of the genre, wild young women are inevitably and relentlessly chastened by grief, pain, and sickness, which, in a final surrender, they admit to having brought on themselves, and once outgoing and happy girls end up alone in squalid rooms, abandoned by everyone except the Virgin and the saints.

Susan Grayson, for instance, in Anne Tansey's "Will-o-the-Wisp," which appeared in the *Voice of St. Jude*, was the pet of her teachers and the darling of a fast crowd of friends. After graduation, she finds glory on the stage (indeed, she changes her name to "Gloria"), but "success went to Susan's head." Ambition attained is invariably the signal for disaster in these stories, and, sure enough, Susan/Gloria breaks down. She is "confined" to a hospital for three years: "careless and extravagant living," Tansey scolds, "exacted its toll." Abandoned now by her many friends and humiliated, Susan comes to her senses.

She turns to the saints for help, but Tansey ridicules her for "rushing" frantically "from saint to saint for succor" (a bitter judgment for those of her readers who were holding her story in their hands exactly because they had rushed to a saint for assistance). Susan finally finds Jude and accepts her lot in life; at the end she is living in a "shabby house in a poor section, . . . placidly happy" and content with the "companionship of no one" but him. Not even young nuns are exempt from this treatment. When a novice's mother in another story objects to the harsh discipline her daughter is undergoing at the hands of her novice mistress, the young religious replies, "Mother darling! It is only what I deserve, and you know it!"[11]

But the most powerful disciplinary strategy of devotional culture was less obvious. Deeply embedded in editorials, short stories, advice columns, popular ethics, and theology—even in the funny fillers and hints for housewives scattered through the pages of Catholic magazines—was a fantasy about Catholic family life, about husbands and wives, parents and children, especially mothers and sons. I will borrow a term from psychoanalysis and refer to this as the American Catholic family romance, by which I mean a domestic dreamscape shaped by specific and identifiable (but not often conscious) desires and denials and presented by cultural authorities as historically authentic, morally imperative, and religiously sanctioned.[12] The romance had a public, discursive expression, in the moral construct of the "Catholic family" held out as the goal of married life, as we will see, but the real power of this creation was in its more intimate and subterranean currents. There were many clues in the way the romance was elaborated that marked it as a creation of desire and need, the clearest being that the "Catholic family" so evoked was always presented as a childhood memory. The Catholic family romance always began "in the old days," before women became what they are today, dangerous and unsexed—back in the days when women were *our* mothers, in other words, and we were their children—and our family experience was wonderful, warm, sacred, perfect. The language of the devotional press was generally precious and sentimental, but in the crafting of the family romance it became especially suffocating, thickened by yearning, loss, and resentment, suffused with anger and regressive passion.

THE AMERICAN CATHOLIC FAMILY ROMANCE

The wise old matrons celebrated in this romance were almost always widows. They had to have been married once, of course, in order to have given birth to sons, but this was a dimly imagined and mainly unhappy circumstance. In the logic of the American Catholic family romance, fathers were not really necessary members of the everyday life of the family: as one writer put it in 1927, "We feel more pity for those children that have lost their mother than for those whose father is dead, because when the mother is gone the heart of the family is gone." Given the prevalence of such sentiments, adult, married men were largely absent from this imaginative construction. When they did appear, they assumed one of two guises. They could be the dutiful, doting sons of saintly older women; more often they were mean, sexually demanding, inadequate husbands to victimized wives (who were also mothers). The "sweet-faced woman who had known little else than poverty and wretchedness since her marriage some fifteen years ago" was a familiar figure in the pages of Catholic magazines. The literary historian Joseph McShane, S.J., reviewing American Catholic popular fiction between 1930 and 1950, concluded that husbands in these tales have a "tendency towards weakness" and are "expected" to fail, and what George Sanderlin, a regular contributor to *Voice of St. Jude*, said of St. Augustine's father was generally true of Catholic husbands in devotional magazines: at their best they were "good but mildly alcoholic."[13]

Sanderlin was evoking one of the great triangles of Christian biography, that of Augustine and his parents Monica and Patricius. Augustine's *Confessions* is, among other things, a moving account of Monica's unswerving commitment to her son's spiritual welfare and of the deepening relationship between the two of them, which culminates in a shared mystical vision in Ostia the day before Monica's death. Patricius's contribution to this story was the disciplining pain (including sexual) he inflicted on Monica. This trope was at the heart of the family romance. The importance of older men, their dynamic contribution to the elaboration of the fantasy, was the holiness they made possible for their wives. The spiritual counsel regularly offered by devotional writers to women (never men) that they accept marriage as the Calvary they had to climb to get to Easter morning was premised on and worked to reinforce the ubiquitous image of the bad husband. "We must give generously of ourselves," Huesman counseled in *Saints in Aprons*, when men demand sexual satisfaction, "for the sake of conjugal peace and happiness," knowing all the time that this surrender (even to the point of tolerating a husband's peccadilloes) was the doorway into the rich "darkness of faith." The issue for women was "how to stay married though unhappy," as Fulton J. Sheen titled one of his widely syndicated articles.[14]

Another structural combination was made, moreover—analogous to the pairing of serene old/dangerous young women—between troublesome or absent married men (like Patricius) and their sons (like Augustine). Here the direction of the contrast was reversed, though: younger men were safe and sober, older ones dangerous, sexual, voracious. In the construction of the Catholic family romance, younger single women were structurally aligned with older married men, younger single men with older widowed (or unhappily married) women.

Devotional writers were not nearly as worried about the immigrants' sons as they were about their daughters. Secular magazines at the time were obsessed with what was identified as the problem of "juvenile delinquency," a response in part to anxieties over the dislocations of war and population mobility, and Catholic writers reflected such concerns. But however tough and unruly bad boys might be, there was an evident fondness and compassion among Catholic writers for "angels with dirty faces"—which was the title of a much loved movie starring Pat O'Brien as a priest working among the hard-bitten but good-hearted Bowery Boys. Such scamps were seen as fundamentally decent and probably salvageable (as indeed the Bowery Boys were). The deeper confidence underlying anxiety about boys is evident in the campaigns of the Catholic Youth Organization, which was specifically founded to redeem the east side kids of various Catholic communities, urban and suburban, by the disciplines of athletics.[15] Tough as they might be, in any case, bad boys ultimately brought ruin only onto themselves; bad girls, on the other hand, threatened the demise of Catholic culture, the stability of the family, and the integrity of Western civilization, an apocalyptic distress not as securely diminished by basketball.

Young men were praised for their caution, steadiness, and stability by Catholic writers—and warned to beware of their dates. Rosie was married to sober, virtuous Jim. Barbara yelled her desire to live on thrills into the ears of loyal and serious Freddy, a responsible young man as long as she was not around. The Liguorian construction of the "female" current in Catholic moral theology was given vivid, dramatic form in these fictional worlds. Young men were also spared the punishments meted out to their girlfriends: "Freddy sustained only a broken collarbone" while Barbara "paid the severe penalty with a crushed chest. . . . [A] splintered bone pierced her lung and tuberculosis set in." These young men (like the old women they were aligned with) were enlisted in the disciplinary campaign against Rosie, Barbara, and their real-life sisters. "As the prevailing fashion of women's dress is unlikely to change," the editors of Ave Maria observed in 1927, "it will be well to remind young men and boys that if they cannot avoid this new occasion of sin—unquestionably it is such—they can nullify it to a great extent" by refusing to look, and perhaps when the girls notice these "indications of a lowering respect" for them "they will have more respect for themselves." Punitive invisibility imposed by good boys would be the first step toward female submission.[16]

The pairing of old woman/young man, in the form mother/son, was at the center of American Catholic devotional culture and piety, which made the relationship between Jesus and his mother the model of the spiritual life, the clearest expression of the encounter between the human and the divine, and the pivot of Catholic cosmology. The American Catholic family romance acquired sacred significance and sanction in this special bond. "To separate the Mother from the Child in religious thought and belief and devotion, is to put asunder what God has joined together, and to make another religion that is not the religion of Jesus Christ," *Ave Maria* warned in 1920. Mary is still a "creature," devotional writers admitted, but "her maternity raises her far above all other creatures, and unites her in the closest and most intimate manner to the Triune God." Admitting that this had not yet been "declared an article of faith," Don Sharkey nevertheless proposed, in his bestselling book, *The Woman Shall Conquer*, that "Mary shared in the work of the Redemption to such an extent that she is call[ed] the Co-redemptrix," so that "all the graces we receive" are distributed by Jesus through Mary—the traditional Catholic formulation of the flow of spiritual and temporal benefits between heaven and earth.[17]

Evocations of Mary's intimacy with Jesus and her place in the drama of redemption reached a high level of spiritual and emotional excitement and intensity in the years just before the Second Vatican Council urged a rethinking of Mariology. Meditations on this bond became the occasion in Catholic devotional culture for the experience and expression of simple and direct childlike emotions and desires. As one writer put it, Mary brings out "the boy in the priest," and these boys (and some girls, too) elaborated all the nuances and implications possible in a piety centered on the relationship between a virgin mother and her man-child. They did so, moreover, in highly erotic language which sometimes became a kind of liturgical baby talk, particularly when the bond between Mary and Jesus served as the opportunity for the elaboration of fantasies about the love between human mothers and sons.[18] It was in such devotional cooing about Mary and Jesus and, through them, about human mothers and sons, that the emotional, erotic impulses of the Catholic family romance found most undisguised expression.

Mary is "that Mother with the sword in her soul," a Franciscan priest told the readers of St. Anthony's Messenger in 1941. Her son "permitted" the sword "to pierce her," knowing that afterward he "would draw it out gently with his loving hand, and heal the wound." The priest who warned that to separate Jesus and Mary is "to put asunder what God has joined together" was appropriating for the mother/son bond a phrase that actually referred, in scripture and Catholic ritual, to the marriage bond. "We say, 'A mother's place is in the home,'" another priest wrote in The Sign in 1949, "by which we imply that a father's is not," and then he also turned to the language of marriage to limn the mother-child relationship. "We are 'two in one flesh' with her by a far more intimate physical union than she can possibly achieve with her husband. She suffers for us as she suffers for no other. In a sense, she dies for us that we may live, for it is of her substance, by the destruction of a part of her, that our physical substance grows, differentiates, matures, and is delivered. Of all this, father is a silent spectator, quite helpless to do anything for his child." Real marriage is that between mother and child; true love is the unconditional love of the mother for her children (not the more difficult and ambivalent love between husbands and wives). In Fulton Sheen's imagining, a pregnant woman became "a flesh and blood ciborium"—the cup that holds the consecrated host—and the sign of "a love which hardly knows a separation between herself and her child." This made of motherhood "a kind of priesthood," according to Sheen, another expression of the intimate identification of mothers and sons in this culture.[19] "If anyone of us could have made our own mother," Sheen concluded in a rather flirtatious meditation on mother-love, the way the God Jesus made his, wouldn't we make our "mommy . . . the most beautiful woman in the world"—just like Jesus created his?

So Mary's bond with Jesus was another way, on the level of cosmology, of situating young women in a subordinate position in, if not actually excluding them from, the Catholic family romance. Mary's role as mother of all the faithful, male and female, was overshadowed and emotionally overwhelmed by the fact that she appeared in history as the mother of a boy-child, not a girl-child. The specific details of a religious tradition's stories and myths have a profound effect on the orientation of desire and imagination of the people who grow up inside it as they establish the public, official limits to the possibilities of spiritual and psychological play and exploration within the idioms of that tradition. The American Catholic family romance might have taken another shape, might have allowed for other fantasies, dreams, and desires, had Mary been the mother of a girl, but she was not, and so the tender and loving evocations of her maternity in devotional culture had to do with mothers and sons, not mothers and daughters.

THE SOCIAL ORIGINS OF THE FAMILY ROMANCE

Older married women were indeed at the center of neighborhood life in the Catholic ethnic enclaves. They collected family paychecks every week, disciplined children (or directed their husbands to), watched over and judged young peoples' romantic attachments and life choices, and generally shaped their families' social worlds. They defined the codes of appropriate behavior and enforced the necessary sanctions when these were transgressed. As John Bodnar writes in his history of this period of European immigration to the United States, "in nearly every immigrant-household economy, the central manager of financial resources, children's socialization, and the entire operation was the married female."[20] Immigrant fathers did not wield the same kind of authority in their homes nor play as central a role in their children's lives as their wives and female relatives did, and they are not remembered with the same emotional intensity and resonance. Preceding their families to the New World often by a considerable stretch of time, married men were not around for their children's earliest years. Even after their families had joined them in the new country, the pressures of contending with periodic unemployment (which frequently demanded that they take jobs away in other cities), their broader opportunities for socializing outside their homes, and the fact that they were, in some Catholic communities, generally older than the women they married, combined to shape a world in which fathers seemed oddly absent even when they were home. This was the basic domestic pattern in all American Catholic ethnic communities.

The family romance was obviously constructed out of the facts of this social world, and the people crafting this psychological fantasy could credibly claim for it the authority and status of "memory." But the romance did not simply reproduce the past. Devotional culture offered the immigrants' children a rich symbolic medium in which to explore and manipulate the latent emotional possibilities of these Catholic family patterns in response to the changing circumstances of their contemporary experience. The romance articulated the latent tensions and hostilities that erupted between men and women of all ages as the enclaves began to dissolve in the late 1920s: it was a transitional creation, an elaboration of emotionally charged memories of the ethnic family as a way of meeting the disorienting experiences of the present.

Unfortunately for women, the satisfactions, justifications, and explanations offered by this dynamic creation in between social history and memory belonged to men. The immigrants' sons and daughters tell similar but subtly different stories about the enclaves. Men recall their mothers as strong, nurturing, powerful, if sometimes difficult and vexing figures, and women say this too—but they also remember that they were tied to their older female kin by more complex bonds of authority and domination that were difficult to break. Men recall families pulling together in tough times, and so do women, but they also remember having to sacrifice their own plans and ambitions on behalf of their brothers. Men tell stories about the good times hanging out in the streets and playgrounds with their buddies; women remember the conflict and tension that surrounded their social lives, and especially their occasional bids for independence, because their missteps outside the house were more threatening to their families' honor than were their brothers' errors.

The romance exacerbated this gendered divergence of memory: it elaborated male fantasies of family life in the enclaves and enshrined male memories as normative as it responded to anxieties about the immigrants' daughters and occluded their memorial processes. Good sons in loving and redemptive alliance with powerful mothers would save the world from dangerous young women without competition from older married men, who were pushed to the edges of memory. The family romance was a male child's dream of immigrant family life, suffused with his needs and fantasies. To enter the world of devotional culture, as American Catholic women regularly did, was to enter a place of very powerful desires and complex nostalgia, but it was a world of male desiring and memory, and so girls became the voracious villains in a cosmic struggle. This was supposed to teach the immigrants' daughters, not their sons, something about who they were, and how they were to live their own lives.

Consequently, devotional culture in its official, public guise was of no help to young women struggling with serious and troubling issues. Unable to shed their fears of and contempt for women, and lost in the excitements and satisfactions of the romance, the writers and editors of Catholic magazines turned the problems and challenges of contemporary American social life into taunts and accusations, which made it impossible for them to offer advice, support, or encouragement to their most faithful readers. The dynamics of this failure were evident in the mid-1960s in two consecutive Mother's Day essays by the venerable editor of *Ave Maria,* John Reedy, C.S.C.[21] Reedy set out in both years to express his sympathy for the plight of modern mothers. But there was no room in the family romance for such compassion, and midway through each essay Reedy's anger at young women got the better of him: commiseration turned to accusation, with all the emotional power of the romance evoked against women.

The circumstances of life today, Father Reedy wrote in 1965, including a "mother's involvement in causes and activities outside the home," have made the tasks of mothering extremely difficult. Girls are right to think twice about undertaking this daunting and unpromising responsibility. (Were Catholic girls thinking twice about becoming mothers? Reedy here may be making an oblique reference to birth control, a theme that will explicitly emerge in the next year's article.) "This isn't a very cheerful Mother's Day column," Reedy confessed, "but then I'm not selling flowers," and he closes on a tough note: "To all of you who are receiving and wearing flowers today, my sympathy—and my prayer that *you* might be able to beat the system."

Father Reedy's Mother's Day greeting the following year appeared under the title, "If You're So Well Educated, So Free, So Respected as a Person, How Come You're Not Happy?" He begins: "My mother would be amazed at the notion of Catholic women [not couples or Catholic men] exercising some judgment about the proper size of their families." Having thus associated women's autonomy with the forbidden domain of birth control, Reedy goes on to say, "My mother had to make a few basic decisions about her life ... but once those decisions were made, the choices were pretty well resolved; the pattern for the rest of her life flowed from them. She didn't have to keep facing new alternatives and new decisions." His mother never had to think about men other than his father, for example (another identification of autonomy with the illicit), or about working outside her home (which by this juxtaposition has acquired the status of birth control and adultery). As for modern women who are indeed faced with choices like these, Reedy can only lament, again, for them—and against them—the loss of "the more stable patterns of the past."

But what past can Father Reedy be remembering here? Millions of young Irish women in his mother's generation went out to work—indeed, they chose to leave Ireland, removing themselves from the authority and control of their male kin, to start new lives for themselves, a choice of remarkable courage, fortitude, and independence. Reedy's use of history here is unfair to this generation of women as well as to their daughters and granddaughters. But the past Reedy evokes, framed by the familiar trope of old woman/young woman, is the imagined past of the family romance, when there was no moral ambiguity, no ambivalence, no decisions to be made or risks taken. All he can offer troubled modern women—and all official devotionalism could offer—were the recriminations of male nostalgia.

<h2 style="text-align:center">FROM RED HAIR TO RED HANDS</h2>

"See the two pictures on this page?" Jim Bishop asked his readers in "Your First Girl," referring to two photographs of his mother, one as a girl, the other as an older woman, printed in the middle of his article. "She's my first girl; my best girl. There she is then—and now. Wasn't she a pretty one, though? I mean, honestly now. The round soft face of her; the blue eyes that seldom smiled; the dark red hair that gleamed like shiny copper when the sun hit it."[22] The plot of the Catholic family romance presented a conundrum: how did beautiful and alluring (and dangerous) young women become serene (and safe) old ones?

The story of wild Rosie Graney is instructive again. One afternoon, sober Jim comes home from work on the railroad to find Rosie out of the house and his mother collapsed on the floor, crushed by the work she's had to do to cover for her daughter-in-law's slovenliness. When Rosie returns, Jim throws her out, saying he never wants to see her again. Rosie responds to this dismissal by indenturing herself as a servant to her own mother's family, and her transformation begins. "Time . . . laid a devastating hand on her bright hair, ruthlessly took the lilt out of the gay voice, and set the giddy feet on duty's rugged path." The once gay and carefree woman slowly becomes "little more than an indistinguishable blur . . . a bent, pale little drudge, with red work-worn hands, the hair that was once her pride drawn back into a dull knot at the back of her head." As it turns out, though, Jim Graney prefers her this way. Hurt in a railroad accident just after his mother dies and lying on his bed one afternoon in pain, Jim hears "a timid voice" asking if he wants supper. He cannot recognize his wife at first, but when he does he yields to the "tender touch of Rosie's roughened but capable little hand." They reunite, raise many children, and at the end of the story gay young Rosie has become a "popular and beloved matron."[23]

This is the answer to the conundrum: wild Rosie and her sisters became venerable matrons in devotional culture by passing through the fires of pain and humiliation. Devotional writers could not have been more explicit about this. "You're a giddy, light-headed little creature," a priest scolds a young woman in another short story, "who's got to be made unhappy to grow into a fine woman." Asking himself how his mother came to be the wise old woman he loved, Jim Bishop recalled the brutal circumstances of her childhood and concludes "if that . . . could produce a flawless diamond like Mom, there must have been something very right about it." This was the message of Anna Maria Taigi's horrible life. There were two categories of women in American Catholic devotional culture: old women who had been broken by time and labor, and young women who needed to be broken by time and labor. Pain was the hinge of the diptych.[24]

Suffering was not only the central social fact of women's lives, in this imagining, but their spiritual destiny and vocation; this was description and prescription. Anna Maria Taigi, Marcy Balaird, Rosie Graney, Susan Grayson, and all their sisters, real and imagined, found domestic and spiritual purpose through suffering (or so they were told). This is how they become the women God wanted them to be. Suffering defined the meaning of motherhood and turned ordinary marriages into the staging ground of sanctity. As late as 1965, Catholic women could be instructed by a (female) devotional writer that their greatest achievement was "the capacity to suffer humiliation."[25]

Women's pain also made the elaboration and enjoyment of the romance possible, moreover, for another mystery of this devotional culture was how adult men could write with such obvious passion and yearning for their mothers. How could Fulton Sheen and Jim Bishop come so close to imagining their mothers as their beloveds? What could make such cloying language possible and enjoyable? Pain transmuted the unpredictable and ungovernable energies, physical and emotional, of young women into the serenity, security, and—above all—asexual love of old women. The hard disciplines of life burned off the threat of women's sexuality, independence, and desire, rendering them safe to be loved and cherished in openly erotic language. They could be embraced then in possessive, smothering baby talk, as sweet old women, who are most real in the embrace of their sons but who have no history, independence, or achievement of their own other than pain. Women's pain was also the hinge, in other words, between the conscious and unconscious levels of the romance. Through the disciplining of women, the inner terrain of devotionalism, alive with primitive desires, had become safe for men, but as a result, it could be quite unsafe for women.

Women's power was not completely denied in devotional culture, of course, as the role assigned to Mary there in the salvation of the world indicates. But the source of Mary's power, too, was suffering and pain: if women, including the Mother of God, were "powerful" in this culture it was because they had suffered or were suffering, usually for their children and their men. Mary was the cosmic woman who endured extraordinary pain. She reported to the children to whom she appeared in the last two centuries that she was experiencing the conditions and attitudes of the modern world as pain in her body; at LaSalette, for example, she said, "for a long time I have suffered for you; if I do not want my son to abandon you, I am forced to pray to him myself without ceasing."[26] Devotional writers affirmed that it was only through this pain that the world could hope to turn aside God's wrath.

The same vocation, and the same discipline, were assigned women on earth. Anna Maria Taigi, whose brutal husband endorsed her sanctity by reporting that "I always found her docile and submissive as a lamb," could heal with "the mere touch of her toil-roughened hands," but she attained this and other supernatural graces only after she had embarked on her devastating regime of physical mortification. Women, following Mary's example, could literally offer up their pain in exchange for the spiritual and physical health of men in need. Even the progressive Catholic periodical *Integrity,* founded in New York City in 1946, proclaimed "women's special vocation to suffering" as the source of their unique intimacy with Jesus.[27]

The path marked out for women was clear: rebellion, autonomy, ambition brought terrible punishment, while suffering and pain made women beloved, graceful, capable of healing and helping. All women had to do is keep silent.

"WHY SHOULD A VOICE LIKE MINE BE HEARD?"

"School my lips, Lord," Marcy Balaird had prayed in a terrible moment of suffering, "not to complain." Women were not just called to pain in devotional culture; they were taught there the spiritual etiquette of distress, the proper manners and comportment of the suffering woman. "Are you allowing worry to show up in your facial expression?" the writer of a column called "For the Ladies" in the *Voice of St. Jude* asked; if so, then replace that frown with a smile and "greet the family pleasantly." Women were supposed to suffer like Marcy Balaird and the other saints in aprons: cheerfully, resignedly, secretly. Their husbands and children were not to know. As Anna Maria Taigi's (endlessly talkative) spouse told the world, "She was always cheerful and pleasant; yet she had a host of maladies. However, they did not keep her from working. . . . She made trousers for me, and overcoats."[28]

But above all, as Marcy Balaird's prayer indicates, women were instructed to suffer silently. Tell your female parishioners who are faced with abusive husbands that a woman's "best sermon is a silent one," a priest counseled his fellows in the *Homiletic and Pastoral Review,* for only in this way can she "raise men to the stars." A young, very sick female character in a story published in the *Voice of St. Jude* muffled her own distress in order not to disturb her brother's rest when he came home from work. When women did complain, they invariably brought spiritual and physical disaster down on their families and themselves. "Let's have no more chitter-chatter," St. Jude scolds a female character who calls on him too often in a short story, and she relents "meekly," afraid that her complaining will get her "crossed off the list" of the saint's hopeless cases.[29]

Mary was the model for this kind of silent suffering. The Virgin speaks in devotional culture, of course, and her devout have collected and pondered her words. But the Virgin's chattiness in the company of the women and girls she has visited has been the source of considerable unease among church officials, and the more garrulous the Virgin has been, the greater this institutional anxiety. Alongside the popular experience of a Virgin who comes with messages and secrets, consequently, there has been a more ecclesiastically comfortable emphasis on Mary's taciturnity. "Be brave then," a priest counseled the women reading *St. Anthony's Messenger,* "whoever you are, be silent, in imitation of her whose heart held the sorrows of the world." "Why were you silent?" a character asks Mary in a poem published in *Ave Maria,* and the Virgin modestly replies, "Why should a voice like mine be heard?" Mary's silent suffering was thus evoked to seal women in their silent rooms. "What mother, before our Sorrowful Mother, or after her[,] has ever been, or ever will be called upon to probe again the depth of sorrow which was hers?" Rose Huesman asked women in *Saints in Aprons.* "We could never plumb the depth of sorrow into which Our Lady's soul was plunged," Huesman says, and so—be silent, stop complaining, accept your lot.[30]

Devotional writers established complex associations between women and voice. Volubility was seen by some as a fact of natural law, a notion rooted in the scholastic emphasis on morally significant natural distinctions between male and female, and this assumption found frequent and varied expression in the devotional press. In a guide for young Catholic men contemplating marriage, for example, published in *Ave Maria* in 1954, Father Robert Sheehan attempted to define the differences between the sexes. Men are aggressive, "self-assured," "domineering," Sheehan observed, whereas women excel in "the use of words, rote memory, imagination, perception of details, and intuition which is sometimes called instinct." Women had a power of speaking that men lacked; their voices could accomplish things that men's could not. Indeed, women could endow men with speech, as Catholic marriage counselors taught, by encouraging their spouses and boyfriends to talk about what was on their minds or by introducing into the evening's conversations delicate subjects that their more reticent men might otherwise avoid. At the same time, the power of women's voices was a source of great anxiety. Father Sheehan warned his male readers that many of the words coming out of women's mouths were dangerous because women "frequently express their thoughts before they let their emotions calm down enough to give reason a chance," a tendency that becomes particularly evident during "the times of menstruation and change of life." Injunctions to female silence were everywhere in Catholic family magazines, in jokes, medical advice, kitchen tips, spiritual counsel, and the biographies of Hollywood stars; silence had to be so pervasively enjoined on women precisely because their voices were so powerful and threatening. It is not surprising given Father Sheehan's association between women's dangerous voices and menarche that another devotional writer approvingly mentioned the custom of "some primitive societies" of segregating menstruating women into "places apart."[31]

But the ideology of the "Catholic home" worked just as well as a menstrual hut. As Catholics struggled in the postimmigration period with the dilemmas of modern life, deep anxieties about the destiny and stability of the "home" in general, and the "Catholic home" in particular, emerged across the culture. "Sin-maddened men," wrote George Sanderlin in the *Voice of St. Jude* in 1949, were destroying the family, which was struggling to survive in a landscape blighted by divorce, juvenile delinquency, homelessness, urban decay, consumerism, industrialism, and racism. Others saw Communism as a direct assault on Catholic families. The American Catholic bishops issued a pastoral letter in 1949 urging Catholics to wield all the resources of devotional culture against the modern world's threat to the family, which they considered "more fearsome than the atomic bomb." The immediate ground of these anxieties, of course, although it was not always recognized as such, was the contemporary dissolution of the immigrant enclaves. Against these terrors Catholic writers posed the secure and comforting counterimage of the "Catholic family": whatever was happening in the homes of other people (like Marcy's sister-in-law), Catholic families should—and could—be sanctuaries of peace and holy serenity in the surrounding darkness. As one commentator typically asked: "Who should more truly realize the perfect marriage than a Catholic man and woman, united as they are in the Mystical Body of Christ!"[32]

Patrick Peyton, C.S.C., founder and promoter of the Apostolate of the Family Rosary, promised anxious parents that if they said the rosary daily, "their homes will become, by God's grace, peaceful, prayerful, places, little heavens, which God the author of home life has intended they should be!" A happy family, Geraldine Macelwane advised the readers of *Ave Maria* in 1952, is like a "little church," with family members carrying out "their responsibilities joyfully, approaching them with faith and a sense of humor. Such persons fairly twinkle when they mention their spouse or children." Macelwane, who also maintained that women were responsible for their husbands' faults and prescribed a discipline of female silence and submission as the foundation of a solid marriage, was a judge of the municipal court in Toledo and had served as the assistant prosecutor of Lucas County, Ohio, in charge of offenses against the family, but all this experience did not prevent her from contributing to the disciplinary myth of Catholic family perfection. When Catholic censors demanded that references to divorce or, especially, happy remarriage be excised from films, they were acting in accordance with this code of domestic silence and occlusion.[33]

It was this ideal image that confronted real women, whose families behaved often enough as something other than little heavens, when they opened the pages of Catholic family magazines that were ostensibly offering them practical and moral advice and support. The ideology of the Catholic family was another medium of silence and discipline, another strategy of denial. Catholic writers seemed to delight in affronting their readers with an extravagantly unattainable prescription of family perfection, often juxtaposing it with real-life concerns as if to heighten its disciplinary edge. During the postwar housing shortage, to cite just one example of this riotous attitude toward the problems of everyday life, George Sanderlin encouraged St. Jude's anxious clients—who were filling the letters pages in the same periodical with their difficulties finding homes—to gather logs, procure shovels, and homestead on the scrubland at the urban margins.[34]

The "Catholic family" took up and elaborated one dimension of the family romance, its projection of a perfect moment of family harmony when there was no dissent, choice, or ambivalence, and the only pain there was was good for women, and it redoubled injunctions to domestic silence and submission. How could one complain about or rebel against family structures that participated in the Mystical Body of Christ? American Protestants may have known such family troubles, but not Catholics. Silence enclosed silence: the silent woman took her place in the perfect home.

American Catholic family magazines were a special kind of cultural space: they brought together the viscerally powerful myths of Catholic religious cosmology with housekeeping tips, moral advice, and social commentary, among other quotidian concerns. Having entered the world of these creations, readers moved easily between vivid imaginings of the drama of human fall and redemption to updates on Bing Crosby and his family and hints for decorating suburban bathrooms. But these were not discrete domains, the sacred and the profane: it was the great ambition of American Catholic culture to inhabit a single unified reality of which every detail, however trivial, bore weighty significance and meaning. This is what gave midcentury Catholic family magazines their strangely grandiose tone. Everything was treated with the same portentous intensity, everything was rich in Catholic truth: there was religious excitement in Bing's story (he was such a good Catholic he initially refused to play the role of the priest in *Going My Way* because he deemed himself unworthy to don the cloth) and practical implications in the dynamics of the cosmos.

Practical implications especially for women: in the varied genres of these magazines (of which they were the main consumers), American Catholic women were offered what anthropologist Clifford Geertz calls a "sentimental education," an intimate schooling in the attitudes, postures, moods, self-perceptions, and emotions that their cultures, American and Catholic, deemed appropriate for them. They were taught here what was real, good, and possible, and it was in these pages that they learned who they were meant to be in relation to others.[35] Women were implicated in devotional magazines in a way of being, exposed to a construal of their subjectivities as silent, suffering figures, whose agency was grounded in pain and whose mission was endurance and submission. It was in devotional culture that this account of the meaning of womanhood received supernatural sanction in relation to the story of Mary's place in the history of salvation.

What made devotionalism so powerful in its work of imagining women was that its vision was not merely proposed or even mandated as a code of moral injunctions or rules (although it was both) but enacted and performed as psychological drama and physical discipline as well. Women entering the spaces of devotionalism found themselves swept up in a compelling religious re-creation (what I have called the family romance) of the realities and problems of their actual social world, an imagining of them that was suffused with desire, denial,

and repression. By entering the domain of devotionalism, women were implicated in the drama. The media of this enactment and implication were quite
intimate, including the highly charged images inherited by American Catholics
within their tradition—dying sons, suffering mothers, pierced hearts, bleeding
wounds—as well as the array of corporal practices characteristic of Catholic
piety. Women touched, burned, and smelled things in devotional culture,
poured oils and waters onto their skins, put things in their mouths, rubbed
various substances into their bodies and onto the bodies of their loved ones;
they touched and were touched, incorporated and were incorporated. The
devout could not stand back from devotional performance or from the romance, and they were summoned into the latter by the former. As they did
these things with their senses in the realm of devotionalism, women incarnated
the story that the culture told about them.

The central political fact of devotionalism is that while it was ostensibly
made for women, directed at their hearts and purses, it was made against them,
too. In the most distressing circumstances—when their children were sick,
their husbands unemployed, when they were unable to find a place to live or a
much-needed job—American Catholic women turned for solace, help, and
meaning into a world that denied their experience and recast them as villains
in a cosmic melodrama. The culture's anger, fears, and disappointments found
expression in this theater, transforming the immigrants' daughters into dangerous viragos and their mothers into healing matrons, the one doomed to
destruction by desire, the other made redemptive by pain and denial. American Catholic women's subjectivity was fundamentally shaped in this dynamic
encounter between the facts of their everyday experience and the re-creations
of this experience in devotional fantasy.

The disciplinary impulse of devotional culture accounts for the uncanny
cruelty of its different genres whenever the subject was women. Devotional
hagiography in particular, as illustrated by the stories of Marcy Balaird and
Anna Maria Taigi with which this chapter opened, was a mean genre: where
else could the vacuous voice of a man so complacently cruel as Anna Maria
Taigi's husband was be called upon so often to witness to and endorse his wife's
sanctity? But the cruelty was not incidental here; it was a function of a world
that addressed women in order to discipline them.

What remains to be said about the piety of the immigrants' daughters?
American Catholic women, at a time when they were tensely negotiating (consciously and not) a difficult transition from one way of being and living to

another, were interpellated (to use the language of structurally oriented historiography for the destiny of "subjects" in history) or implicated in a crafting of their identities that encouraged them to be passive, submissive, and dutifully suffering. This discourse was shaped and promulgated by anxious and threatened figures, male and female, who used the considerable resources of the Catholic devotional tradition in a subtle and complex psychological, religious, and cultural strategy of domination. Catholic women's choices in this context, presumably, would be to submit to this imposition or reject it. But how capable they would have been to reject it is unclear, since all Catholics were encouraged from childhood on to enter the domain of devotionalism regularly, but especially in times of need. The whole culture directed the immigrants' daughters into devotionalism, and there they were remade against the movement of their own times.

What remains, then, is to see how Jude fit into this scenario.

But women were not passive consumers of devotions. They engaged their tradition actively: they took objects away from the Shrine in Chicago, for example—its oils, waters, holy cards, prayer books, and, above all, its many representations of St. Jude—and used them in ways unforeseen, and often unsanctioned, by the clergy in Chicago. The devout told stories about the saint, and about themselves in relation to him, in their own voices; they spoke to him in their own words, besides saying the published prayers of the Shrine, addressed him with their often secret, barely acknowledged needs. Jude was not imposed on women, in other words, nor did they simply inherit him; they invented him, too. They took him away from the Shrine out there and brought him into their lives and homes, for better or worse.

I have been concerned in the past two chapters with the forces converging on and against young Catholic women, with the circumstances of their hopelessness, the ideologically occasioned disjunctures in their experience, and finally with the fantasies others entertained of them. Now I want to turn to the way the women so imagined were at the same time, in the same domain of devotionalism, imagining Jude.

The way into this devotional relationship for women—and so for us, too—is through Jude's eyes.

4

"I Recognize Him When He Turns"
Women Imagining Jude

Clara was driving in Chicago one afternoon on family business that was taking her, as usual, from one end of the city to the other. She stopped for gasoline at a service station in an unfamiliar neighborhood and made a quick telephone call. As she was edging her way back into the heavy rush-hour traffic, distracted by the many things she still needed to get done before dinner, her car suddenly stalled and came to a standstill.

"Just then, a huge semi-truck went speeding before me. If I had pulled out, I would have been hit broadside. There is no way I could have survived an impact like that."

Trembling and shaken, Clara leaned back in her seat and "my eyes came in contact with my statue of Saint Jude," a small plastic dashboard figure she had picked up at the Shrine many years ago. Still looking in the saint's eyes, she turned the key in the ignition and "the car started right up. It never stalled

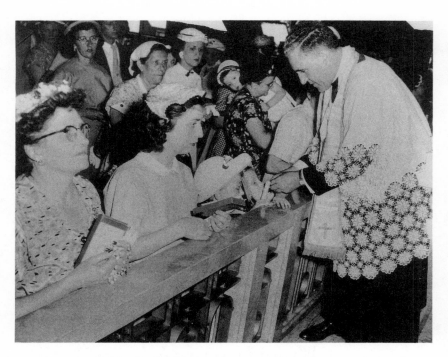

Venerating Jude's relic during the June novena, 1954. Father DePrada presides.

before nor has it ever stopped since." Clara says that she understood through this exchange of glances that the saint who had been protecting and caring for her already for so many years had just intervened again in her life, this time to save it.

When they describe how they imagine Jude to look, his devout emphasize the saint's face and eyes; when they pray to him they search to see his face, either on the statues and prayer cards before them or in their imaginations. Faces and eyes are the features most carefully examined by the devout in deciding whether or not particular representations of Jude are good likenesses.[1] Although she keeps statues of many other saints in her home, Isabel told me, she has never had one of Jude there, although she loves him most of all, because "I don't like the statues they have of [him at the Shrine] and I don't want to put up something that doesn't look the way I would like it to." I asked her what makes a statue look like Jude or not? "The face," Isabel said, "and the eyes and stuff."

Women say that Jude turns his face toward them when they need him and watches over them kindly and attentively. "I feel mighty fortunate with Saint Jude's picture looking down on me," one client wrote the Shrine, and another testified that the saint "has never turned his head when I asked him for help." One of my sources, who called herself disabled and said she was bedridden most of the time, began her description of Jude by imagining herself slowly approaching a man with his back to her. Just as she reached this apparent stranger, he looked round and "I recognize him [as St. Jude] when he turns."[2]

The point of many of the practices associated with the material world of the devotion—the statues of various sizes sold by the Shrine, its holy cards, medals, stationery and greeting cards, dashboard medallions, and so on—has been to focus Jude's caring and protecting gaze. The devout site Jude, arranging their images of him at home and work so they might exchange comforting, consoling, and encouraging glances as they go about their daily tasks. The devout believe that images of Jude can *see,* and they address their prayers directly to the saint's eyes. "I carry his Prayer Card with me always," a woman said in a letter to the Shrine in 1968, describing a common practice, "and turn to him frequently." One devout purposefully wrote his or her letters to the Shrine in sight of Jude's image at home; another taped a holy card to the back of a picture of her son in the Navy for the saint literally to keep an eye on the boy overseas; another propped his image up on her kitchen windowsill so she could talk to him as she washed dishes and cleaned vegetables. Worried mothers trained the saint's gaze down on their sick children. Sometimes in addition to writing to the Shrine and talking to the images in their homes, women sought out Jude's statue in neighborhood churches, slipping off to experience his eyes upon them in these special settings apart, outside their homes, away from the regular course of their days.[3]

Although they have never reported aural or visual experiences of Jude and do not expect to encounter him in these ways, his clients believe that he communicates directly with them, either through a voice they hear or feel inside themselves or by the way he looks back at them while they pray. The look on Jude's face is thought to hold clues to the outcomes of their petitions, so the devout are also practicing a kind of divination when they seek the saint's gaze. "This may seem strange, I know," Judy told me, but "a lot of times I'll look at his face [on a statue], and I'll see if he's smiling, everything will be OK." The prospect that Jude would not be smiling so terrified her that "sometimes I'm afraid to look up there." What she longed to glimpse was a "smile or [that] serenity look." Women also believed that Jude could see directly into their hearts. One told me that Jude's eyes are knowing and "penetrating," and many others affirmed that the saint saw them clearly for who they were and knew their secrets.[4]

But though there is this real risk involved in imagining the saint—for who could be sure what the future holds?—the anxiety with which women search Jude's face in times of trouble is softened by the evident love and care they also see there. Jude's eyes may have held threatening information, but his face was gentle and compassionate. If women experience themselves as revealed in his sight, they never feel completely vulnerable because the man they are looking at looks back at them with understanding and acceptance. With Jude's eyes on them, women have felt truly seen and recognized—and loved and held in the recognition.

Who was this man, then, who gazed so compassionately and affectionately, and with such discernment, upon his hopeless supplicants?

"THE VOICELESS AND INARTICULATE, THE SPEECHLESS AND SILENT SAINT"

Almost nothing is known with any certainty about Jude Thaddeus, and the tradition preserves few legends, so over the years the clergy in Chicago have had to improvise stories about the Patron Saint of Hopeless Cases for his American devout, working from the testimony of the apocrypha, occasional remarks of ancient theologians, and the visions of a medieval mystic. This is what they have said about him in Chicago:

Jude was Jesus' cousin. His father, Cleophas, was St. Joseph's brother, and his grandfather, Jacob, was the Virgin Mary's uncle, so Jude was related to Jesus through both the latter's earthly parents. Chicago's hagiographers delighted in describing how the two boys played together in the alleys of Nazareth with their other cousin, John the Baptist. Born of a "sturdy race," Jude grew up to be a farmer. His hands were callused, yet "through his veins course[d] the royal blood of the kings of Israel." Jesus chose him to be one of the apostles. At their last meal together, Jude asked his cousin what was to be done about the Gentiles, an ecumenical compassion he would express again in his canonical epistle.[5]

Jude occupied a place of prominence among the apostles because of his kinship with Jesus, an arrangement resonant with the values of the family enclaves (and with Chicago's ward culture of nepotism). According to one of the few legends about him, Jude was entrusted with a special mission toward the end of Jesus' public ministry. His "divine cousin" had received a message from Abgar, King of Edessa, who was suffering from leprosy, begging him to come and perform a cure. Moved by this expression of faith from a person who had never seen him, Jesus pressed a cloth to his face, miraculously imprinting it with a likeness of himself, and sent it back to Abgar with Jude. This is why the saint is traditionally represented holding a small image of Jesus' face against his chest.[6] After Jesus' death, Jude traveled through Syria, Mesopotamia, and Chaldea, proclaiming the gospel and debating religious matters with pagan priests. Writers at the Shrine liked to emphasize the contrast between the saint's opponents, who were worldly, sophisticated, and accomplished intellectuals, dressed in fine clothes and possessed of elegant diction, and the peasant-preacher, who always defeated them in contests of miraculous power and silenced their specious eloquence with his simple message of love and redemption. It was after one of these encounters that his humiliated rivals revenged themselves by clubbing Jude to death, which is why the saint is also commonly shown gripping a huge bludgeon at his side.

Now silence and obscurity enfolded Jude Thaddeus. Because of the unfortunate assonance between his name and that of Jesus' betrayer, the apostle was "lost," as the Shrine puts it, "forgotten" by the faithful, never properly venerated even though as Jesus' relative and trusted companion he was one of the most powerful of all the saints in heaven. "His memory had all but perished" in the tradition, and Jude had "almost lost his identity," despite Jesus' own appearance to St. Bridget of Sweden in the fourteenth century to encourage devotion to his cousin.[7] By the time Father Tort came across the holy card in the pew in Prescott, Arizona, Jude had become "the Voiceless and Inarticulate, the Speechless and Silent Saint," "the Forgotten Saint," the "Obscure and Unknown Saint," as his earliest titles at the Shrine named him.

All because "Jude" sounds like "Judas." The occlusion of the powerful apostle by Christendom's great traitor is the most important feature of the saint's biography and a unique aspect of this devotion. Nowhere else in Catholic popular culture is Judas assigned such an important and central place. He was responsible for Jude's "unfortunate handicap" and "sad predicament," in the words of the first hagiography published in Chicago, and in this sense Judas constituted the devotion to St. Jude, for without his obscuring presence the cult of lost causes would not have been necessary. Judas's more vivid and compelling character, furthermore, as recorded in scripture and legend, became the pivot around which Chicago's storytellers, struggling to make the unknown Jude more real to his devout, elaborated his own less-distinct personality. Judas was treacherous and underhanded, Jude is loyal, dependable, and straightforward; Judas "was a victim of personal anguish that consumed him in despair," while Jude "realized that he should always depend upon the strength of Christ" and never give up. Judas shaped the devotion on this level, too: Jude became visible in relation to him. Jude and Judas are mirror figures in the devotion: in an image printed at the Shrine in 1954, the two are shown in specular diptych, with Judas's hand resting on Jude's shoulder. They are inseparable; the Patron Saint of Hopeless Cases is Judas inverted.[8]

The Jude/Judas trope was the first in an interlocking chain of inversions that structured the way Jude was imagined, both at the Shrine and by the devout around the country. Jude the forgotten, whose name Thaddeus means "meek" and "amiable," was actually the most powerful of all saints. The simple farmer with roughened hands, coarse garb, and plain speech triumphed over the sophisticated priests of pagan courts. The saint celebrated for his bodily purity served as the refuge for "those in the depths of impurity." To pray to Jude— whose titles included "the Saint of the Impossible" and "the Patron of Hopeless Cases and Matters Despaired Of," and whose particular role in the American Catholic pantheon was to make the impossible possible, the hopeless hopeful— was to enter upon the path of reversal. As one woman exclaimed after her faithful Jude had come to her assistance in a difficult situation, "the trick has been turned again."[9] This could be a daunting, and even terrifying, prospect, as we shall see, however much it was also desired.

ST. JUDE GOES TO CHICAGO

In his incarnation as a modern American hero, Jude was born during the Depression, and as his clients were marked by the time, so was he. When his biographers at the Shrine extrapolated from the meager tradition and recast the saint in more American idioms, Jude emerged as a humble and unassuming man—Judy referred to him once as "a stand-back kind of person." He is, in the colloquial descriptions of his devout, a regular fellow, a swell guy and a real pal, "God's right-hand man," who gets the necessary jobs done right, but who is at the same time so modest that he does not even mention in his epistle that he is related to Jesus. Jude is a scrapper, steady and uncompromising, afraid of no one and intimidated by no situation. Tremendously powerful, he has the common touch, caring equally for everyone who calls on him. He may not be a smooth talker, but he can be an effective communicator when he needs to be; his customary reticence, like Gary Cooper's, comes from the fact that he is usually too busy helping people to say very much.[10]

The American Jude obviously resembled other Depression-era popular heroes, real and imaginary. The hope that help would come from a hidden and unexpected quarter was shared in many different venues at the time of the Shrine's founding. Jude came suddenly on the scene, apparently out of nowhere, just when he was most needed—like Huey Long ("an angel sent by God" to his followers) or Father Divine (whose earthly origins remained mysterious to his flock) or Superman. Like the Lone Ranger (who had twenty million fans by 1939), Clark Kent, and other radio and comic book superheroes, and like shy Mr. Smith, who went to Washington to set things right with his dogged, simple integrity, Jude cloaked his awesome power with an amiable public persona, so amiable that people in trouble overlooked him initially as a source of help. Jude had suffered, moreover, had known disgrace and humiliation and the misunderstanding of the crowd, and he was constantly at risk that this fate would enfold him again. He was the once-hurt and always vulnerable saint, in short, and in this, too, he resembled other heroes of the time who had to be handicapped in some way before they would be trusted. Frank Capra's comedies, for instance, according to Warren Susman, "all, in some degree, depend[ed] initially on a kind of ritual humiliation of the hero, a humiliation that is often painful and even cruel but from which the hero ultimately emerges with some kind of triumph." The wounded "St. Roosevelt," who was perceived, according to a study done after the Depression, as "a warm, understanding man, a man with great power and status, a man with competence who was, withal, a champion of the little man," was counted on to lead the nation back to health.[11] In idiom and impulse, then, the American Jude was a recognizable figure, cobbled together out of the same needs and fantasies and expressing the same hopes of inversion and redemption as other figures on the cultural landscape.

But Jude was a distinctly American Catholic hero, too. The social and cultural position of the immigrants' children in the 1930s and 1940s, who were just edging their way uneasily into a society they had been raised to mistrust (not always without reason), added its own shadows to this portrait. There was a subtle undercurrent of resentment, aggrieved defiance, and hostility in the way Jude was first imagined, although this shading diminishes over time. "It's good to see poor Saint Jude come into his own occasionally," one of the saint's devout groused in an early letter to the Shrine, and others regularly expressed the same sentiment: their patron saint had gotten a bad deal, a bum rap, and was never appreciated for who he really was and what he could do. "Sometimes it happens that precious caskets richly ornamented contain trash," Jude is said to have taunted the Persian priests, "while valuable jewels are guarded safely in chests of rough wood."[12] A similar spirit was evident in the sketches of Catholic movie stars and nightclub entertainers that were a staple feature of devotional family magazines. These figures were invariably better than the tinsel world they inhabited, inured to its blandishments, excess, and decadence by their resilient Catholic faith (regardless of their luxurious homes and elegant clothes), although this quality about them was predictably overlooked by the cynical (non-Catholic) reporters on the Hollywood beat.[13] All this hostility was obviously suffused with guilt. See, these portraits proclaimed, however much we may look like other American success stories (or however much we may desire to), we are always different, better, sounder—and still Catholic. And if we happen not to look like American success stories, if we still look like the enclaves—if we are still discernibly Catholic—do not be fooled; we have made it, too. The emergent Catholic middle class had made heroes out of its bad conscience and holiness of its resentment and insecurity. Jude was the misunderstood hero of an ambivalent community.

Saints are always shaped by the intellectual crosscurrents, ethical conundra, politics, and social-psychological impulses of their times, and so, obviously, was Jude.[14] But saints always have a more intimate genesis, too: they emerge out of the private, everyday emotional, spiritual, and physical needs of the people who imagine them into being. This is another site of in-betweenness in the phenomenology of this devotion. We have already seen that the immigrants' daughters who imagined Jude into being were situated at the intersection of the old and the new, between the expectations of others and their own desires, in the broader context of generational, cultural, and geographical transition, and that the prayers they made in this fluid social history moved fluidly between the "personal" and the "public." So, too, the man to whom these women directed their prayers was an in-between figure, made by the Shrine's official caretakers and thus of "culture," but made as well from the intimate needs of the women calling on him, and thus a "private" figure. There are no secure boundaries in the cult of saints.

In 1947, the director of the Shrine, Father Joseph Puigvi, sought to respond to a problem that had arisen in the devotion. "The national office of St. Jude's League in Chicago, not so very long ago sent a statue of St. Jude to a person who asked for it," and "a few days later the same office received the package back with a note: 'We return the statue because it is not a statue of St. Jude.'" Father Puigvi conceded that there was a real difficulty here: "How shall we know a statue or picture is one of Saint Jude?" Since we can assume Jesus looked like his cousin, Puigvi proposed, the most authentic statues of him would be those that looked most like Jesus (and Puigvi assumed that everyone would recognize the resemblance).[15]

But the devout had their own, more personal criteria, for recognizing Jude. Before they determined to acquire a statue of him for themselves, they would already have had some direct experience of him; the acquisition of a three-dimensional representation (which was not inexpensive) was a gesture of love and gratitude generally undertaken *after* some important event had occurred; it expressed a desire to have the saint who just acted for them at a crucial moment near them always in a visible and tangible way. This is in part what has made the devout so uneasy at the first sight of their long-awaited and desired statues: once the *real* St. Jude had been encountered on such charged occasions, others would just not do. By way of dealing with the discomfort provoked by this discrepancy, the devout often attempted to make the official images their own in some way, usually by working on them with skills and techniques typically associated with women's crafts, like sewing and decorating. One woman latch-hooked rugs with Jude's face on them to give to friends. Others assembled complicated floral arrangements for their statues at home or painted them in warmer and more satisfying colors than the Shrine's official hues.[16]

Even when they claimed to accept the official representations of Jude as authentic, furthermore, women tended to see something different—and more —in them. "Exactly as the pictures and statues of him indicate!" one woman replied to my question about the saint's appearance, and then recalling the circumstances of her first encounter with Jude, when she was in "severe pain," she went on to describe how the saint really looked to her: "bearded, [with] a slight smile [and] long artistic fingers."[17] "How do you describe love?" Clara retorted when I asked her about Jude's looks, suggesting that no iconography was equal to the emotion she enjoyed whenever she prayed to Jude, a "feeling of knowing you have someone special who helps you when all else fails." Such iconic dissatisfaction has been a subtle but persistent theme in the devotion. The printed prayers distributed at the Shrine were similarly unsatisfying to the devout. "I'd much rather talk to [Jude]," one woman told me, "than say the formal prayers," a preference shared by many others. Jude's devout usually say they "talk" (rather than "pray") to him because, as this same woman put it, "I think Saint Jude is truly my friend."[18] Another woman described her way of approaching Jude: "I use the novena booklet and I use the [prayer]-card, but I also just talk to him. It's almost not like praying so much as saying, 'Hey, St.

Jude, you know something, I got up this morning and I really can't deal with these mundane things,' whatever the thing is; 'You've got to help me with this.' " Concerned that I might misunderstand her, she quickly added, "I don't mean to be undevout, but it's just a very comfortable, you know, a more comfortable relationship than I really have with God, because with God, I'm a little bit more formal. [Jude] is like a bigger brother or a trusted friend or somebody that you know."[19] The devout have always described their communications with Jude in such intimate terms. "Prayer" to him has always meant a daily, extended conversation, a continuing connection, a way of "keeping in touch."[20] "I just talk to him [all day] and thank him and love him," I was told, and "I talk a lot to him and I know he hears me because I feel that he does."[21] As Clara said: "Sometimes I just say thank you; other times I carry on a full conversation. Periodically I plead and become angry."

Women did not simply inherit Jude, then: one way or another, they appropriated him for themselves, in their own idioms and styles, in their own spaces, and in response to their most pressing needs and experiences. They engaged him emotionally and imaginatively, bringing him into their lives for themselves, and in the process of this transposition, the "official" Jude acquired another set of meanings, qualities, and associations, unthought of by the priests in Chicago. The dissatisfaction Puigvi encountered emerged out of the discrepancy between the two processes of improvisation by which Jude was imagined into being: the Shrine's extrapolation of the slender historical record and the devout's appropriation and extension of this for themselves.

Jude was an especially good figure for this kind of imaginative intervention precisely because he was the unknown and forgotten saint, with no ethnic ties, European roots, institutional affiliation, historical tradition, or local identification. There were none of the legends about him of the sort that made other holy figures, like St. Anthony or St. Thérèse of Lisieux, such vivid, appealing, and trustworthy figures, but that also inevitably constrained, or at least oriented, the imaginative play possible with them. These other saints, furthermore, all of whom had definite assignments (Anthony helped find lost objects, for example, Blaise cured sore throats)—unlike Jude, who was a generalist— were deeply implicated in kinship structures and neighborhood bonds. A young woman growing up in a Catholic home in 1936 would have known that her mother had a special love for St. Paulinus of Nola, perhaps, while one grandmother was devoted to the Infant of Prague and the other to St. Anthony. The images of the saints filled familiar domestic niches and became part of the experience of home and place in the old enclaves, resonating with rich familial associations, stories, and feelings, for better or worse. But Jude was an unencumbered figure, a new presence on the American Catholic landscape as of 1929. Catholics generally thought of saints as helpers in difficult times and Jude would have been familiar enough in this formal sense, but he was an empty form and his emptiness in the tradition inherited by the immigrants' daughters opened a space for the exercise of their imaginations there. The unknown saint stood at that place in a religious culture where desire, imagination, and improvisation are possible, and the devout set about filling in the outlines of his portrait with their needs.

"ALL I KNOW IS I NEED HIM VERY MUCH": ENCOUNTERING THE UNKNOWN SAINT

The immigrants' daughters usually came across St. Jude for the first time in one of two ways: either they happened upon him by chance, discovering one of the Shrine's holy cards on a bus, for example, or seeing a reference to the saint in a newspaper, or, more commonly, they heard about him from someone else, a friend or relative or even someone who just briefly crossed their paths—the person in the next hospital bed or the one sitting behind them at the unemployment office. But the defining character of these first encounters was extreme need—the saint was said to "wait for the very last minute" before acting —and the intensity of the moment fundamentally shaped both the way Jude was experienced and the details of his imagining.[22] This was a charged moment, marked in memory and experience both by the intensity of its need and the suddenness of Jude's intervention, and every woman I spoke with could remember the details of these occasions clearly and specifically however long ago they may have been.

The devout themselves explicitly made the connection between the extremity of their distress and the timing of Jude's arrival. "Whenever I need Saint Jude," a woman wrote me, "he is there," and another, charting the saint's many interventions in her life, concluded, "all I know is that [when] I need him very much" he comes. The appearance of the saint in this specific emotional context took on the quality of destiny. Jude seemed to come unbidden, as if he were watching and waiting for just the appropriate moment to make his presence known; the devout interpreted their feeling that this was so as the disclosure of a hidden divine design beyond human calculation. "Sometimes when I pray to him for something I need desperately it seems like he is standing right there next to me," an eighty-nine-year-old woman wrote me from a nursing home. "I believe that [St. Jude's] bubbling over trying to help people." The saint was said to be thrilled when his intercessions worked, so eager was he to be of assistance. "If you wish to announce [the outcome of her prayers to Jude] in the *Voice of St. Jude*," a woman wrote the Shrine in 1941, "you may do so as I think that St. Jude feels happy to know that through his intercession God has granted a favor to one who has the utmost confidence in him."[23]

At the same time the devout also reported being startled by Jude's interventions. His appearance may have been destined, almost ontologically coincidental with the extremity of distress, but the devout always insisted that they did not know this in their hopeless times and so never took his help for granted. Jude was someone new and unexpected in their lives, but he had been there all along, too, poised to help; his arrival had the quality of a recognition or a timely intuition. One woman told me that although she had never called on the saint before and was barely aware that she even knew who he was, when she saw her nine-year-old son hanging by his neck from the twisted chains of a backyard swing set she heard herself screaming out Jude's name. This unthinking summons was to her an essential dimension of the miracle of the boy's rescue.[24]

So, in fact, a series of subtle contradictions or paradoxes characterized the way Jude was imagined by his devout: his appearance was expected but startling; he was newly encountered but familiar; he responded to their pleas for help but was always there. The most intimate contradiction of Jude's imagining, though, was that women's engagement with him represented an experience of trust in a male figure just at the moment when the actual men in their lives were failing them. The devout made it clear in their narratives that Jude entered the space vacated by men; often they referred to Jude as being like "a very loving big brother or father" or having "a very fatherly disposition." When they recalled the saint's first engagement with them, moreover, they were also very often remembering an occasion of male disengagement. Women reported calling on the saint when their husbands, sons, or boyfriends abused or mistreated them, when their doctors left them alone in unfamiliar settings with bad news, when their priests proved unavailable for counsel or comfort, when their fathers were dying. One woman wrote me that she was "desperate over a son completely lost to alcoholism" and "on his way to Skid Row" when she first prayed to St. Jude. "I spent hours weeping, praying and trying to find him," which she eventually did—but first she found Jude.[25]

The relation here between Jude and men recalls that between the saint and Judas, and again the imagining of the saint acquired some of its specific qualities in the mirror of betrayal and disappointment. The men in women's letters to the Shrine are often weak, insecure, incompetent, or at least unequal to some challenge; Jude gets things done—he is "capable of handling the most serious problems in life." Men may be undependable and disloyal, but Jude is reliable, secure, and loyal: "wart or worry," as one woman put it, "that noble saint always comes around." Husbands, sons, fathers, and boyfriends absent themselves from the bonds they made with women by drinking, philandering, being assigned to distant ports, losing their jobs, or dying. Jude is always there. "I enjoy Saint Jude," a young woman recalling the breakup of an old relationship wrote me, "and I pray to [him] when I [am] alone."[26]

"TO ME HE IS TALL, HANDSOME, WITH A CLEFT IN HIS CHIN"

St. Jude, as his devout have pictured him to themselves, is a "tall thin man," "about 5 feet and between 9 to 11 inches in height with a good and average build." He is strong but also "gentle and kind," "powerful," "compassionate and caring," "a great friend to have when in need." A woman who described herself as "single, and very ill and scared" when she first turned to St. Jude imagined him as "kind, personable, and loving," a man she could "relate to"; another woman who said her situation was "up for grabs" at her first encounter with the saint, a reference to problems of health and romance, called him "quiet, soft-spoken, sure of himself—a kindly man." Other women told me they thought of Jude as "very handsome," "nice looking [with] a perfect" and "pleasant" face that shows "concern . . . for all who seek his help." He has "dark" and "penetrating eyes" that are "warm," "friendly," "soft and pleasing," "kind and sad," and "a gentle smile" that radiates "a look of Protection—SomeOne to Lean on." "A gentle, kind, loving person," one woman concluded her description, "who you would like to embrace."[27]

The saint's manly good looks have been important to the women praying to him; they obviously enjoy the sensation of this man's dark and warm eyes lovingly held on them. This is another answer to Puigvi's dilemma: some statues were just not handsome enough. "I have seen a statue of [St. Jude] at Saint Peter's Church in the Loop," Judy told me, "but I don't particularly like that statue of him." It makes the saint seem too "old," she complained, whereas she sees him as "tall, handsome, with a cleft in his chin [the chin on the statue at the Shrine is bearded] and [with] soft, sympathetic eyes and a gentle smile." Spanish statues of Jude, like the one Judy saw downtown, generally depict him as an older, bald man; the younger saint in South Chicago has a full head of wavy hair, and his rugged good looks, reproduced on countless holy cards, helped orient the fantasies of his American devout.

There have actually been two representations of St. Jude at his Chicago shrine. Sometime in the mid-1940s (the date is uncertain, even in the memories of people who were present during the transition), Rose McDonald's statue was moved to the correspondence room in the devotion's downtown offices, where it still stands, and replaced by another image of Jude. The two figures share common physical features, but the second statue is more modern in feel, less European. Jude now has a squared chin and shoulders, his posture is more upright, and there is somewhat less movement in the folds of his garments, giving him a greater sense of stability and poise. The Shrine seems thus to have Americanized Jude even further.

This handsome, hirsute, and robust young St. Jude is an intuitive and attentive man who knows how his devout feel even when they are too anxious or uneasy to say so for themselves. Writing from Niagara Falls, New York, in 1969, a woman told the Shrine: "My son had a severe eye hemorrhage from which he is almost completely recovered, but had not passed General Science once this school year. I jokingly remarked that if Saint Jude would stand behind him during the exam and give him a nudge in the right direction I would send a donation. Not only did my son pass a very difficult exam, thus passing the subject for the year, but he passed quite high. I think Saint Jude took me seriously and I am so very grateful." Jude can respond this way even to unspoken or casually mentioned needs because he is so deeply interested in his devout and so "aware," as several women told me, of what is best for them. "He is very sincere," one wrote me, "and has an awareness of how we feel when we are going through desperate situations"; in a later conversation she added that she knows St. Jude "is listening to me [and] he knows what I am going through." The saint is kind and comforting; he offers support and consolation. Women tended to think of Jude as being concerned exclusively with them, at least when they were addressing their needs to him; afterward they would happily spread the word about him and express satisfaction that thousands of other people had discovered him to their own benefit too—but not right away. "In enjoying friendship with Saint Jude," I was told, "you feel an intimate personal feeling almost like you are the only one praying to him and he will answer you personally."[28]

The love the saint has for his individual devout is "unconditional," many say, a word Clara defined like this: "Well, I don't think the saints walk around

The remodeled Shrine, in a photograph from the mid-1950s.

and one day they like you and the next day they don't. That's not unconditional love. [Jude] doesn't judge me by my outbursts, whatever the case may be. You have unconditional love for your children, your husband, your loved ones. You may have a big argument with them one day and tell them that they're a pain in the rear end, or something, but that doesn't mean I don't love them anymore. I don't like their actions, but I love them as a person. That's what I mean by that." Jude not only knows them, Clara and other devout believed; he accepted and loved them for themselves, faults, "outbursts," and all. They need never worry about *this* bond. The devout were not embarrassed by what they said or did with Jude watching, by what they asked him, or by the intensity of their needs for him, because he loved them without qualification.

This saint, imagined in this way, has been an inexhaustible and unfailingly generous source of good things for his American devout, giving more than they had asked him for, sharing their happiness and joys, and attending to their sorrows and needs.[29]

"AN ONGOING RELATIONSHIP"

The devout believe that once he has helped them in their most awful times, the saint becomes "a very dear friend to whom I [can] run with all my troubles," "a good friend that's at my elbow," "a living friend," someone with whom they were in an "ongoing relationship."[30] Jude came in a moment of crisis and stayed; the movement here was from a contingent, even contractual, association predicated on extreme need to a more lasting, less desperate bond, and very many women have remained faithful to this relationship for decades. Crisis lent a special feeling to the tie: like friendships made with other sick people and their families in hospitals or with the nurses caring for one's children, friendship with Jude had a particular intimacy and intensity for having been forged in terror. But the connection lasted long after the danger was past.

Several years ago Judy had a double mastectomy, and in the weeks after the operation she used to sit in the warm morning sun on the enclosed back porch of her house with St. Jude for company. "He's back there," she told me, referring to a statue of the saint she kept beside her in the room, and "it's quiet and warm." She appreciated the saint's gentle, steadfast companionship during her convalescence. The devout have a vivid sense of Jude facing difficult times with them, standing with them (literally, although invisibly) in hospitals, at job interviews, as they rushed off to work in the mornings, or in nursing homes, some of the locales of Jude's "loving presence." "I just knew [St. Jude] was going to be there with me," a woman said of her trips to the hospital for chemotherapy, "that he was going to help me."[31] Jude puts their minds at rest, and later, as the years pass, he helps them with unhappy memories and the complex consequences of old circumstances and decisions.

As befits the bond between friends, the devout insist that Jude is not a guest in their homes; he lives with them and is treated like a member of the family. I asked Clara, who is a businesswoman, whether she removed the very large statue of Jude she normally keeps in her dining room, the most public spot in her home, when professional associates or prospective clients come by to see her. "No! I wouldn't move him!" she said. "That's where he belongs in my household. They're guests, he isn't. There's a difference. They are guests in my home, and he isn't. He belongs there, he's part of the family. They aren't."[32] The two most common places for keeping images of Jude, according to the devout's stories, have been, on the one hand, family rooms and bedrooms—the small, at times close, spaces where the difficulties of domestic life were most intimately and claustrally encountered—and, on the other, in women's purses and desk drawers at work. The devout have worn medals of the saint on charm bracelets, affixed there beside tokens of family events, or pinned to their dresses and undergarments. They set the saint up on their dashboards, and on bedside tables in sickrooms at home and in hospitals; they planted his statue on their lawns. So Jude participates in family gatherings, looks on at backyard barbecues, and watches over the daily round of household comings and goings. Neighbors greet him in the hall. Pat told me she keeps one image of Jude in her dining room "because it is an obvious place where all who enter will see it" and others "under my pillow . . . by my chair where I work at home (read, watch television) . . . in my car . . . on my desk at work . . . in my purse." Her statue of St. Jude, Clara said, is "the oldest thing I have" and the most cherished.

By touching his statue, whispering to it and kissing it, keeping it within or bringing it into the nooks and crannies of their everyday lives, the devout physically engaged Jude, literally stayed in touch with him. Many women told me that they reserved their favorite images of the saint for their bedrooms; some said that they took statues or holy cards of Jude into bed with them at night so they could touch him while they talked to him.[33] "I usually talk to him in the quiet of the evening," one woman explained, "laying awake at night before falling asleep."[34] Kathy told me, "I always do my praying in my bedroom [where her statue of Jude is] so we're in the same room together." "I carry his prayer card with me always," a woman wrote from Detroit in 1968, "and turn to him frequently." They "hold on tight" to Jude, in another woman's words, as they describe their needs to him.[35]

Critics of devotionalism within the church, reflecting certain theological and (more recently) psychological and sociological assumptions, have interpreted the cult of the saints primarily as an expression of magical thinking to which men and especially women resort when other ways of acting and understanding have been frustrated.[36] I will return to this critique in the last chapter, but here it needs to be said that the intimacy of the bond with Jude belies such a simple and narrowly instrumental understanding of the devout's practices. Women certainly asked Jude for help with vexing problems ranging from real tragedies to minor annoyances, and they did manipulate particular cultic objects like holy oil in order to get impossible things accomplished, just as the practitioners of magic are said to do. But their requests and actions always came out of and referred back to the "ongoing relationship" they were establishing with the saint and drew on this deeper source of devotion and commitment; the relationship established both the possibilities and the limits of what could be achieved through the practices. So, too, for the material objects of the cult: there was no inherent power in the Shrine's cards and liquids, medals and candles, nor was their efficacy bestowed solely by official consecration. Rather, their agency was relational: they were tokens of a connection, reminders of a beloved friend whose presence was experienced in them. This is what governed how women used and interacted with these objects, and this is why things could be done with them: because the friend so present was Jesus' cousin and the powerful saint of hopeless causes and matters despaired of. Just as Jude was animated by women's needs, desires, fantasies, and love, so were these markers of his presence.

As she finished telling me about her long association with Jude, one of my sources addressed herself past me directly to the saint, writing: "Dear Saint Jude, I love you, I've known you and asked for your help and intercession for over 40 yrs. Be with me always."[37] The structure of this woman's prayer is characteristic of the way the devout approached their friend, and reveals the quality and complex motivations of their petitions. Intimacy with Jude is cited twice—"I love you," "I've known you"—before any mention is made of favors, which appear third and are syntactically and emotionally joined with and subordinated to the reference to friendship. We ask our friends for help when we need them, many of the devout reminded me, and Jude is no different; if this is manipulative magic, then it is the manipulative magic of human relationships.

A wider range of feelings can be expressed to a companion this intimate than to other sacred figures—or even to many human ones. Women have not only told Jude that they loved him and appreciated what he did for them; they have also raged against him, cursed him for betraying them, and turned away from him when they felt he was dishonoring their bond. They could do these things because they were so close to him and could trust his love for them so completely. I asked Clara, who had just been talking about the unconditional nature of Jude's love for her, how she dared to get mad at the saint. "Because he's my friend. You can get mad at a friend. Everything isn't hunky-dory in friendships anywhere. You know, husbands, wives, children . . . there's anger involved in all friendships. I was angry at the last novena [and] . . . I told this priest this. I said, 'I'm angry.' And he said, 'Look, remember one thing: you need him, he doesn't need you.' And when he said that, I got madder." Clara's pastor did not understand the quality of mutuality that characterized her relationship with Jude. Isabel told me that when she was angry at Jude she threw his statue in the back seat of her car and forced him to ride around town like that, ignominiously lying on his side, until she was satisfied he had gotten the message of her displeasure.

But such familiarity has its limits, even with the amiable Jude. The devout never forget that he is a figure of power, and they always approach him with a special kind of devotional tact or courtesy that bespeaks an underlying reticence, or even caution. "Today I received a letter from you thanking me for my kindness during your last Novena," a client wrote the Shrine in 1951, but "it is I who should be thanking you for giving me the opportunity to make this Novena to Saint Jude." Popular piety has its canons of etiquette, too. The devout keep track of the number of requests they have made to Jude in any period and worry that they are asking too much of him sometimes, "abusing his generosity" or bothering him for petty favors.[38] They forever remind themselves to stay in touch with Jude when things are going well, too. They say that they were humbled by the gifts their patron secured for them and pray to be worthy of his assistance and attention. The devout are also careful to tell Jude how much they value and love him because they believe his feelings would be hurt if they did not.

The warm and intimate tie between heaven and earth shaped in the cult of lost causes, furthermore, entails moral responsibilities; entering upon the path of reversal is to accept an ethic of reciprocity. One client's feeling that "I can never do enough for that wonderful Saint" is shared by all of the devout.[39] "I have received so much help from [St. Jude]," another client wrote from Brooklyn in 1951, "that I feel I am obliged to do what I can to make him known more and more." "I owe him quite a bit in thanksgiving prayers," a woman worriedly noted in a letter to the Shrine, "which I shall try to give him in the future." The devout clearly understand that they are in Jude's debt and must do something for him in return for his interventions. The cult of saints posited an ethical cosmology in which human beings and sacred figures were bound to each other by ties of mutual responsibility, involvement, and entailment. It was in this spirit that women made donations to the Shrine. "I don't buy my requests," one woman scolded me (although I had not suggested that she did), "but I always offer a donation . . . in thanksgiving."[40] The metaphor of the slot-machine used by critics of devotionalism missed this point, because it overlooked the intimate and morally implicating bonds of friendship between saints and clients.

The devout have also acknowledged that they had to reciprocate the saint's faithfulness by displaying loyalty and generosity to other people in distress of the extreme sort that they had known. The moral ties forged with sacred figures yield moral responsibilities among humans; in this regard, the Shrine's efforts to render the devotion morally conscientious during the reformulations of the 1960s were otiose and a little condescending. The devout always believed that they had at the very least a responsibility to tell others about Jude after he had helped them so that others could also benefit from the saint's kindness. This commitment actually had the status of a vow in the cult of lost causes.[41]

But Jude is not exempt from this ethic of reciprocity and responsibility, either, as his rides on the back seat of Isabel's car indicate. The tie established in a hopeless time between heaven and earth, Jude and a devout, makes demands —and sets constraints—on both parties.

THE VULNERABLE BUT DANGEROUS SAINT

The devout have always known that Jude needed them as much as they needed him; this was one of the initial attractions of the new cult in the early 1930s and has remained an important feature of it since. Without his clients, as the Shrine has repeatedly cautioned in its promotions over the years, Jude would slip back into obscurity. As Clara put it, "I want [St. Jude] to think, 'I do need her to talk about me and carry my name to other people to be devoted.' You like to think that you're doing something for him, too." This was one of the reasons why Jude was a good saint to pray to: he could be bartered with, promised something he really *needed* in return for his own favors. It was also what made Jude so accessible—he was vulnerable, too. So when Jude's devout prayed to him for a favor they always promised that if he helped them, they would tell others about him so that he would never be the unknown saint again. This was the official prayer of the cult. The devout have always written in to say how happy they were to be participating in the work of rescuing and restoring Jude.

The subtext of this prayer, however, only just unspoken, is the threat that if Jude does not behave reasonably and do what is expected of him, his sad predicament awaits him again. Jude is vulnerable in two ways: he has to rely on the devout to keep his name alive and he has to keep proving himself by acting efficaciously so that his clients have something to talk about with other potential bearers of his fame. "I pray to Saint Jude," one of my sources explained to me, "because I think he desires to be known [and] then people might get their prayers answered." The devout assume that Jude has earned his title and esteem as helper in causes despaired of and expect him to keep working hard in order to retain it. Jude wants to be put to the test, one of my sources proposed, because he is eager to show the world how powerful he is.[42] He has a reputation to defend, and women have cajoled him with a special kind of barbed flattery, invoking and thus ensnaring him in his own titles.

So Jude's peculiar vulnerability has made it possible for his clients at least to attempt to coerce him into giving them what they wanted, and they evolved several strategies to that end. The most common is the threatening promise: the devout tell Jude that they will do something good and generous for him or the Claretians *if* he accedes to their wishes. But if he disappoints them, they caution obliquely, they will do nothing. The devout have also sometimes increased the terms of their initial promises at the first sign of a change in their circumstances, just as Jude has begun to work for them, as a way of raising the ante for the saint and encouraging him to finish the job. A third ploy is to append to their thanksgiving donation for a favor received an additional request as a way of getting a double grace for the price of one. At other times they remind the saint of his faithfulness in the past to shame him into responding again in the same way in the present, or they recall earlier donations they made to the Shrine as if to suggest that Jude and Chicago were in their debt. If these relatively subtler gambits fail, then the devout openly barter with Jude: you give me this and I will give you that, the familiar pact of Catholic piety. And because people turn to Jude in very bad moments, when they are willing to do just about anything to get help, they have often resorted to all of these strategies at once. The following letter, sent to the Shrine in 1953, is a catalogue of the arsenal of ploys Jude's devout have wielded in their dealings with him over the years:

> My father has been a habitual drinker for years and has shown no inclination to change his ways. I prayed to Saint Jude that he would change and promised to acknowledge publicly his help if my father stopped drinking. At first my prayers seemed to have no effect whatsoever, but I pleaded and prayed to Saint Jude as did the rest of my family reminding him that he was the patron of hopeless cases and therefore he could not turn down my request. Suddenly my father did change almost overnight and I thanked Saint Jude for his interces- sion in our behalf. . . . For this and many other truly difficult requests which Saint Jude has helped me obtain, and to whom I shall entrust all future re- quests, I wish sincerely to thank Saint Jude.[43]

They are all here: the promise, the threat, and the expression of gratitude that hints at more petitions in the future and establishes an expectation of fulfillment.

But the devout have never been completely and securely confident with these gambits, and the very array of strategies deployed is evidence of a real apprehension that the saint would either not respond to their prayers or not respond in the way they hoped. However vulnerable he may have been, after all, Jude is a saint, indeed the most powerful of them all (and ominously associated with Judas), and for all of their strategizing and manipulation the devout clearly are not only uneasy with this power but also fearful of bringing it into their lives. They worry that a successful outcome of their prayers might represent disaster for someone else. They fear that if they do not phrase their requests properly and precisely, or if they do not really want what exactly what they ask for, they might be unpleasantly, even tragically, surprised by what they get. "I would never dream of asking [St. Jude's] help if I were not absolutely sure I wanted the favor to be granted," a young woman admitted to the Shrine, "because once turned over to him, my 'despaired of' case seems to right itself inevitably." Jude is ultimately free to act or not as he thinks best, and because he can discern what is good for his clients beyond their own most immediate sense of what they themselves want or think they need, they realize that they do not completely know what to expect once they have called on Jude. His inter- ventions might be shocking, challenging, even painful, hard to take. Inversions might be dangerous.[44]

This dread of the unpredictability and danger of Jude's enormous powers has been a dark, persistent undercurrent in the experience of the devotion since its inception. Its expression has taken many forms. Chain letter prayers have regularly circulated among Jude's devout with the usual threats of dire consequences if the circle is broken. We have seen that there was fear at the Shrine that some clients were using the material objects of the cult, especially its blessed liquids, in rituals intended to exercise secret, coercive influence on others. The devout have also sometimes expressed the belief that their afflictions in the present were the result of not having adequately thanked Jude for something he had done in the past. "He's not listening" to me, one of my sources said of Jude, "because I didn't keep my promise" to take her husband back into the church; "he's forgotten me," and so her husband had slipped into alcoholism.[45] The most common expression of this terror has been the belief that for every good thing Jude does for a client he takes something of equal value away as a sort of inversionary payment in kind. A child's life saved could mean that his or her parents would lose their home; a sickness healed might entail a job lost. The Shrine clergy continually reassured the devout that this was not the case, but the belief persisted.[46]

These various fears and the steps taken to ward off their consequences are not incidental to the experience of the devotion, nor are they aberrations and perversions on its margins. They developed directly out of its central beliefs and values and from the nature of the devout's relationship with this particular intercessory figure; they have constituted an essential component of the structure and experience of the cult. Fear of Jude represents an acknowledgment of the dangerous edge of sacred power that could never be completely controlled or sublimated (despite all the efforts to do so) precisely because it was sacred and so beyond the conventions and expectations of human moral behavior. Fear also points to a peculiar instability at the heart of this cult of inversions: to enter the world of the devotion is to enter upon the path of reversal, as we have seen, and the devout are clearly afraid that once the inverting has started, once the upside-down world of hopelessness has begun turning right-side up again, the process might not stop where they want it to stop. The image of Judas returns here in a kind of hagiological pentimento, and reciprocity reveals a sinister face. The amiable Jude is also, potentially, the betrayer for whom he had been so long mistaken.

On still another, social-historical, level, this fear of the vulnerable saint is rooted in the peculiarities of American Catholic women's experience from the time of the Depression and the breakup of the enclaves onward. It emerged out of and articulated a fear of men, or, more precisely, it made apparent women's dreadful knowledge of their dependence on vulnerable and threatened—and so also threatening—men, a circumstance that we have seen was harshly disclosed in the hopeless moment. Dependence on Jude, for all his compassion and competence, could be as dangerous and risky as dependence on earthly men. The devout were making themselves vulnerable in a very familiar way, as women, when they allowed themselves to depend on the male being they had conjured up out of the depths of their needs. They had permitted their deepest desires to take shape in front of them in the figure of a man they were calling on to help them achieve goods that everyone else—their doctors, families, supervisors, teachers, and so on—were telling them were not only impossible but maybe even wrong for them.

This may have been the most dangerous of all the inversions worked by the devotion to the Patron Saint of Hopeless Causes: that through a relationship with a man, desperate need could become the source of strength, and surrender could become a move toward personal agency. If this is indeed what happened: we need to turn now to a consideration of what the immigrants' daughters actually *did* with the help of the man they had imagined into being.

5

"She Would Tell Me Her Troubles, and I Mine": Hagiography as Stories in Two Voices

"Oh, Judas," devotional writer Sister Marguerite lamented in the *Voice of St. Jude* in the summer of 1948, "if only you had gone to Mary." The Mother of God would have consoled and comforted you, made you less lonely and desperate, less confused about your master's mission. Even after you had kissed the Lord's cheek in the garden she "would have devised a plan for you" if you had called on her. There was still hope as "you were breathing out your twisted, gasping life" at the end of the rope if only you had turned "interiorly" with your "last earthly thought" to Mary, "the Refuge of sinners." By attending to you, Jesus' betrayer, Sister Marguerite allows herself to speculate (in a theologically questionable but characteristically American Catholic vein), Mary might have averted her son's terrible fate (and utterly transformed salvation history). But the "despairing end" came at last, and "it was too late, then, Judas, to go to Mary." "When the death on the Cross had freed the world," Jesus' "mangled

Petitions and thanksgivings from Jude's devout stacked high around the Shrine's reliquary, early 1950s.

Body," washed clean of "blood, spittle, and defilement" and wrapped in "sweet, clean linen," was laid in a "new-hewn tomb," while Judas's body, discovered "creaking dismally as the wind swung it to and fro," was dumped in a ditch.[1]

As Mary was making her way from Jesus' grave, leaning on the arm of her son's beloved apostle, she came upon another woman crouched down sobbing in the middle of the road. Mary bent to embrace the distraught figure, but St. John tugged her sleeve. "How could any sorrow be like to your sorrow?" he complained. "How can you spare time and energy now from your own grief?" The Blessed Mother turned to him reproachfully. "Oh, my son," she said, "[this is] the mother of Judas."

In this story elaborated out of the association of Jude and Judas in the cult of lost causes (and known only to its devout: Sister Marguerite is improvising a narrative within the devotion here, not retelling an ancient legend), Good Friday ends with two women embracing each other at the foot of Calvary as a man in the background petulantly protests the display of female loyalty and mutual concern. The consolation Mary could offer Judas's unnamed mother would have been especially heartfelt, as Sister Marguerite tells the tale, because it came from shared experience: whatever else had happened on Good Friday, two women lost their sons that day—just as whatever the patriots claimed, war meant loneliness, struggle, and the death of brothers, husbands, sons; and whatever economists taught about markets and cycles, depression meant domestic conflict and devastating feelings of loss, vulnerability, and disappointment. It was to this experience of history that Sister Marguerite was speaking.

If knowledge of the place of Mary's love in salvation history is Catholic gnosis, hidden within this was another secret, known to the women who participated in devotional culture: in times of trouble, women helped other women. In this remarkable image of Mary bending to Judas's mother, Sister Marguerite was disclosing the fundamental bond of the cult of lost causes and hopeless cases.

NARRATIVES OF PETITION, NARRATIVES OF GRACE

The most obvious characteristic of devotion to St. Jude has been the impulse of this saint's devout to narrative: the proliferation of "Thank You, St. Jude" notices in the classified sections of local newspapers around the country is only the most public and widely known expression of the cult's dedication to publication. This devotion more than others encouraged narrative activity because of the way it was promoted by the clergy and imagined by the devout, and there has always been a voluble quality to talk about St. Jude, so insistent that it would tolerate no obstacle to its unfolding. The cult of lost causes and things despaired of can be thought of as a national chain of interlocking stories of hopelessness and hope, encouraged by the Shrine for pastoral and financial reasons, anxiously joined by new clients in desperate times, and faithfully upheld by the saint's longtime devout.[2]

Talking to and about St. Jude has taken many forms, intimate and public, colloquial and formal, but two occasions of storytelling in particular within the cult were distinctly stressed by both the Shrine clergy and devout. The cycle of storytelling began when a woman in need admitted to a friend or relative (and to herself) that a bad situation had become truly awful. (Sometimes this acknowledgment came only *after* she encountered Jude, as if his title authorized her to designate her own experience as "hopeless.") Then this woman, encouraged by the person speaking to her about Jude or by the Shrine's literature, addressed herself directly to the saint, describing her circumstances and asking for help. This was the first occasion for articulation within the devotion. I will call these prayers *narratives of petition*. They were stark, simple statements of what was happening to the woman speaking or writing—my husband is unfaithful, my son is an alcoholic, my child has cancer, I am lonely and afraid—in the woman's own words or on the petition forms provided by the Shrine. The unadorned facticity of these expressions of pain is what gives the letters pages of the Shrine's periodical their cumulative power. Some women wrote their prayers on scraps of paper and tucked them around statues of Jude in their local parishes, improvising private rituals of communication. To speak so straightforwardly was already an achievement in most cases: the saint's new clients had to arrange the inchoate and perhaps never fully acknowledged circumstances of their hopelessness into words that could be communicated to others, on earth and in heaven, sometimes in the face of resistance, anger, or denial (their own as well as others'). Because Jude was the Patron Saint of Hopeless Cases—and because his power could be more clearly seen if the depth of need were adequately exposed—the devout were encouraged to be explicit about their situation.

The second occasion for articulation within the devotion came after Jude had acted, when the saint's clients assumed responsibility for the promises they had so desperately made to advertise his name far and wide. The devout responded eagerly to this obligation; as one woman told me, "I could write forever about Saint Jude."[3] In their letters to Chicago they said that they were "anxious" to make their stories known, that they could hardly wait to tell everyone what Jude had done for them. Often they noted that they were sitting down to write on the very day Jude acted for them; those who waited apologized for the delay. The devout often pointed out that they were writing in spite of severe physical limitations, like impaired eyesight or almost paralyzing arthritis, as if to emphasize that nothing could stop them from putting down their stories. Women whose accounts were not published in the *Voice of St. Jude* (an obstacle to disclosure over which they had no control) were deeply disappointed; many wrote back to the Shrine angrily demanding publication. The clergy in Chicago sometimes seemed overwhelmed by what they had (perhaps inadvertently) unleashed. They tried to convince the saint's clients that the "writing of a letter and our receipt of it is sufficient to fulfill your promise of publication" or even that an intention made in good faith to tell the story of Jude's actions was enough. Occasionally they went beyond these gentle admonitions. An uncharacteristically sharp notice began to appear on the letters page of the *Voice of St. Jude* in June 1943, scolding correspondents, "if your letter of thanksgiving has not appeared here, do not waste time wondering why."[4]

I will call these later expressions of what Jude had done *narratives of grace*, a category that includes any account a woman gave of his interventions in her experience: the letters sent to the Shrine but also the stories told to friends and kin, to strangers in hospitals and churches, to needy colleagues at work, to anyone the saint's devout thought might benefit from hearing about Jude, often decades after his initial appearance in their lives. All talk about Jude is purposeful in this way, meant to further his renown and fulfill promises. Almost all of the women who came to tell me about the saint, braving the harsh predawn cold, snow, and freezing rain of Midwestern winters to meet me before work and usually staying well past the hour they had originally mentioned they would have to leave, said that they were doing so because they loved the saint, were grateful for the help he had given them, and wanted others in desperate straits to learn about him. They transformed our conversations into narratives of grace too.

Although this enthusiasm to publish narratives of grace reflected the thankful, exhilarated relief of desperate people who wanted to do something good for Jude and for other needy people in turn, the darker, more threatening, side of the devotion made its presence felt here as well. Some correspondents acknowledged that their not writing immediately after Jude's intervention had become a source of guilt and fear to them. They were afraid of retribution. Silence was a betrayal of the saint; angered, he might turn against them. The desire to proclaim what Jude had done sometimes took on a compulsive quality. "I feel ten pounds lighter," a woman confessed after finally composing her story, "for a debt that has been paid better later than never."[5] Some combination of emotions—fear of retribution, dizzying relief, an acknowledgment of reciprocal responsibility, desperate hope, sheer exuberance, and the impulse to protect the saint against further obscurity—all together drove Jude's devout to tell their stories.

However strong the impulse to narrative, women did not always find either idiom—of grace or petition—easy to use for themselves. The devout sometimes admitted to being reluctant to tell their stories publicly, inhibited by embarrassment or fear of ridicule. It was not a simple matter, moreover, to express what one was hoping for in a desperate time (as anyone who has tried will know). In making narratives of petition women had to contend with ambivalence, fear, perhaps an unwillingness to accept responsibility for their own hopes; they had to confront the contradictory desires of others and even their own reluctance openly to admit (to themselves as much as to others) what they wanted. Some anticipated the hostility of family members who did not share devotion to Jude and who, lacking both the impulse to disclosure and its sanction within the cult, may have preferred that their mothers, wives, or sisters keep quiet about the family's bad times. A fellow worker, especially one who was not Catholic, might find a woman's bond with this figure odd or be offended by the suggestion that Jude could help him or her, too, regardless of religious affiliation. By the mid-1960s, furthermore, as devotionalism came into disrepute, Jude's clients could no longer be sure that the Catholics they were speaking to, their neighbors in the pew or even (perhaps especially) their parish priests or the sisters in school, would have any patience for tales of Jude's wonderful doings. The reticence or shyness occasionally alluded to in the letters should serve to remind us that talking to and about this saint in particular, whose specialty was desperation, entailed risks of various sorts. Still, women told their stories.

Devotional culture accused women precisely of talking too much, as we have seen, of having voices too insistent and powerful; they were enjoined to silence as discipline and calling. It was more than rhetorical convention when Jude's devout began their narratives to the Shrine with apologies for not being "good with words": the immigrants' daughters were not "good with words"— or felt themselves compelled to disavow their voices like this—because they had been warned, by the very devotional culture in which they were encountering Jude, not to say what was on their minds. The words they needed most—those to speak and complain about their pain, about things at home, about their fears and new ambitions, the problems and possibilities of their everyday lives—were precisely the ones denied them by both their cultures, American and Catholic.

But it was not just that others would not listen to them or were explicitly denying them speech. One of the most disturbing discoveries women made in hopeless moments was of the inadequacy of their own linguistic resources for conceptualizing and expressing their distress, a consequence at least in part of the ideological roots of despair. Hopelessness, as we have seen, erupted at the site where the social experience of the immigrants' daughters had fissured, where they most intimately experienced the contradictions between the values, orientations, and expectations of the enclaves (which they shared), and their own wishes and hopes on the new social landscape; between the world as it was said to be and as they knew it. These ruptures were largely hidden, made up of unacknowledged or suppressed inconsistencies in the way reality itself was constructed and engaged. Even if the social historical causes of their distress were not clear to them, women certainly experienced the emotional cost of these submerged conflicts: the anger, panic, and recrimination of the people around them and their own frustration, confusion, disappointment, and guilt. The ruptures were evident as well in the contradictory demands and impossible expectations made of women. But precisely because the ideological and social historical fissures that women found themselves in were hidden, they were initially unable to speak about what was happening to them, incapable of naming their distress or their hopes. Instead, they talked about the darkness, loneliness, and obscurity of their circumstances. Hopelessness meant entry into a space of denial, repression, confusion, and inarticulateness; women were in danger of losing their voices in the undertow of experience.

But here they were, talking constantly to and about Jude in the various media of the devotion, talking, indeed, about just the things that they were supposed to keep to themselves and that they had once found it difficult to express.

The Shrine's myth of origins encouraged and sanctioned women's speaking within the devotion: St. Jude *needed* the prayers of desperate people and the stories they told after he had proved himself to them. This was one of the implications of the name of the Shrine's periodical: the voice of St. Jude was the voice of the women describing what he had done. Jude "spoke" on the letters pages in women's narratives of petition and grace.[6] This was the first doubling of voice to occur in and through the medium of the devotion: two voices— women's and the saint's—were inextricably intertwined in the practices of the cult. Hagiography, traditionally defined as stories *about* the saints, becomes here stories about the saint but also about the circumstances the women telling the stories had found themselves in when they called on him. Hagiography as narrative practice first delineates the troubles on earth before it recounts the interventions of heaven. By means of a kind of hagiographical ventriloquism, women had found their own voices while restoring Jude's.

"A STRANGER SAW ME CRYING": WOMEN'S NETWORK OF STORIES ABOUT JUDE

One of the features that marked women's initial encounters with Jude as extraordinary in their own retrospective understanding of them was the sudden and propitious appearance of another woman just when she (and Jude, who comes through her) was needed the most. The woman whose son was refusing to settle peacefully into kindergarten, for example, making it impossible for her to go off to work with an easy mind, had just about given up when, outside the boy's classroom "a stranger saw me crying" and "told me to pray to Saint Jude for help."[7] The pregnant woman who found herself trapped (as she tells her story) in the care of unsympathetic physicians was visited early on the first (and only) morning of her hospital stay by a female social worker who returned later "after she finished her work and brought me a Saint Jude prayer card and told me to pray to Saint Jude."[8] Again and again women documented in their letters the timely interventions of other women—"my husband's mother gave me the prayer to Saint Jude," "my sister-in-law told me that help may be had by praying to Saint Jude," "my sister-in-law recommended Saint Jude"—into their terrible experiences.[9]

Just as Mary and Judas's mother had shared a common grief on Calvary, the women who spoke about Jude to distressed strangers, friends, or kin were often themselves in equally painful, sometimes identical circumstances, or had just come through them. A woman explained to me that she gave prayer cards "to other family members that have been so depressed, that are in the very same situation that I've been in." Another said she first heard about St. Jude just after being diagnosed with cancer from "a friend [who] has had cancer, too."[10] One of the Shrine's correspondents described this encounter in a hospital corridor:

> Five months ago my baby girl was stricken with one of the most deadly types of meningitis. The doctor could give us no hope for her recovery and in the event

that she did recover there was the very real possibility that she would be left with some horrible after effect of this dreadful disease. I could never find words to tell you of the agony I went through as I stood outside the door of that hospital room that awful day. A young woman whose name I never learned, but whose face I shall never forget, came up to me and slipped a Saint Jude prayer card into my hand. This girl too was waiting to learn whether her baby would live or die.[11]

The correspondent's story has a happy ending—her child recovered (we do not learn the fate of the stranger's baby)—and she is writing to say that she is sending the prayer card given her "that awful day" to another woman now whom she does not know personally but "whose little daughter is dying with leukemia."

Jude brought women together. In times of war and economic trouble, sickness and domestic crisis, female friends and family members gathered around the figure of the saint, at the Shrine if they lived in Chicago, more often in kitchens or parish churches elsewhere. Women prayed *for* each other on these occasions or made their own requests to the saint alongside other women making petitions like theirs. A woman writing from Lafayette, Indiana, in 1952, reported that when her husband was "desperately in need of work" her "sister-in-law suggested we make a Novena to Saint Jude, the helper of desperate people," so "we did—taking our babies to Church each morning." She closed, "We knew Saint Jude had heard our prayer." The use of the plural pronouns throughout is important: one woman's experience of distress is opened out to be shared by others. Jude belonged to the daytime world of women's friendships; as a seventy-six-year-old woman explained to me, "I grew up with young ladies who like to pray to the saints as much as I did."[12]

Women used these devotional conversations to encourage one another, to offer support, consolation, and advice; talking about Jude gave them a way to share confidences, to trust each other in bad times, to uncover hidden or only partly acknowledged feelings. They could divulge intimate and embarrassing matters in the idioms of this devotion that they might otherwise have felt constrained to keep secret: mental illness, the humiliating side effects of certain medical procedures, male betrayal and failure, and the fear of childbirth. "I have a friend who was terrified because the doctor discovered a lump on her breast," one woman told me, "and she came to me because I just had my right breast removed and I gave her the prayer book and told her she must have faith in Saint Jude and she will come thru." Another woman described her feelings when her hair started falling out as a result of an unspecified medical intervention. "I was desperate," she wrote. "But I was lunching one day with a friend and she said her hair came out too but the doctor told her to get a bottle of A-Vitamin tablets at the pharmacy and her hair came in beautifully again. I tried it and it worked. That's the way St. Jude gets around."[13]

Many social factors militated against this kind of conversation among the immigrants' daughters. The stringent sense of family honor among southern and eastern European Catholics demanded that domestic problems should be discussed only with one's own. The shame that generally attends open expression of certain matters, like addiction to drugs or alcohol, marital infidelity, and financial difficulty—all regular topics in stories about St. Jude—also inhibited talk. In his sensitive study of the mores of Polish American Catholics, historian Paul Wrobel observes that women in the neighborhood he studied wanted and needed conversation with other women but were afraid of it, too. They accounted for this ambivalence by telling Wrobel that talking with women friends interfered with their housework, but it is clear that they were intimidated by the risk of broken confidences and of taking friends too deeply into embarrassing circumstances. All this worked against women's friendships, especially in the unfamiliar world outside the old neighborhoods.[14]

But Jude allowed women the safety of sharing confidences within the secure boundaries of genre. In talking about Jude women were disclosing their most intimate experiences, but they were also telling tales of what a saint had done for them, a well-established Catholic idiom. Just as Jude's voice was enclosed in theirs, so was theirs in his, and if they felt shy or uncomfortable about what they were saying—about their admissions of domestic discord or drug-addicted children—they could take refuge in the ostensible reason for their disclosures, to spread the word about St. Jude. They could even say they were talking not by choice, but in fulfillment of the devotional promise. The comforts of genre may not always have been necessary, but they were always available. That such conversations were taking place around a holy figure, moreover, lent them a special kind of sacred privacy, like admissions made in the confessional, and women may have been more able to trust their friends in this context. It could be dangerous as well as unseemly, after all, to gossip about such matters, and to tell malicious tales about a figure like Jude.

Women were deeply attached to the tokens they had obtained of Jude's bond with them in bad times. These emblems embodied complex memories and associations and evoked personal histories of despair, hope, and recovery; to give someone a prayer card just like the one you had used in your bad time, or actually to loan an especially disturbed friend your own beloved image of Jude, was to make a very intimate gift that linked one's own experiences to a friend's. One devout physically enacted this joining of stories by painstakingly copying out the Shrine prayer for her (or his) neighbors because the original was so faded from use.[15] "Two weeks ago," a woman reported to the Shrine in 1953, "a friend who knew I was worried about the spiritual welfare of my 15-year-old son loaned me her prayer to Saint Jude."[16] The devotion's material objects, which were souvenirs of Jude's love and enactments of his presence as well as artifacts of individual women's own histories, became in turn expressions and enactments of mutual support, compassion, and solidarity among female relatives and friends.

To give a desperate friend an image of Jude then was to offer a relationship (with the saint) within another relationship (with the woman making the gift and telling her own story). The face and eyes of the saint, so central to women's memories of Jude's actions in their hopeless moments, were superimposed upon the face and eyes of the caring girlfriend. Prayer cards of Jude can perhaps best be thought of as holograms—turned one way, the saint's face appears; tilted back, the face of the friend who gave you the image and brought the saint's healing power into your life.

Devotion to St. Jude created a network of women caring for other women in this way. A group of women in Indiana traveled to Chicago every week to pray at the Shrine with a friend who was starting chemotherapy.[17] Women of other religious traditions were included in the network, the impulse to compassion surmounting denominational borders. The devout also understood the network to include all the women who prayed to St. Jude around the country, united through shared affiliation with the Shrine.[18] Finally, the network extended beyond the grave as well to embrace deceased relatives and friends.

The devout acknowledged this network when the time came to give thanks for graces received: they were as grateful to the women who had brought Jude to them as they were to the saint himself. As one woman reported to the Shrine, "I gave a St. Jude Prayer Card to a friend who is not Catholic, and she received a favor she wanted very much. She is so grateful to St. Jude, and she couldn't thank me enough for giving her the Prayer Card." The Shrine itself recognized (and endorsed) such expressions of gratitude among devout in January, 1967, with a notice in St. Jude's Journal that read (in part): "Mrs. Sally Lee of Philadelphia suggests that we include in our intentions the person who first introduced us to devotion to St. Jude. This is an excellent recommendation by Mrs. Lee, worthy of our prayerful consideration." A new petitioner often understood Jude's intervention to have taken the form of directing another woman to her with word of the saint or to have led her to an unexpected meeting with a devout.[19]

The network of women's talk constituted by the devotion was one of the ways that the immigrants' daughters and granddaughters reconstituted the patterns of female reciprocity and mutual support they had seen among their older relatives in the enclaves. Women of different ages shared problems and strategies with each other in the devotion just as their mothers and aunts had done in the hallways and local shrines of the neighborhoods. Sometimes Jude resolved petty conflicts between neighbors that were preventing them from helping each other.[20] Women who would otherwise have been in tense, competitive relations because of the dissolving family economy—young women and their husbands' mothers and sisters, for example, quarreling over family loyalty and place—were able to find common ground through the medium of the devotion. The saint brought female relatives together at passages in their lives when they were confronting problems that alienated them from each other: during times of tension between adolescent mothers and daughters, or when young women moved away to start their own families, or later in life when mothers found themselves unexpectedly dependent upon their daughters. Older women stayed connected to their families and contributed something of value in difficult times by praying for troubled kin to St. Jude or talking with them, in the idioms of the devotion, about their problems. They also asserted their disappointments and desires in prayers to Jude at a time when their families had stopped listening to them as they once had.

The importance of these exchanges between women of narratives and the material objects connected with them to the success and national prominence of the cult of lost causes has been obscured by the predominance of men in its public promotions. Catholic periodicals regularly featured profiles of famous male athletes and entertainers who prayed to Jude, and certainly some of the devout discovered him through these accounts. But the primary fact of the social history of the cult is that Jude has been most often engaged by women in the presence and voice of other women. The saint lived and thrived in women's conversations with each other about him, and his devotion grew and spread in spirals of empathy, understanding, and communication among them, moving out from its center in Chicago along the tracks of interconnected dialogues between women about distress and hope. The national chain of conversation that constituted the devotion was linked with women. As I was told, "To be honest, I know very little about Saint Jude, [but] one of my lady friends had a few picture cards [of the saint], and we got talking."[21]

But what did these exchanges about St. Jude look like? How did one woman "suggest" to another a common prayer? What did it mean for women to introduce each other to the cult of hopeless causes?

In the spring of 1954, a woman wrote the Shrine from Lake Charles, Louisiana, to say that she had reached the end of her endurance of her husband's drinking, gambling, and (she suspected) unfaithfulness. She was desperate. Should she leave him? If she did, could she and her children survive on their own? "I talked things over with a dear friend," the woman told Chicago, "and she gave me the wonderful help I needed in the form of a Saint Jude Prayer Card." But this second woman did not simply hand her troubled friend St. Jude's image. She talked to her and confided her own experiences of hopelessness, the times when Jude had helped her. "She went into great detail," the Shrine's correspondent wrote, "explaining how much help she had received from Saint Jude's intercession and how he was always ready to help the needy."[22]

Stories about St. Jude are stories in two voices in this second sense, too: the voice of the woman in need, who is speaking her troubles aloud, and the voice of the woman responding, who listens and then tells her own story about what had brought her to Jude and what he had made possible for her. "Three years ago I started to pray to St. Jude," a woman began her story for the Shrine in 1952. "I was very despondent, for my husband was alcoholic. . . . I was working at the time and a girl friend of mine knew that he had been drinking excessively for eleven years. So she brought a prayer of St. Jude to me at work."[23] The devout never forgot these exchanges—no one I spoke to had trouble remembering who had first introduced her to Jude—and it is not difficult to understand why. It was in this moment that the terrible grip of hopelessness was loosened.

What made these devotional duets so exhilarating was the convergence in them of the devotion's two primary narrative idioms, of petition and grace. Roman Catholics have long written, spoken, and painted tales about interventions of the saints in their experience, and Jude's devout were bound by (as they found voice within) the conventions of this genre. Hagiographical tales are accounts of the miraculous; they are *always* about wondrous and startling turns of events, surprising twists, and abruptly happy endings just when everyone else, observing events from a human perspective, thought the story was over. The woman in crisis would have just heard one of these special narratives:

Jude came to her in another woman's story of hope that had begun in awful circumstances just like her own. The narrative of petition that she was invited to speak now was thus anticipated and occasioned by and enclosed within a narrative of grace. She was urged by the idioms of the devotion to tell the saint not simply what was happening to her—the difficulties of her present circumstances—but what she wanted to happen, too, her hopes and desires, as well as her fears and sorrows. The Shrine's petition forms literally offered a space for the inscription of wishes and needs.

Narratives of petition were poised thus between the acknowledgment of desperation and the vision of an alternative, between "reality" and desire. They necessarily began in an organized and detailed description of distress, but just as necessarily, within the conventions of genre, they gave way to expressions of hopefulness. This was the dynamic of devotional speaking. Like the immigrants' daughters—and like the saint to whom they were addressed—narratives of petition were characterized by in-betweenness, which made them both frightening and exciting to articulate. This enclosure of petition within grace (and the tension within narratives of grace between "reality" and "fantasy") encouraged hopeless women to reimagine and replot their experiences as the potential and likely site of the surprising and wondrous: to say a narrative of petition within the idioms of the devotion—knowing who Jude was, having just heard what he had done, having grown up with stories of the saints' miraculous powers—was already to anticipate the opportunity of crafting one's own narrative of grace. The woman from Lake Charles was encouraged by her friend not simply to narrate her troubles to Jude but to reimagine her story transformed by Jude's intervention just as hers had been once.

This is not to say that women believed that Jude was going to act immediately or give them whatever they wanted; Jude was unpredictable, after all, and not controllable. But the arrival of the saint in the voice of another woman speaking about grace subtly shifted the hopeless woman's relation to her circumstances. Once the devout began telling their stories within the devotion, the flow of events was replotted against the unexpectedly glimpsed horizon of hope that opened in the presence of the saint. Petition and grace were contemporaneous: one woman's grace became another woman's petition which anticipated grace. This powerful conjuncture was most clearly expressed in the promissory form that narratives of petition most often took. Speaking to Jude at her friend's suggestion, the woman in trouble says: this is what is happening to me, this is what I want to happen, this is what I know you can accomplish if it is God's will. The typical sequence of the devout's petitions—"if you will do . . . I will do . . ."—which we saw was a strategy for implicating Jude in the obligations of a promise, represented the eruption of the future into the sealed space of hopelessness. The narratives of hopeless women were cast now in another mood, the conditional, and another tense, the future, as they pictured for themselves different endings to the ones they had previously thought inevitable, given the bleak circumstances of the present. As one woman's narrative of grace opened the space for another's narrative of petition, so by the entry of the conditional the present was taken up into alternative possible futures. Even as women told Jude that they would be resigned to whatever he did for them, they were anticipating an end to their trouble, a future they were saying they could accept; even the saint's unpredictability worked against the stifling confinement of hopelessness. Religious narrative was here to time what religious ritual is to space: it organized the otherwise disorderly field of human experience into a coherent sequence and situated this within a broader frame of meaning opening out toward purposefulness. The hopeless moment had actually become the middle section of a larger plot rather than what it had been before, the suffocating entirety of the story.

Women sensed this subtle shift promised by the narrative practices of the devotion, and they identified it as something they wanted for themselves. "I am a constant reader of 'St. Jude's Mail,' " a client wrote the Shrine in 1950. "Reading of the many favors Saint Jude grants those who invoke his aid with confidence, I also asked him for a favor." Another woman described the effect of hearing stories about Jude like this, "Just a year ago this month, I found myself on the verge of a nervous breakdown. The love of my family and husband didn't seem to matter much and I found I was getting nowhere. During this time I picked up your magazine and read of the wonderful help people received from praying to Saint Jude." Encountering these narratives of grace and recognizing the possibility of replotting her own story this way awakened hope and courage in this woman. "From that date on," she concludes, "I started my prayers to this Saint"—started organizing her experience, in other words, in the conditional idioms of the devotion—"promising to write about it, if ever my prayers were answered."[24]

There was a nested quality to these narratives. One woman's story would be enclosed in another's, which in turn might have been told by a third as part of her account. One devout explained this process to me: "A young lady friend of mine sent me the picture of St. Jude with [the] prayer on the back. When we write to each other she would tell me her troubles and I mine." This interleaving of voices could be so thorough that it is difficult in some narratives to sort out who has prayed for whom and who is telling whose story. One of my sources reported, for example, that she first learned about Jude when a friend of hers gave her a prayer card, "and she [the correspondent's friend] said, I gave one of these to my friend [a third woman, who] was quite sick and her husband quite grumpy. She had bad backaches and her husband had started to raise cain why it was so untidy in the house and why isn't she going to work."[25] In response to a question about one woman's devotion, three women's stories emerged.

In every way, the cult of lost causes and things despaired of offered the woman entering it encouragement and sanction for speaking and assurance that her account of herself was already heard (by the friend speaking to her and by the saint who knew her needs before she articulated them) and would continue to be attended to, on heaven and earth. It gave her the authority to tell her story and then retell it in the idioms of inversion—gave her, in other words, the authority of plot, and women's response to this is best indicated by the enthusiasm with which they have wielded it. Jude's devout have always been (and still are) practiced, committed storytellers, using the full repertoire of narrative devices to recount what the saint had done for them. This is evident even in the truncated excerpts published in the *Voice of St. Jude,* but especially so when women have an opportunity to speak or write about their experiences with the saint at greater length. They obviously delighted in the play of narrative. Their stories are suspenseful, engaging, and compelling. They seem to enjoy shocking their listeners with the grimness of their circumstances just before Jude acted for them. Women telling me about Jude invariably paused after describing their hopeless situations to see whether I had been sufficiently dismayed. The equivalent of this pause in the printed accounts are phrases like "you cannot imagine how I felt at this time," which invite the reader into the story as it simultaneously alerts her to the extraordinary nature of the events about to be recounted. The reader or listener is primed by this catch in the narrative voice to be astounded by the inversion worked by Jude. When they are finished telling their stories, the devout are proud of their handiwork. "I think I wrote a pretty good letter," one woman told me, recalling a message she had sent the Shrine some years before. "I explained it's been many years that I've been devoted to St. Jude, and [told the Shrine clergy how] I've put my favors in public in the paper."[26]

Women frequently sent their narratives to the Shrine in installments, posting serial reports of Jude's response to their petitions. They kept the Shrine apprised of impending medical tests and procedures, job interviews and prospects, and of the ups-and-downs of their circumstances in general, and then jubilantly dashed off the last episodes of their crises, sure that the clergy in Chicago and the readers of the *Voice of St. Jude* were anxiously awaiting to learn the conclusion of these dramas.[27] "It will be undoubtedly a source of great gratification to you," a client wrote in June 1935, "to know that this week I hope to break down the barrier which has kept me away from confession for sixteen years." Another happily announced to the readers of the *Voice of St. Jude* that "the baby and I are well" after a difficult labor, as if she were completing a domestic saga they had all been tensely following.[28]

Clients of St. Jude marked the successive moments of their replotted experience—their first meeting with the saint, for example, a positive change in events, or an unexpected feeling of peacefulness and resignation—by lighting votive candles either at the Shrine or before a statue of Jude (if there was one) or of the Virgin in their local churches.[29] The candles were meant as gifts to the saint and part of the bargain cut with him, but they also served to give visual expression to the new mapping of the crisis made possible through Jude. The Shrine itself referred to the candles as tongues speaking people's stories to the saint before whom they flickered, and this identification of flame and narrative runs throughout the devotion. In the candles, the narrative work of the devout took visual form in space: it was as though the crisis of hopelessness was literally a landscape though which women were moving in Jude's company, stopping now and then to signal with a candle where they had been and to illuminate where they might go.

In narrative and flame, in time and space, women's inner experiences of hopelessness found expression outside of themselves. This was an important movement: the devout had found a way—what philosopher Elaine Scarry has called an "avenue of objectification"—of taking their inner experience and bringing it out of "the inarticulate pre-language of 'cries and whispers'" into the realm of shared objectification, where it could be recognized, shared, and acknowledged.[30] In narrative and candle women found ways of connecting themselves—precisely at the point of their deepest isolation and inarticulateness—with the world outside of themselves, with the Shrine, with other women, and also with themselves, countering the self-estrangement that was one of the most terrifying aspects of hopelessness.

THE CENTER OUT THERE—NARRATING AS GOING

Women reported that once they had entered the world of the devotion they no longer felt overwhelmed by circumstances; composing their stories they composed themselves. In the process of telling her story a woman in distress moved from being the victim of circumstances to the narrator of them. She realigned herself in relation to what was happening and assumed the authority of identifying cause and effect, of mapping the sequence of events, imposing and discovering for herself a pattern and order in her situation that seemed chaotic, meaningless, and threatening before she began speaking. By way of concluding this chapter, I want to study a little further this transition from raw, threatening experience to narrative.

Devotion to St. Jude was structured in practice as a series of intercessory relationships, not a single one (as it may appear from the Shrine's promotions). Most evident in the public life of the Shrine, of course, was Jude's intervention on behalf of his clients with his divine cousin. But this heavenly exchange was anticipated on earth by a woman's intervention in the difficulties of a friend or relative: women were there before Jude and served as the occasion of his presence. Christ was the ultimate source of grace, Jude the penultimate, women friends the proximate. In heaven too, moreover, a female intercessor was pivotal in the popular cosmology of the cult. Again this feature of the devotion is not obvious since it was gratitude to Jude that the Shrine was most interested in making known, but the devout's expressions of thanksgiving have commonly included both Jude and one or another female holy figure, usually the Virgin but sometimes another female saint, like Thérèse or Anne.[31] Occasionally the devout said that Jude intervened for them *with Mary,* who in turn presented the supplicant's petition to her son; at other times they saw the saint and the Virgin working together.

Women's participation in the devotion was not limited, therefore, to petition and donation, as priests who had scruples about "slot machine" religion feared. They were as central to what was accomplished through the cult as the saint himself. In their relations with each other, in the care they took to mention and thank the friends who brought Jude to them, in their generous promotion of the saint, women reenacted on the local level the bonds of reciprocity established by the cult between heaven and earth. Ethnic patterns of reciprocity are usually thought of as distinctly male forms of connection, at work, in politics, business, and the church, but the history of the devotion to St. Jude reveals that the immigrants' daughters were as schooled and skilled in this practice as their male kin. Through the exchange of stories and "Judes," lonely hopelessness gave way to an intricate pattern of obligations, debts, responsibilities, and gifts on heaven and earth.

The layering of stories characteristic of devotional narrative—one woman's story nested inside another's inside another's—allowed the devout to begin to get some perspective on their experience by seeing their lives in wider frames of reference. Because women first met Jude in other women's experiences of him, their discovery of the saint was also always the discovery that they were not alone, not in heaven, but also not on earth. Their experiences were shared, familiar to other women, and the gift of Jude from one to another was, among other things, a sign of recognition between women that whatever was happening to one was not aberrant, regardless of what anyone else may have been saying about it. The devout were not so lonely once the saint had arrived in the voice and story of another woman. Just as the failure of hope was an event between people, so was its reawakening in the cult.

The future anticipated through Jude in the hopeless moment (if . . . then), narrated to friends (in stories) and to Jude (in prayer), and given visual expression in flame, did not obliterate the unhappiness of the present or the memory of it afterward. Neither women in distress nor the friends or relatives who directed them to Jude minimized the unhappiness. Indeed, just the opposite was true: women were particularly careful to limn the coordinates of hopelessness with precision so Jude's power could be seen more clearly by others in need. Women knew that their connection with Jude would sooner or later give them (indeed require of them) a recounting of their worst experiences, and within the conventions of devotional speech they learned to be explicit about their troubles. By encouraging talk about Jude's interventions in matters despaired of, the devotion offered women a discipline of disclosure and a poesis of hopelessness.

The letters pages of the *Voice of St. Jude* and the stories shared among friends about the saint were unique narrative spaces in twentieth-century American Catholicism. Nowhere else in the culture were the difficulties and complexities of modern family life so unambiguously disclosed. While popular moralists and preachers fulminated about young Magdalenes in short dresses and fast cars, storytelling within the devotion recorded the less spectacular but more authentic troubles of Catholic families in a transitional period. It was to the saint and to their friends in talk about the saint that the immigrants' daughters defined the difficulties of their everyday lives and assessed their strength for meeting them. Perhaps most striking about these stories was the appearance in them of the figure explicitly excluded by the fantasies of the Catholic family romance: the married woman struggling in the middle of her life with real problems. There were few wild and capricious girls here, high on thrills, and few household saints silently climbing domestic calvaries. The women telling these stories to each other *complained* about their insensitive male relatives, brought them to Jude's attention as problems; they described the difficulties they were having finding work and child care and admitted their fears of pregnancy; and they publicly expressed and privately imagined an end to these woes. Women in the devotion showed themselves contending with circumstances, not submitting to them as discipline.

Looking back over their lives from the perspective of their association with St. Jude, devout in their sixties and seventies do not present themselves as having been broken to holiness by life's pain, nor do they cast a warm, nostalgic glow over the challenges and sorrows they confronted. Instead, they proudly say that thanks to St. Jude's help they were able to accomplish many things. "I have had a hard life," a woman wrote me in an autobiographical reflection typical of Jude's older devout. "My husband spent 34 years in a Mental Hospital thru an accident. I had to raise 3 small children (3 yrs. 4 mos.[,] 18 mos. [and] I was 6 months pregnant). Thru the *help of St. Jude* I was able to get a job and raise them. (One boy was killed at the age of 20 in a car accident.) They are happily married and I have 6 grandchildren. I have good health and am enjoying retirement. Thanks to St. Jude."[32] The memory of Jude's company in difficult times offered older women other autobiographical possibilities than those available to them in American Catholic popular culture.

Another woman, whom I will call Helen, the mother of two grown children living close to her in a New England town, began her account of her life by noting that she had chosen to write me "because Saint Jude has been sharing all of my burdens, giving me peace of mind and generally being with me for more than 30 years."[33] Helen first encountered the devotion in 1954 when "I was newly married, pregnant and living in my husband's family home with my mother-in-law," with whom she was not getting along. She prayed to St. Jude for "improvement," and "these prayers resulted in a very close friendship developing between myself and my mother-in-law (which lasted as long as she lived)." Helen and her husband were able to buy the older woman's house after their first child was born. "From that time on I very seldom made a decision or took any action in my life without asking St. Jude for his guidance." Helen continued: "I am now a happy, healthy woman, 62 years old. I have been married 34 years to a wonderful man who is now 69. Our life together was not perfect, but all problems were minor and handled quickly by prayer to St. Jude. I have a 33 year old son and a 29 year old daughter who were raised during the years of drugs and dissension. We were a very close family due, I am certain to continued aid from St. Jude. Particularly at times when the children were teenagers and out on their own for an evening. I would ask St. Jude to care for them while I could not—he always did!" Helen is pleased with her children's marriages, believing they were led to their spouses by St. Jude; assessing her own, she called her husband "a good provider and a hard worker with no major vices."

St. Jude also aided Helen in her professional life: "I started to work with only a high school education. Over the years I progressed from a typist in an insurance company office to a position as Town Administrator for a town with 35,000 residents. I retired in 1985 with a testimonial dinner attended by more than 500 people including many local and state officials. I could not have accomplished this had not St. Jude been with me all of the way, putting the correct words and actions into my head whenever I requested assistance." Helen kept St. Jude prayer cards in her desk at work and "said many daily prayers of request and thanks to him." "If co-workers had problems I would suggest prayer to St. Jude and most were aware of my great trust in this saint."

There was a postscript to the letter: "Before I completed this correspondence last June, my husband was diagnosed as having bladder cancer!" The future is uncertain now, although "with the constant help of St. Jude, we have had the best summer I can remember," and Helen rests in the "complete confidence that Saint Jude will care for us both."

The melodrama of the family romance has given way here to a more tempered view of married life. Helen does not ignore her troubles; elsewhere, listing the occasions she called on Jude, she mentions car accidents, cancers, and her daughter's brief estrangement from her husband. But her reason for including these troubles was to affirm that with Jude's help such times were engaged, not merely endured. Jude has served many American Catholic women of Helen's age and younger as the "articulatory pivot" of an alternative autobiographical practice through which they constituted their lives not as records of the grim discipline of endurance but as having been lived well through pain, hope, sacrifice, and satisfaction alike.[34] In the understanding of the Shrine (which was shared by the devout, too), stories like Helen's *proved* Jude's power; these narratives of grace served as evidence of his special place in heaven and secured his voice and presence on earth. Jude's reality thus established proved in turn the truth of Helen's and other women's experience: just as they anchored Jude's existence by talking about him, so by talking about him they claimed the reality of their experience. These life stories stand as counterhagiographies, the immigrants' daughters' answer to the saints-in-aprons.

The cult of lost causes appears to have offered the immigrants' daughters media of closure, ways first of controlling their experience (through narratives of petition) and then of resolving and integrating circumstances that were otherwise terrifying and disorienting into the larger flow of their lives (through narratives of grace). The latter practice in particular seems to seal the crisis, fixing it safely in the past; the lighting of a votive candle at this point marks the definitive *end* of something, the burning flame constituting an impassable barrier between the disorienting time of hopelessness and whatever peace, confidence, and resolution that the women were able to achieve.[35]

But the end of the crisis was also the beginning of a relationship. Women's exquisitely maintained loyalty to Jude over the years lent a persistent immediacy to the experiences that had brought them to him. The experience of hopelessness was not forgotten or repressed over time; rather, the ongoing vividness of the hopeless moment in the narrative practices of the cult is one of its most striking features. Every time a woman told someone else about St. Jude, or looked at the image of him she had acquired in a desperate time, or for years afterward sent in donations first promised in such a time, she had occasion to recall the circumstances of her unhappiness. "Please send me a statue of St. Jude," a woman wrote the Shrine in 1967, "so I can be reminded of what he has done for me every time I look at it."[36] By promising never to forget what Jude had done for them the devout assumed the responsibility and discipline of never forgetting the worst moments in their personal histories.

This, in turn, offered women another opportunity: as long as they kept talking or writing about what had happened to them there was always the possibility of rethinking and reinterpreting their experiences. Language has a dual nature: it is both regularizing (because individuals must submit to the constraints of syntax and grammar, for example) and opening (because of the arbitrariness of the relationship between signifier and signified and of the ever present ambiguity of connotation). All narrative, oral and written, is an invitation to interpretation; meaning is not so much contained *in* narrative practices as it is worked toward through them, in relationships between people. When women talked to each other over the years about Jude, they were engaged in a dialogue making sense of their lives. Sometimes such talk happened without much reflection, perhaps simply as duty to the cult or as a casual reference to a friend; but at other times, depending on their own circumstances, women would have occasion to think anew about their experiences. Past conclusions were undermined when women had the chance to see their own lives through the prism of someone else's. This was especially true of exchanges that took place across generations: younger women learned the history of what they were going through, uncovering links to older female relatives, while the latter were enabled to see what had happened to them from the critical perspective of alternative expectations. As Helen's accounting of herself suggests, the auto-biographical practices possible in the devotion countered the authority and fixity of other cultural construals of women's experience that they encountered in the secular and devotional press and in the stories their doctors, priests, and families were prepared to tell about them. Women were enabled not just to interpret but to successively reinterpret the meaning of their own experiences.

The central movement of the devotion was outward from the closed space of hopelessness toward self-expression, dialogue, companionship, disclosure, and hope. The anthropologist Victor Turner writes that religious pilgrimages offer the sick or harassed or frightened person a "center out there," a reference point outside the world of his or her immediate, local—usually unhappy— experience.[37] The opening up of this space-away provides the relief of distance in two senses, geographical first, but then perspectival, too: viewing his or her experience from the center out there, the person in crisis might discern pat-terns and meanings in—and ways out of—that distress, possibilities otherwise hidden by proximity and anxiety. Typically pilgrims avail themselves of the power of special places by going, but Jude's Chicago Shrine was a placeless site in the imaginations of the devout, as we have seen, a locus of power that did not compel journeying. In place of going, however, there was narrative: the primary connections between the Shrine-out-there and the dispersed devout in their everyday experience—and *through* the Shrine with each other—were the narratives of grace and petition that women spoke and wrote about the saint, to the Shrine and to each other. These functioned in their experience as journeying. As they spoke about themselves to Jude and other women, en-countered their experiences and themselves from the alternative perspective of these other eyes, and imagined other scenarios and other endings to their crises, women found a way to the understanding and therapeutics offered by standing in the center out there.

The next chapter will examine how the immigrants' daughters used the media of the devotion to heal themselves and others of various illnesses. But it was necessary to see how they were authorized and encouraged to talk within the devotion about themselves to understanding and sympathetic figures. This was the first and most fundamental transformation worked by the cult of lost causes; whatever else happened with Jude's help, this was the first healing.

6

Healings

St. Jude has been as much a part of the immigrants' daughters' experience of illness since the 1920s as doctors, laboratories, and drugs. More than half of all the narratives received by Chicago had (and still have) to do with sickness, according to the women who sort through the Shrine's correspondence, and their estimate is confirmed by the evidence of the letters pages. Many devout thought of sickness as Jude's domain; sometimes they identified him as the patron saint of whatever specific disease was afflicting them. The healing of Sarah Muldowney, one of Jude's earliest American miracles, was widely advertised in the Shrine's promotions and celebrated on the anniversaries of its founding. The clergy in Chicago used language drawn from the Catholic tradition of thaumaturgic healing sites to identify Jude's devout as "crippled . . . paralyzed . . . blind . . . sick," though women prayed as often for work, successful marriages, and prom dates as for good health. Attracted by this emphasis, pitches for hospital insurance and home remedies appeared in *Voice of St. Jude* alongside notices for healing oil, the Shrine's own home remedy. The history of popular devotions, in Chicago and elsewhere, is inevitably also the history of medicine.[1]

Jude was called on to respond to many different kinds of physical distress, a generalist in sickness as he was in other forms of trouble. Some of the suffering brought to him was (and is) apparently psychogenic, although such distress is no less real, painful, or embarrassing: exhaustion, gastric troubles of various sorts, headaches associated with domestic or work-related stress, small "lumps" that appear and disappear suddenly, skin rashes, mysterious inflammations, and so on. The devout reported in these cases that their doctors could find nothing organic wrong with them despite the persistence of their distress; sometimes their symptoms came and went so quickly that they did not have time to get medical attention. But the saint also heard somatogenic complaints, including heart ailments, eye problems, arthritis, cancers of all sorts, and neurological crises.[2]

Because it is the common destiny of all human beings sooner or later to get sick, it is possible to construct a phenomenology of the experience of sickness not necessarily tied to a specific time or place.[3] On this universally shared level, sickness is always a confrontation with the limits of the body: the sick person feels betrayed by the closest thing to her, by what she knew best, her body, which now shows itself to be the enemy of her real self and soul. The interior regions of the body become menacing places. At the same time, the sick person comes to feel absolutely identified with her sickness because the body calls attention to itself in a new and unavoidable way in distress; the sick body is at once radically other and painfully me. I am the one-who-is-sick, she thinks, her unique and distinct subjectivity eroded by pain.

What happens to the core of the self also happens to space and time. The ordinary, taken-for-granted flow of everyday life is disrupted; there is no more simple movement from what was to what is to what will be. Disease and pain cloud the horizon of the future and obliterate even the loveliest moments of the past. Now there is only sick time, the medicines at the bedside, the long gray days out of time. Space constricts, too: the sickroom, the waiting room of the doctor's office, the hospital admissions office, and the space of the body become the limits of experience. Then sickness sickens the social world; it severs a person's normal ties to other people. Love becomes anxiety. Relatives and friends must now tend the sick body in its intimate distresses. The need for relief and comfort make the boundaries of privacy and reserve difficult to maintain, and this embarrasses everyone. Some turn away from the message of the sick body or its demands. Others who cannot absent themselves become bitter and angry toward the sick person and perhaps toward life itself. They weary of complaint and responsibility and the closed smell of the sickened world. It becomes impossible to imagine any life other than sickness, which seems to fill up the spaces and times of the world after it has emptied them of everything else. To be sick, paraphrasing the philosopher Simone Weil, is to be hammered into one place.

The logic of devotionalism would seem simple here—especially here: sick people (or the women caring for them) pray to get better. What else is there to say about devotional healing?

But sickness is not always and everywhere the same experience. Particular respiratory diseases may invariably appear in the body as fevers, chilling sweats, and weight loss, making possible a science of diagnosis; how these are talked about and experienced, what range of healing practices are brought to bear on them, and how the person sweating and shivering feels about what is happening to him or her are matters of social, cultural, and scientific history. *Illness* (as opposed to *disease,* which is the biology of what is happening to the body) and its relief are experienced and expressed in culturally available idioms.[4] For the immigrants' daughters, these were drawn from two sources: the values and orientations of modern American medicine and the treatment of pain and suffering in Catholic devotional culture. How they got sick and better—and what role Jude played in the process—must be understood in relation to these two culturally and historically specific grammars.

THE SPACES AND TIMES OF SICKNESS IN MODERN AMERICA

Just as the immigrants' daughters were leaving the enclaves to begin life on their own, American medicine was itself entering a new moment in its history. By the 1920s, physicians, in alliance with educators, muckrakers, and progressive politicians, were finally successful in their long campaign to eliminate alternative and competing practitioners from healing work.[5] By setting and enforcing new national standards for medical training, hospital accreditation, and professional advancement, and by sharply restricting the flow of information about healing techniques and drugs to the lay public, these activists discredited the many nonmedical healers popular in the United States (a group that included midwives, chiropractors, chiropodists, osteopaths, and folk and faith healers) and curtailed what had once been a widespread culture of self-treatment. One healing paradigm—the biomedical—and one very well-organized and supervised caste of healers would now dominate medical care in this country. These changes were not simply imposed from on high, however. A convergence of factors—new attitudes toward marriage, family, and children that emphasized bonds of love and nurture; the challenge of the progressive and labor movements to the harsher consequences of capitalism; and improved standards of living—made people want better health and happier lives for themselves. By the late 1920s Americans of all social classes were anxiously identifying an ever expanding range of symptoms as needing medical attention; expecting more from their healers, they began to yield more authority to the men from whom they wanted so much.

A major transition in the ecology of healing accompanied these shifts. There were fewer than two hundred hospitals in the United States in 1873, according to a government survey; by 1920, the number stood at six thousand. The newer hospitals were awesome citadels of technology and science, located outside the ordinary settings of most people's everyday lives. This move to the hospital further deepened the social distance between doctor and patient and enhanced the latter's authority. As hospital care was increasingly restricted to acute cases, furthermore, "the boundary between staff and patients in hospitals, once crossed by convalescents and the less seriously ill, now became more fixed," in medical historian Paul Starr's words. A critic of modern hospitals was already complaining by 1907 that the patient had been reduced to the status of a "medical subject," a lament that would grow louder and more insistent over the next sixty years.[6]

The consolidation of medical healers' power and prestige and the relocations of care had tremendous consequences for the construction and experience of illness. Sick people and their families came to rely primarily on doctors to define the nature of their distress and its appropriate treatment, mistrusting their own judgments and inclinations in the complex, intimidating, and mysterious world of modern scientific medicine. It became almost impossible for patients to challenge doctors' judgments or to know when to "disengage" from them, in Starr's word. Exchanges between physicians and patients were radically unequal, reflecting divergent levels of education, social class, access to power, and prestige; patients were in awe of their doctors. Nurses, once independent of doctors and able to question sickroom decisions, were gathered under the institutional authority of hospitals and effectively silenced. Professional codes of conduct limited even what doctors might say about the methods and choices of their colleagues; it was only in the 1970s that physicians began to acknowledge a legal and moral responsibility to discuss alternative procedures with their patients.[7]

The awe inspired by the modern doctor had varied sources, but the most important was his powers of diagnosis: identifying disease was what physicians did best for most of this century. Tools like the stethoscope, introduced in the mid-1880s, and, later, X rays and biomedical laboratory science enabled physicians most of the time to tell patients exactly what was wrong with them. Diagnostic skill contributed to the medical mystique by creating what Starr calls an "asymmetry of information": patients could see that their doctors knew more about the insides of their own bodies than they did. This had several implications for the lived experience of sickness. First, as diagnostic technology improved, the actual speaking voice of the patient became increasingly otiose. Physicians dreamed of devices that would free them from patients' unreliable (as they saw it) descriptions of their own distress; as such tools became available the rift between doctor and patient widened. The medical consultation slowly waned in importance and patients' idiosyncratic descriptions of what they were feeling, informed by all sorts of personally meaningful (and medically useful) emotional, cultural, and moral detail and understandings, became irrelevant. Diagnostic virtuosity limited the range of acceptable discourse in medical settings by narrowing the meaning of "illness" to what registered on a meter or appeared in laboratory tests. Anything else that patients had to say about their experience—the story they wanted and needed to tell—was defined out of bounds.[8]

Second, the priority of diagnosis contributed to the geographical displacement of sickness, as patients waited in one place for the results of tests made in another to come back from a third before setting out to be taken care of by specialists in still another. Medical practice in this century was steadily severed from its local connections, a development analogous to the broader eclipse of the local that we have already seen at work shaping the National Shrine of St. Jude. The sites of discernment and healing moved from the sickroom at home to the hospital and then to the laboratories and clinics beyond; medical news, good and bad, now came from afar. By the 1930s, according to historian Edward Shorter, family doctors were already functioning as referral services.[9]

Finally, and very important for understanding Jude's place in modern medical history, diagnostic sophistication altered the temporal, as well as the spatial, experience of sickness. The future became the dominant tense of sicktime. Sick people waited anxiously for the results of tests and—once these arrived from the laboratory out there—had a clearer sense of their destinies than ever before. The questions sick people had for their physicians were oriented toward the future: When will I get better? When will the pain go away? When can I leave the hospital?[10] Prognoses became a popular obsession, the lay complement to medical diagnostic virtuosity.

Patients and their families believed their doctors could answer these questions. They also expected that the men who could so accurately tell them what was wrong with them could do something about it. But the fact of American medicine until the Second World War was that doctors could not cure what they could so skillfully identify.[11] Until the arrival of wonder drugs after the war, the hopes raised by diagnostic acumen were most often dashed. This is not to say that doctors could not bring relief to their patients, but it is an irony of this history that what comfort and help they could provide depended precisely on those features of the doctor/patient relationship that were being eclipsed by the increasingly narrow scientific orientation and institutional structures of modern medicine—conversation, trust, familiarity, touching, being present in the middle of the night, and so on.

The introduction of penicillin after the war, antibiotics in the late 1940s, and then psychoactive drugs like Miltown and Valium in the 1950s and 1960s, along with the growing sophistication of medical technology in the same period, vastly improved the capacity of medicine to cure and sealed the hegemony of the organic interpretation of sickness. Conversation and history taking were all but replaced by what Shorter calls "the impersonal collection and interpretation of laboratory data," as doctors became thoroughly disease- rather than patient-centered. Medical education overlooked the broader social and emotional contexts of sickness. The inevitable result was the gradual disempowerment of the patient and the "depersonalization and dehumanization of [health care]," in the words of a prominent physician commenting on the "death of the clinician" in these years.[12]

THE INSTALLATION OF WOMEN IN THE SICKROOM

Most of the patients constituted by and situated in the developments sketched here were women: the history of modern medicine must be read through the lens of gender because the majority of "medical subjects" were female. Women outnumbered men as clients in doctors' offices and hospitals (as they did at saints' shrines); as Shorter says, by the turn of the century, women were virtually "installed" in the doctor's office (as they had been in devotional culture).[13] This represented the culmination of a century-long process in which women's various experiences and emotions were cast into medical idioms, what one critic has called the tendency to "medicalize" the woman.[14] Modern medicine (like modern advertising) encouraged women to be preoccupied with their bodies, training them to identify a wide range of internal sensations and existential distresses, from family troubles to problems on the job, as organic complaints to be diagnosed and treated by male medical practitioners. Modern women came to be dependent on this group and on this one language—that of the body—to define their troubles, while doctors depended on the female patients constituted by their own discourse for their prosperity, power, and prestige, a symbiosis that resembled the bond between shrine clergy and their female devout.

Encouraged to medicalize their distress, whatever its etiology, modern American women were identified with sickness. The changing circumstances of their lives put the immigrants' daughters under extraordinary emotional and physical stress. The signs and consequences of this pressure, seen in devotional culture as evidence of moral decay requiring submission and repentance, were read in medical idioms as sickness needing diagnosis and treatment. Medical anthropologist Arthur Kleinman points out that the sick are often made into "an alien other, upon whose persona are projected the attributes the group regards as opposite to the ones it values."[15] Young women were already the alien other of the devotional family romance; the identification of women with sickness in the wider society gave this religious trope the sanction of the organic. Medical and religious discourses converged on women, reinforcing each other with their respective authority. It is not surprising, then, that devotional journals should be filled with medical advice, that shrines should promise bodily healing, or that correspondence with the saints should appear alongside advertisements for nostrums: in the social construction of modern women, both devotionalism and medicine relied on metaphors of disease, decay, infection, and sickness, and the girls whose living on thrills endangered Western civilization often wound up in devotional fiction just where they belonged, in the hospital.

These morally/physically sick women were encouraged to go to their clergyman/doctors to learn the truth of their experience and the remedy for it, but there was little chance that either authority would be listening to them. The more they were taught to think of their experience in medical terms and to seek assistance from medical practitioners, the less they were listened to by the men to whom they had turned and the less their accounts of their distress were trusted. Instead, women found themselves medically "diagnosed" (as they had been morally diagnosed) by men whose diagnostic vocabularies purposefully excluded most of what was important about their experience. "The logic seems to be this," cultural historian Mary Ann Doane writes: "if the woman must assume the agency of speech, of narration, let her do so within the well-regulated context of an institutionalized dialogue—psychoanalysis, the hospital, the court of law" (or devotional culture). Doane refers to this permissible narrative activity as "a very carefully constructed relation to enunciation," presided over by a male interpreter whose control of the languages of distress "dominates and controls female subjectivity."[16] Only certain matters could be spoken, and only in particular ways.

The more women moved into the medical domain as patients, finally, the more they lost their own healing authority: embedded in the history of modern medicine is a reversal of male and female agency and competence in the work of healing. Health care in the home had been under the supervision of women who either practiced healing arts themselves or could call on other women who did; male medical practitioners in this setting found themselves surrounded by women who freely commented on and challenged their work.[17] The mothers and grandmothers of young Catholic women brought indigenous curative arts to this country and treated female (and male) complaints of all sorts with practices ranging from simple home remedies to complex and secret cures that resembled and sometimes drew upon religious rituals and idioms. But the "reform" of American medicine (like the reform of Catholic ritual half a century later) had the result of eliminating such female roles. So the immigrants' daughters found themselves dependent, as they entered adolescence and early adulthood, on the singular authority of the male doctor's voice.

There is no evidence that Jude's devout openly challenged the arrangements or orientations of modern medicine. The letters pages show that they turned first to medical doctors in times of physical distress and that they shared the wider culture's high evaluation and expectation of physicians. Such respectful compliance was endorsed, furthermore—and at times harshly prescribed—by the devotional press, which took a sentimental and even pious view of physicians, whose patron saint was the evangelist Luke, by legend a doctor himself. In 1936 and 1937, the *Voice of St. Jude* published a series of articles by a Chicago physician, Frederick B. Balmer, about the way to good health. In a typically boosterish passage, Dr. Balmer announced that disease was completely under the control of modern doctors, adding that "nowadays, the average intelligent individual submits to a surgical operation, whether of a major or minor nature, without much apprehension, fear, or unnecessary delay."[18] Many of Dr. Balmer's readers, of course, would have subscribed to the periodical in the first place after a fearful and apprehensive encounter with some sickness that modern medicine was most likely not in control of, during which they had indeed delayed submitting to a surgical operation, but they would have found little support for their hesitation in his prescriptive ruminations.

As one might expect, women turned to St. Jude when their physicians could not cure them or someone they loved. Disappointment in such times was inevitable, given medicine's relative powerlessness, but it was so much more bitter because of the high and unreasonable expectations encouraged by medical culture, exemplified by Dr. Balmer and shared by so many women. When they called on St. Jude in circumstances of medical limitation, the devout were asking him among other things to heal them of the pain of their own exaggerated desires. But what troubled women the most, according to the letters, was not simply that doctors were more limited than expected but that having encountered these limits, they turned away. The letters record the silence and absence of doctors. There was nothing perennial about this: it was constituted by the ethos of modern medicine. If there was nothing (organic) "wrong" with a patient, if nothing showed up on an X ray or in a test, or if indeed something did show up but was inoperable or untreatable with drugs, then there was nothing more for physicians, particularly specialists, to do or say. There was little in their training or science to prepare them to deal either with other kinds of wrong than the organic or with the broader sorrows and disruptions of organic disease, and the acceptable diagnostic languages and the social hierarchy of the medical world precluded women from speaking on such occasions about what was really wrong with them anyway.

Some might say that this was not the physicians' responsibility—there were other professionals, after all, whose specific task it was to help sick people and their families with spiritual and existential dilemmas. Visiting parish priests and hospital chaplains brought an ancient and complex theology of human suffering, pain, and sorrow into the places of sickness for support, consolation, and edification. But here again the immigrants' daughters were to experience silence, disappointment, and abandonment in times of great need.

THE DEVOTIONAL ETHOS OF SICKNESS AND PAIN

Physical distress of all sorts, from congenital conditions like cerebral palsy to the unexpected agonies of accidents and illness, was understood by American Catholics in the middle years of this century as an individual's main opportunity for spiritual growth.[19] Pain purged and disciplined the ego, stripping it of pride and self-love; it disclosed the emptiness of the world. Without it, human beings remained pagans; in physical distress, they might find their way back to the Church—and to sanctity. "Suffering," one hospital chaplain told his congregation of sick people, "makes saints of many who in health were indifferent to the practices of their holy religion." Pain was a ladder to heaven; the saints were unhappy unless they were in physical distress of some sort. Catholic nurses were encouraged to watch for opportunities on their rounds to help lapsed Catholics renew their faith and even to convert non-Catholics in the promising circumstances of physical distress.[20]

Pain was always the thoughtful prescription of the Divine Physician. Thomas Dooley's cancer was celebrated in Catholic popular culture as a grace, a mark of divine favor. Dooley himself wrote, "God has been good to me. He has given me the most hideous, painful cancer at an extremely young age." So central was pain to the American Catholic ethos that devotional writers sometimes went so far as to equate it with life. "The good days are a respite," a laywoman writing in *Ave Maria* in 1950 proclaimed, "granted to us so that we can endure the bad days."[21]

Catholics thrilled to describe the body in pain. Devotional prose was generally overwrought, but on this subject it exceeded itself (as it did in presenting the equally exciting family romance). There was always an excess in devotional accounts of pain and suffering of a certain kind of sensuous detail, a delicious lingering over and savoring of other people's pain. A dying man is presented in a 1937 issue of *Ave Maria* as having "lain [for twenty-one years] on the broad of his back, suffering from arthritis . . . [his] hands and fingers were so deformed and twisted that he could not raise them more than an inch . . . [his] teeth were set . . . so physically handicapped that in summer he could not brush away a fly or a mosquito from his face because of his condition."[22] It was never enough in this aesthetic to say simply "cancer," stark as that word is; instead, it had to be the "cancer that is all pain." Wounds always throbbed, suffering was "untold," pain invariably took its victims to the very limits of endurance.

The body-in-pain was itself exciting: flushed, feverish, and beautiful—"the sickroom is rather a unique beauty shop," one priest mused, where "pain has worked more wonders than cosmetics"—it awaits its lover. A woman visiting a Catholic hospital in 1929 came upon a little Protestant girl who was dying and reported: "He has set His mark upon her. Somehow you guess; those frail little shoulders are shaped for a cross, those eyes are amber chalices deep enough for pain, that grave little courteous heart is big enough to hold Him! He will yet be her tremendous lover, drawing her gently into His white embrace, bestowing upon her the sparkling, priceless pledge of his love—suffering." Pain had the character of a sacrament, offering the sufferer a uniquely immediate and intimate experience of Jesus' presence.[23] Walking amid the "couches of pain" laid out for the sunset service at Lourdes, an American visitor suddenly sensed that "He is here now. . . . Almost I can hear him speak,—almost I can reach out and touch his garment." Another writer reported that she knew "a very holy nun who is herself one of God's chosen ones [that is, afflicted with the most severe pain], and one day she said something to me that I have never forgotten. She said, 'Sometimes God's hand seems to rest so heavily upon our shoulder, and we try to squirm away, and we cry, "Oh, let me be!" And then we begin to realize how tender as well as how heavy is His hand, and we want it there.' "[24]

This was a darkly erotic aesthetic of pain, one expression of the wider romanticism of American Catholicism in this period; but for all this culture's fascination with physical distress, the sensual pleasure it took in feverish descriptions of suffering, it was also deeply resentful and suspicious of sick persons. A nasty edge of retribution and revenge is evident in these accounts. In one priest's typical cautionary tale of pain, "a young woman of Dallas, Texas, a scandal to her friends for having given up her faith because it interfered with her sinful life, was severely burned in an explosion. Before her death, through the grace of God, she returned to the church." According to a nursing sister, writing in the leading American Catholic journal for hospital professionals, *Hospital Progress*, in 1952: "Physical disability wears off the veneer of sophistication and forces the acceptance of reality. It is difficult for a patient imprisoned for weeks in a traction apparatus to live in a state of illusion."[25] Pain gives people their comeuppance; it serves as chastisement and judgment.

The Catholic tradition was ambivalent about the moral status of the sick. Despite constant injunctions to the contrary, a persistent identification was made between sickness and sin—not only sin in general or Original Sin, but the specific sinfulness of the person in pain—and the suspicion of all physical suffering as merited was never completely absent from devotional culture.[26] "You may complain and moan about a simple toothache," Father Boniface Buckley chided the readers of *Sign* in 1945, but be "woefully forgetful of the fact that this particular pain may be due in justice for some sin of that very day." God always has a reason for sending pain. Theology's restraint is evident here in Father Buckley's use of the conditional; devotional writers commonly threw such theological caution to the winds in order to score moral points with pain.

Learn to take your pain the way a man takes a hangover, another priest scolded, and admit you "asked for it."[27]

The association between physical sickness and moral corruption was reinforced throughout American Catholic popular literature by the persistent use of metaphors of illness to describe threats to the social fabric and sources of political and moral decay. As the editor of *Ave Maria* put it, aphoristically, in 1932, "error is due to thought germs" against which only mental and moral hygiene is an effective prophylactic. Another writer even suggested that to visit the sick was to stand at "the bedside of our soul-sick world."[28] The persistent metaphorical use of leprosy to excoriate various moral dangers was so egregious in the Catholic press that missionaries among sufferers of Hansen's disease regularly complained of the effect this usage was having on the people in their care. This was not an unusual rhetorical device, of course, but it achieved its own peculiar, disorienting resonance in Catholic devotionalism, where images of the body-in-pain were used to suggest both the depths of corruption and the highest reaches of spiritual glory. In the case of the leper, the two discrepant usages converged: the leper was at once physically—and morally—scrofulous and (potentially) sacred.[29]

As American Catholics interpreted an ancient tradition in their contemporary circumstances, the idea that sickness was punishment for something the sufferer had done took deeper hold. The more sentimental view of sickness as the training ground for saintliness was commonly reserved for people with congenital conditions, like cerebral palsy: their distress could not be attributed to any personal moral failure since they were born this way. The innocence of handicapped people made them central to the elaboration of the gothic romance of suffering; because they were "innocent," unalloyed spiritual pleasure could be taken in the brokenness of their bodies. There was a cult of the "shut-in" among American Catholics in the middle years of this century, a fascination with "cripples" and a desire to be in some relation to them, which was thought to carry spiritual advantages. In the summer of 1939, *Catholic Women's World* set up a pen-pal system so that readers going away on vacation could write to shut-ins about their trips; the project was so popular that "many readers have written to us requesting that we put them in touch with not only one, but as many as three or four shut-ins." There were a number of organizations dedicated to harnessing the spiritual power of shut-ins and putting it to work for the rest of the church, such as the Catholic Union of the Sick in America (CUSA), which formed small cells of isolated handicapped persons who communicated with each other through a round-robin letter and whose spiritual assignment was to say prayers, more powerful by virtue of their pain, for some specific social good.[30]

But the mistrust of the sick, the suspicion that their physical distress was the manifestation of a moral failing, lurked just below the surface even of the fantasy of the holy cripple. The eleventh-century "cripple" Hermann, who composed the Marian hymn "Salve Regina," is described in one article as having been "pleasant, friendly, always laughing, never criticizing, so that everybody *loved* him." Concluding, "What a record for a cripple!" the author implies that just the opposite could have been expected from a man like this.[31] The subtext here is that if Hermann had not been so delightful, he would not have deserved love—there was nothing unconditional about this culture's affection for cripples.

Apart from these "fortunate unfortunates," a favorite Catholic term for the handicapped, however ambivalently construed, sick people were guilty people, and, not surprisingly, they behaved as such. Sick people were generally depicted as malingering, whining, selfish, overly preoccupied with their own problems, indolent, maladjusted, and self-destructive. They exaggerated the extent of their distress; they were quick to yield to despair and loneliness. Wake up to the fact that life is a vale of tears, one priest scolded the ill, and get rid of your "Pollyanna attitude," by which he meant stop hoping for relief. Above all, the sick could not be trusted. Without the astringent of religion, for example, lepers—even beloved lepers—would be "spiteful, cynical and debauched," according to one visitor to Molokai, and this was generally maintained as true of all sick people. As late as 1965, a Dominican priest writing in *Ave Maria* derided a sick person as a "spoiled child" and warned against "the tendency to remain in our suffering, to exaggerate the injustice, to pout."[32]

But what exactly constituted complaint? Were devotional teachers warning in these passages against the dark and self-defeating human impulse to protest the will of God or to rebel against the facts of life? "Complaint" meant any sound that the sick might make, any use of their voices, whether it was to ask for a glass of water in the middle of the night, to question a doctor's decisions, to express a spiritual doubt, or to request that their bodies be shifted in bed. Hospitalized sick people who complained of physical discomfort were referred to in the *Voice of St. Jude* as "c.t.m.p.['s]" ("cantankerous, tempestuous, maladjusted patient[s]"), an imitation of the slang acronyms of residents and interns.[33] There was only one officially sanctioned way to suffer even the most excruciating distress: with bright, upbeat, uncomplaining, submissive endurance.[34] A woman dying horribly of an unspecified cancer was commended by

Ave Maria for having written "cheerful, newsy notes" home from the hospital, with "only casual references to her illness." In the style of a fashion editor, a devotional writer counseled the chronically ill to "learn to wear [your] sickness becomingly. It can be done. It has been done. Put a blue ribbon bow on your bedjacket and smile." Visitors were instructed to urge their sick friends and kin to make the best use of their time; the sick should be happily busy and productive even in the most extreme pain. "Only two percent of the various types of pain are permanent and continual," wrote Mary O'Connor in an *Ave Maria* article for the sick in 1951. She was onto their games; she knew they were likely to be "wallowing in the muck of self-pity or sympathy": "If the sieges of pain let up a little now and then, take up an interesting hobby and throw yourself into it with all you've got. You'll be delighted to find that your pain is lessening as a result." Her own experience was exemplary in this regard: since the onset of her pain a decade earlier she had written over two thousand poems, articles, and stories.[35]

If such pitiless badgering failed to arouse the sick, against their sinful inclinations, to saintliness, there was always the scourge of the suffering of Jesus and Mary: no matter how severe your suffering, the sick were told, Jesus' and Mary's were worse, and *they* never complained. What is a migraine compared to the crown of thorns?[36] How could any sorrow be like Mary's? Jesus' suffering served the same purpose as Mary's virtue in devotional culture: to diminish the integrity and meaning of ordinary persons' difficulties and experiences. Indeed, there was a hierarchy of scorn for sick people: just as Jesus' suffering outweighed all human pain, so truly awful pain was used to dismiss anything less, and all physical distress was greater than any psychological trouble, in a pyramid of suffering with Jesus, all bloody, and Mary, modestly sorrowing, at its top. Leprosy, in particular, functioned as a means of denying other forms of physical distress. The message to sick people was: someone else is suffering more than you are—look at the lepers!—and besides, Jesus suffered most of all, so be quiet!

Thus devotional writers waged a campaign against men and women in physical or emotional distress. The saint offered as patron to the sick in this century was Gemma Galgani, who used violence against herself when she was ill so that she might "subdue even the faintest suggestion of rebellion on the part of the flesh against the spirit"; and if sick people would not subdue their own flesh as St. Gemma did hers, if they could not bedeck their pain in ribbons, it would be done for them. The language used against people in pain was harsh and cruel, devoid of compassion and understanding, and dismissive of their experience. As one priest demanded, if a child spends "seven years or nine" in an iron lung, "what of it?" There was only scorn, never sympathy, for the sick who failed to become saintly through pain.[37] Bending the images and idioms of popular religion against them so that even the suffering Christ emerged as reproach, devotional writers crafted a rhetoric of mortification and denial for the sick, an especially cruel work because they were doing it in the language and venues of popular devotionalism to which sick people customarily turned for spiritual and emotional comfort.

The consequences of this rhetoric was that pain itself—the awful, frightening reality of something going wrong in the body—disappeared. It was hidden behind the insistence that the sick be cheerful, productive, orderly; it was masked by the condescending assurances offered to shut-in handicapped by those who were not that it was better to be a cripple; it was occluded by the shimmering, overheated prose, the excited fascination with physical torment, and the scorn and contempt for the sick.[38] There is not nearly as much suffering in the world as people complain of, a writer chided in the pages of *Ave Maria*—two years after the end of the First World War.[39]

"I enjoyed my week with the lepers of Molokai," a traveler exclaimed, as if he had not been sojourning among people he had just described as looking "more like decomposing corpses than human beings." Chronic illness brought families together in special joy and intimacy, according to these writers. Even Jesus' pain could be denied: lest they find in his Passion an expression of the reality of their own experience, the sick were occasionally reminded that because he was conceived without Original Sin, Jesus was never sick (the risk of Docetism apparently less troubling than that of compassion). It was in this spirit that William P. McCahill, executive secretary of the President's Committee on National Employ the Physically Handicapped Week, reported with approval a child's question to a handicapped person: "Mildred, is it fun to be a cripple?" Yes, it is! McCahill assured his readers.[40]

Physical distress that had been thus purged of its everyday meanness, of the limitations it imposed on the body, and of the dreariness of its persistence could be transmuted into its opposite: "pain" became a "harvest" ripe for the gathering, a spiritual "powerhouse" that could light the church, a vein of gold to be mined, minted, spent. "It isn't suffering that's the tragedy," one of CUSA's mottoes proclaims, "only wasted suffering." In a 1953 meditation that mixed several transformative metaphors, Florence Waters urged the readers of *Ave Maria* to "travel the length and breadth of the country and add them up—the cardiacs, and arthritics, the cerebral palsied, the paraplegics, the amputees, the blind, the congenitally malformed, and the victims of countless other ills that tie human bodies to beds, wheelchairs, crutches, to one room or one house." What does all this add up to?—"a vast storehouse of spiritual power." In "stark, unadorned pain, mental and physical," Waters concluded, there is "a subtle but true coin that may be exchanged for spiritual goods for ourselves and others."[41]

So pain was alienable: coined from the bodies of the (untrustworthy) sick, it could be taken away and applied to the welfare of the healthy in a redistributive economy of distress. God apparently sent pain to some people so that others might be edified, making the bodies of the sick conduits of communications and benefits from heaven to earth. "The pain of the weak," according to one priest, "is the occasion for self-sacrifice and growth in virtue on the part of the strong."[42] But, again, the actual sick people, the real persons suffering from specific illnesses in precise ways, got lost in this process.

Because all pain was god-sent and good, and because it was never in any case as bitter as weak, whining sick people made it out to be, there was no need to account for its place in the universe, to respond to the spiritual and intellectual distress it might have occasioned. Protestants required this, perhaps, but not Catholics, who knew that God sent pain always for a purpose.[43] Priests, who might have been expected to sympathize most compassionately with the spiritual and physical dilemmas of the sick, were said to be cheerful in the presence of suffering because, unlike their counterparts in other faiths, they knew that the problem of pain had been "solved." In any case, as American devotional writers reminded the sick, comprehensible suffering was not real suffering. Catholics were said to prefer to suffer humbly and submissively, in recognition of their own guilt, rather than attempt to lessen the sting of it through understanding. Only spoiled children required such assurance.[44]

Devotional writers did not shrink from the hard God implied by their celebrations of pain; indeed, they delighted in him. In the winter of 1949, Jerry Filan, a young man with cerebral palsy, was badly burned in a fire at his home in Brooklyn, New York. Filan had made two arduous trips to Lourdes in the hope of a miracle sometime before this, capturing the imaginations of devotional writers so that, by the time of the fire, Jerry Filan was a well-known and admired "shut-in." The young man died after two months of excruciating pain. In their stories of his last days, Jerry Filan's admirers calmly affirmed, with the pride that American Catholics took in making such hard statements, that the fire was God's will; that God would burn to death a young man in a wheelchair never seems to have occasioned any doubt or grief.[45]

This God reflected all the anger, resentment, scorn, and denial of the Catholic ethos of suffering and pain. A paralyzed woman, bedridden since she was seventeen, admonished herself to remember that "it is God who sends such things as cold toast." Writing about a nun dying slowly of cancer, a priest concluded that God "had planned to fill her last days on earth with pain so that she might have greater glory in heaven." The family of a little girl stricken with polio was told to marvel that God loved them (not necessarily her) so much as to send them this gift. Anyone who dared to register dismay at the handiwork of a deity mean-spirited and petty enough to chill a sick girl's toast or torment an old nun would have met with derision from devotional writers, and with even harsher injunctions to silence. American Catholic religious teachers practiced an antitheodicy in which a cheerful, compliant silence was deemed the only appropriate response to human sorrow.[46]

American Catholics in these years were enraptured and enthralled by physical distress. They presented themselves to the rest of the nation as a people experienced in pain. This was what set Catholics apart and above others: in such an elitism of pain, rebelling against illness, whining and complaining were seen as characteristically Protestant responses, while Catholics were stronger, better able to endure, better prepared to suffer. "It's how I react to cancer" that is important, Dooley wrote, not the suffering itself, because "people will see how I react" and draw spiritual lessons from it. This was one of the things that Catholics could teach American Protestants and, beyond them, the world.[47] There was a specular quality about the way in which Catholics understood their suffering. The devotional press severely and coldly admonished Catholics to suffer well in the sight of others, particularly Protestants, as if everyone were taking note of how they handled their distress. Pain served in this way as both a test of Catholic presence in the United States and a guarantee of it.

At a time when several American industries were dedicated to the desperate work of helping people avoid or deny pain—which was increasingly understood as an obstacle to performance, achievement, and consumption in a culture that treated physical distress and difference as sources of embarrassment and shame as well as signs of personal failure—the Catholic ethos posed (as Catholics themselves recognized) a powerful alternative. Catholics offered to make a storehouse for what everyone else was disposing of; the notion of sickness as a source of spiritual energy for the whole church recast the uselessness and isolation of sickness into participation and belonging. Organizations like the Catholic Union of the Sick in America assigned the physically distressed a privileged place in the spiritual economy and offered them a way to reconnect themselves to the world around them literally *through*, not despite, their illnesses.

But there is an irony here: these romantic evocations of pain without analgesia and of the spiritual glories of leprosy were appearing just as the immigrants' children were leaving the enclaves. Physical distress was regularly, but ambivalently, counterpoised in devotional culture to middle-class achievement. What good is success, money, power, fame in this vale of tears? Catholic writers asked, over and over again—in the same periodicals that regularly celebrated the success, money, power, and fame of Catholic film stars, business tycoons, and athletes. James Terrence Fisher suggests that the pervasive preoccupation with pain in American Catholic culture of this time was a way for the children of immigrants to articulate and respond to their uneasiness with their success.[48] Their American world proclaimed that ambition was good and that material achievement and consumption were worthy goals, but they had grown up in cultures, religious and ethnic, that advocated self-control and self-denial, sacrifice and delayed gratification. These were the values of the Catholic family economy; they were taught by parish priests and nuns, expressed in the stories children were told about the saints and the old countries, and evident in the iconography surrounding them in church. This clash of moral sensibilities was exacerbated by the fact that the immigrants' children were trying to make it—and were by then succeeding—in a society that had not welcomed their parents and in which they were uncertain of their own places. These were the roots of the anger, resentment, and ambivalence that found expression in the early imaginings of St. Jude, and also in the discourse of pain and the broken body.

The modern American Catholic cult of pain and suffering cannot simply be attributed to the European heritage, in other words. This was not peasant fatalism: the parents and grandparents of the people writing about how wonderful it was to suffer cancer without recourse to painkillers had come to America to escape pain, not make a fetish out of it. Second- and third-generation Catholics improvised an ethic of suffering and pain out of the elements available in their tradition in conscious and unconscious response to their contemporary circumstances. What they made lent an aura of spiritual heroism to the frustration they experienced in moving, with guilt and uncertainty, out of the enclaves, and assured them of their moral superiority over the culture they were ambivalently striving toward. The constant refrain that pain mocked the pretensions of the world transformed their resentment of people who appeared to be more successful than they were (among whom they were not sure of finding the place they desired) into a satisfying reaffirmation of traditional Catholic values.

But however satisfying it may have been on this level, the devotional ethos of suffering and pain failed actual sick people. It deepened the silence already threatening persons in pain with its constant injunctions to be quiet and intensified their isolation and claustrophobia. By making pain a test of spiritual capacity, devotional culture added a layer of guilt and recrimination to the experience of bodily disease as it proclaimed that most human beings would fail it. The ethos denied the social, communal, and psychological consequences of illness. Devotional writers literally drew a curtain across the sickroom: addressing him- or herself to an imaginary person in severe pain, an anonymous author in *Ave Maria* intoned: "You enact your monotonous drama of pain in such a divine technique of self-suppression, you make us think that, after all, there is joy in suffering, with sunshine, summer and rose bloom behind the half-curtained windows of a sick room."[49]

Not surprisingly, given all this, few priests undertook ministry among the sick as their main work, and visiting hospitals was not always a high priority among parish clergy, as the periodic admonitions in clerical journals suggest. Parish clergy of the time held hospital chaplains in contempt, as the latter well knew; often enough, there was some reason for their disdain. The Catholic hospital chaplaincy has been a scandal until relatively recently, having been treated as the place to assign—and to hide—men with emotional or physical troubles of their own, particularly alcoholism, and as the dumping ground for priests who could not make it in the high-pressure, big-business, hearty male world of the American parish. As late as 1965, when the National Association of Catholic Chaplains was founded, men (and women, although their spiritual work in the hospitals was generally accorded more respect from the first) who had chosen the hospital ministry as their vocation were complaining that they were forced by local church authorities to accept "a semi-invalid or problem personality" on their increasingly professional staffs.[50]

Even the most conscientious hospital chaplains defined their ministry in carefully proscribed terms, though: as one put it in an advisory note to his fellows, "your main purpose in calling on the sick is to anticipate the need of the Sacraments." Home visits were likewise intended for the administration of the sacraments: precise instructions on the preparation of the sickroom and the appropriate demeanor for greeting the priest at the door—reverently, holding a lighted candle, and above all, silently—were reviewed in the devotional press, which also advertised "sick call sets" of ritual objects needed by the priest. Just as the priority of the organic set definite limits to what could be said in the doctor's office, so this sacramental emphasis constrained talk between priests and sick people. Pastoral visits to home and hospital were characterized for the most part by a carefully cultivated sacerdotal aloofness and by the formality required by sacramental protocol. Chaplains believed in keeping their distance, seeking to be "friendly to all, but never just a regular guy," mindful that, as one put it, "people watch [us] like a hawk." Be "human, yet not lax," another advised, "friendly yet not familiar, reserved yet not distant."[51]

The efficient administration of the sacraments to patients in large hospitals demanded a no-nonsense manner, Donald L. Barry, an experienced chaplain, counseled, because "if you pulled up a chair and visited each even for a few minutes, the day would be gone."[52] Like their parish counterparts, chaplains tended to measure the meaning of their work by volume, keeping careful accounts of souls "harvested" which they could show to bishops oriented to the bottom line. "4000 personal visits were paid to Catholic men," a chaplain at a California tuberculosis sanitarium tabulated for his four-year ministry, "and 5000 to Catholic women . . . 3100 quarterly Confessions and Communions of men and 4400 of women," 50 converts (which required an additional 400 visits to the hospital), 20,000 Catholic periodicals distributed. It is no wonder given this ethic that one man, in a statistical elaboration of Barry's warning, fretted about what would happen "if the chaplain of a large hospital with, say, 350 beds, were to spend but one minute with each patient," calculating that this would "require six hours, besides the time spent in going from door to door, from floor to floor, in answering the telephone when paged, in stopping to speak with people in the halls, in waiting for the elevator, in hearing confessions, or trying to resolve a doctor's or nurse's problem which just can't wait until later." When a priest proposed in 1942 that chaplains sit with the sick a little, he was conscious of making an unusual suggestion, explaining that it was "perhaps the Southerner in me"—not the priest—"that made me take my time."[53]

Set within this preoccupation with sacramental statistics was the familiar clerical apprehension of emotional trespass, the anxiety of intruding and of being intruded upon that generally informed priests' relations with lay people, especially lay women, but particularly so in sick times. "We priests have no right or wish to walk where we may in your home," one priest observed in a 1958 discussion of the right conduct of a sick call, "or you in ours." But how was it that the prospect of lay people aimlessly wandering through rectories (the most unlikely of all possibilities) even emerged in an article about priests visiting the sick? The secure boundaries first erected in seminary and subsequently fortified by the male culture of the parish house were threatened in sick times because illness, pain, and death demanded more emotionally frank and engaged responses than these limits permitted. The author of this article almost pleaded with lay people to restrain themselves: "while pain slowly overcomes life, and death approaches, the members of a Catholic household must not lapse into a hectic state of hopeless helplessness punctuated by senseless remarks." He ends by curtly ordering them to "say the Rosary," in other words, to transpose their own cries and laments into the safer (for him) and more controlled idioms of devotional piety.[54] Vulnerable and exposed, clergymen relied on the solemnity of sacraments and sacramentals to do the work of encouragement and consolation for them, if indeed they did not stay out of the sickroom completely, leaving it to drunks, "semi-invalids," and other men whose masculine and clerical identities were already corrupted.

And indeed there might have been some comfort in the awesome rituals for the sick (as there was in the equally awesome conduct of medical rites)—in the procession of the priest down the hospital corridor, preceded by a Sister Sacristan ringing a bell to announce the presence of the sacrament or the touch of oil on the limbs and head of the sick person—were they not so thoroughly terrifying. Everyone knew that priests were primarily concerned, by theology and clerical culture, with the dying. The Tridentine definition of Extreme Unction—last rites—reserved the sacrament for those ready to die, stressing the spiritual (not corporal) assistance it offered in this extremity.[55] Priests dashing into hospitals were popularly imagined as racing against time on a soul-saving course; it was this, not the consolation of the sick, that lent whatever drama, importance, and dignity there was to the hospital chaplaincy.[56] A priest working as a chaplain as late as 1966 referred to the hospital as the "anteroom to eternity," where people "shuffling off the mortal coil" were ripe for spiritual salvation. The appearance of the priest at the bedside signaled doom, and most people delayed summoning him for as long as they could.[57]

The rapid shift in the reorganization of health care from the home to the hospital in the first three decades of this century posed a daunting challenge to an already overburdened church, and the inadequacy of spiritual care for the sick can be at least partly attributed to this. But American Catholics succeeded in building a network of modern, technologically sophisticated hospitals; Catholic doctors and nurses were well trained in denominational schools; Catholic hospital professionals in the United States were up-to-date and well informed on matters ranging from the latest surgical equipment to the best cafeteria designs, as the publications of the American Catholic Hospital Association show. The Church was also capable of providing—and of treating as heroes—military chaplains in several wars. All of this contrasts sharply with the dismal level of pastoral care for the sick and suggests that the latter reflected the impact of the ambivalent ethos of suffering and pain rather than the economic or social state of the community.

The ethos also shaped the culture's stand toward religious healing, although this needs to be set briefly in a wider historical and cultural frame. Power over disease was considered a gift of the Holy Spirit by the earliest Christians and a sign of their goodness and spiritual charism.[58] By the early Middle Ages, this power had been reserved to the saints and the Virgin Mary in the Western church, channeled, as other forms of charismatic expression and authority had been, into official idioms (more or less) under the authority of popes and bishops. Popular belief in healings flourished—as the historian Stephen Wilson has observed, medieval saints' shrines were always healing sites above all else—but the place of healing in the Church remained contested because it posed such difficult and dangerous questions of authority and control.[59] Who healed? Who declared a particular place a site of healing and who then controlled it? Many thaumaturgic cults developed without Rome's approval (or often its knowledge), some without even local consent; healing practices were often related to ancient regional folk medicines and pre-Christian customs. Rome had always struggled to maintain its control over these cults and rites, but in the years after Trent especially the Church reserved to itself the right of investigating and deciding upon miracle claims. After the rise of modern science, a new elite appeared to review the miraculous for its own purposes: scientists, rationalists, and political radicals pointed to what they saw as the uncontrolled excitement of healing places and the exploitation of people in need by greedy clergy to discredit religion and publicly display and establish their own intellectual and moral authority.[60] Religious healing in the Catholic tradition is best understood, then, as the focus of multiple contests and conflicts. The official definition of Extreme Unction is an unintentional expression of this ambivalent history: although the sick body was anointed with oils and water in the sacrament in a most impressive display of religious power, sick people and their families were explicitly cautioned *not* to expect physical healing of the rituals.

Healings had taken place at American shrines before this century, and charismatic healers, usually members of religious orders who scrupulously muted their own place in the thaumaturgic event in deference to ecclesiastical authority, were not unknown in the community before the widely publicized revival of faith healing among Catholics in the 1970s.[61] Catholicism's suspicion and mistrust of religious healing was evident here as well, however. The traditional curative arts of Irish and southern and eastern European women were mostly lost within a generation of their immigration to this country under the combined pressures of their children's assimilation to the world of modern medicine and the clergy's denunciations of "superstition" and "magic."[62] After the revival of faith healing among American Protestants in the early part of the century and its subsequent association with flamboyant and disreputable characters, many American Catholics sought to distance themselves from what they saw as an example of Protestantism's tendency toward excess and anarchy. Insecure enough in their own middle-class status, Catholics had no desire to get out on anyone else's margin, and faith healing was definitely on the American margins.

But it was the romance of pain itself that made it so complicated for Catholics to hope for healings. Their yearnings were supposed to be pointed in the opposite direction, toward a deeper, sustained engagement with the promise and loveliness of "pain" (as opposed to the distress and loneliness of pain). Devotional culture taught that to alleviate pain was to deny the cross, understandable, perhaps, but still an instance of human selfishness, a denial of the soul's superiority to the body and a rejection of the opportunity for saintliness. In a meditation published in *Catholic World* in 1929, a very sick woman warned others in similar distress that to be healed meant that "you might lose the shining thread of Him" in a misplaced quest for happiness, "only to discover that you had it once when you were bedridden, poor and alone." Some Catholics opposed pain killers and anesthetics even for extreme distress on the grounds that they interfered with an experience intended by God for the good of the afflicted person and intruded upon the intimacy with him available only to those in pain. Father Jerome Dukette celebrated a man "quite crippled with rheumatism" who, after traveling all the way to the Shrine of St. Anne de Beaupre in hopes of a cure, decided that his suffering was a sign of grace after all and turned away. Thirteen years later, according to Father Dukette, this man came back to the Shrine to tell St. Anne that he was grateful to her "for not curing me" because "healthy, I stood a chance of damning myself, [whereas] I prefer to crawl up to Heaven on hands and knees than to run off to Hell on two good legs."[63] The Dominican theologian Bede Jarrett told a story with a similar theme:

I remember a woman once in a parish where I worked, down in terribly poor streets. I remember her dying of cancer—a terrible cancer, that type of cancer that is all pain. One day she said to me: "Need I take morphia? The doctor wants me to. Need I?" "No," said I, "there's no need to; but why not?" "I think it would be better for me not to. You remember my boy?" Yes, I knew and remembered all about her boy. "It would be much better for me not to because then I could offer all my sufferings for him. I'd love to make an offering of them. I can, can't I? That is the teaching of our faith?" What could I answer except that this was indeed our faith. She died in very great agony but wonderfully happy. The worse her pains grew, the happier she became.[64]

What other answer, indeed? In the devotional understanding, healing would shut off the spiritual dynamo of pain and stop the flow of its exploitable energy; it would be like turning off Niagara Falls.[65]

TRANSITION: WOMEN IN THE HOSPITAL

Although these teachings on pain were directed to all sick people, it is necessary to recall here that devotional culture was in fact primarily addressed to women and that women were fundamentally identified with pain in devotional culture. They would thus have been the main consumers of this discourse and its primary subjects. As if to seal this connection between the imaginative construction of pain and sickness and its intended audience, it was women's pain that figured most prominently in devotional presentations of the meanings of suffering. It is not simply that suffering women were more often depicted in devotional culture or that women's distress was seen as more clearly illustrative of the meanings of pain (although both are true). Rather, it is that the discourse on pain was gendered: to suffer pain well—which meant cheerfully, silently, submissively—was to suffer like a woman; conversely, the good woman had the same character as the person-in-pain. It is difficult to imagine substituting a man for the woman-in-pain in Bede Jarrett's story, since it was precisely women's responsibility in this culture to make such bodily sacrifices of themselves for others, especially for men; it is also impossible to imagine a devotional writer celebrating the searing by fire of a wayward boy as in the story told about the young woman in Dallas. (The fire that burned Jerry Filan was not punitive.) These are idiomatically unimaginable substitutions because the devotional discourse on suffering was in fact identical with its discourse on women. Sickness was a beauty parlor, not a barber shop.

This did not mean that women in pain would therefore be treated with special consideration. Sick women were very dangerous figures in this imaginative construction. Once again, the identification between the two discourses is clear: the sick have the characteristics of women—they talk too much, they complain and whine, they are preoccupied with matters of the body to the detriment of their souls, overly susceptible to outside influences, emotional, they are even seductive. Sick women were thus doubly alienated in this culture. "Satan transmitted the germ of error to Eve when he deceived her," the editor of *Ave Maria* wrote in his discussion of "thought germs." Eve is sinful and sick. Father Barry, the chaplain who generally discouraged visiting for efficiency's sake, specifically cautioned against visiting young women not merely for the obvious reasons but also because "older [sick] women will notice and resent it," whereas sick men do not mind if the priest stops at other men's bedsides.[66]

But women were present in other ways in the hospital and sickroom than as devotionalism imagined them there. The everyday spiritual care of the Catholic sick was left to, and competently assumed by, women, lay and religious, in many different capacities and roles: as social workers, nurses, hospital sisters, as relatives and friends of sick people, or as patients in the next bed, women provided spiritual encouragement and consolation. An explicit distinction was made by Catholic writers between the hospital work and responsibilities of males (priests and doctors) and females (nurses, lay and religious, and sisters) based on the gender categories of scholasticism. Jesuit Father Edward Garesché, an authority on Catholic nursing and founder in 1916 of the first International Catholic Federation of Nurses in the United States and Canada, taught that a nurse's female nature, her "motherly instincts . . . qualities of pity, gentleness, and serviceableness," made her the primary figure of mercy and compassion in hospitals. Doctors, acting from the "male qualities of authority, dominance, strength, and assurance," "merely pay visits to the sick," whereas nurses attend to them lovingly through the nights.[67] Well-trained nurses will be ready to "respond automatically to the patient's spiritual needs," a nursing educator wrote in *Hospital Progress* in 1958, "praying aloud at the dying patient's bedside . . . whispering aspirations into his ear . . . and comforting his loved ones. A number of spiritual associations, like the Nurses' Apostolate, were founded to support nurses in this dimension of their work. "Sister-visitors" paused to talk with patients after the chaplain had moved on to the next bed with the sacrament. Nurses, female hospital administrators, and sister-visitors sometimes registered sharp complaints about the quality of personal care that priests and doctors were providing.[68]

One of the most common ways that nurses and women religious ministered to the pastoral needs of the sick was by bringing devotional culture into the hospitals. At St. Vincent's Hospital in New York in the 1950s, for example, sisters placed holy pictures and prayer cards on patients' meal trays in observance of major feast days; kept a small shrine to St. Gerard on the maternity floor and gave medals of the saint to women in labor; and handed out St. Jude prayer cards to patients and their relatives. Each year student nurses staged a May Crowning on the hospital terrace at a Marian shrine erected especially for the ceremony; dressed in formal gowns, they recited the rosary together and then each placed a rose in an arch above Mary's head.[69]

The lay and religious women who brought the Virgin and saints into hospitals and sickrooms were not merely complementing the sacramental work of the clergy (or the medical efforts of physicians), however. Underlying their distribution of prayer cards and medals, the saying of rosaries and novenas, and their maintenance of hospital shrines was an alternative understanding of what was possible for the ill, medically and religiously, in the spaces of the hospital and sickroom. The experiences, relationships, and understandings opened to sick persons by the holy figures and devotional practices women introduced into the spaces of their distress were subtly subversive of the authority of male hospital elites. They also stood in marked contrast to the devotional ethos of suffering and pain. It was such alternative possibilities to those presented by official medicine and religion that women were offering each other when they took Jude into the spaces of sickness.

PATTERNS OF CARING FOR THE SICK IN THE DEVOTION

Sick women or women caring for sick people called St. Jude directly into the experience of physical distress by putting devotional objects associated with him into immediate contact with the afflicted parts of their own or others' bodies. They slept with medals and holy cards pressed against aching teeth or held to lumps they feared were malignant; they pinned medals onto their own or relatives' hospital gowns so Jude would go into operating rooms with them.[70] One woman fixed a medal to her father's pajamas in the middle of the night as he thrashed about unconsciously in a mysterious seizure. Others massaged St. Jude's Oil into the parts of their bodies that had just been operated on to help the healing process, spread it onto the places for which their doctors either held out no hope or with which they could find nothing wrong, and applied it to embarrassing skin eruptions that were keeping them home-bound.[71] The following account was sent to the Shrine in 1953 by a woman writing from Tampico, Illinois:

> Three years ago my father was struck by an automobile and very seriously injured with fractures and internal injuries. For two days and nights he was in intense pain, conscious in part and begging for relief. Being a registered nurse, I was with him on the third night with no improvement in his condition. I was desperate indeed; everything had been done and nothing helped. As I put my rosary in my purse my fingers felt a vial of Saint Jude's Oil. A neighbor returning from a visit to the Shrine had brought it to me two years previous. I had carried it with me but had never used it. I took the oil and used it on my father's head, heart, hands and limbs, reading the prayers and asking St. Jude to please intercede for us that my father might recover or die a peaceful death. Dad stopped his delirious moaning and crying and almost instantly fell into a peaceful normal sleep. . . . He was one and a half years regaining his health, but he walks today with scarcely a limp and works every day.

Stories like this appeared in every issue of the *Voice of St. Jude.*[72]

Once he had entered the sick world, Jude stayed for the duration of the crisis. "I shall never fail to pray and tell others of the wonderful help St. Jude gave to us," one woman wrote, describing his faithfulness, "not only in my husband's recovery but also in seeing the children and me through those desperate days during his illness."[73] The saint attended alcoholics in their withdrawal; accompanied patients to hospitals, laboratories, and clinics for various treatments and tests; stood nearby during long, difficult convalescences; and gently presided over peaceful deaths. He kept the sick and their families company while they waited for the laboratory results or anxiously watched to see whether particular medical procedures would work.[74] Judy told me that Jude stayed with her during her chemotherapy when she felt she would rather die than endure the treatments any longer, and many others acknowledged the saint's help in this context. Another woman remembered that she wore her medal of the saint "all the time" when she went to the hospital for radiation treatment for breast cancer "because I just knew that he was going to be there with me, he was going to help me."[75] Jude journeyed with his devout over the dispersed spaces of modern medicine and sat with them in its waiting times.

It is possible to sketch out a map of the specific times and places within the calendar and geography of an illness when Jude's help was most desperately sought: at its onset, when the taken-for-granted, everyday world was suddenly and fearfully rent; just before and after medical interventions; at moments of intense pain, especially when nothing could be done for even momentary relief; in the middle of the night, when sick and alone or sitting up with a sick person; while waiting for test results, operations, procedures; when the sick person's prognosis suddenly improved or worsened; when there were changes in medical plans or personnel; during convalescence, particularly if it was anticipated that this would be an especially trying period. Occasions of social transition within overall sick-time were difficult—when the sick person left his or her immediate local world for the hospital or laboratory, for example, or reentered it as a convalescent. Jude's company was anxiously sought when women had to take care of their children in emergencies, especially if they could not reach their doctors or husbands. In these situations, women felt the weight of their nurturing responsibility most acutely and saw with dismaying clarity the limits of their protective powers. One woman in such circumstances affixed a medal of St. Jude on her infant's incubator (a common gesture), another gratefully reported the saint's help with her son's earaches.[76] "My son was taken ill two years ago with a rare and fatal bone disease," a parent in Rochester, New York, began a long letter to the Shrine in 1950:

> At the start of the sickness doctors at one of the largest hospitals for children in the country said he had but a 50–50 chance for recovery. As time went on he grew steadily worse: he was put in a complete body cast. The predictions were that if he ever pulled through he would never be able to sit up or walk again.... When he first got sick, I bought a statue of Saint Jude and burned a vigil light constantly before it.... When we told hospital authorities we didn't have any more money, we were told there was no hope for the boy anyway; we might just as well bring him home. I did not know where to turn. I did not want him to suffer any longer, but to think of losing him was torture. I took him home and cared for him the best I could. All this time the statue of Saint Jude was on the dresser beside him. He would never go to sleep without kissing it goodnight. I taught him to say, "Saint Jude, make me better, and make my pains go away."

This mother eventually found, through Jude's help, a doctor able to care for her son, and the letter closes, "I am very happy to say that [my son] is now walking, running, and climbing like any normal child."[77]

Calling on Jude made such moments less lonesome because now he was there in caring attendance and also because entry into the devotion meant access to widening, concentric circles of mutual support and encouragement, as we have seen, constituted and marked by the rounds of medals, vials of oil, pictures, and prayer cards that circulated among the sick and their families and friends in the hospital and between one household and another. The Shrine itself was a link in this chain of concern and consolation. The devout kept candles burning there while they waited for news or as a loved one's life hung in the balance; they sent pictures of themselves sick and then well, progress reports, diagnoses, and accounts of their illnesses, or their families did so for them. In addition to acknowledging these missives and placing the letters and petitions under Jude's statue, the Shrine recognized its far-flung sick in a public benediction at each of its four annual novenas. The center out there was sending its own message of encouragement, concern, and hope back through the chain.[78]

WOMEN IN THE HEALING PROCESS

Just as they were responsible for the physical care of the sick at home and comfort and consolation on hospital visits, so women were *always* the ones to bring Jude into the spaces of sickness: not a single account is preserved in any of the Shrine's publications of a man's using the cult's devotional objects for the physical relief of another stricken person. Women, in their roles as wives, mothers, sisters, and fiancées, took the necessary steps to secure the saint's attention, rushing into action with medals and oil, organizing and sustaining prayer circles of family and friends, and voicing the sick person's needs to the saint.[79]

Women were well aware of their essential role in mediating between the natural and supernatural in the care of sick people, and they communicated a sense of personal healing agency in the way they narrated Jude's interventions in sick times. "One of our five children had a skin disease which neither the doctor nor every salve on the market could cure," a mother began her account for the Shrine in 1941. "We were very much discouraged and the poor child suffered so much. Finally I prayed to St. Jude, the little prayer you sent me, and in a few days, she was cured." This is a typical organization for devotional healing stories: my relative was getting sicker and sicker (and, it was usually noted, there was nothing doctors could do about it), then I intervened and prayed to St. Jude, who responded to my prayers. Another woman told me this story:

> When my son was 5 months old he developed a virus. When I took him to the hospital he was dehydrated and very ill. He had not eaten for about a week and a half. On Sunday our doctor came to tell me my son was very sick and to prepare me for the worst. My husband and I immediately went to the Shrine [from Munster, Indiana]. I remember it was during Mass I asked Saint Jude for

a sign that my son would survive. I have never prayed so sincerely . . . [elision in the original] I heard the church bells ringing. Meanwhile at the hospital my son started to eat. He's 12 yrs. old today.

The elision here emphasizes the importance of the correspondent's prayers in Jude's response.[80] Women often noted that Jude acted *while* they were praying, or emphasized that they prayed *until* he acted, or asserted that greater physical improvement occurred during their novenas than as a result of medical effort.[81] "My daughter wasn't able to conceive," a woman told me, "and she wanted a child so much. I began novenas to St. Jude, and she has the most beautiful year-old child you ever saw." Isabel called herself a "facilitator" in Jude's healing her husband's migraines. "I started him on vitamin E," she said, after her husband had pleaded with her to help him, "and I started praying to St. Jude. . . . I gave him twenty-six hundred units of E a day and I gave him two thousand Cs, and within a week, between that and St. Jude, the pressure eased up and he was able to do things."[82] In another common healing plot, a woman's secret intercession on behalf of sick relatives and friends brings relief though the afflicted continue mistakenly to believe (unless corrected) that they owe their improvement to their doctors or to nature.[83] Finally, women sometimes simply said that Jude was acting for *them* when he responded to their prayers for someone else.[84]

Jude's devout were not directly claiming to be healers in these stories, as certain women in their old neighborhoods might have; the immigrants' modern, well-catechized daughters understood the difference between their intercessions and Jude's. But the distinction was never absolute. As we have seen (and as these healing accounts indicate still more clearly), the narrative practices of the devotion, the intensity with which the devout imagined Jude as their intimate companion and protector, and the immediacy of his apprehension of their needs and wants permitted a blurring of the lines between the saint's powers and those of the women who brought him into particular circumstances. At times this identification could go far. "I have a lady friend who is a Protestant," a woman wrote the Shrine in May 1952, "who has a little boy two years old, who suddenly developed a bone disease. . . . I explained to her about Saint Jude and asked her if she would mind if I said a novena for her little boy." The boy's mother agreed, the correspondent prayed, and then her friend "received the good news from the doctors that her little boy [had] started to walk." The writer concluded, "I feel so happy and grateful to St. Jude and Our Blessed Lady that through my prayers a child walks again."[85] "Through my

Father DePrada placing narratives of petition and grace beneath Jude's Shrine altar in preparation for a novena, ca. 1954–1955.

prayers," a woman told me, "my husband gave up drinking after ten years of drinking and he never went back to it for 30 years until his death a couple of years ago." Another wrote the Shrine in 1958, "My little girl was very sick but my prayers to Saint Jude have improved her greatly and I know if I keep praying she will soon completely recover." Women kept track of the sick people they were tending through the devotion, monitored their progress, and made sure they followed directions for using the devotion's material objects correctly.[86]

The devout were most explicit about their healing roles in relation to the Shrine's Holy Oil. Fearing that her daughter had been exposed to infantile paralysis, a woman reported from Iowa in December 1940, "I rubbed her back and head with the Oil you sent me, and she is well on the road to recovery." Another wrote that her youngest son "was constantly subject to nose-bleeds," so "one night I rubbed some St. Jude Holy Oil on his nose and forehead" and "since that time last August, he has had only one slight case." A woman told me that she sends for ten bottles of oil at a time from the shrine in Baltimore

(Chicago no longer offers it) for her own complaints and for a friend living far from medical assistance in a rural area who uses the oil to tend her children's minor injuries. Certain devout were recognized by neighbors and relatives as being especially efficacious in their ministrations of the Holy Oil.[87] Perhaps it was because the blurring of women's powers and Jude's was so pronounced in this context that the Shrine felt it necessary to deny that the oil had any healing properties at all, even though it promoted it as such.[88]

HEALINGS

Using techniques and materials available in the devotion, women lessened the pain of headaches as Isabel did; controlled panic during late-night attacks of chest pain; treated infections and rashes; massaged away the pain of aching, bruised, arthritic limbs; recovered or restored breath during asthma attacks. "St. Jude's Mail" recorded hundreds of such healings over the years.[89] But the devout did not merely want this one thing from Jude—the miraculous removal of symptoms of illness—and that as soon as possible. Acknowledging that the saint might not act as quickly or in the exact way they hoped, they recognized that they were entering upon a process of praying that could turn out to be very long, its outcome open, and that they would have to endure many things as it unfolded. Physical endurance was supported by love now because Jude was going to be with them through their experience, and as they addressed the saint sick people and their families began to reconfigure their experiences into narratives of petition, a form of speaking and imagining that was (as we have seen) dynamically poised between acceptance and acknowledgment of reality on the one hand, and hope and desire on the other. So their prayers were more likely to be: this is what I want, if it is God's will to grant it; but I trust St. Jude, who loves and knows me, and so if I cannot have this, then I will accept whatever God intends for me. One woman told me that Jude's greatest gift to her when she was sick was the knowledge that "he's there, to guide you, to strengthen you," not always to give you what you want.[90]

Women found the courage in the devotion to prepare themselves for medical procedures and the confidence and hopefulness to facilitate their recoveries; they also discovered in their relationships both with Jude and with the women who had brought him to them the spiritual resources to endure what could not be healed, to live with chronic illness, and to persist through painful treatments. One of my sources told me this story:

Some years ago I hurt my knee seriously in a fall. I prayed to Saint Jude a long time and I kept going somehow, but the problem seemed to get worse and besides it tricked me so I fell so many times. I went from doctor to doctor, but none of them offered much, except one and he wanted to cut in right away, but I had no confidence in him. Finally, a very good doctor was recommended and he looked at the x-ray, saying—"you didn't break a bone, you seriously stretched a muscle." It was a life-saver and gave me more confidence with the oil. I kept on praying, and finally on St. Anne's day I got relief and a steady curing process. I believe St. Jude led me to St. Anne, and I have told others about it.[91]

The saint helped his devout contend with periodic setbacks in their conditions and with discouragement and disappointment.[92] These were "healings" too.

Such a broad understanding of what constitutes a "healing" is necessary because "illness" itself is an inclusive experience. "The disease may be localized in the tissues of a single individual," medical anthropologist Arthur Kleinman writes; "the illness incorporates his social circle."[93] Most health care is provided by families; this was certainly true in the ethnic enclaves, where sick people were looked after at home, and it remained so into the years of the institutionalization of medicine, when Catholics' move to the more isolated and dispersed suburbs put new and special pressures on families in times of sickness, which now entailed more transportation (within the new settlements and back and forth to the old), time, and family coordination. The history of medicine is thus always also the history of families, in their various forms, taking care of sick kin in changing social, cultural, and geographical circumstances.

Among his other roles in sick times, Jude served as the pivot for the experience and expression of family responsibility and loyalty. The devotional idealization of "pain" proclaimed that sickness deepened family bonds, but the devout knew better. Shared prayer was a special way for families to come together and stay in touch with each other during protracted physical crises, sometimes over long distances, and often despite long-standing estrangements, hostilities, and resentments. "My son had to undergo a very dangerous operation—a spinal operation," a devout reported in 1949. "I wrote to our relatives asking them to pray for a successful operation. My little grandsons served Mass every morning in honor of Saint Jude."[94] Family members and friends met in hospital corridors and waiting rooms to pray to Jude. Married couples having problems conceiving, struggling with seriously ill children, or going through other health crises that might otherwise have separated them came together to call on the saint. The devout reported that Jude's presence helped them cope with the protracted or chronic illnesses of kinfolk, which can be the most corrosive of illness experiences for a family.[95] After the illness had passed, memories of the saint's presence (often commemorated by a newly purchased statue) allowed families to integrate an experience that might have been quite bitter and divisive into their narrative of themselves.

Sick people and their kin are often embarrassed by the intimate details of their daily lives, by their preoccupation with the body's fluids and movements, its smells and betrayals. They are unable to talk about them however much they may want to: they sense (or imagine) that their healthy friends and neighbors are annoyed or frightened by their stories, unsure of how to respond, uncomfortable with unfamiliar and unwanted information about people they have known in other ways. Cancers in particular (among the most common of the illnesses brought to Jude in this industrial society) were viewed with such moral repugnance that people suffering with them, their families, and even their doctors refused until recently to speak its name openly, and the same was true for other forms of physical and psychological distress.[96] Disease bore the added shame of moral stigma in Catholic culture. Illness is so absorbing an experience, moreover, that even apart from such cultural constructions it stifles expression. Pain is aversive to language, according to Elaine Scarry: the vocabulary available to describe it is impoverished, on the one hand; on the other, it undermines the human will to speak and confidence in communication. Sickness is paradoxically an experience of exposure (of the body's secret places and inner workings, of hidden moral guilt, of need and incapacity) and enclosure, as the sick person and his or her family hide, by choice or compulsion, from what is betrayed of them to others.

Making narratives of petition together offered families a safe context for naming and describing physical and emotional distress. The devout were careful to get the names of diseases right so they could specify them precisely in their petitions; they asked relatives and friends to pray for them so that these others would also in turn articulate the names of the illnesses. "St. Jude's Mail" was a catalogue of precisely described symptoms. The forbidden and morally marked terms—tumors, cancers, swollen lymph nodes, infertility, lumps on the breast—could be spoken in the idioms of the devotion, and the inner experience of illness, its profound fears and disorientations, represented, by the sick person to him- or herself as well as to others. Prayer became the occasion for the acknowledgment of reality. The lit candle in the sickroom, the medal on the hospital gown, the oil glistening on a sick person's forehead all served as avenues of objectification (to borrow Scarry's term again): visible, tangible expressions of the otherwise mute and solitary experience of pain. It was particularly important for women taking care of sick persons to disclose the seriousness of the illnesses they were contending with because their families might otherwise never know, especially if the women at home honored the bond of silence expected of them. Caregivers extended the circle of responsibility outward through prayer; sickness lost some of its power to isolate and trap them.

The quality of compassion and attention offered the sick person changed once the secrecy of sickness was broken. Care and commiseration need not be embarrassed any more; distress could be talked about openly, with a detachment made possible by the liberating frankness of prayer. One woman told me that her daughter and son-in-law appreciated knowing that she was "bombarding heaven" in the many years they were struggling to have a baby; they openly mentioned her efforts to their friends. The more they talked about her talking to Jude, the less secret and shameful this young couple's own experience became: the ventriloquial voice of the devotion was a healing instrument just for its having been raised. Naming illness, furthermore, "lends credibility to the patient's suffering, hones attention in on particular parts of the body."[97] One person's illness may be easily doubted by another: Scarry points out that pain is both the sign of absolute certainty (for the person feeling it) and absolute doubt (for the person not); as we have seen, the devotional press encouraged attitudes of mistrust and suspicion toward the sick. But when family members, friends, and neighbors prayed to Saint Jude together for a woman who was ill, her needs and troubles were publicly acknowledged and authorized. Clara told me that her family knew that something was seriously wrong when they saw her praying to Jude; there could be no doubting it now. Women often reported that when they were anxious about a personal health problem they asked their husbands to pray with them, getting them thereby to assent to the reality of their experience and to share their understandings of it.[98] A woman's complaints could not be ignored once Jude had been called, especially if her whole family was praying to him on her behalf.

This was a particular kind of attention, different from the scrutinizing of sick women by both medical and devotional authorities. These two discourses identified women with their complaints as they denied the validity of them. Jude sanctioned the reality of their troubles but also opened a way past them: to complain to Jude was not to be bound either to him or to the complaints, but to have hope that the troubles would end. This was an attention that liberated.

The words spoken in the devotion and the markings of illness by its material culture were not simply representational of the illness itself: they also expressed and made the hope for a future beyond the times and spaces of sickness.

Sickness, even short bouts of it, can come to overwhelm any other reality—or identity—that sick persons may have known; it becomes the medium of their self-presentation to the world and the confines of their subjectivity. But Jude intruded upon the intimacy of sick persons with their own illnesses. The sick person's experience of herself was multiply mediated as a result of his presence—by the saint's concern for her, by the connection of her story to others' narratives of sickness, and by the cosmic drama of inversion at the heart of the cult. As the devotion opened the sick person's world out to these other ties, possibilities, and stories, it severed the awful connection that bound her exclusively to herself. This may be one of the reasons why women often reported that after turning to Jude they discovered they did not have to see a doctor after all: they no longer needed to have their image of themselves as sick persons ratified.

With Jude's help, finally, women prepared themselves for the death of seriously ill spouses and found enough calm and peace of mind to anticipate and plan for what lay ahead. They anointed their dying husbands' bodies with oil, asking Jude to relieve the men's pain, and in this way kept their hands on their husbands through the worst times, soothing them and comforting themselves with the same gestures.[99] They worked with Jude to bring their husbands' or fathers' lives to a peaceful conclusion. One of the most common requests made to the saint was to restore dying men to the church. These petitions make it clear that men's religious estrangement was an expression of a more diffuse anger and alienation, so that bringing them back to the faith also meant reconciling them with their children, siblings, in-laws, and sometimes also with their wives (and daughters), who seemed to have experienced their men's anger against God with special intimacy. Then, in Jude's company, women took leave of their husbands. One woman told me that she used to pray for her husband when he was out traveling on business in the early days of their marriage; she made sure he always carried the medal of St. Jude she had given him. "And when he died, I put the little St. Jude medal in his pocket."[100]

RE-CREATING THE SPACES AND TIMES OF SICKNESS

We need to shift our attention now from women's more private experience of illness to its institutional settings. Women brought St. Jude with them into the specific spaces and times of modern American medicine. What did they hope for and accomplish in these contexts with Jude's assistance?

Jude certainly enabled women to renegotiate the role assigned them by medical culture (and eagerly embraced by many of them in their preoccupation with their health) of the awestruck and compliant sufferer of many organic complaints that only medical doctors could define and treat. Calling on Jude for encouragement and support, women openly and regularly challenged their doctors.[101] They critically assessed their medical care, made decisions for themselves even if these went against physicians' recommendations, and changed practitioners if they felt they were not being treated properly or were not getting what they wanted.[102] Sometimes women cast the saint into direct competition with their medical caregivers, aligning him with themselves against the medical establishment.[103] Jude even referred women to other doctors who proved to be more amenable to their requests. Often enough he enabled his devout to avoid doctors altogether. However powerful and authoritative doctors were, Jude was more so, and however mysterious and threatening a set of symptoms appeared to be, Jude knew what to do about them. "I had a large growth on my eye," reads a characteristic account of a woman avoiding a medical intervention she had thought was inevitable. "The doctor said I would have to have it burned off. I prayed to St. Jude to intercede for me also to the Blessed Virgin. Thanks to both it disappeared. . . . My husband asked me what I did to get rid of the wart. I told him nothing as I had done nothing but pray." "Early this spring," a woman told the Shrine in 1936, "my husband had a lump or boil on his right arm above the elbow. What the medical term is I don't know. I prayed to Saint Jude to help him the last time he went to the Doctor. He was told he would have to operate. My prayers were answered and my husband was able to avoid the operation." "To the amazement of her doctors," another woman reported, "my sister made a perfect recovery from major surgery. Having prayed to Saint Jude, I was not surprised."[104]

These women may not have been making good choices when they ignored their doctors' advice or resisted recommended treatment, nor can these stories be univocally interpreted as medically installed women liberating themselves from the grip of male medical authority by reclaiming power over their own bodies. In many cases the doctors involved were undoubtedly making appropriate recommendations; because the Shrine never tracked the devout over time, we cannot know whether women who did not do what their doctors told them to do suffered for their choices later, but surely some did. The relationships among women/doctors/Jude cannot be neatly organized around the axes of submission/autonomy, or male control of women's bodies/female control of their own bodies, or biochemical medicine/holistic care, because none of these axes was unambiguous in the devotion. Still, the fact is that with Jude's help women made choices in the medical setting itself (where the discrepancy, as Starr pointed out, between their physicians' authority, dignity, and power and their own was most starkly represented and institutionally sanctioned). In the sociology and history of medicine in this country, male doctors and female patients formed the essential dyad; but Jude stepped between them.

He could do this, in part, because once he came on the scene, the experience of illness was set into another narrative framework than the one proposed either by medical or devotional culture, an alternative story that decentered the doctor and recast the meaning of healing by declaring that it was Jude who led physicians to the appropriate diagnoses, guided surgeons' hands in successful operations, revealed to doctors what was required by the patient's condition and enabled them to complete delicate procedures.[105] Powerful physicians became Jude's assistants in this narrative realignment, and in a final twist the physicians themselves, "even the biggest," were called on to confirm that it was Jude who healed, not them.[106]

Just how much could be attributed to Jude in a healing and how much to medical skill was a matter of interpretation. The claim that a miracle may have occurred was not casually or quickly made.[107] The devout were modern women, after all, with faith in medicine as well as in the saints; they had to make sense of the multiple causal possibilities of their experience.[108] Clara told me that when she arrived at the hospital after her visit to the Shrine and found her suddenly healthy mother sitting up in bed, she quizzed the older woman carefully to determine whether or not the change had come while she was kneeling before Jude. "I wanted to know," she said, "if this was just something that came about during the night" naturally or as the direct result of her prayers. As they crafted narratives of petition and grace in the medical setting, the devout determined the shape of their stories for themselves. A woman concluded a long account of her struggle with bone cancer with the reflection that "while I think the X-ray treatments helped, we, my husband and I, both know we owe most of our thanks to the Sorrowful Mother and our new and true friend," St. Jude. "I recently made my first petition to Saint Jude," another devout with an "incurable illness" reported in 1935, "and [I] am glad to say that either I am responding to the doctor's treatment or Saint Jude has listened to my plea."[109]

This reclamation of authority over the plotting of one's medical experience served a healing function itself when the stories being told at the same time by physicians (their authoritative, culturally-sanctioned diagnoses and prognoses) were hopeless. Women simply refused to accept their doctors' version of the future in such cases, to live the medical script proposed for themselves or their loved ones.[110] "A year ago my brother was injured in an auto accident," a young woman wrote the Shrine in 1935, "and was not expected to live. When his recovery became evident the doctor said he would always be crippled. I sent his membership into the Saint Jude League and said several novenas and now he is as well as before the accident." "I was very sick for six months," another correspondent recounted, "without hopes from doctors. . . . I made the novena [to St. Jude] and God worked a miracle. I am up now and improving every day." Such anti-prognoses have been among the most common of the devotion's medical narratives. "I wish to acknowledge publicly my gratitude to Saint Jude," or to cite another example, "My baby who is now in perfect health, was given up entirely by the doctors at the time of his premature birth."[111]

Women were clearly posed against male medical professionals in these stories. They went into action right after their doctors gave up all hope, applying devotional remedies, praying to Jude. "My father was very ill with pernicious anemia," a woman wrote the Shrine in 1940. "The doctors had given him up, and they said he couldn't possibly live but for only a few months. So my mother and I started the Novena, and prayed continually for nine months. Then like a miracle he started to get well and strong again. Today his blood is normal and he has gained in weight."[112] In another instance, a whole group of women refused a doctor's gloomy prognosis:

My baby was born with an intestinal obstruction and from all indications an operation was necessary. He was indeed a sick child, and we were all sure he would not live. The surgeon refused to operate until the child was ten days old and then he was doubtful about the child living through it. Fortunately I was in a room with two Catholic women, and my doctor and nurses were also Catholic. One of the women suggested that I pray to Saint Jude, the other said to pray to Our Lady of Perpetual Help. . . . Immediately after the relic [of Blessed Kateri Tekawitha, a Native American holy figure] was applied the child retained his food for the first time. . . . My baby was christened "Thomas Jude" and the operation was scheduled to take place on a Monday afternoon at 2:00. At 10:00 that morning the obstruction cleared up. The operation was therefore not necessary and the baby immediately improved.[113]

At the end of these stories there is usually a muted but heartfelt sense of vindication.[114]

Women also resisted when the other male professionals they encountered in sick times and spaces—visiting parish priests and hospital chaplains—proposed their version of the hopeless prognosis, the sacrament of the last rites. While priests readied the oil to anoint the bodies of the dying for their last journey, the devout were praying to St. Jude in the same room for another ending to the story.[115] Indeed, the practice and imaginations of men and women in sick-rooms moved in completely opposite directions. Male doctors and priests passed authoritative, institutionally based judgments of hopelessness while women went on believing in the power of their relationship with Jude. Women found ways of speaking and making new personal bonds through the devotion in contrast to the sacramental silence of the priest and the professional reserve of the physician. Jude excited hopes of healing in a setting in which both the Catholic ethos of pain and the science of prognoses sought to dampen such expectations and offered the possibility of action while the protocols of the doctor/patient and priest/lay person relationships encouraged acquiescence, acceptance, and submission.

It is little wonder that women preferred the company of the saint. With his help, they fundamentally remade the meaning and experience of the spaces and times of modern medicine.[116] By taking him with them into the hospital, the devout transformed the setting from an alien, neutral space in an un-familiar landscape, where men spoke an incomprehensible language, where women's bodies or the bodies of people they loved were attached to big, un-fathomable machines, into a place of recognizable values and meaning.[117] There was no location in this apparently impersonal, institutional world that was beyond Jude's reach, so his devout were never really alone in it.[118] They marked the most technologically sophisticated (and intimidating) spaces of the hospital with the saint's image, literally affixing medals or cards to incuba-tors, oxygen tents, and other life-preserving or -sustaining machines, and extended their care and protection into places they were otherwise prohibited from entering.[119] They distributed objects associated with the devotion to their doctors and nurses, to unfamiliar specialists and medical students, to X ray technicians and physical therapists. Sometimes the devout persuaded nurses and orderlies to apply Jude's Holy Oil to them or their relatives; on the eve of operations they assured their doctors that they would be praying for them during the night; and as they left the hospital they promised everyone who had taken care of them that they would light candles and makes novenas for their intentions. In this way, St. Jude's devout shaped communities of attentive caring women inside the male spaces of the hospital as they incorporated hospital professionals in their understanding of things.[120]

Healings

The devotion opened the isolated and constricted spaces of illness out to the world beyond, offsetting the body's confinement. "I had my prayers with me in the hospital," I was told by a woman whose family rarely visited her, "and I would say them every day in the hospital." This ritual helped diminish the bouts of claustrophobia that had been terrifying her.[121] Devout expressed great relief when some simple communication came back from the Shrine, thankful that a caring voice reached them from outside the circle of illness.[122] By the vigil lights they burned in the center out there, the petitions they requested be placed under Jude's statue, and the prayers they asked be said for them there, the devout connected themselves with the placeless place outside the sick space. The peculiar spatial identity of the "National Shrine" turned out to be just what was needed, as though the constricted world of modern medicine (and of the experience of illness) required a correspondingly open place out there as its antithesis. The devotion allowed women to create and represent for themselves and their families in the material culture of the devotion a series of spatial interconnections—hospital/shrine/home/heaven.

Just as they reasserted themselves over the experience of sick space the devout also took hold of sick time through the practices of the cult. Instead of waiting passively for the results of tests to come from faraway laboratories, the devout said novenas, over and over, turning these times of apparent inactivity and powerlessness into occasions when they could do something for themselves or people they loved. They used the waiting time to articulate (and discover) what they wanted and to explore what kinds of future they were prepared for. Jude's devout took the future back from unknown technicians, refusing to wait to be told by others what was in store for them; they became diagnosticians of their own futures.

The assertion of the preeminence of the supernatural over the natural has always been the theme of Catholic healing stories. In the nineteenth century, this served as a powerful and popular expression of antimodernist feeling.[123] But the immigrants' daughters were not simply setting themselves against modern science. The devout experienced illness in two registers: the official, scientific, and medical, on the one hand, and the personal, connected, supernatural, trusting and hopeful, on the other. The two were never completely distinct: in the practices of the devotion, by all the things they did with Jude in hospitals and sickrooms, by what they said about him and hoped for through him in those spaces and times, the devout brought the two levels of their understanding and practice into relation to each other. (As one of my sources, just recovered from intestinal problems, put it, "Thanks for [the] saints in heaven and modern medicine."[124]) The devotion to St. Jude was not simply an anti-modern impulse, in other words: it was the way that American Catholic women negotiated a relationship with the values and procedures of the modern world, including modern medicine, in which they had no choice but to live.

Sickness is always discursive; or, more precisely, sickness is always the site of conflicting discursive practices situated in different relationships of unequal social and cultural power. As Kleinman writes, illness is "transactional, communicative, profoundly social." From the meaning of symptoms to strategies of care to the prospects of healing and the experience of convalescence, sickness is a contested and negotiated reality. The sick have things to say about themselves as they struggle to figure out what has happened to them and what the future holds (if they can imagine a future), an ongoing "self-reflective grappling," again in Kleinman's words, "with illness meanings." But the people around them—their caregivers, doctors, spiritual helpers, families and friends —also have things to say about them, and frequently these others speak with louder voices. All this talk, Kleinman writes, "encases the patient in a visible exoskeleton of powerfully peculiar meanings."[125] The sick are spun into many-leveled webs of meanings, in circumstances of inequality.

The devotion to St. Jude, in all its narrative tenses, spatial reconnections, and material idioms allowed women to tell and enact other stories about their illnesses (or those of their loved ones) than the ones told for and about them by doctors and priests (and than the despairing ones they may have been tempted to tell themselves). As they transformed sickness into illness (in Kleinman's terms) within the idioms of the devotion, they made another reality for themselves and their families.[126] Missing from their narratives was the assumption that only biological language was appropriate for understanding disease and health, or that the doctor's word was final, or that the doctor knew definitively what was happening or would happen, or that modern medicine had the answers to all their problems. Missing, too, was the association between sin and sickness and the idea that all suffering was deserved, the contempt for the hope of relief and healing, and the insistence that silence and submission were the only acceptable responses to sickness. Gone was the God who sent fire to Jerry Filan and cold toast to a bedridden girl. In his place was the loving, empowering, and consoling Jude. The devotion inverted the illness meanings available in culture: isolation became connection, hopelessness hope, submission confidence, silence voice. The inverting saint turned the cultural experience of illness inside out.

Kleinman and other contemporary medical scholars have sought to revive what he calls "empathetic witnessing to the existential experience" of illness as a healing art among doctors.[127] Jude has been so witnessing since the 1920s. The saint can be seen as a precursor of figures who have emerged in recent years out of the critique of Western scientific medicine, like patient advocates (who authorize the patients' choices), family members (who are no longer excluded from hospital settings and whose role in the care even of hospitalized patients is recognized), the hospital ethicist (who sets medical decisions into a broader narrative framework), and even the new, attentive doctors called for by Kleinman and others. Research by medical anthropologists and social psychologists has shown that talk within the medical setting, especially the lost art of taking the patient's "history," actually serves to initiate the healing process.[128] Narrative has a curative role. It is recognized now that more or less intangible factors—from the color of a nurse's uniform to the amount of preoperative touching a patient gets to the landscaping of hospital grounds—make significant contributions to healing. But these are recent discoveries; for most of this century, the curative role of such factors was not appreciated or acknowledged. Scientific and social factors converged to make modern doctors forget simple but essential dimensions of their craft, their most effective healing tools. But as doctors were forgetting these things, there was Jude, to be held, touched, gazed at, to be clutched before operations and murmured to in the long days of convalescence. Doctors and priests might have both been, for different historical and cultural reasons, not good at listening to sick women; but Jude was. He unraveled the threads that wove sick women (or women caring for sick relatives) into webs of defeat, shame, passivity, guilt, isolation, and surrender.

Liberated like this from its constricting and limiting social construction, "disease" become "illness" in the devotion was amenable to cure. In the years when American medicine was pulling body and soul apart, the immigrants' daughters found a way of reintegrating them in an anticipation of holistic healing: if American medicine healed during the season of forgetfulness (as it did), it did so in part because of figures like Jude and the practices associated with them. Devotional healing practices did not thrive in place of scientific medicine but alongside it, the necessary complement to increasingly sophisticated but evermore narrowly construed methods and orientations. Recognition of this should temper assertions about the secularization of healing in the industrial world: if the world of medicine had been truly secularized, no one would have gotten better in it.

7

"There's Miracles, and Miracles, and Miracles": The Cult of Hopeless Causes

As the devout have told their stories over the years to each other and to the Shrine in Chicago, in desperate circumstances they prayed to St. Jude and . . . something good happened for them. Errant husbands came home, medical procedures proved unnecessary, children passed exams, dying fathers reconciled with their families, and so on, thanks to St. Jude. The women involved did not query the elision in the narrative further. Such reversals of fortune occurred because Jude loved them unconditionally and knew their needs without their having to speak them. But it is precisely into this space between the social facts of hopelessness and the changes wrought thanks to St. Jude that we must go now, at the end of this study of women's practices of praying to the Patron Saint of Hopeless Cases and Lost Causes, with questions the devout themselves might not have asked.

The least helpful way of thinking about this would be to try to account for what happened when women prayed to St. Jude in the way that last century's scientists explained the cures at Lourdes, finding "common sense" causes for "religious" phenomena. More useful is to review how these women created and sustained a world in relation to Jude, based on the evidence of the past three chapters, how they imagined reality and its alternatives, and how they lived in this imagined and reimagined world through their devotions. Women believed themselves to be "different persons" after encountering Jude. Without the saint's help, one of his clients wrote me, "I don't think I would be as good a person"; according to another, "thanks to St. Jude's intercession once more I am a complete person."[1] These women and many thousands of others discovered what they wanted, needed, and hoped for in sight of Jude's eyes, as they made their narratives of petition; this is where desire erupted and where its limits were set. They gave form and meaning to the inchoate flow of events, created memories, crafted accounts of themselves as women in their narratives of grace. The narrative practices of the devotion do not represent the recasting of mundane experience in another "symbolic" or "religious" key, but the reexperiencing of everyday life in a new way.

Women who say that they became new and different persons in their encounters with Jude in terrible moments are alerting us to a central feature of devotionalism studied specifically as women's practice. How do human beings become certain kinds of "men" and "women" in particular historical settings? What are the cultural disciplines that shape and constrain some desires as they permit others, that allow and disallow different experiences of life, and how do the persons so inhibited or disinhibited participate in the processes of their own becoming or subvert them, or both? The practice of Jude's cult takes us directly into the construction of women's subjectivities at a time when what it meant to be a woman was a tense and bitter matter in American Catholic cultures. Because Jude's province was hopelessness, furthermore, it also brings us to the limits of women's agency, of their capacity, or incapacity, to do things for themselves and others, as these limits were marked in culture.

Prayer is not an innocent social or psychological activity. It is always situated in specific and discrepant environments of social power, and it derives its meanings, implications, and consequences in relation to these configurations. Indeed, praying is one of the most implicating social historical practices because it is in and through prayer that the self comes into intimate and extended contact with the contradictions and constraints of the social world. It was to Jude that women brought their frustrations and disappointments as mothers, wives, daughters, patients, or office workers; this is where they came when the complexities of their social circumstances became oppressive. Persons at prayer are working to negotiate—or renegotiate—meaning, purpose, a sense of the possible and the good, usually in situations in which the givenness of the world has been undermined, and as they work on the world like this, the world is also working on them.

The lives of the immigrants' daughters were characterized by disjuncture, tension, and discrepancy on several levels, and it was amid these cracks and fissures that they had to make lives and selves in the changed circumstances of their times. For very many of them, the world and the self were remade in relation to Jude, but what was the world and who was the self so constituted?

THANK YOU, ST. JUDE:
ONE INTERPRETATION OF WOMEN'S PRAYERS

The past two chapters presented devotion to St. Jude as basically good for American Catholic women. To recapitulate the argument simply here: whatever the Claretians had in mind for the cult they founded in a Mexican neighborhood in Chicago in 1929, devotion to the Patron Saint of Hopeless Causes and Things Despaired Of encouraged and enabled the immigrants' daughters to tell their stories in a religious culture that otherwise would have denied their voices; it provided them occasions for the experience and expression of solidarity among their female relatives and friends; and it offered them resources for contending with the emotional and physical effects of the increasingly hierarchical, male, and institutional shape of American medicine. The prospects of young Catholic women finding such an idiom for themselves on the hostile ground of devotional culture did not seem good. But by taking Jude into their own lives, inflecting the Shrine's official portrait of him with their needs, desires, and hopes, the immigrants' daughters were able to make something out of the devotion for themselves. Desire was the implicit pivot of the argument between Chapters 3 and 4: the power of women's need for Jude seemed to release him from implication in the strategies of gender construction and domination otherwise so obvious in devotional culture. But another, quite different reading of the same evidence is not only possible but necessary here before any "conclusion" can be reached about what happened in the elision.

The basic patterns of the devotion seem to have been set in the Depression. We saw that women assumed primary responsibility for the economic and moral maintenance of their homes in this time; they were expected to be sources of domestic strength and energy. Nowhere in the published letters (or in my conversations with the devout about these times) was there any expression of anger against an economic system that could make families feel hungry and threatened and hold workers responsible for their own distress, just as there was no explicit protest against the organization of modern hospital medicine or against any of this country's wars. Instead, during the Depression, women prayed to Jude for his help in finding work for their husbands; when the latter did get jobs their wives attributed their success to Jude, not to the men's skill, diligence, or dedication, or to changes in the economy. "I started a Novena on Easter Sunday so my husband would find work," one woman informed the Shrine. "I am so happy to say that he went to work the other day. I am sure that without St. Jude's help he would have failed to secure employment."[2]

This is the characteristic pattern of Depression narratives: they open with an incomprehensible event (unemployment), describe a woman's turning to St. Jude, and end in another incomprehensible event (finding work), reinforcing—by finding religious meaning in—an alienated understanding of the social process. There is a pervasive sense of passivity and impotence throughout: men are fired, men are hired. "Some time ago," another woman wrote the Shrine in 1935, "I wrote and asked you to remember my husband in your prayers for the novena that he might secure work. At the same time I prayed hard at home and placed Saint Jude's picture in my front window and asked him to call my husband to work. A few days later he was called to work."[3]

The devotion bore the trace of these Depression-era origins down through the years. Through the practices of the cult, the immigrants' daughters made a reality for themselves in which all they had to do was pray to St. Jude for awful situations to come out all right in the end, wonderfully and surprisingly (although once they became regular clients of the saint, they began expecting such inversions from him). Too poor to send her kids to parochial school, a woman enrolled them in public school—and then "that same night a friend came to tell me that I was to send the children to Catholic school the next day, for some people of the parish would pay for their education." Thank you, St. Jude. Another's husband had long dreamed of opening a photography studio but was without capital and could not find a location—and then "we received a phone call from a friend telling us of an ideal location [with] nominal rent, spacious quarters," which the town's zoning board unexpectedly had approved for commercial use. Thank you, St. Jude. "Like a star from heaven," another reported, her boyfriend had found a job; "help seemed to come almost overnight and from entirely unexpected quarters," according to another. When one of my sources told me that she had prayed to Jude at the race track, "Help me win today and I'll give you ten percent of my earnings," she was disclosing the basic impulse of the devotion: make things come out the way I want them to! "I whisper a desperate prayer to St. Jude," an older woman who lives in a nursing home wrote me, "and the problems disappear."[4]

The devout regularly denied their own capacities, motivations, and accomplishments when they thanked St. Jude, giving him credit for what they had achieved themselves, as if they refused to acknowledge their own competence and authority. Kathy attributed her success as owner of a plastics company entirely to St. Jude; with the same self-effacement, her best friend, a mother of several small children, confided to her once that "I wouldn't be able to make it without [St. Jude]." A woman who held her family together after her husband left them used this same phrase to describe her bond with the saint. Whenever she makes any decision at home or in her position as inventory control supervisor at a large corporation, she told me, she "fingers" the medal of Jude, whom she calls her "lifesaver," around her neck. If a large shipment is misplaced in the warehouse "I'll walk around muttering and say 'OK, St. Jude, where is it?' And 99 percent of the time I can walk right up to it and put my hands on it. I feel he controls my life."[5]

Ironically, however,—or perhaps perversely—at the same time as they were diminishing their sense of personal agency in relation to Jude, women were also intensifying the pressure of their domestic responsibilities on themselves in the same way. Women did all the necessary devotional work for their families in times of distress. When a couple was in trouble or a man's business failing, it was up to the woman involved to make whatever sacrifices were thought necessary to propitiate the sacred; it was her task to negotiate with Jude, bartering her devotion and commitment for her family's welfare. Women often called on the saint in grueling prayer marathons that lasted all night or for several days; as one woman wrote the Shrine, she prayed "until my throat ached" for a relative's cure.[6] Many believed that Jude's response to them was dependent on the intensity of their prayer: it had to be strong, sustained, impassioned, and, above all, self-sacrificing and self-denying. When I asked Judy why her husband had been called back to work and not other women's, even though they had prayed to St. Jude, too (as she saw at the Shrine during the U.S. Steel strike), she said that maybe it was because she had prayed more fervently than they had, making a greater "sacrifice" on her husband's behalf. Writing from Brooklyn in 1964, Mrs. E.C. told the Shrine: "My little grandson fell off the bed and hit his head very hard. The diagnosis was clot on the brain. The doctors all said the case was hopeless, the child would be retarded or blind. Each day I prayed a little harder and thanks to St. Jude our baby is perfect."[7] The implication of these stories is that if the women involved had not prayed as hard as they did, their families' sorrows would not have been mitigated; this was to impose an awful responsibility on women praying to St. Jude.

So intimately connected to another's inner world that she speaks his or her needs, usually over and over until the saint responds, indeed so connected that she becomes personally responsible for the satisfaction of those needs through prayer, the person praying is inevitably affected by the process, especially when she has been taught since childhood that this satisfaction of others' needs by her own self-sacrifice is her duty. Prayer is not a unidirectional practice; there is always a reflux of implications, consequences, and entailments for the person praying. By the intensity of their prayers to Jude for other people's pain, women absorbed the anxieties, needs, and distress of others into themselves, into their bodies and hearts. Prayer to Jude rendered them porous; in the practice of the devotion, women dissolved the boundaries of their own subjectivities and lost sight of the difference between themselves and their spouses, parents, children. Their everyday tie with St. Jude, which they experienced as so sustaining, bound them to the Catholic ethos of women's infinitely extended and intimately assumed responsibilities. So the more they prayed to Jude, the more they needed him, in an endlessly implicating cycle of demand and dependence.

The devotion did not necessarily encourage women to be as attentive to their own needs as it trained them to be of others', however. The devout prayed to be able to serve their families regardless of their own distress and pain, as they had been instructed to by the tales of the saints-in-aprons. "For some months I've been having hemorrhages," a woman wrote from Wisconsin in 1954, "when finally the doctor took me to the hospital and said I'd have to undergo surgery, at least minor and very possibly major." But there was "no help at home" for her four children (though she signs herself "Mrs."), and she says that she is grateful that with Jude's help she avoided major surgery, although we have no way of knowing whether this was a medically sound decision. Jude's sanctioning of the devotional discourse of female heroic self-abnegation was especially evident during the baby boom when with his help women took terrible risks with their bodies and spirits to conform to their culture's mandate to bear children. It is difficult to understand one woman's jubilant prayer—"My gratitude to St. Jude for a miraculous delivery; fifth Caesarian on a diabetic mother!"—as anything other than her complete surrender to an awful discipline. Jude's devout secured other women's compliance with the severe demands of the culture, moreover. Every time a woman did not tell a distraught friend to leave her alcoholic and abusive husband, protest the treatment she was receiving at work, insist to her children that she needed rest, or stop risking dangerous pregnancies, but instead gave her a prayer card that recalled her to the familiar cycle of sacrifice and submission, she was deepening patterns of women's alienation, surrender, and oppression. The devotion can be seen from this perspective as the medium through which women were mobilized to enforce on themselves and others the standards and psychological orientations that were bearing so heavily down on them.[8]

Although they prayed for many people, Jude's clients have been most pre-occupied in their devotions with male need. They recognized this themselves: when I asked women at the Shrine which family members they prayed for most consistently, all of them listed menfolk, not wild and wayward daughters. So most often it was male need that became women's responsibility in the practice of the devotion. Grateful that her husband has found a job after "I [not "he" or even "we"] had prayed to St. Jude for quite some time," a woman promised that "I will continue to pray for his [not "our"] success." The problem and the sacrifice are hers; the happy ending his. Another woman ended a narrative of petition that her husband and his brother might be reconciled after a long and bitter estrangement by thanking St. Jude "for this and all past help he has given me"—again, not "my husband" or "us." The wife of a Notre Dame grad-uate student who simply could not pass his qualifying examinations "urgently begged" Jude for his help; when the young man finally succeeded she wrote the Shrine, "I am so glad that I [not he] was introduced to St. Jude." This was the gendered substitutionary ethic pervasively enjoined on women in devotional culture: like the old mothers of the romance who fortified their families by their own pain or the young women who yielded their vitality to save a man's life, the devout offered to trade Jude their own fervor and intensity for their men's desires.[9]

Women prayed most often for men because what men were doing was most often the root of their vulnerability: in the devotions they undertook on behalf of their men, the devout seem to be peeking anxiously—and helplessly—over the saint's shoulder at behavior that threatened to ruin their lives. "I am writing this letter," one woman began in 1951, "to thank St. Jude for all his wonderful favors received during the past two years; especially for bringing my husband safely through a terrible temptation, for being with him through an investigation of all his business transactions, and for getting him to make a retreat he said he would never make." But what if the man had not been able to resist the temptation? What if Jude had not stopped him, and he had gone on, despite his wife's concerns, to make a compromising choice? Another woman told me that during the worst time of her husband's alcohol abuse, when he was almost insane with drink, she would slip off to the bathroom at work, close the stall door behind her, and talk quietly to Jude. Prayer was a way for otherwise helpless women to hold their breath in dreadful suspense.[10]

Among the saddest stories brought to Jude over the years were those that recounted the emotional and economic consequences of male abandonment. The women involved seem doubly bereft: they have lost not only their companions but their confidence and dignity, too. "I wish to acknowledge a great favor received from just praying to St. Jude for little over a week," a woman wrote the Shrine in November 1949. "My husband walked out of our home after we had been married for twenty one years to go with another woman." Frantically she made "novenas" to other saints, but her husband remained with his new girlfriend. Then one afternoon a man came to the door selling subscriptions to the *Voice of St. Jude.* This was the first time the correspondent had heard of the saint, but right away she "knew then that there was still hope that my husband might return." "I started to pray to St. Jude. Not long after, near midnight, the phone rang. It was my husband saying that he wanted to return home. . . ." "I promised publication," another abandoned wife wrote in 1969, "if my request was granted—that my husband would drop his divorce suit and return home. He has been home for two months and everything is working out fine—better than ever. Thanks to St. Jude." Still another told this story: "My husband started drinking a good deal and spent many nights away from home. Needless to say, my four children and I were lonely. After many prayers to St. Jude and Our Blessed Mother my husband is home every night and is not drinking. We are a happy family and I know it was made possible through the intercession of St. Jude."[11]

These stories exemplify in a stark way the themes of women's self-abnegation, denial, and submission that I have been tracing through the devotion. Abandoned wives never expressed any anger toward their faithless men or indicated any recognition that something had been revealed about their marriages that needed attention. Rather, they seem overly eager at the end to assure themselves that everything is wonderful, "better than ever," thanks to St. Jude, apparently with no necessary intervention on their part. They never even confront their husbands with the hurtful and humiliating consequences of their irresponsibility. The confident conclusions of an earlier chapter seem misplaced: the speaking that took place in the devotion occurred in place of other, more direct and efficacious, speech, and we can see now that the devout's narratives of petition and grace were actually expressions of a more familiar genre—the devotional narratives of women's alienation and submission of which Anna Maria Taigi and Marcy Balaird were heroines. From the Depression forward, the immigrants' daughters have been trained by devotion to St. Jude to recast their most distressing experiences into the passive voice.

Hopelessness now seems like the experience of a certain kind of freedom. It erupted where the culture's authoritative explanations and procedures broke down, where the tensions implicit in women's everyday lives reached the surface and became unendurable, and where established authorities—doctors, priests, husbands, parents—showed their inadequacies. This was an opportunity for the women involved, and their anxiety on such occasions may have expressed the recognition that they would have to make up (dream up) new possibilities for themselves, configure novel choices and relational patterns, and take unexpected steps. But when these women, at this precise moment, sought refuge in Jude they surrendered the freedom of the inchoate that had been thrust upon them by the changing circumstances of their times. Desire became surrender: whatever complex impulses brought them into the cult, whatever configuration of anger, disappointment, hope, longing, fantasy, and recognition of better ways of living constituted what they named "hopelessness" was transformed—by praying—into capitulation, resignation, and, worst of all, self-delusion, which from the harshest perspective is what the past two chapters were about.

SICKLY, CHILDISH DEVOTIONS: THEOLOGICAL AND PSYCHOLOGICAL CRITIQUES

Most commentators on the cult of saints, even the most sympathetic, designate some of the practices associated with it as childish, regressive, and "unwholesome," the word used by Jesuit theologian Paolo Molinari for the less seemly aspects of the bonds between human beings and saints. Father Molinari, who has been responsible since 1957 for presenting the causes of Jesuits for canonization at Rome, wrote an influential apologia after the Second Vatican Council defending the cult of saints against the "aversion and repulsion" of modern theologians for it.[12] *Saints: Their Place in the Church* was addressed at the same time, however, to those naive practitioners of the cults who displayed a "wretched reliance upon the saints in order to obtain every conceivable kind

"There's Miracles, and Miracles, and Miracles"

193

of help other than that which would contribute to a growth of true religion and Christian devotion." To Molinari (and other theological critics of devotionalism), it was unwholesome to turn to the saints "solely to obtain favors of a material nature" (like finding apartments or selling homes, getting a better job or a prom date—all the boons that Jude's devout typically sought) and especially for assistance in "certain enterprises which can even be at variance with the will of God" (like winning at the track). Devout must realize, Molinari cautioned, that they call on the saints primarily in order "to arrive at a greater intensity of spiritual life" and a deeper religious and psychological maturity, not "to negotiate with them for temporal blessings."[13]

Another Jesuit theologian, William Meissner, who is also a psychoanalyst, has proposed a psychological etiology for devotional unwholesomeness; his account is important both as an influential psychological anatomy of stages of religious experience and as an expression of a broader modern orientation toward certain kinds of religious practice. Meissner (like Freud) locates the ground of all religious experience in a person's "symbiotic union with the mother," specifically in those "experiences of the mother as a loving and caring presence, in nursing, and in the mother's participation in the act of mirroring by which the child finds himself narcissistically embraced, admired, recognized, and cherished . . . that can serve as the basis for an evolving sense of trust, acceptance, and security." Out of this bond comes the first mode of religious experience, which Meissner describes as a "primitive and/or deeply regressive state that is dominated by the conditions of primary narcissism," in other words, by the infant's absorption in his or her mother and the attendant feeling of omnipotence. The infant desires, the caretaker responds (to unarticulated desires, too), and out of this dynamic comes a feeling of extraordinary powerfulness that shapes the first religious sentiments, which are characterized by the absence of boundaries between the self and God, feelings of "absolute dependence" and "unconditional omnipotence," and a "disposition to accept the conditions of life." As the child matures and begins to take shape as a separate person and as reality impinges on his or her fantasy world with increasing insistence, these infantile religious impulses may be modified. A more "spiritualized" God image emerges, clearly distinct from the self and an active judge of right and wrong; believers at this more mature level are less preoccupied with the eyes and face of God (let alone with whether or not he is bearded or handsome). Not everyone reaches this stage of religious experience, of course, either on the level of culture (Meissner points to "primitive polytheisms" in contrast to more sophisticated monotheisms) or individual personality. Many persons remain fixed in the egocentric bond with the sacred that expresses itself in feelings of magical omnipotence. For this kind of believer, there is the "expectation that God will hear and answer the petitioner's prayers," since this God serves as an extension of the individual's will. Meissner puts into technical psychological language the discomfort and unease many feel when they look in on devotions like Jude's, the almost embarrassing sense that there is something unseemly and childish about a woman's whispering her needs to an omnipotent figure who steps into the place of her father or husband and then making believe he grants her wishes.[14]

The quality of women's bond with Jude, the things they sought to do through the media of the cult, and the fantasies they entertained in Jude's sight obviously resonate with what Molinari and Meissner, in different critical languages, have identified as the most problematic dimensions of devotional practice. The terms women used for describing the saint, their focus on his eyes, face, and hands, and their sense that Jude was there for them alone and so intimately connected to them that he would satisfy their unspoken needs, clearly indicate the primitive roots of the devout's relationship with this figure who came to them in times when they were as helpless as babies to do what they needed for themselves. In this bond, furthermore, the devout obviously experienced something like "unconditional omnipotence." One woman claimed to have dug a well with the saint's help. When workers hit quicksand on her daughter's property and came to tell the younger woman that she would have to sink an artesian well, the Shrine's correspondent intervened. "I said to the man, 'No, you go and clean the well out again and I will ask St. Jude to help us clear this trouble up.'" She concluded: "today my daughter is having plenty of water and it is very clear." Another reported that Jude "helped me fix a faucet that doesn't work." Isabel opened spaces in the rush-hour flow on Chicago's highways with Jude "riding on my shoulder." One of Jude's clients saved her daughter and son-in-law from debt ("I prayed to St. Jude and they are almost on their feet again"); another won a difficult case for her cousin, a lawyer; still another got her son a scholarship to the Naval Academy. The extravagance of one woman's report in 1952 that her prayers to Jude had ended the war in Korea actually discloses the delusional quality of women's devotional self-understanding in general.[15] Like children, these women were mistaking their wishes for the world; they closed their eyes, and everything turned out all right. But also like children, the devout were trapped in an odd conjuncture of contradictory feelings of magical agency and resignation. They could do everything; they could do nothing.

"There's Miracles, and Miracles, and Miracles"

Although this is not exactly what critics of devotionalism like Meissner and Molinari meant by the word, the inclination of the immigrants' daughters to turn to the saints in times of trouble was in fact literally childish. They first learned this way of living from their mothers and grandmothers; relations with the saints in Catholic cultures are matrilineal, handed down as consolation, legacy, and charge from female kin to their sons and daughters. Jude's devout always acknowledged this hagiological genealogy by identifying the saints their mothers, aunts, and grandmothers had prayed to before discussing their own tie with the unknown saint; many had been introduced to Jude by a female relative, especially after the 1940s and 1950s, back in the enclaves presided over by women. But children did not simply hear stories about the saints; rather, they entered the emotional currents of adult lives when they accompanied or observed their relatives in their devotions. A particular holy figure, the adult whose protecting patron he or she was, and the child in care or company of the adult, came together in a devotional triangle alive with the adult's needs, hopes, anger, and disappointments, with his or her present circumstances, relationships, and history. All this found expression in the medium of the saints and was subtly communicated to the child along the connecting lines of the triangle.

A woman's bond with Jude had ancient sources, then; enclosed within this intimacy were other intimacies, on heaven and earth. When she turned to Jude as an adult in hopeless need, she entered upon a path of associations, feeling, and sensation that led straight back to the enclaves, to the women who took care of her there and taught her how to be in the world, and to the heavenly figures these women had spoken their own needs to in those worlds. The bond with Jude revived the devotional triangles of their childhoods, so that women felt safe and comforted again, secure and connected, watched and protected. Not completely safe, though: because adults in the enclaves addressed the saints in difficult times, the bond with Jude was never free of a subcurrent of unease and anxiety, as if reawakening the comforts of their childhoods also inevitably entailed reviving its terrors too, including the fear of losing one's own identity in the embrace of this all-seeing figure. The devout enacted this primitive level of the devotion by their handling of its material culture, taking Jude's image into bed at night or into the rooms of medical treatment and murmuring their needs and desires while holding on to him, experiencing his gaze on them as they went about their days, his touch in the oil on their bruises.

Certain social-psychological and social-historical conclusions about women's devotion to St. Jude seem inevitable here, a deepening and elaboration of the perspective briefly considered at the end of Chapter 3. Young women struggling out of the ethnic enclaves toward emergent modern American subjectivities were resituated or reimplicated in the old ways by their practices of engaging Jude. Prayer was a regressive conduit backward to the most primitive moments of their experience. As women availed themselves of the primitive satisfactions of relationship with this saint, allowing their desires and needs to become transparent to the saint and making themselves vulnerable to and dependent on him, prayer became a discipline for the making of female subjectivities of just the sort demanded by devotional culture.

At the same time, women detached themselves from their everyday reality and surrendered themselves to the realm of fantasies, dreams, and wishes. But these dreams of opening spaces on the Dan Ryan Expressway, digging wells, and healing the sick masked what was in fact a deeply passive and alienated experience of reality; responsible for everything but unable to do anything, women turned to subterfuge, self-delusion, and magical omnipotence. They entered a regressive relationship with a male protector who filled the spaces vacated by others they had depended on (their fathers and mothers, husbands, priests, and doctors) and brought them deep satisfactions, but at the cost of an authentic engagement with their circumstances and of the renunciation of their adult selves.

Jude turns out to have been Judas after all.

THE IN-BETWEENNESS OF THE UNKNOWN SAINT IN HISTORY AND WOMEN'S EXPERIENCE

While this identification of the risks and even dangers of women's praying to Jude is a useful corrective to any understanding of popular religion generally and this devotion specifically as unequivocally empowering, oppositional, or subversive, clearly it is incomplete. The old woman whose whispered prayer to Jude appears to typify the impulse of the devout to withdraw with Jude into childish satisfaction and security began her letter to me by identifying herself as "89 years old and in a nursing home on the *independent care* floor so I still take care of myself." Her devotion to Jude went back decades (some of her experiences have already been mentioned) and reflecting on this long association she said, "I am sure I pester St. Jude too much but he keeps me going and he never fails, although I do try to help myself first." She may whisper her needs to him and believe he hears them, but this woman has not lost her autonomy in her connection to Jude, nor does she seem to be living delusionally through him. He has been her constant companion—"he keeps me going," as she and many other women have seen it over the years—but he has apparently not subverted her own agency, diminished her pride in her achievements, or undermined her capacities to make choices for herself. Somehow she is able to hold together gratitude for the essential assistance she believes Jude has given her, the feeling of an ongoing intimate bond with him, and a sense of her own dignity and autonomy in the way she understands her life.

Most devout have described their relationships with the saint like this, emphasizing that he helped them do what they needed to do—in other words, that he brought them into an active and efficacious engagement with their circumstances. The woman who slipped into the bathroom to kiss the saint's image told me that she did this to gather her resources before going back out to contend with her husband's alcohol abuse. "The saints work with us," she reflected, "to help us to be stronger and to keep our faith." With the encouragement she derived from these moments apart in Jude's company she found the literal as well as moral strength to carry her husband, who was so "saturated" he "could hardly walk," to the hospital for the treatment program he had been avoiding.[16] Clara believed that Jude would respond to whomever called on him, but she also felt that hopeless people would have to take the first step toward the saint with some degree of confidence and courage, however uncertain or inchoate. "Something doesn't appear to you," she said, "something with wings, you know, [and say] this is it—this way, through those doors and you'll do fine." She herself did not really know what she was doing when she stopped her car in front of the Shrine on her way from her son's tennis match to her mother's hospital bedside, only that she was doing something; later on she understood that this was the movement she had to make toward Jude for him to turn toward her. When Judy saw that a strike was inevitable at U.S. Steel, she set aside part of her husband's regular paycheck as a personal strike fund, even though she was praying to Jude to avert the disaster. It was necessary to show the saint you could help yourself even as you counted on him to help you; just as Jude spoke through women's voices in their narratives of thanksgiving, so they acted with hope and courage borrowed from him when they made their narratives of petition, in a brave, anticipatory movement of faith.

Clara's written response to my question about what St. Jude looked like was "fear turns to confidence," as if Jude embodied the transformation that took place within her when she prayed to him. In their letters to the Shrine and the stories they told about him to their friends, women expressed their gratitude to

Jude for dispelling their fears and doubts and thus enabling them to act in circumstances that were making them feel weak and powerless. "I greatly needed guidance," a woman wrote the Shrine in 1969, "in making a decision which will affect the rest of my life. I asked St. Jude to guide me in making the right decision. I arrived at a decision in which I feel secure and happy." "When I have a problem," another woman told the Shrine, "I always say a prayer to St. Jude and it seems that I can face that problem with more courage."[17]

An interpretation that emphasizes how women made themselves porous to the needs and desires of others through the practice of the devotion (which they certainly did) does not help us understand how they came to free themselves from the same needs and burdens by means of the same devotional practices. And we can see how women exposed themselves to real dangers and risks in the devotion, but it is not clear yet how they were enabled by the same risky means to free themselves from hurtful ties. The stories of the baby boom years frame this ambiguity most sharply. Women's desperate prayers for conception appear to offer definitive support for the interpretation that the devotion enforced women's submission to their cultures' (American and Catholic) construal of female identity and bodily destiny at a time when parturient women were fast losing control over the birth experience. As Judith Leavitt writes, "the physical removal of childbirth from the woman's home to the physician's institution shifted the balance of power. Birth . . . had become instead a medical affair run by medical professionals," and women "could not decide what kind of births they would have."[18] But this was not so for Mrs. P.K. of Louisville, who described the birth of her eighth child in a 1953 letter to Chicago. "I was going to have a baby," she wrote, "and I had high blood pressure. The doctors came to my house and rushed me to the hospital where they examined me further; they found I had toxemia poisoning." The physicians insisted that she stay overnight, and although she "put up an awful fuss," Mrs. P.K. finally surrendered. She was now in the male, medical place of power—but she was not alone, on earth or in heaven. In the devotion's most familiar exchange, Mrs. P.K. was given Jude's image by a female social worker who visited her on the morning of her admission, when she was feeling particularly vulnerable and trapped. Now Mrs. P.K. began to get what she wanted. The doctors told her that her fetus was dead inside her, but she refused to believe them and, against their wishes, she insisted on leaving the hospital. "A few days later at 1 a.m.," Mrs. P.K. continued her story, "I awoke with a terrible pain, but I thought it was false, so I just laid back and prayed." She was determined to have her baby at home, with St. Jude's help, which she did: "a

"There's Miracles, and Miracles, and Miracles"

few hours later my baby was born with no doctor or anyone but my husband around, a big twelve and a half pound boy as healthy as anyone would want and I got along fine."[19] "I was told by my doctor that I would have to undergo a Caesarian operation," another woman wrote the Shrine, "in order that my baby and I could avoid any complications at the time of my delivery," but then she turned to St. Jude and was able to hold out for "birth in the natural way."[20]

How are these and all the other stories women told about Jude to be understood? What kind of a conclusion can we come to here? The earlier theological, psychological, and social theoretical interpretations of the devotion were implicitly organized around a series of dichotomies that reflect the values and worldviews of these different modernist critical perspectives. A shorter list of these polarities would include, on the psychological level, mature/immature, adult/infantile, separate and individuated/symbiotically enmeshed; on the social historical level, active/passive, self-determining/oppressed, public/private, work/home, freedom/submission; and on the theological level, spiritual/material, unselfish/selfish, magic/religion, aniconic/anthropomorphic, moral/amoral. These are clearly not neutral categories; nor are they free of gender assumptions: at one time or another, as the voices of different women telling their stories about Jude or of women speaking about various moments of their relationships with him have been heard here, it may have seemed more or less clear that particular women belonged to one or the other side of these normative dualities. But ambivalence and ambiguity persist. Is Mrs. P.K. the agent of her own story or a victim? Did the social worker empower or endanger her? Did women like Mrs. P.K. live delusionally or realistically?

The instability and in-betweenness of the devotion and the ambiguity of its effects on women's lives that makes it so difficult to come to a single conclusion here mirrors the in-betweenness, ambiguity, and instability of Jude, the unknown and forgotten. He was the most powerful but also the most vulnerable saint, most efficaciously present in Chicago but just as much so wherever women found him; he was officially represented by the Shrine but imagined into being by the women who needed him; he was recognizable to Catholic girls who had grown up among the saints, but he was a new figure, too, unencumbered by the associations of their childhoods in the enclaves but resonant with the emotions that characterized other bonds there, on heaven and earth; his devotion was presided over by men and shared between women; he was a private figure, brought under the covers at night to hear women's murmured desires and tucked away in purses or office drawers but brought out into the most public places by them so they could tell others who needed him all about their own histories with the saint. Women expressed Jude's ambivalent place in their experience when they said that they were startled by discovering him but that they expected his help, too, or when they claimed never to have heard of him but then recognized him when he turned to them. Any interpretation that would place women on one or the other side of those critical dichotomies is incomplete because it ignores the in-betweenness of Jude in history and women's lives. The challenge here is to consider how it could be that intimacy and dependence of the intense sort that characterized women's bond with Jude (and that so troubled critics of devotionalism) could apparently be the ground of action, choice, autonomy, and healing, for that it was is the historical record of the cult's narratives.

We can begin to explore this strange paradox by looking again at Jude's movements across the landscapes on which the immigrants' daughters dwelled. The saint moved back and forth, in women's purses or cars, for example, or on medals around their necks, between home and work, the enclaves and the suburbs, between the spaces of intimacy and of public responsibility, performance, and achievement. He accompanied the immigrants' daughters—who were themselves in-between figures—as they negotiated their way across the unfamiliar geographies of their new experiences and hopes. By his simultaneous and connecting presence in such disparate environments he served as a bridge among these domains while other figures in women's lives were telling them not only that these hopes, plans, and desires and these different sites of experience were mutually exclusive but that any convergence of them represented a grave spiritual and cultural threat. The devout felt calm and supported knowing that the saint had accompanied them into these places of distress and disorientation.

The power of this in-betweenness to reshape experience is evident in Jude's place in the lives of working women. The devout almost always kept some image of the saint with them at work, usually scattered among other personal effects in a desk drawer. A drawer is both a private place and not: they are opened, co-workers can see into them, and over time—without their having had openly to transgress the rules of workplace decorum—the devout would have made their bond with Jude known to others, which allowed them to tell something of their life histories to their co-workers, often as a way of encouraging them to tell their own in a difficult time. In this way a space was opened at work for storytelling, the exchange of confidence between women, and the expression of compassion and solidarity. Helen wrote me: "My religion is private and I am not considered by others to be any type of 'fanatic.' I did however always have a St. Jude prayer card on my desk and said many daily prayers of request and thanks to him. If co-workers had problems I would suggest prayer to St. Jude and most were aware of my great trust in this saint." Women encouraged each other in the workplace with Jude. One devout, for example, left her prayer card in her desk for her replacement to find on her first day at work. Jude has been so important to American Catholic women at work that some believed this was his special domain; as one told me, "It has been my experience that [St. Jude] is especially good with finding employment and in solving problems related to employment."[21]

But Jude was not there solely as a source of secret, hidden consolation and security (although he certainly was this). In their intimate and comforting bond with the figure tucked away in their drawers or purses the immigrants' daughters have found the confidence to look for work, master new technologies, and cope with office responsibilities, while being told by the various media of their two cultures that they should not be working at all, but if they did they should know their place there, too. Jude helped young women starting out in the 1930s and was with them again in the 1950s and 1960s when they attempted to reenter the workforce after raising their families. He accompanied them to interviews and relieved them a little at least of the distress of leaving their children in the care of family or friends. He helped women with disabilities find suitable employment despite obstacles and prejudice. One woman reported that when she found herself "unjustly removed from my position at my office" and "shifted around," she shared her concerns with a female co-worker, who told her to make a novena to St. Jude; with this encouragement "my case was won and I was restored to my position."[22]

Jude's literal movement across the landscape and between the distinct and discrepant spaces of women's lives was a material representation of a deeper process at work. Any understanding of what transpired in the elision must hold together two things about devotion to St. Jude. First, women imagined Jude with all the childlike, regressive feeling that critics said they did, but at the same time they never lost sight of the difference between him and them. As much as he was the creation of their needs (and so "inside" them), he was separate from the devout imagining him too, independent of their wishes even as he embodied them, free of their control as they struggled to assert it. Remember that the devout *never* hallucinated Jude, aurally or visually; the Shrine has never had to issue a caution about this. Women were *in relation* to Jude, not merged with him. This is the second point: whatever else it is, popular devotionalism is the practice of relationships. Praying is not simply a narrative practice, but a narrative practice addressed *to* someone—who looked back and responded. Prayer is always a relational imaginative activity.

Jude was not a single figure, though. The saint was made of relationships in the past (because he embodied memories and feelings associated with the saints women had prayed to as children and the women they had prayed with), present (because Jude always arrived in the voice and concern of another woman), and even future (because the devout anticipated in their prayers different or better interactions with loved ones). The older devotional triangles were enclosed in contemporary ones, like that of Mrs. P.K., Jude, and the social worker, which accounts for the special intimacy of women's devotional exchanges, even the most fleeting (in schoolyards and hospital corridors).

This multiplicitous figure existed "inside, outside, and at the border," in the language of the British psychoanalyst D. W. Winnicott. Winnicott was describing other sorts of border figures (like a child's invisible companion, or the internalized image of a parent or other relative; others have included in this special pantheon of human creations characters in literature or Scripture or historical figures) that served as ways of anchoring the self as it explored the world in transitional times.[23] The saint did not stand inertly as a kind of hinge between the polarities (between private/public, for example, or childhood/adulthood, past/present, or the enclaves and the America outside them) nor did he dissolve the boundaries between them. Women continued to feel the contradictory demands of the enclaves and their new homes, for example, or the tension between their aspirations and the injunctions of the devotional press. Rather, the saint moved back and forth between the satisfactions and comforts of childhood and the challenges of adulthood, between the mentalities and values of the enclaves and those of the "America" outside, allowing women to draw deep from one to confront the other. Jude was in between, and he allowed the immigrants' daughters to play across the borders others would have made for their experience.

Because the devout never forgot that Jude was separate from them, however much they may have tried to influence his behavior to their advantage, their tie to him had the effect of setting boundaries, not dissolving them. In praying to this other, the devout learned to recognize what they ultimately could not control and to surrender what was beyond their powers. The devotion allowed them to guard against an overwhelmingly intrusive intimacy and curtail the loss of their subjectivities to others. One woman told me that while she was saddened that the marriages of two of her children had ended in divorce, despite her prayers to Jude for them, she "realized that they have separate lives and I have accepted them," an understanding she came to as she reflected on her disappointment with Jude's not giving her what she had wanted. Clara was upset at the time of our conversation that one of her sons had successfully competed to be the goalie on his hockey team, but she also recognized that "we're different people. There's a lot of things I'd like to change [but] you don't interfere with somebody's life. But what I do is pray, 'dear Jesus in heaven, in the name of St. Jude, watch him, because it's dynamite out there.'" Helen wrote that "when the children were teenagers and out on their own for an evening I would ask St. Jude to care for them while I could not." Women found peace for themselves this way and discovered and acknowledged their separateness from their families while they fulfilled their responsibilities as good wives and mothers, too. This capacity to let go in trust and hope was particularly important for the aging parents of handicapped men and women.[24]

The process of setting boundaries in prayer is evident even in women's petitions to Jude for their men. Divorce is not mentioned in the narratives of petition published by the Shrine. The topic was generally off-limits among Catholics and especially so in a devotional culture that, as we have seen, presented abusive husbands as the occasion of women's sanctity; a divorced Catholic who remarries is legally marginalized in the community. But Jude has stood by American Catholic women as they ended hurtful ties. One woman told me that she first called on the saint in the early 1960s, when "I was in a very unhappy marriage," to "help me either straighten it out or get out of it." She continued, "All of a sudden [after praying to St. Jude] things turned around. I had filed for divorce twice before [but] I had always gone back. I didn't have any self-confidence. I never thought that I could support the children [or that I would be] able to get into a job where I [could] have a regular income." Now she went through with it. "I took on all the bills. . . . I was working three jobs, but there were times that I didn't have money in the house for food. And it was very odd, because I'd say to St. Jude, 'I've got to feed these kids,' and people that I hadn't heard from for years, I mean some of them ten [or] fifteen years, and all of a sudden I'd get cash, just enough to buy the groceries that I needed."[25]

But we can see women working on their marriages with Jude even in the accounts printed by the Shrine. Speaking in the company of the saint, women let alcoholic husbands know that their abuse of their families could not continue. The decision to pray to the Patron Saint of Hopeless Causes was a public declaration that a limit had been reached, as men knew when they saw images of the saint appear before them in their homes. The candle lit before the statue in the bedroom or the prayer card taped to the refrigerator signaled new expectations and a new willingness not to hide from the truth anymore. The in-between saint tracked between inside and out, allowing women to represent emergent desires and resolutions as they went on with their lives as they had to. Often such prayers were women's first acknowledgment of the problem to themselves and a crucial step in breaking patterns of denial or overidentification; constant prayer in such crucial times steadied women as they dealt with their husbands' subsequent duplicities, evasions, and anger. When they asked other members of their families to pray to Jude with them, the devout were also insisting that these others recognize the problem as they did, respect the new limits, and end their own contribution to the perpetuation of a situation that was bearing down most heavily on women.[26] One woman told me that she kept Jude's statue in her living room specifically as a reminder of his assistance when she was dealing with her husband's alcoholism; every time this man passed the saint in his house he was reminded of the pain that he had caused his family and of his wife's resolve to end it. Jude has accompanied women to Al-Anon meetings as a trusted witness and companion.[27]

The letters pages mostly describe "hopelessness," of course; not all women faced such extreme difficulties in their marriages. But it is clear from the Shrine's correspondence and especially in conversations with the devout that Jude played an essential role in the way American Catholic women lived their marriages in a time when their own expectations for married life were outpacing what their men may have anticipated and wanted and what Catholic authorities were teaching. With Jude they resisted their parents' choices of spouses for them in the enclaves; as married women, they brought their husbands into their prayers with Jude (sometimes to the Shrine itself), communicating to them their desires and needs, as well as their understanding and experience of particular moments in their common lives, in the idioms of the saints. One woman described this kind of devotional sharing to me: "I became angry at my husband and to please me he took me (26 miles) to the south side of Chicago for a daily novena."[28] Not every man could drive to the Shrine like this, but all could acknowledge the seriousness of their wives' concerns. This was another of the devotional triangles constituted by the devotion. Women thus secured their husbands' participation in their struggles and took them into the world as they imagined it to be. With Jude's help the immigrants' daughters made the marriages they wanted for themselves, or at least more closely approximated them.

This is not to say that everything women accomplished with Jude's help was benevolent or that their impulses were always benign. Isabel was forever praying to Jude for her children and forever telling them that she was—which meant that she was constantly letting them know that whatever they were doing had driven her to the extremes of worry. Her prayers were unsublimated expressions of what she thought was best for them. Clara was more scrupulous. She told me that she would never ask Jude to prevent her son from becoming a hockey goalie because she knew how much the young man wanted this; she would pray instead for his safety if he made the team. These are two quite different ways that women could bring Jude into their family lives, and the devout did both. Women obviously wielded Jude against family members in their determination to get what they wanted them to do; he enabled them to be intrusive, domineering, demanding. Consider the dynamics in the following story from a longer letter sent me by a woman from an Eastern state:

> I have two sons from a previous marriage (24–25). The youngest, Eric, has been a burden all of his life. Before I started praying to St. Jude, Eric was overweight, homosexual and did not work half the time. Since I started praying to St. Jude, Eric has lost about 100 pounds, started dating girls, and is working steady. At first, I did not tell Eric that I was praying to St. Jude for him. The day that I told him he laughed and said, "You don't believe in that 's——' do you?" Later that day he had an automobile accident. It was not his fault, but the car was pretty badly damaged. Nothing was ever said, but my husband and I brought him a St. Jude medal to wear around his neck. When we gave it to him he put it on. It has since worn out and he asked me to get him another.[29]

Jude is asked here to serve as the conductor of this family's currents of resentment, disappointment, anger, and recrimination. He is forced on Eric, called to judge and shame him, and although the young man appears to surrender at the end (I am a little suspicious, though, about his medal "wearing out"), it would not be surprising if Eric—and everyone else who has been thrust into this kind of relationship with Jude—came to hate the saint with as great a passion as others loved him. Devotional practice is never innocent; it may be effective, but it is not always decent, respectful, selfless. Jude emerged as a powerful figure in family conflicts and crises, which meant that often enough he bore the marks of these conflicts. So the point here is not that women were always right and good in what they did with Jude, but that with Jude's help they were always working on their family lives, for better or worse.

WHEN JUDE SAID "NO":
THE PROBLEM OF THEODICY IN THE DEVOTION

The devout did not start out from the perspective that life was going to be easy. "There is going to be illness," Judy told me (from her own considerable experience of it), "there is going to be death, you cannot escape that. Sometimes I think making the novena is just to give you the strength to get through what you have to get through." Isabel put it more bluntly: "Nobody ever promised you a perfect life here." The devout acknowledged the inevitability of bad times and so they never blamed Jude for them. They believed the saint did what he could for them in a hard world; expecting pain, they were grateful when it was not too bad, like the woman who thanked Jude for saving her son's life in Vietnam, even though he was gravely wounded.

The devout have been grateful for small consolations, "half-granted" requests, and "almost immediate help."[30] One woman wrote the Shrine that although she missed her husband terribly, she was "happy" Jude had answered her prayers for his reconciliation with the church on his deathbed. Another was grateful that even though her nephew was still drinking, he was managing to hold on to his job. "After losing their home and the death of their 4½ year old daughter," another wrote, "my son and his wife were hopeless in debt. I prayed to Saint Jude and they are almost on their feet again." There was an unexpected grace amid life's difficulties, thanks to St. Jude.[31]

Women made different petitions to the saint as their various crises unfolded. They struggled in their narratives of petition to ascertain the limits of what was possible to them in light of what was already happening. They elaborated earlier prayers, reformulated their requests as circumstances changed, voiced new understandings and needs, and contended with disappointments and setbacks. They warned themselves not to be "selfish" in their prayers, by which they meant not clinging to their initial hopes.[32] They prayed to be able to understand unforeseen turns of events. Prayer was thus an ongoing process of discernment, self-examination, reconsideration, and adjustment, a flexible and supple medium for living with both hope and clarity. The devout themselves called their praying to Jude "realistic." You have to remember one thing, Clara cautioned me:

"There's Miracles, and Miracles, and Miracles"
207

St. Jude is not God. He may request [something for you] or he may be trying to help you, but maybe you can't get what you're asking for. I'm a realistic person. I would always like to put steak on the table for my children, that would be my goal. Definitely the best. But if I can't give them the best, I give them the next thing to it. Not excellent, but very good. I put pork chops [on the table]. . . . All life is not steak, but there are other things you can fill in with that are just as good. That's the way I look at it. I mean, I haven't got a well mother, there was no: Your mother is completely cured. But my mother is alive and existing. What more could I ask for?

You do not pray for what you want, another woman explained, but for what is best for you, and then you take life as it comes. Jude is there amid life's "breaks," not in place of them. As we saw in the previous chapter, the devout sometimes did not even request the saint directly "heal" them or give them a specific grace, only that he help them with the courage to endure.[33]

Prayer was thus also an intimate pedagogy in how to comport oneself in terrible times: by praying women learned patience, steadfastness, determination, commitment, and courage, the necessary virtues of adulthood. They discovered what they could do for themselves and others in unfamiliar circumstances. They learned how to attend to their hopes and speak their needs precisely and, most importantly, they were taught that it was appropriate to hope, to be confident, and to speak. The movement of the devotion, as we saw in the past two chapters, was always outward, from private to public, from the closed spaces of sickness, hopelessness, abandonment, and anxiety to the openness of saying what one really wanted. In this way, devotion to St. Jude worked against the shaming disciplines of the devotional press: there was no story too terrible to tell St. Jude. At the same time, though, the devotion also instructed women in preparing themselves for grief, sorrow, and defeat. The devout have been grateful to Jude for trimming the insistent pressure of their desires, which left unchecked could have defeated them most profoundly.[34]

The discipline of praying to Jude was not the harsh stoicism endorsed in devotional culture, however, but a courageous response to life's troubles undertaken with love and trust. In the company of the figure in between, women moved back and forth during crises between hope and acceptance, fantasy and an acknowledgment of the inevitable. "I turned to Saint Jude," a woman wrote me, "in Feb. [1981] when my 15 yr. old son was diagnosed as a victim of cancer. Naturally my first petition was [for] my son's cure. My faith was strong so I believed this miracle could happen. Never before in my life had I needed a miracle. I believed he could be cured and that he would survive." But "God's plan was different" and the boy died. Still, this women did not feel that Jude had abandoned her. In time she played a role in opening a Ronald McDonald House for young cancer patients in her community, and she attributed her strength in this endeavor to the novenas she had been making to Jude since her son's cancer was discovered. The saint *had* heard her prayers, she was able to say bravely, but in a way she had not expected. It was never a matter of simply enduring in the devotion, but of enduring confidently in the saint's continuing love.[35] To accept God's will, as this was experienced in Jude, was not the end of the story or the imposition of silent submission (as the devotional press had it), but the opening up of the story to unexpected developments and unforeseen movements of love.[36] In Clara's words, "there's miracles, and miracles, and miracles."

DIALECTICS OF GENDER AND HOPE IN AMERICAN CATHOLIC DEVOTIONALISM

St. Jude, the unknown but familiar saint, stood at the points where distinct zones of human experiencing, as many tend to think of them, converged: inside/outside, spiritual/material, past/present/future, the political and the psychological, fantasy and reality. Because figures like Jude are both outside in culture (in the control of the Shrine clergy, in the wider domain of devotionalism) and inside the hearts and imaginations of the people who need them and live their lives with them, they serve to connect levels and domains of experience. This is what made Jude and other figures like him such powerful conduits of gender structures and social impositions.

But Jude was not stable: indeed, he was so alive with powers, feelings, and resonances on so many different levels, so filled with relationships, that the devout were themselves sometimes afraid of him. This apprehension surfaced in the nearness of Judas to the imagining of Jude: the beloved saint might not be who he appeared to be; he might betray the trust a needy person placed in him. It also emerged in the ideas that Jude would take something away for everything he gave or that once he had entered a person's life there would be no stopping the chain of inversions initiated by him. To come before the saint, in other words, was to come into an exciting but also dangerous place where it was sensed that the fixed and frozen experience of hopelessness could be dissolved.

Jude was the site where "reality" and "fantasy" converged, where play, illusion, and hope intersected with the constraints of the present. It was not that

"There's Miracles, and Miracles, and Miracles"

women became infantile in the devotion but that the past and the present interpenetrated and in this way made possible alternative experiences of a "future" that had previously seemed closed. In his company, before his eyes, women found their desires and the voice to speak them, the security to acknowledge them even if they were not satisfied. This was the devotion's dialectic of hope, enclosed within its dialectic of gender.

So the dialectic of gender could never do its work the way structurally inclined analysts of women's social experience imagine. Jude did not suture women into gendered roles, nor subject them to particular gender destiny, because Jude was too volatile for this. It is best to think of figures like Jude as supple, multidimensional idioms for working on the self and the world in an oscillating dialectic between "fantasy" and "reality," self and other, objective and subjective, past and present, submission and resistance. Inflected by desire, Jude was not a stable agent of the culture; born in culture and history, he was not a completely trustworthy ally of the self. Figures like Jude are cultural double agents, constituting and destabilizing both culture and self.

Devotional culture was itself made of many voices and of many competing values and perspectives. The immigrants' daughters not only discovered who they were in the dense devotional world that developed in American Catholicism after 1925 but created and imagined themselves, too, manipulating and altering the available grammars of gender they found there. Religious traditions are zones of improvisation and conflict, and making meaning within a tradition is a dialectical process. Much of the raw material of devotional culture was poisonous to them, as we saw, and Jude's cult was not free of this poison. Still, the analysis must be dialectical: through the power of their desire and need, awakened by and in response to the new challenges and possibilities of their American lives, and with the flexible media of devotional culture—the images they could take away with them into their rooms and beds, the water and oil they could touch to their pains in gestures and rituals of their own improvising—the immigrants' daughters could do much with what they inherited. The political philosopher Göran Therborn has pointed out that the word "subject" has two contradictory senses: to be subject to (in the sense of domination) and to be subject of (in the sense of autonomy, as in the subject of one's own story).[37] Devotionalism made women subjects in this dual sense.

Praying is the practice of making and entering alternative stories. For a moment in their prayers, the devout could enter the world as they wanted it to be, in the company of the figure whose gaze legitimated and encouraged their hopes. "Reality" itself is a construct, although this is not how it is commonly experienced by those who must live within it. Particular arrangements of gender, class, race, are treated as natural or given, part of the taken-for-grantedness of the world, even though they are made and sustained in culture. But in their prayers to Jude in disorienting times women experienced the "reality of the reality-refusing imagination," to borrow social theorist Joel Kovel's phrase for this sort of creativity: they refashioned the world and then directed themselves toward this new horizon become real in the moment of praying.[38] This is why the Shrine's blessed oil and water were thought to be so powerful by the devout and so dangerous by those whose responsibility it was to control the cult: they were the solvents of the givenness of experience. The material culture of the devotion—its prayer cards, statues, medals, dashboard figurines—were the media with which women played on their world. Over and over again in different words Jude's clients have written to say that "seemingly impossible cases" revealed themselves to be not so with Jude's help. As women prayed to Jude they sensed a subtle shifting of the axes of their experience; the closed space of hopelessness was opened. "When I pray to St. Jude," a woman wrote the Shrine in 1961, in a sentence that may stand here for all the narratives this saint's devout have written, spoken, whispered, cried to him over the years, "I once more feel that there is hope and to despair would gain me nothing."[39] He heard them, he saw them, he loved them, and for this, realistically, the immigrants' daughters thanked St. Jude.

Notes

Works frequently cited have been
identified by the following abbreviations:

AER	*American Ecclesiastical Review*
AM	*Ave Maria*
CD	*Catholic Digest*
CM	*Catholic Mind*
CW	*Catholic World*
CWW	*Catholic Women's World*
HP	*Hospital Progress*
HPR	*Homiletic and Pastoral Review*
MSH	*Messenger of the Sacred Heart*
SJJ	*St. Jude's Journal*
StAM	*St. Anthony's Messenger*
VSJ	*Voice of St. Jude*

I have identified my sources in the following ways. Written responses to questions about devotion to St. Jude prepared by devout during novenas in 1987 and 1988 are identified as *Per.comm.*; letters received from devout as *Per.corr.*; and telephone conversations as *800*. Each of these prefixes is followed by the devout's initials (fictitious but consistent throughout), gender, age, place of residence, and marital status. A question mark by itself in any of these categories indicates that definite information was lacking; a question mark followed by an entry in a category means that I had sufficient grounds to guess but am not absolutely certain. A fuller discussion of these sources may be found in the Preface.

Correspondents to the *Voice of St. Jude* and *St. Jude's Journal* were usually identified by their initials and place of residence; sometimes they were also given the titles Mrs., Mr., or Miss—but not always, to my great frustration. Correspondents whose gender I could not determine from textual evidence are indicated by a question mark (for example, ?F.K., Brooklyn, N.Y., *VSJ* [July 1949]); I added the title Mr. in brackets to those writers I could identify as men. All other letters came from women. In other words, if a letter is cited without specific gender information (for example, L.E.S., San Pedro, Calif., *VSJ* [September 1951]), the writer was definitely a woman. Readers will notice that occasionally I support an observation about some aspect of women's participation in the devotion with reference to a letter or letters written by devout whose gender I could not determine. The letters in all of these cases contained useful and unambiguous information *about* women, even though they were not clearly written *by* women.

PREFACE

1. My point here is not to impugn the honor of the men responsible for the devotion, who invented Father Robert in an effort to simplify their dealings with Jude's extensive and far-flung clientele. My respect for the Claretians will be clear throughout this book, but I will emphasize it now: the priests and lay people who have tended devotion to Jude over much of this century in Chicago have been thoughtful, careful, and scrupulously honest in their charge. I have discussed the devotion's history frankly, in this matter of Father Robert and others, and leave it to readers to come to their own judgments about the business end of this particular devotion. But I want my own assessment to be on record.

2. I have changed the names of all my sources.

3. See Giddens, *Constitution of Society,* 122–130.

4. 800: Frank K.-M-66-Los Angeles-D(?); "better pray-er": 800: AB-M-55+?-Pittsburgh-D.

5. I was extremely conservative in making these gender determinations, restricting myself to those cases only where there was absolute textual evidence to do so, such as a reference to "my husband" or "my boyfriend." It would not have been unreasonable to have identified several hundred of the letters that offered less certain grounds for making determinations as coming from women, too, either because of particular usages (like

calling a child "my baby"), allusions to the correspondents' everyday life (including comments about staying home all day to take care of children) or descriptions of devotional practices that I knew more generally from my research were performed only by women (rubbing a sick person's body with Jude's oil, for instance). But I did not number these in my tabulations of women correspondents, which means that the gender discrepancy cited in the text is probably underestimated. Letters from the years 1942 to 1944 are not included in this gender survey, because I did not initially have access to them. The same patterns hold for these years, however.

6. The specific questions I invited devout to respond to in writing were: 1. When did you first turn to St. Jude? 2. How would you describe your circumstances at the time you first turned to St. Jude? 3. How would you describe St. Jude? What do you think he looks like? 4. Do you think it more likely that a man or a woman would pray to St. Jude? Why? 5. Have you ever shared your devotion to St. Jude with another member of your family or with a friend? Can you describe an occasion on which you introduced someone else to St. Jude? 6. How often do you pray to St. Jude? 7. Who else do you pray to? 8. What kinds of requests is St. Jude particularly good at answering? 9. For which family member have you prayed most often? 10. Do you ever pray to St. Jude when you have no specific request to make? 11. Do you have a statue of St. Jude at home? Where do you keep it? 12. Why do you keep it there? 13. Do you have a prayer card to St. Jude? Where do you keep it? What do you do with it? 14. How do you show your gratitude for St. Jude's help? 15. When you pray to St. Jude for someone, do you usually tell that person you are praying for him or her? Why or why not? 16. Do you think that women need a friend like St. Jude more than men do? Why or why not? 17. Please add anything you wish about your friendship with St. Jude.

I left ample space for replies, and almost everyone who chose to write did so at great length. The language of the questions (the phrase "pray to St. Jude," for example) intentionally reflects common devotional usage.

7. To avoid confusing readers who may have first encountered these sources in one of my earlier articles about the devotion, written as the book was evolving, I will note here that I mistakenly identified an aspect of Clara's story in "Have You Ever Prayed to St. Jude?" 136. Clara first prayed to St. Jude when she found herself torn between her responsibilities as a mother and a daughter, a story I will return to later, not—as I write in this article—when she was nursing a dying father. For a while I considered mixing up little details of these women's stories in order better to conceal their identities, even from their own kin (maybe even from themselves), but I eventually decided that this was becoming an instance of academic scrupulosity, a variant among researchers of the familiar venial sin. There is really nothing so compromising in any of these accounts or so secret that close family members would be shocked to learn of it if they did not already know about it.

8. See Dolan, *American Catholic Experience,* 394. I have also been helped in preparing this brief introductory review of modern American Catholic journalism by Arnold J. Sparr, "The Catholic Literary Revival in America, 1920–1960," Ph.D. diss., University of Wisconsin-Madison, 1985; and Baumgartner, *Catholic Journalism.*

1. This history of South Chicago is based on Año Nuevo de Kerr, "Chicano Settlements in Chicago"; Jones and Wilson, *Mexican in Chicago;* Reisler, "Mexican Immigrant"; A. Jones, "Mexican Colonies in Chicago"; Gamio, *Mexican Immigration;* and on the recollections of people in the neighborhood with whom I spoke.

2. This correspondence is cited in Joseph M. Puigvi, C.M.F., "Historia de la Parroquia de Ntra. Sra. de Guadalupe," in *Dedication of Our Lady of Guadalupe Church* (Chicago: John H. Hannigan, 1928), unpaginated. It is also mentioned in Victor Julian, C.M.F., "Necrology: Father James Tort, C.M.F.," unpublished ms., p. 7, Claretian Provincial Archives [henceforth: PA].

3. Mundelein's interest in Mexican Catholics is noted in Shanabruch, *Chicago's Catholics,* 210–211.

4. Eugene Sugranes, a member of this first team of priests, identifies the location of these in a brief history he wrote of the church: "Catechism centers were established at strategic points; in Clyde on the C[hicago]. B[urlington]. and Q[uincy]. R.R.; at Gresham and Blue Island on the Rock Island R.R.; at Franklin Park; at 38th Street of Santa Fe R.R. [*sic*]; at 83rd and Vincennes on the Western Indiana R.R.; at Waukegan and at Milwaukee, Wisconsin." See "History of Our Lady of Guadalupe, So. Chicago, Ill.," in *Dedication of Our Lady of Guadalupe Church.*

5. This sketch of Tort's biography is based on Julian, "Necrology"; F. Smith, "Load of Bricks Stumps Priest"; James Tort, C.M.F., "Passion Flowers and Easter Lilies," *VSJ* (April 1935): 7; George Hull, "Life Begins at Forty," *VSJ* (June 1935): 7–10; Joachim DePrada, C.M.F., "Our Founder is Dead," *VSJ* (June 1955): 34. The claim of Tort's noble birth is made in "Fr. Tort Able to Attend Mass," *VSJ* (July 1936), p. 16.

6. That this was Tort's explicit strategy is confirmed by Julian, "Necrology," 10, and by Father James Maloney, a former director of the National Shrine and recent pastor of Our Lady of Guadalupe Church. Father Maloney has graciously given me permission to cite our conversation, which took place in January 1988. Mundelein's fiscal philosophy is discussed in Shanabruch, *Chicago's Catholics,* 162–163.

7. "Throngs Witness Breaking of Ground for Our Lady of Guadalupe," reprinted in *Dedication of Our Lady of Guadalupe Church.* The ethnic composition at the cornerstone ceremony is described in "Bishop Diaz Lays Corner Stone of Our Lady of Guadalupe," in ibid.

8. "Bishop Diaz Lays Corner Stone."

9. My understanding of the financial history of the church comes mainly from a manuscript history of the Claretians' work in the United States written sometime in the 1940s by Reverend Joseph Berengueras, C.M.F. The study, which is written in Spanish, is preserved in the Claretian Archives in Rome. An English translation is kept in the Provincial Archives in Chicago, and all of my references are to this version. Berengueras puts the archdiocese's contribution at $80,000, whereas Julian says it was $90,000. Mundelein's insistence on parochial financial autonomy and accountability was not unusual among

this generation of businessmen-prelates; see O'Toole, *Militant and Triumphant*, 149, for evidence of similar demands by Boston's Cardinal O'Connell. Berengueras comments on Mundelein's position: "The Cardinal's commitment had been verbal, and perhaps our people had misunderstood it."

10. Reference to Chile is made in "How Devotion to St. Jude Began in America," *SJJ* (December 1960): 1; and "St. Jude: The Saint of the Impossible," *SJJ* (May 1963): 2. The latter dates the origins of the Chilean shrine to 1911 and describes it as "a large shrine . . . which still attracts many petitioners even today." The association between obscure holy figures and marginal elements of a population is evident in other religious contexts as well. C. Stevan Harrell, for example, writes that prostitutes in Taiwan are often associated with an intermediate class of underworld being, part god and part ghost ("When a Ghost Becomes a God," in *Religion and Ritual in Chinese Society*, ed. Arthur P. Wolf (Stanford, Calif., 1974), 195.

11. The earliest accounts of the founding of the devotion are James Tort, C.M.F., "Dedication Anniversary of the National Shrine of Saint Jude," *VSJ* (February 1935): 12–13; Hull, "Life Begins at Forty," 8, and Schneider, "Tenth Anniversary." None of these mentions the side altar as the location of the two competing statues. On the other hand, a comic book about the devotion published in *VSJ* in October 1954, "Jude: The Forgotten Saint," highlights the switching of the statues on the side altar as an indication of what Jude and Thérèse themselves wanted. Two later accounts simply mention that Thérèse was in a "prominent position" somewhere in the church ("How Devotion to Saint Jude Began in America"; and "Personal Devotion to a Saint," *SJJ* [May 1963]: 2). Julian, "Necrology," 11, emphasizes the competition between the two saints, but differs from all of the other accounts by putting Thérèse in the inferior place. The detail about Mother Cabrini (who died in 1917 and was canonized in 1949) comes from James Maloney, C.M.F.

12. Tort's awareness of the Carmelite shrine was mentioned by Father Maloney. A brief sketch of the origins of the devotion to the Little Flower in Chicago may be found in *The Sword* (May 1948): 106–116; information about the national devotion is in the *Little Flower Magazine*, which was published monthly by the Carmelite Fathers of Oklahoma City until the mid-1970s. The Claretians' struggles with devotional pirates is described in Robert J. Leuver, C.M.F., to John M. Kiely, April 26, 1961, and Leuver to Mr. Charles Cannon, May 5, 1961, Archives at the National Shrine of St. Jude (henceforth SA). For other examples of devotional competition see the warning in *AM* 49 (January 7, 1939): inside front cover; and "From the Shrine," *VSJ* (December 1941): 17.

13. For evidence of the participation of people of many different ethnic backgrounds in the devotion's first decade, see, for example, "A Nine-Day Triumph," *VSJ* (December 1942): 3–4; and "Novena Closing at National Shrine," *VSJ* (December 1943): 5. The first classes at the Claretian seminary in Momence, Illinois, were made up of boys from many different neighborhood enclaves as well; see "First St. Jude's Seminary Claretians from Chicago Ordained," *VSJ* (June 1943): 9. The phrases about competition between Jude and Thérèse are from, respectively, Schneider, "Tenth Anniversary," 13, and Julian, "Necrology," 11.

14. This figure is recorded in "Jude: The Forgotten Saint."

15. Julian, "Necrology," 12, mentions St. Jude's Chicago address. The figures for 1935 are from James Tort, C.M.F., "Bishop Preciado Presides at Novena," *VSJ* (November 1935): 15, 17; see also the note from the Shrine clergy on the letters page, *VSJ* (December 1935): 17. Information about the novena in 1937 comes from James Schons, C.M.P., "St. Jude's Feast Celebrated at National Shrine," *VSJ* (October 1937): 5–6; and Anthony Catalina, C.M.F., "The Saint Jude Novena," *VSJ* (March 1938): 10. For the economic context of that year's celebration see McElvaine, *Great Depression*, 298.

16. Information on the founding of the League of Saint Jude is from Hull, "Life Begins at Forty," 8; "Jude: The Forgotten Saint"; Julian, "Necrology," 13–14; and Berengueras, manuscript history. On the Police Branch see Julian, "Necrology," 13–14; Hull, "Life Begins at Forty," 8–9; Schneider, "Tenth Anniversary," 15–18; "Jude: The Forgotten Saint"; "Guns and Missals," *VSJ* (October 1954): 28–29.

17. John O'Brien, C.M.F., "An Outstanding Visitor," *VSJ* (August 1936): 11–12. The *Voice* was preceded by a less ambitious publication, the *St. Jude Bulletin*, in the summer of 1934, according to Hull, "Life Begins at Forty," 9.

18. This emphasis on the strong immigrant family is widely shared among contemporary American historians of the "new immigration" who set themselves in opposition to the tragic historiography of immigration best exemplified by Oscar Handlin's *The Uprooted*. For an important expression of the newer orientation see Bodnar, *Transplanted*.

19. The picture I draw here of the changing nature of the organization of American Catholic family history and social life in the years after World War I is based on Dolan, *American Catholic Experience*, 349–417; Shanabruch, *Chicago's Catholics*, 155–232; J. Thomas, *American Catholic Family*; Brinkley, *Voices of Protest*, 82–106; Gordon, *Heroes of Their Own Lives*, 168–203; Fisher, *Catholic Counterculture*, 71–99; O'Toole, *Militant and Triumphant*; Tentler, *Seasons of Grace*, 297–527; Jones and Holli, *Ethnic Frontier*; and the following studies of particular communities: J. Smith, *Family Connections*; Nelli, *Italians in Chicago*; Yans-McLaughlin, *Family and Community*; Cinel, *From Italy to San Francisco*; Baily, "Adjustment of Italian Immigrants"; Mormino, *Immigrants on the Hill*; Bukowczyk, *And My Children Did Not Know Me*; Obidinski, "Ethnic to Status Group"; Ostafin, "Polish Peasant in Transition"; Polzin, *Polish-Americans*; Wrobel, *Our Way*; Parot, *Polish Catholics in Chicago*; William J. Galush, "Faith and Fatherland: Dimensions of Polish-American Ethnoreligion, 1875–1975," in Miller and Marzik, *Immigrants and Religion*, 84–102; D. Clark, *Irish in Philadelphia*; McCaffrey, *Irish Diaspora in America*; McCaffrey et al., *Irish in Chicago*; A. Olson, *St. Louis Germans*; Josef J. Barton, "Religion and Cultural Change in Czech Immigrant Communities, 1850–1920," in Miller and Marzik, *Immigrants and Religion*, 3–24; M. Mark Stolarik, "Immigration, Education, and the Social Mobility of Slovaks, 1870–1930," in Miller and Marzik, *Immigrants and Religion*, 103–116; Ducharme, *Shadows of the Trees*.

20. Kerby Miller describes Irish Americans in this period as "Janus-faced, divided between bourgeois aspirations and proletarian realities, torn by conflicting loyalties to the United States and Ireland" (*Emigrants and Exiles*, 524); see also McCaffrey, *Irish Diaspora*

in America, 152. On divided loyalties among Polish Americans at this time see, among others, Polzin, *Polish-Americans*, 133; Bukowczyk, *And My Children Did Not Know Me*, 66–67.

21. For a general perspective on this particular development see Gordon, *Heroes of Their Own Lives*, 188–189; on the emergence of adolescence in Polish American communities see, for example, Ostafin, "Polish Peasant in Transition," 267, 312. Cinel, *From Italy to San Francisco*, 125–126; J. Smith, *Family Connections*, 73–75, discuss the subject among Italians. Almost all studies of immigrant communities in the 1920s and 1930s include some mention of this emergent tension between the first and second generations.

22. J. Thomas, *American Catholic Family*, 99–169. On intraethnic marriage by Polish Americans see Polzin, *Polish-Americans*, 167. Bukowczyk notes that by the late 1920s, second-generation Polish Americans did not object to interethnic marriages (*And My Children Did Not Know Me*, 71); see also Ostafin, "Polish Peasant in Transition," 254. On ethnic groups see J. Olson, *Catholic Immigrants in America;* Rosenzweig sees this pattern of intermarriage among ethnic groups as well under way in Worcester in the 1920s and 1930s (*Eight Hours*, 182 n. 27). Italians in St. Louis, for another example, began marrying persons from families outside their parents' regions in southern Italy as well as non-Italians in the late 1930s and 1940s, according to Mormino, *Immigrants on the Hill*, 73. O'Toole found increasing rates of Irish-German intermarriage in Boston after 1917 (*Militant and Triumphant*, 150). All of the sources cited in note 19 above have some discussion of this movement.

23. J. Smith, *Family Connections*, 118–121. Dolan, *American Catholic Experience*, 357. Dolan also describes the loss of the sense of community that had developed in the immigrant enclaves and generally considers the years 1920–1960 as a period of many exciting but also disorienting transitions in American Catholic social life. "The new social environment" of the suburbs and areas of second settlement within cities "challenged the immigrant church to change," he writes, and "how it met this challenge constitutes the most important chapter of American Catholic history in the first half of the twentieth century" (362). Greeley sees a "profound modification" in American Catholic culture as a consequence of this geographic shift (*Church and Suburbs*, 52). On the movement to the suburbs in this period generally see Miller and Nowak, *Fifties*, 133. Miller and Nowak date the beginnings of suburbanization in the Northeast, the cities around the Great Lakes, and on the West Coast to the 1930s and 1940s. The quotation about Irish Americans is from K. Miller, *Emigrants and Exiles*, 522; see also McCaffrey, *Irish Diaspora in America*, 158–159. Ostafin says that while family loyalty remained strong among Polish Americans in these years, it had become a matter of personal decision and value ("Polish Peasant in Transition," 280); see also Polzin, *Polish-Americans*, 135; Obidinski, "Ethnic to Status Group," 51–52. Cinel, writing about Italians in San Francisco, refers to this as a "mass movement" and estimates that between 1938 and 1961, 40 percent of married Italian Americans left their old neighborhoods in the city (*From Italy to San Francisco*, 125–130); see also Baily, "Adjustment of Italian Immigrants," 292.

24. Ostafin observes, for example, that "in place of tried and tested behavior, the

younger generations of the Polish peasant have to face the burden of painful thought, disturbed and conflicting feelings, and contradictory action," as they make their way out of the enclaves ("Polish Peasant in Transition," 283). James Fisher sees a "gradual but persistent transformation" of American Catholicism in these years "from a defensive subculture to a widely diffused body, vulnerable to the insecurities freedom and mobility produce" (*Catholic Counterculture*, 82).

25. Writing about the 1950s, Mintz and Kellogg note the culture of anxiety about children in isolated suburban families (*Domestic Revolutions*, 188). For examples of people praying to St. Jude for some member of their family to succeed in this culture of credentials see: ?W.J.O., Chicago, *VSJ* (April 1935); ?H.C.L., Chicago, *VSJ* (April 1935); Mrs. J., Wisconsin Rapids, Wis., *VSJ* (April 1935); Mrs. A.C., Bronx, N.Y., *VSJ* (August 1937); ?C.W., New York, *VSJ* (April 1943). Petition slips prepared by the Shrine, which enabled the devout conveniently to check off the things they wanted to call to Jude's attention, included categories for professional and educational success. See, for example, "My Thanksgivings and Petitions," *VSJ* (May 1948), 7. On Catholic desire for more education for their children in these years see Greeley, *Ethnicity, Denomination, and Inequality*, 60. On intergenerational tension among Polish Americans in this period see Ostafin, "Polish Peasant in Transition," 281; and especially Bukowczyk, *And My Children Did Not Know Me*, 72. I have discussed this aspect of Italian American culture more fully in "Fault of Memory."

26. Mahony, "Our Friend, the Hospital Chaplain," 1261. A survey of Catholic sermons in the 1950s revealed that half of them were devoted to the subject of money (Dolan, *American Catholic Experience*, 382); Greeley says that suburban priests lived in "a never-ending financial crisis," *Church and Suburbs*, 64–65; see also O'Toole, *Militant and Triumphant*, 159, and, for quotations, 211, 241.

27. Dolan writes, "The thirty years after World War I was the time when devotional Catholicism hit its peak" (*American Catholic Experience*, 384); see also O'Toole, *Militant and Triumphant*, 21. Nolan and Nolan point out that the formation of new devotional cults peaked in European Catholicism in the middle years of the twentieth century as well (*Christian Pilgrimage*, 104). On the specific devotions mentioned in the paragraph see "Tickets to heaven for persons of all creeds," *VSJ* (July 1946): 20; Donovan, "Perpetual Help Wafers"; "Join the League"; R. Miller, "Lourdes of the West"; Gluckert, "Slice of Heaven."

28. The pamphlets on good health are mentioned in *StAM* 48 (June 1940): 48; information on the lilies comes from "St. Anthony's Lilies," ibid., 40 (June 1932): inside front cover. On the Shrine of the Little Flower see the advertisements in *Little Flower Magazine* 14 (January 1934): 24, 31; the night-light is offered in "Bedroom Nightlight for Private Devotions to the Little Flower," ibid., 14 (March 1934): 29.

29. Donovan, "Novenas and Devotional Tastes." The radio demagogue Father Coughlin began his public career at least in part to pay off a mortgage (Brinkley, *Voices of Protest*, 82–92), and the well-trained readiness of American Catholics to contribute to priests in financial need, especially when these needy men were affiliated with shrines and saint

devotions (as Coughlin was initially), helps explain the rapidity of his rise. Warning against sale of shrine in Father Breen to Father Provincial, September 6, 1922, Shrine of the North American Martyrs file. Fordham University Archives, New York.

30. "Burn A Novena Vigil Light," *VSJ* (January 1939); "Purgatorial Society of the Immaculate Heart of Mary," *VSJ* (November 1947): 13. On women and advertising in this period see Cowan, "Two Washes"; Marchand, *Advertising the American Dream;* and Lears, *Fables of Abundance,* esp. 209. On the miraculous in the nineteenth century see Taves, *Household of Faith,* 66–67.

31. Rudolph M. Ellensohn, "Personally Yours," *VSJ* (August 1947): 23. Ellensohn worked at the periodical. For an example of the way Tort promoted the Purgatorial Society see James Tort, C.M.F., "November: Month of the Holy Souls," *VSJ* (November 1935): 5. Lay people who volunteered their services as "promoters" of the cult in its earliest days received a free gift of a statue of Jude ("Join the St. Jude's League," *VSJ* [January 1935], inside front cover). Subscribers to the magazine also received small gifts. The promotion for the statue of the Infant of Prague appears in advertisement, "This Beautiful Image of the Miraculous Infant Jesus of Prague," *VSJ* (October 1951): n.p. A headline proclaims that the statue is "ABSOLUTELY FREE," but the fine print explains that it is free for a ten-day trial period, after which the Infant costs five dollars (six for the "Deluxe Statue"). The wartime shrine is from advertisement, "First Time Ever Offered! Home Shrine of St. Christopher[,] Patron of Travelers," *VSJ* (September 1944): 20.

32. The reference to slot machines is from Delaney, "Tuesday Night Novena"; the second quotation comes from F. C. Smith, "Spurious Piety," 15. For a stinging attack on devotionalism, first delivered at a conference of the American Catholic Hospital Association in 1920, see Schlarman, "Ite, Missa Est." Schlarman, who was Bishop of Peoria at the time, derided individual devotions, especially those involving some sort of financial component, as "a sort of *spiritual capitalism.*" Donovan's comments about the suspicions of chary churchmen are from "Perpetual Novena." For expressions of clerical anxiety about the effects of devotionalism on the quality of faith see F. C. Smith, "Spurious Piety," 17, and Gillis, "Are Medals Superstitious?" Smith complains that "one comes across leaflets, printed usually without ecclesiastical approbation or the 'imprimatur' of the bishop, proclaiming the power of some relic or medal or other object to obtain all kinds of spiritual and temporal favors" (16). On clerical racketeers see, for example, "Law of Faith"; F. C. Smith, "Spurious Piety," 16; Gillis, "Are Medals Superstitious?" 14–15. The word "rackets" is used by one of Donovan's correspondents, quoted in "Perpetual Novena," 254.

Very little work has been done on American Protestant devotionalism in these years, despite a new concern for the subject among historians of colonial religion, but Harrell, *All Things Are Possible,* has useful information on Protestant piety in the twentieth century. Popular devotions served Paul Blanshard well in his vicious attacks on the church after the Second World War. "The hierarchy professes enthusiastic admiration for science on the upper cultural level," Blanshard taunted, while on the lower levels, "the exploitation of scapulars, ancient knucklebones, rusty nails from 'the true cross,' and pictures engraved on grave clothes by urea goes on continuously." Catholic devotionalism, according to Blanshard, constituted a "religious-commercial fraud" that served to impede the nation's progress toward "efficient democracy" by keeping the laity in a "perpetually depressed cultural tradition," while it exposed the hypocrisy of the hierarchy and revealed the constraints under which all Catholic intellectuals labored, disqualifying them for full participation in national culture. The sentence about the hierarchy's hypocrisy is from Blanshard, *American Freedom and Catholic Power*, 223; all others from idem, *Communism, Democracy, and Catholic Power*, 233–234. For Catholic celebrations of the possibility that the saints constituted a barrier between themselves and American (or more generally modern) culture, see Walsh, "What Are Saints?"; James, "Saint as Controversialist"; and Woywod, "Peculiar Use of Images."

33. Donovan, "Novenas and Devotional Tastes," 643–44.

34. Berengueras, manuscript history; also "Copy of the Report on the Residence at Our Lady of Guadalupe at South Chicago. For the Provincial Chapter, 1947," n.p. (SA). Such small donations also funded Coughlin and Gerald L. K. Smith; see Jeansonne, *Gerald L. K. Smith*, 50, 149. Plans for the new shrine are broached in "Proposed National Shrine Altar," *VSJ* (June 1949): 10.

35. The observation about the obverse relationship between devotional popularity and economic distress is from Christian, *Person and God*, 65. For some examples of Depression-era prayers to the Shrine, see Mrs. C.G.F., Chicago, *VSJ* (January 1935); Mrs. M.E., Chicago, *VSJ* (January 1935); Mrs. V.R., no loc. cited, *VSJ* (March 1935); Mrs. V.K., Whiting, Ind., *VSJ* (April 1935); M.G.C., Chicago, *VSJ* (April 1935); Miss. M.E.A., Baltic, Conn., *VSJ* (December 1935); Mr. and Mrs. B.C. [written by Mrs. B.C.], Detroit, *VSJ* (August 1936); Mrs. J.T., Swissvale, Pa., *VSJ* (September, 1936); Mr. and Mrs. M.J.B. [written by Mrs. M.J.B.], Chicago, *VSJ* (October 1936); Mrs. B.H., Richmond Hill, N.Y., *VSJ* (February 1937); Mrs. F.M., Bronx, N.Y., *VSJ* (March 1938). I was told about the monthly donation in Per.corr.: BC-M-50-New York, N.Y.-M.

36. On correspondence to and from the Roosevelt White House see McElvaine, *Down and Out*, 5–6; idem, *Great Depression*, 171–172, 367 n. 5. McElvaine notes that "the Depression provided the strong motive that the poorly educated needed to write," in *Down and Out*, 7. Hickok is cited in ibid., 6; the quote about FDR's personal government is from idem, *Great Depression*, 325. On Father Coughlin see Brinkley, *Voices of Dissent*, 119–120; the figure is for 1934. People were also writing to Gerald L. K. Smith, see Jeansonne, *Gerald L. K. Smith*, 40, 63. Fulton Sheen received six thousand letters daily from listeners to "The Catholic Hour" (Dolan, *American Catholic Experience*, 393). For example of Depression-era petitions to the Shrine see Mr. J.F.D., Chicago, *VSJ* (January 1935); Miss M.S., Toledo, Ohio, *VSJ* (June 1935); [Mr.] T.K., Niles Center, Ill., *VSJ* (June 1935); Mr. and Mrs. M.J.B. [written by Mrs. M.J.B.], Chicago, *VSJ* (October 1936); ?A Friend of St. Jude, Chicago, *VSJ* (May 1937); Mrs. I.C., Pittsburgh, *VSJ* (September 1937); ?F.J., Ames, Iowa, *VSJ* (February 1937); B.M., Minneapolis, *VSJ* (January 1940); ?W.A.B., Muse, Pa., *VSJ* (August 1940).

37. For examples of wartime prayers see Mrs. J. Konrad, 8818–212 Place, Queens Village, N.Y., *VSJ* (May 1942); ?L.S., Pennsylvania, *VSJ* (September 1942); ?T.D., Wisconsin, *VSJ* (October 1942); ?E.M., Michigan, *VSJ* (November 1942); M.D., Maryland, *VSJ* (March

1943); ?M.M., Illinois, *VSJ* (March 1943); ?R.L., California, *VSJ* (April 1943); ?J.C., Ohio, *VSJ* (August 1943); ?M.E., California, *VSJ* (August 1943); A.W., California, *VSJ* (September 1943); ?M.F., Illinois, *VSJ* (October 1943); ?J.G., Wisconsin, *VSJ* (October 1943); C.M., Los Angeles, *VSJ* (October 1943); [Mr.] J.M., Chicago, *VSJ* (November 1943); and Per.corr.: DI-F-56-Dubuque, Iowa-M; CG-F-65-Chicago-M; and BE-F-66-Chicago-M. The latter described the circumstances of her first prayer to Jude as simply, "The War. We were newly engaged at the Time." Jude helped find at least one woman wartime work (F.R., Massachusetts, *VSJ* [March 1943]). My understanding of these years has been helped by J. Thomas, *American Catholic Family*, 274–275, Mintz and Kellogg, *Domestic Revolutions*, 152, 167–168; and Chafe, *American Woman*, 135–173. For the Shrine's wartime activities and promotions see, for example, advertisement, "Send Him a Rosary Ring," *VSJ* (April 1943), n.p.; advertisement, "Clients of Saint Jude," *VSJ* (July 1943): 13, which offers heavy-coated prayer cards "ideal for men and women in service; "Pocket-Size Personal Shrine," *VSJ* (March 1945): 18. (This last was not sold by the Shrine.) For a gripping story of the power of St. Jude's medals in wartime in the experience of the devout see Capt. James F. Bertie, "St. Jude in Korea," *VSJ* (April 1952): 22–23. Throughout the war years, the Shrine urged devout to "send in the name of Your Boy in Service that his Protection and Safe Return may be prayed for," Novena Notice, *VSJ* (September 1944): 16.

38. This is Dolan's understanding of the decline of the Sorrowful Mother novena, *American Catholic Experience*, 385; Dolan also attributes the decline of devotions after the war to the influence of the liturgical movement, 388.

39. For an interesting view of the work of sustaining, and redefining, an old neighborhood—in this case, Italian American—ethnic festival through years of change see Beth Harrington's video-documentaries, *Ave Maria: The Story of the Fisherman's Feast*, prod. and dir. Beth Harrington, 24 min., University of California Extension Center for Media and Independent Learning, 1986, and *The Moveable Feast*, prod. and dir. Beth Harrington, 28 min., University of California Extension Center for Media and Independent Learning, 1992.

40. See, for example, Greeley, *American Catholic*, 50–68; Dolan, *American Catholic Experience*, 356–357; Hennesey, *American Catholics*, 283. Hennesey emphasizes the important role of the G.I. Bill in Catholic economic success after the war.

41. For a description of the devotion in the immediate postwar years see Puigvi, "Jottings on Devotion." The membership figure for 1954 is from "Jude: The Forgotten Saint." For information on Father Catalina see George Hull, "Our New Superior," *VSJ* (August 1936): 6; and "Father Anthony Catalina, C.M.F., Becomes An American Citizen," *VSJ* (January 1939): 15. On Catalina's immediate successor, Joseph Puigvi, see "From the Shrine," *VSJ* (September 1942): 9; "Joseph M. Puigvi, 1898–1968," *SJJ* (May 1968): 2. There is helpful information on the transition from Tort to Catalina in Schneider, "Tenth Anniversary," 16. The *Voice of St. Jude* was edited from 1949 to 1984 by Robert E. Burns, a former public relations man who was intellectually attuned to the major currents of modern Catholic culture, dedicated to the promotion of St. Jude's cult, and skilled in the distinctly American arts of mass communication. Burns helped Father Maloney rethink

the devotion in the 1960s and presided over the transformation of the *Voice of St. Jude* to *U.S. Catholic*. See "R.E.B. Retires June 30," *Claretian Newsletter* 14, no. 3 (June 1984): 1–4.

42. The director of the Jesuit Shrine of the North American Martyrs in 1926, Francis X. A. Byrne, S.J., for example, recorded in a letter to John J. Wynne, S.J., "You will be interested in knowing just what was said in the Village church last Sunday morning. There were three statements;—that it was an act of disloyalty to the parish priest to attend Mass at the shrine and a personal insult; that there never was and never would be a miracle at the shrine as long as it was conducted on its commercial basis as had been the case, and the faithful were exhorted with very much oratory and animus to put this deep in their hearts; that the present director whose name was mentioned from the altar, had tried to take both altar boys and the organist from the church. That is that." Father Byrne to Father Wynne, July 5, 1926, Fordham University Archives.

43. "Copy of the Report," Section VIII, Part 3 (SA).

44. For an example of the representation of Guadalupe as the "site" of the devotion see "Silver Anniversary for Pastor of Shrine Church," *SJJ* (June 1969): 3. That there were no Spanish-language devotions at the Shrine until the 1970s was emphasized for me by a Mexican American woman who grew up in South Chicago as a member of Our Lady of Guadalupe parish and now works in the church, conversation January 1988. A Spanish-language prayer book was available, along with ones in Italian, Croatian, and Polish.

45. Conversation with MC-F-55-Chicago-?, January 1988.

46. Tort, "Dedication Anniversary," 12–13; conversation with Rev. James Maloney.

47. The arrival of Jude's relics in Chicago is described in Hull, "Life Begins at Forty," 8.

48. See Christian, *Person and God,* 73–75, 99. Christian says, "The more clear-cut the sociogeographic unit, the sharper its boundaries, then the more likely it was to have a cultural symbol, a protector, a patron in a shrine image. The jurisdictions, the territories of grace of the images in the valley and the region, could be no more clear than the boundaries of the sociogeographic units themselves" (99). Wilson comments on the close affinity that has existed between saints and their special places, in his introduction to *Saints and Their Cults,* 11.

49. Rice says that as a saint's cult develops, his or her power is understood by the devout to reside in objects increasingly further from the saint him- or herself. St. Jerome's power, for example, moved in medieval and Renaissance Europe from the saint's relics, to the sound of his name, to his image. See Rice, *Saint Jerome in the Renaissance,* 24, 44, and 59. The classic discussion of the portability of holy artifacts is Geary, *Furta Sacra.*

50. There is now a huge and superb literature on the modernization of Europe; for specific discussions of the cult of saints in this period see, Christian, *Person and God,* passim; idem, *Moving Crucifixes in Modern Spain;* Nolan and Nolan, *Christian Pilgrimage;* and Pope, "Heroine Without Heroics."

51. For a useful discussion of these conflicts in contemporary European popular devotionalism, see Badone, *Religious Orthodoxy.*

52. Chinnici, in a useful but unfortunately judgmental statement, observes that immi-

grant devotionalism in the United States "looked backward to a time when church and society had been integrally connected" (*Living Stones,* 127–128).

53. Taves discusses nineteenth-century American Catholic piety in *Household of Faith,* 57–61. See Floyd Anderson, *The Incredible Story of Father Baker* (Hamburg, 1974): 43–51, for the origins of the shrine of Our Lady of Victory. On the popularity of Lourdes grottoes in the United States see Kselman, "Our Lady of Necedah." For a vivid description of the process of reconstructing Lourdes on these shores, see R. Miller, "Lourdes of the West," passim. There is a reconstruction of Lourdes at St. Lucy's Church on Mace Avenue in the North Bronx, built in 1934, which is now a popular healing site for Italian American, Hispanic, and African Caribbean New Yorkers.

54. Tort's statements are recorded in Hull, "Life Begins at Forty," 9. The resonance between the devotion and American identity reached its most intense expression, not surprisingly, during World War II, although the way to this had been prepared in the decade before. See Father Joseph, C.M.F., "A Letter from the National Shrine," *VSJ* (October 1942): 3; and Puigvi, "Jottings on Devotion." The devout quoted is D.S., Buffalo, N.Y., *VSJ* (March 1949): 6. This commitment to making Jude better known around the country is also the motive for the ubiquitous notices thanking the saint that appear in the classified sections of local newspapers. On this impulse see also ?H.R., Brooklyn, N.Y., *VSJ* (July 1951). The petition slip with Jude's global title appears under the heading "My Thanksgivings and Petitions," *VSJ* (May 1948): 7. For examples of Protestant participation in the devotion, drawn from either end of its history, see Miss A.H., Sommerville, Mass., *VSJ* (April 1938); Mrs. D.L., Meadville, Pa., *SJJ* (February 1968); and Mrs. R.F., Akron, Ohio, *SJJ* (August 1969).

55. For the Shrine of St. Anthony see Hermann, "If Miracles Thou Fain Wouldst See": 171–172; on the Shrine of the Little Flower see "Shower of Roses," *Little Flower Magazine* 14 (January 1934): 3, 30.

56. Susman, *Culture as History,* 159–161. Roosevelt emphasized the theme of national "interdependence" in his first inaugural address; see McElvaine, *Great Depression,* 140.

57. Dolan, *American Catholic Experience,* 353–354; see also J. Olson, *Catholic Immigrants in America,* 146, 194; Fisher, *Catholic Counterculture,* 90. The latter in particular offers a creative interpretation of the many ambivalences in this period of American Catholic history.

58. Ducharme, for example, complains of the loss in this period of a sense of place among third-generation French Canadians in New England (*Shadows of the Trees,* 60–61, 210). On the making of Cardinal O'Connell as a national figure see O'Toole, *Militant and Triumphant;* for Spellman see Cooney, *American Pope.*

59. Bukowczyk, *And My Children Did Not Know Me,* 70. Bukowczyk notes that by the 1930s, Polish American workers felt a greater affinity with their Italian and Hungarian American counterparts than with local, self-consciously Polish entrepreneurs and professionals (*And My Children Did Not Know Me,* 83); see also Polzin, *Polish-Americans,* 157–158; and more generally Rosenzweig, *Eight Hours,* 172, 217. On the subject of ethnic pride as a path to American identity see, for example, J. Smith, *Family Connections,* 169; Obidin-

ski, "Ethnic to Status Group," 69–70, 87–88, 115–119; K. Miller, *Emigrants and Exiles,* 510–511; Bukowczyk, *And My Children Did Not Know Me,* 66–67; Yans-McLaughlin, *Family and Community,* 254–255; J. Thomas, *American Catholic Family,* 116–117, 139; Ducharme, *Shadows of the Trees,* 184, 208.

60. Per.corr.: AB-F-70-Aurora, Colo.-W. In the earliest days of the devotion, the Claretians regularly described the Mexican Catholic customs celebrated at "the National Shrine" for readers of the *Voice of St. Jude.* Although this may seem to have set the National Shrine in the familiar ethnic context, I believe it had the opposite intention and effect. The tone of these articles was folkloric and romantic; they seem to be evoking the vanished world of readers' childhoods, not of their contemporary experience. The articles belong in this sense less to the literature of the Mexican migration than to that of second- and third-generation American Catholic ethnic nostalgia, and indeed their appearance (as fund-raising devices) coincided with the first of several ethnic "revivals" in American Catholicism. See, for example, Eugene Sugranes, C.M.F., "Los Pastores: Old Christmastide Play Given at the National Shrine of St. Jude," *VSJ* (January 1935): 9; James Tort, C.M.F., "Christmas at the National Shrine," *VSJ* (January 1936): 10; "From the Shrine," *VSJ* (January 1942): 16–17. On shrines as geographical reference points see Christian, *Person and God,* 44. This tension between the local and the national was characteristic of other popular movements at the time. Brinkley, for example, sees a conflict between the national visions and aspirations of Huey Long and Father Coughlin, on the one hand, and the local concerns and aspirations of their followers, on the other. The Chicago shrine allowed the devout to play across this tension in their own experience (*Voices of Dissent,* 192–193). A number of popular Protestant faith healers and evangelists first gained national reputations in the 1920s, too, also as a result of their sophisticated use of the new communications technologies; see Harrell, *All Things Are Possible,* 16–21.

61. James Olson, for example, describes devotionalism in this period as "popular, ethnically narrow paraliturgi[cal] and preoccup[ied] with saints," and contrasts these idioms with more modern "ethical religion" (*Catholic Immigrants in America,* 225). Dolan is equally harsh, referring to "the liabilities of devotional Catholicism and the culture it created" for Catholics in the United States (*American Catholic Experience,* 401).

62. For a list of devotional radio programs available to Boston's Catholics in 1948 see Dolan, *American Catholic Experience,* 393.

63. Hendrickson, *Seminary,* 36–37.

64. MacEoin, "Has the Rosary Survived?" 12. The call to a new "Christian maturity" is seen in a ten-part series published in *AM* in 1962: James Kilgallon and Gerard Weber, "The Christian and the Rules," beginning *AM* 96 (September 22, 1962): 4–7. On piety as a detraction from worship see, for example, Benedict, "Liturgy vs. Private Devotions." "In the hierarchy of importance," Benedict writes, "our reverence and appreciation must go first of all to those actions of Christ in his Church which we call the Sacred Liturgy" (25). Some commentators, attempting to account for the preconciliar popularity of devotions that now appeared to them as a great mystery, pointed out that as long as the Mass was in an incomprehensible language, Catholic liturgical life was trapped in something like

"deep freeze," and so "to fill the void left by the silent Mass and the closed Bible, there arose a multiplicity of private devotions" (Trese, "Hold Onto Your Beads"). Benedict and others suggested that the proliferation of devotional practices reflected human spiritual and intellectual deficiencies; see Benedict, "Liturgy vs. Private Devotions," 25.

65. Marbach, "Liturgical Customs," 14; R. Griffin, "De Senectute," 22, 28. For an intimate and moving sketch of one woman's commitment to sewing a nightie for the Infant Jesus of Prague in the devotional years, see Freshman, "Star-Light of Faith." On the new perception of the strangeness of devotionalism see, for example, Calkins, "Our Lady of Childbirth."

66. MacEoin, "Has the Rosary Survived?" 14. The article is an account of this important conference. For other reflections on the postconciliar fate of the rosary see McInnes, "Liturgy of the Word"; O'Flynn, "Rosary and Liturgy"; Rush, "Rosary and the Christian Wake." On the reimagining of the saints as moral exemplars see McNaspy, "Fracas About Saints"; MacEoin, "Has the Rosary Survived?" 28; and "The Case of Therese Neumann," *AM* 96 (October 6, 1962): 17. One of the most comprehensive and thoughtful engagements with the cult of saints from the perspective of the postconciliar ethos is Molinari, *Saints.*

67. This theme of the word runs throughout the literature of the period; see, for example, McInnes, "Liturgy of the Word," 650–651; and Longley, "Make Christian Burial Christian."

68. Joachim DePrada, C.M.F., "The Meaning of Saint Jude," *VSJ* (October 1954): 8; see also Sister M. Marguerite, "The Definite Article," *VSJ* (January 1949): 7, 29, 33; and Dennis J. Geaney, O.S.A., "Tools for the Christian," *VSJ* (August 1954): 12–14. "Personal Devotion to a Saint," *SJJ* (March–April 1963): 2. Ten years before DePrada's apologia, an article emphasizing the centrality of the liturgy in Catholic life—and making no mention of the cult of saints—appeared in *VSJ*, reflecting perhaps an earlier moment of theological concern at the Shrine; see Buechel, "My Catholic Keepsakes." In April 1942 the Shrine offered the devout, amidst all its other promotions, *The Mass Year,* a liturgical almanac published by Abbey Press, to deepen their participation in the Eucharistic liturgy.

69. This paragraph is based on "Next Solemn Novena to St. Jude," *SJJ* (August 1969): 1; "New St. Jude Novena Book," *SJJ* (January 1967): 2; "Director's Column," *SJJ* (August 1968): 2; "Father John Devany, C.P.," *SJJ* (January 1967): 1. The Mother's Day speaker at the Shrine in 1969 was commended to the devout as having "kept aware of developments in doctrine and theology" ("Father Lawrence Calkins, O.S.M.," *SJJ* (April 1969): 1. For the new format of novena prayers see "Director's Column," *SJJ* (June 1966): 1–2. On the new Eucharistic emphasis at the Shrine see "Director's Column," *SJJ* (October–November 1962): 1–2; "Director's Column," *SJJ* (March 1964): 1; "Director's Column," *SJJ* (April–May 1964): 1; "Director's Column," *SJJ* (June 1966): 1; and "Sunday Devotions Discontinued," *SJJ* (October 1967): 3.

70. The effort to lighten up the church is briefly described in "Director's Column," *SJJ* (March 1962): 1; the spirit of the remodeling of Guadalupe is discussed in "Director's Column," *SJJ* (May 1968): 2; there is a photograph of the new plaque in *SJJ* (April 1969): 3. The plaque reads, "These burning lamps symbolize the devotion and prayer of many

people to the Apostle Saint Jude. Let us with confidence place our petitions at his shrine and unite with them our prayers to this great Apostle of Christ." See also "Director's Column," *SJJ* (August–September 1962):1–2; "Petition to St. Jude," *SJJ* (June 1966): 2; "Director's Column," *SJJ* (October 1967): 1–2.

71. "Director's Column," *SJJ* (August 1966): 1–2; "Director's Column," *SJJ* (October 1969): 2. The caution about scattering prayer cards is in "Director's Column," *SJJ* (October 1967): 2. If the devout were determined to distribute cards around their local churches, the director urged them to make sure to get permission first, another real break with the past. For the theological recasting of the devotion, see, for example: "Why Pray to the Saints?" *SJJ* (January 1961): 1; and in the same issue, "Why A Novena?" 3; also "A Good Name to Keep in Mind," *SJJ* (February–March 1961): 1; "St. Jude is for All of Us," *SJJ* (April–May 1961): 2; "Director's Column," *SJJ* (June 1962): 1–2; "St. Jude: The Saint of the Impossible," *SJJ* (October–November 1962): 3; "Director's Column," *SJJ* (March–April 1963): 1–2. For the broader theological context of this moral reimagining of the saints see Molinari, *Saints,* passim.

72. Father Maloney's opposition to the Vietnam War found muted expression in the *Journal* too, one of the few breaks, if not the only one, with the narrower, devotional focus of the pamphlet; see "Director's Column," *SJJ* (August 1966): 2; "Director's Column," *SJJ* (May 1968): 2; and the small note that begins, "As mentioned in the Director's Column . . ." *SJJ* (June 1968): 4.

73. No one at the Shrine could tell me exactly when the oil was discontinued, and no one could (or would) specify the suspected abuses, except to say that they had heard the oil was being used either in harmful rituals or incorporated into love potions. The first expression of concern about the healing oil appears in *VSJ* (April 1954): 33.

74. Quotations from, respectively, "Director's Column," *SJJ* (April 1967): 2; and "Director's Column," *SJJ* (May 1968): 2.

75. The arrival of the relic is described in "Our Director's Column," *SJJ* (October–November 1961): 2. It is not surprising that Tort's name is mentioned frequently in this column, which so clearly echoes his spirit. Jude's genealogy is discussed in "St. Jude's Family," *SJJ* (August 1964): 4; and "A Beautiful Symbol of Your Devotion," *SJJ* (August 1968): 3.

76. Nolan and Nolan, *Christian Pilgrimage,* 144. Father Maloney's reassurance is in "Director's Column," *SJJ* (August 1969): 2; for another contemporary reflection on this, in a spirit quite different from that evident in Father Maloney's remarks, see McNaspy, "Fracas About Saints," 608.

2. HOPELESS CAUSES AND THINGS DESPAIRED OF

1. Helmbold, "Beyond the Family Economy," 639. See also Milkman, "Women's Work," 78. Kerby Miller writes, in relation to Irish American communities, that "American conditions reinforced the gender segregation characteristic of the post-Famine countryside, and Irish-American females enjoyed markedly greater upward mobility and more successful adjustment to American society than their male peers," in *Emigrants and Exiles,*

494. This fact of Irish American social life is emphasized as well in two excellent studies, Diner, *Erin's Daughters*, and Nolan, *Ourselves Alone*. On Italian American women see Miriam Cohen, *Workshop to Office: Two Generations of Italian Women in New York City, 1900–1950* (Ithaca, N.Y., 1993), and J. Smith, *Family Connections*, 167–168; for Polish American communities, see Wrobel, *Our Way*, 58; Ostafin, "Polish Peasant in Transition," 268; and Polzin, *Polish-Americans*, 187.

2. Helmbold notes that marriage rates dropped during the Depression, which also served to keep younger women at home longer, in "Beyond the Family Economy," 641. Bukowczyk makes the same point specifically about the Polish American community, in *And My Children Did Not Know Me*, 75–76. Gordon comments on the high incidence of violence directed at the adolescent daughters of working-class immigrants as the family economy began to fragment, in *Heroes of Their Own Lives*, 188–190.

3. J. Thomas, *American Catholic Family*, 119. Bukowczyk notes that in the post–World War II years, Polish American women were more likely than their male counterparts to marry outside the group (*And My Children Did Not Know Me*, 108–109). For some examples of women contending with the issues raised by marrying outside the Catholic Church, see Mrs. M.A.K., Pickering, Ontario, *VSJ* (September 1955); L.H., Washington, D.C., *VSJ* (November 1955); Mr. and Mrs. F.E.M., Minneapolis, *VSJ* (July 1958).

4. J. Thomas, *American Catholic Family*, 144–145, 239. Thomas is discussing families of all ethnic groups here. Catholic families were reflecting in this regard broader social trends toward more equal and companionable marriage relations. Mintz and Kellogg point out that the first marriage counseling centers opened in the 1920s (*Domestic Revolutions*, 115–116). Wrobel observes that in second- and third-generation Polish American families there was a greater spirit of mutuality and "more egalitarian" social arrangements (*Our Way*, 77); see also Obidinski, "Ethnic to Status Group," 102. On marriage problems among Italian American families in this period see, for example, Cinel, *From Italy to San Francisco*, 190.

5. J. Thomas, *American Catholic Family*, 186–187. Thomas observes that modern Catholic women were especially disinclined to tolerate their husbands' drinking (220). Many American married people reported dissatisfaction with their domestic circumstances in the 1950s, belying the public image of a nation of happy families; see Mintz and Kellogg, *Domestic Revolutions*, 194. Thomas himself believed that Catholics were sharing in a national crisis of domestic relations (173–175). For his discussion of the causes of marital breakup among Catholics see p. 220. I have also learned from Coontz, *The Way We Never Were*.

6. Wrobel, *Our Way*, 58; Bukowczyk, *And My Children Did Not Know Me*, 103–104. Judith Smith observes, "Perhaps men ceded to women the central role in maintaining contact with parents as a way of resolving the tension between the American cultural ideal of the independent nuclear family and the ethnic culture's practice of mutual dependence on kin" (*Family Connections*, 118–121).

7. Per.corr.: REA-F-63-Dracut, Mass.-M. John Thomas reported that a major source of marital conflict in these years was the tension between a married couple, on the one hand, and their more traditional in-laws (*American Catholic Family*, 233–234).

8. Per.comm.: FA-F-68-Indiana-S. On the isolation of American women in the post-war years see Mintz and Kellogg, *Domestic Revolutions*, 197; and Rothman, *Women's Proper Place*, esp. 224–226. For the importance of these networks of neighbors and kin in women's history see Ross, "Survival Networks"; Ryan, "Power of Women's Networks"; and Kaplan, "Female Consciousness."

9. Mintz and Kellogg, commenting mainly about the 1950s, see a "widespread sense of discontent among American women," arising out of conflicts of roles, expectations, and aspirations they were experiencing (*Domestic Revolutions*, 195.)

10. See, for example, Mrs. I.M., Chicago, *VSJ* (February 1937); ?J.A.D., Detroit, *VSJ* (February 1953); B.A.B., Beverly Hills, Calif., *VSJ* (August 1954); Mrs. W.B., Reading, Ohio, *VSJ* (September 1954); Miss J.M.R., Chicago, *VSJ* (September 1955); Mrs. M.R.P., Nutley, N.J., *VSJ* (October 1958); Miss S.R., New Rochelle, N.Y., *SJJ* (October–November 1961).

11. Quotations from, respectively, No initials, St. Paul, Minn., *VSJ* (December 1941); Miss M.P., Detroit, *VSJ*, October, 1954; ?R.A.P., Weymouth, Mass., *VSJ* (April 1952); Miss J.F., Baltimore, *SJJ* (January 1967). One woman told me that she first turned to Jude when "making life decisions after maturity," Per.comm.: DI-F-56-Dubuque, Iowa-M.

12. Mrs. B.O., Springfield, Mass., *VSJ* (September 1953). John Thomas observed that women's in-laws featured as problems in 47 percent of marital conflict brought to the official attention of the Chicago Archdiocesan marriage court; men's in-laws accounted for 38.3 percent of the cases (*American Catholic Family*, 235). Mintz and Kellogg note that by the end of 1945 "adequate housing was nearly impossible to find," a difficulty compounded, of course, by rising fertility rates (*Domestic Revolutions*, 173). For some examples of (rather desperate) prayers for places to live in the late 1940s and throughout the next decade see ?R.Z., Milwaukee, *VSJ* (November 1949); ?A.W., Middle Village, N.Y., *VSJ* (December 1949): [Mr.] J.T., Chicago, *VSJ* (June 1950); E.W., Detroit, *VSJ* (November 1950); ?A.M., Loraine, Ohio, *VSJ* (February 1951); D.R., Flushing, N.Y., *VSJ* (May 1951); ?R.K., Berkley, Mich., *VSJ* (October 1951); ?C.E., Lamberville, Mich., *VSJ* (November 1951); R.W.C., Oak Lawn, Ill., *VSJ* (December 1951); ?A.M., Lincoln Park, Mich., *VSJ* (January 1952); ?W.B.T., Owensboro, Ky., *VSJ* (January 1952); ?B.M., Winnipeg, Manitoba, *VSJ* (January 1952); ?C.E.C., Little Falls, Minn., *VSJ* (February 1952); Mrs. A.S., Baltimore, *VSJ* (October 1953); ?R.O., West Chicago, Ill., *VSJ* (August 1958).

13. Bea, whom I introduced earlier, told me that the greatest number of petitions come from women who find themselves in marriages in very serious trouble. They pray either for reconciliation with their husbands or for satisfactory conclusions to these bad situations. Bea writes back to many of these women to say that the Shrine is praying with them for a happy resolution of their marital troubles, or, if this is not God's will, then that the woman involved will be given the strength "to get on with her life without him." The second–most frequently cited domestic problem in the letters, Bea added, was wife-abuse. In these cases, Bea said, she had to restrain herself from just writing back to the women and telling them to kick their husbands out. For a description of Catholic annulment procedures for the period of the study see J. Thomas, *American Catholic Family*, 82–90.

14. 800: KL-F-65+-Hernando, Fla.-M.

15. Mrs. A.C., for example, of Dorchester, Mass., enrolled her great-nephew in the League after the young man had "left home, become a hippie, and [started] taking dope." *SJJ* (October 1968).

16. Bea identified older married women whose husbands had just died as a major category of Shrine correspondent. These women often mentioned in their letters how lonely they were. For examples of letters from widowed women see Mrs. L.U., Chicago, *VSJ* (January 1937); Mrs. G.E.M., St. Paul, Minn., *VSJ* (October 1937); Mrs. H.J.O., Boston, *VSJ* (November 1941); Mrs. A.P., Perryville, Mo., *VSJ* (April 1953). The young widow quoted is Mrs. M.V., no loc., *VSJ*, June, 1954. For an example of a woman dealing with the practical consequences of her husband's death see A.O'B., Grand Rapids, Mich., *VSJ* (March 1952). The last comment in the paragraph is from F.R., Massachusetts, *VSJ* (March 1943).

17. Per.comm.:CD-F-75-Milwaukee-M; CG-F-65-Chicago-M; DH-F-67-Indiana-M; DG-F-76-Chicago-M.

18. Rapp, Ross, and Bridenthal, "Examining Family History." Rapp's comment is on 175.

19. McElvaine, *Great Depression*, 7.

20. Wrobel discusses this expectation among Polish Americans in *Our Way*, 68. When he asked contemporary Polish American women what they valued in a spouse, they replied "a hardworking man who wasn't afraid of work" and "a guy who's got a job that can support the family. And he better be the kind of guy who can keep the job." These sentiments would have been shared by immigrants' children in the various Catholic communities. For this evaluation of work among Italian Americans see Orsi, *Madonna of 115th Street*, 25–26, 197–202.

21. McElvaine, *Great Depression*, 172–174; the phrase quoted in the text is on 82. See also Komarovsky, *Unemployed Man*, 23–27, 35, et passim; Ware, *Holding Their Own*, xiii; Elder and Liker, "Hard Times." Komarovsky notes that if family members could not blame a man directly for his situation, they were left "mystified about the unemployment situation" (35). On the severity of this judgment in Polish American contexts see Wrobel, *Our Way*, 43.

22. This paragraph is indebted to Elder and Liker, "Hard Times in Women's Lives"; Helmbold, "Beyond the Family Economy"; Westin, *Making Do;* Bennett and Elder, "Women's Work"; and McElvaine, *Great Depression,* passim. See Bennett and Elder, "Women's Work," 165, for a discussion of middle-class women's entry into the workforce in the 1930s.

23. Mrs. N.G., Tucson, Ariz., *VSJ* (July–August, 1938). One of my sources told me that women needed St. Jude more than men did, and as her evidence for this generalization added, "be it [for] a husband who is unemployed or sick" (Per.comm.: DD-F-62-Whiting, Indiana-M). See esp. Bennett and Liker, "Women's Work," 156, on this point. In *It's Up to the Women*, Eleanor Roosevelt commented on women's "constant anxiety for fear of some catastrophe such as accident or illness which may completely swamp the family budget." Cited in Ware, *Holding Their Own*, 2. On the Depression-era crisis of the family see Mintz

and Kellogg, *Domestic Revolutions*, 133–149; Ware, *Holding Their Own;* Westin, *Making Do;* and Helmbold, "Beyond the Family Economy," esp. 643. McElvaine comments on the higher rates of illness among the unemployed in *Down and Out*, 18.

24. Quotation from Mrs. J.W., West New York, N.J., *VSJ* (June 1938). Komarovsky observed a terrible fear of aging and workplace obsolescence among working-class men and women in the 1930s who feared they would not be able to find work after turning 40 (*Unemployed Man*, 9). Elder and Liker emphasize the importance of the movement from terror to authority in shaping women's lives in the 1930s ("Hard Times," 260–261). They say that for middle-class women—those who did not enter the period destitute—Depression struggles served as the crucible of their responses to crises for the rest of their lives. Women who were closer to the edge in 1929 already were more apt instead to encounter feelings of "passivity" and "helplessness." Elder and Liker did not know about St. Jude, though. Even if the saint's clientele were not absolutely desperate (as they do not seem to be), still the saint was there during those years for Catholic women (and men) of all social classes and economic conditions—there to help them deal with their passivity and helplessness.

25. The last woman quoted in this paragraph appears in Ware, *Holding Their Own*, 8, and the man in Bodnar, *Workers' World*, 116. On women's necessary emotional work see Helmbold, "Beyond the Family Economy," 638–639. Helmbold writes, "To soothe frightened men unaccustomed to unemployment, coordinate the activities of increased numbers of people living in a small number of rooms, and cope with changes in their own lives—all required women's stamina and ingenuity." See also Ware, *Holding Their Own*, 17, and Komarovsky, *Unemployed Man*, 40–41; for contemporary discussions of the problem of family morale, and women's role in this dimension of the crisis, see Slocum and Ring, "Industry's Discarded Workers"; and Woolston, "Psychology of Unemployment," 338. The devout quoted is Mrs. I.C., Pittsburgh, *VSJ* (September 1937). Mrs. P.A.F., Watsonville, Calif., *VSJ* (January 1937) wrote the Shrine that her "son-in-law was very much dissatisfied at his work and that made it unpleasant at home too." See also Mrs. M.G.C., Chicago, *VSJ* (September 1936); S.M.T., Chicago, *VSJ* (June 1935).

26. See Westin, *Making Do*, 77; Helmbold, "Beyond the Family Economy," 629; Komarovsky, *Unemployed Man*, 35, 66–70; and esp. McElvaine, *Great Depression*, 180–181. For an incisive critique of the tendency to frame discussions of the Depression-era families with either-or questions, see Helmbold, "Beyond the Family Economy," 635.

27. McElvaine says that as a result of this discrepancy between financial necessity and the cultural injunction against their working, women lived under extraordinary "psychological pressures" in the 1930s (*Great Depression*, 183). See Chafe, *American Woman*, 135.

28. Quotation from Mrs. J.T., Swissvale, Pa., *VSJ* (September 1936); for other examples of women's great relief when their unemployed husbands find work through St. Jude, in the Depression period and after, see Mrs. V.R., no loc. cited, *VSJ* (March 1935); Mrs. V.K., Whiting, Ind., *VSJ* (April 1935); M.G.C., Chicago, *VSJ* (April 1935); "A Devoted Client of St. Jude," Chicago, *VSJ* (April 1935); D.G., Bourbonnais, Ill., *VSJ* (April 1951); Mrs. V.G., McKeesport, Pa., *VSJ* (September 1941); L.L., San Gabriel, Calif., *VSJ* (May 1950); L.P.,

Eunice, La., *VSJ* (June 1950); Mrs. F.S., Chicago, *VSJ* (March 1953). For an example of a later expression of gratitude for Jude's help in the Depression years see ?L.K., Ossining, N.Y., *VSJ* (November 1949).

29. For some examples of later petitions from women for male employment see E.F., Detroit, *VSJ* (February 1942); R.S., Dayton, Ohio, *VSJ* (August 1950); Mrs. W.B., Waukesha, Wis., *VSJ* (March 1953); Mr. and Mrs. T.W.S. [written by Mrs. T.W.S.], Allen Park, Mich., *VSJ* (December 1954); C.R., New Milford, N.J., *VSJ* (October 1955); W.A.T., Detroit, *VSJ* (February 1958); Mrs. T.H., Royal Oak, Mich., *VSJ* (October 1958).

30. ?E.M., Michigan, *VSJ* (November 1942); ?R.L., California, *VSJ* (April 1943); A.W., California, *VSJ* (September 1943); M.F., Brooklyn, N.Y., *VSJ* (January, 1944); ?I.W., Detroit, *VSJ* (May 1944); L.G., Pittsburgh, *VSJ* (June 1944); C.M., Milwaukee, *VSJ* (November 1944); ?M.S., Miami, *VSJ* (November 1944); C.D., Beaumont, Texas, *VSJ* (December 1944). For examples of this impulse during the Korean War years see Mrs. B.O., Springfield, Mass., *VSJ* (September 1953); A.McD., Philadelphia, *VSJ* (November 1951); Mrs. J.P.N., Fremont, Ohio, *VSJ* (August 1953); Mrs. A.R.E., New York, *VSJ* (November 1953); Mrs. J.L.P., Dorchester, Mass., *VSJ* (May 1954); K.K.E., Bronx, N.Y., *VSJ* (November 1951). There are two letters during the Second World War clearly about men praying to be stationed near home (although one of these is reported by the man's wife): [Mr.] A.O., Chicago, *VSJ* (May 1944); E.O., Milwaukee, *VSJ* (January 1944).

31. Madden, "Army Gets a Mother," *VSJ* (September 1942): 6–7, 15, 17. The phrase about Mary as "homefront heroine" appears in "From the Shrine," *VSJ* (December 1944): 8. For men's wartime prayers see P.F.C., R.V., Fort Bragg, N.C., *VSJ* (May 1953; this man is recalling Jude's help in 1946 when he was having difficulties enlisting because of a "broken arm"); ?J.M., Texas, *VSJ* (August 1943); ?Corporal J.H., Lowry Field, Colo., *VSJ* (January 1944); [Mr.] W.H., Naval Aviation Station, Salem, Va., *VSJ* (January 1944); [Mr.] A.F., St. Louis, *VSJ* (March 1944); Pvt. J.R., Camp Cooke, Calif., *VSJ* (March 1944); ?G.K., Baltimore, *VSJ* (October 1944; the correspondent is praying for his or her son). See also the story told by Father Jerome S. Becker, O.P., about his experience praying to Jude in combat during World War II, in *SJJ* (October 1967): 1. One of the few men to respond to my request for stories at the Shrine said that he had first prayed to Jude "back in early 1944 when I was in the Army Air Force and was sent to the European Theater of Operations. I wound up with the 15th Air Force in Southern Italy and flew 50 combat missions" (Per.comm.: DE-M-67-East Chicago-M.).

32. See Mintz and Kellogg, *Domestic Revolutions*, 161–162; and Chafe, *American Woman*, 159–160.

33. Mrs. J. Konrad, 8818–212 Place, Queens Village, N.Y., *VSJ* (May 1942). I am unable to identify the gender of the correspondents for most of the citations that follow: of all the issues discussed in this study, only these wartime petitions have so thoroughly frustrated me in this regard. It is possible that during this war, male devout undertook the responsibilities of prayer and correspondence; I cannot absolutely rule this scenario out. But if they did, it would be the only time in the Shrine's history when this was so. Where gender *can* be determined (in four of the sixteen cases cited), the correspondents so identifiable

are women: ?L.S., Pennsylvania, *VSJ* (September 1942); ?M.M., Illinois, *VSJ* (March 1943); ?F.B., Wisconsin, *VSJ* (June 1943); J.B., New York, *VSJ* (June 1943); ?M.E., California, *VSJ* (August 1943); A.W., California, *VSJ* (September 1943); ?M.F., Chicago, *VSJ* (October 1943); J.G., Wisconsin, *VSJ* (October 1943); ?M.F., Chicago, *VSJ* (February 1944); ?A.B., Steger, Ill., *VSJ* (May 1944); L.L., Dayton, Ohio, *VSJ* (June 1944); ?J.M., Minneapolis, *VSJ* (October 1944); ?P.A., Long Island, N.Y., *VSJ* (October 1944); ?M.N., San Antonio, Texas, *VSJ* (October 1944); ?L.D., Stockton, Calif., *VSJ* (November 1944); ?I.V., Pittsburgh, *VSJ* (November 1944).

34. Quotations from, respectively, M.B., Vergennes, Vt., *VSJ* (June 1949); and ?R.D., Jackson, Mich., *VSJ* (December 1951). See also ?N.B., Chicago, *VSJ* (November 1944), which begins, "I have a boy in a Veteran's Hospital who suffered a complete nervous breakdown in the Army." Another woman reported that she was grateful to Jude for bringing her husband home to her from the war "in perfect health of mind and body completely unscarred" after twenty-six months overseas, C.M., Milwaukee, *VSJ* (November 1944).

35. Mrs. V.S.S., Worth, Ill., *SJJ* (October 1967).

36. Miss L.M., Baltimore, *VSJ* (July 1953). Miss L.M. points out that she has "heavy financial burdens and not too much financial sense." For an instance of a woman thanking Jude for "safe journeys and [a] wonderful vacation" see Mrs. W.K., Cincinnati, *VSJ* (December 1958).

37. J. Thomas, *American Catholic Family,* 141; on national rates see Mintz and Kellogg, *Domestic Revolutions,* 178–179. On young Catholic women's earlier marriages and child-births see J. Thomas, *American Catholic Family,* 195. In 1940, the median age of those marrying for the first time was 24.3 years for the groom and 21.6 for the bride; in 1949 the respective ages were 22.7 and 20.3. Catholics were participating here again in the national trend; see Miller and Nowak, *Fifties,* 147.

38. Leavitt, " 'Science' Enters the Birthing Room," 301, 297. The statistics quoted in the paragraph are from Leavitt as well, 301. See also Mintz and Kellogg, *Domestic Revolutions,* 120. On the successful campaigns of obstetricians in these years to institutionalize their exclusive authority over childbirth, see Sandelowski, *Pain, Pleasure, and American Child-birth,* 46–47, 69–70.

39. Sandelowski comments on the increased use of painkilling drugs beginning in the 1930s in *Pain, Pleasure, and American Childbirth,* 32–36. She points out that women asked for these drugs, which in turn required further medical intervention. Leavitt argues that the move into hospitals did not necessarily make childbirth safer in the early 1930s, although it did have this effect in the 1940s and afterward as technologies and procedures developed further. See " 'Science' Enters the Birthing Room," 299–301. Sandelowski makes the same point, 42–44. DeLee is cited in Sandelowski, *Pain, Pleasure, and American Childbirth,* 40–41. The material from *Ladies Home Journal* is quoted and discussed in Leavitt, " 'Science' Enters the Birthing Room," 301–302.

40. The phrase "sick, damaged, perverted" is from Miller and Nowak, *Fifties,* 155.

41. Quotations from, respectively, P.R., St. Louis, *VSJ* (July 1950); and D.D., Detroit,

VSJ (April 1952). The account of the woman confined to bed in her fourth pregnancy came from Per.comm.: ER-F-74-Chicago-M.

42. The story of the woman discouraged by seven doctors is told by Owenita Sanderlin, "Saints in Their Lives," VSJ (November 1954): 30. She claims to have been in the maternity ward when this took place. Mrs. A.B.A., Baltimore, VSJ (September 1953), had the friend whose children die. The woman warned of miscarriages is Mrs. G.J.F., St. Louis, VSJ (October 1953). For other examples of women's childbearing distress in these years see Mrs. G.M.W., Braddock, Pa., VSJ (September 1953); Mrs. J.L.P., Dorchester, Mass., VSJ (May 1954); F. and J.K. [written by Mrs. K.], Cicero, Ill., VSJ (January 1954); T.G., Covington, Ky., VSJ (January 1954); Mrs. R.L.C., San Jose, Calif., VSJ (January 1954); Mrs. E.B., Evansville, Ind., VSJ (January 1954); Mrs. R.M.S., Chicago, VSJ (January 1955). The last two quotations in the paragraph are from Mrs. H.C.F., Baton Rouge, La., VSJ (January 1953); and Mrs. N.G., Wisconsin, VSJ (August 1958).

43. Quotation from R.W., Newton, Mass., VSJ (July 1949). The statistics on women in the labor force between 1940 and 1960 are from Cookingham, "Working After Childbearing," 773. On women's appetite in this period for the goods and services newly available, see Cowan, "Two Washes," 156–157. On the increase in the number of women at work outside their homes in the 1950s see Miller and Nowak, Fifties, 162–163; Helmbold, "Beyond the Family Economy," 642–643; Rothman, Woman's Proper Place, 229–231; Mintz and Kellogg, Domestic Revolutions, 198; Chafe, American Woman, 190–191. Schatz discusses both women's desire to work and the Catholic clergy's criticism of it in "Connecticut's Working Class." J. Thomas cites the injunction against married women working outside their homes as one of the foundations of Catholic family teaching (American Catholic Family, 330–332). For a helpful discussion of the widespread anxiety among American Catholic intellectuals in this century over the state of the family, a concern mainly centered on and articulated through a concern for women and more broadly for the stability of gender roles, see Burns, American Catholics. On the broader American ideology of the home after World War II see, for example, Scharf, To Work and to Wed, 43–65; Miller and Nowak, Fifties, 155; Sandelowski, Pain, Pleasure, and American Childbirth, 73–74. Women are generally expected to "absorb any tension generated by those forces" of the economy that converge on the family, according to Milkman ("Women's Work," 73–74).

44. For examples of these sorts of petitions see ?S.A.S., Steubenville, Ohio, VSJ (June 1940); ?R.S., Toledo, Ohio, VSJ (December 1949); L.K., Waverly, Kan., VSJ (January 1952); Miss L.G., Coalton, W.Va., VSJ (April 1953); Mrs. M.B., Bristol, Conn., VSJ (May 1953); Miss D.M.S., St. Paul, Minn., VSJ (June 1953); Mrs. H.J.G., Toledo, Ohio, VSJ (July 1953); Miss E.M.L., Bellevue, Ky., VSJ (August 1953); ?B.I., Los Angeles, VSJ (September 1954); Mrs. A.V.M., Elmhurst, N.Y., VSJ (January 1955); Mrs. M.F., Cincinnati, VSJ (July 1955); Mrs. A.A., Jackson, Miss., VSJ (March 1958).

45. Mrs. G.H., Chicago, VSJ (July 1953); see also ?M.C., Providence, R.I., VSJ (June 1949).

46. ?S.A.F., Louisville, Ky., VSJ (December 1958).

47. "Prayer in Affliction," *SJJ* (October–November 1963): 2. This language was toned down somewhat in a later revision of the prayer.

48. Mrs. J.B.M., Lake Charles, La., *VSJ* (March 1954).

49. N.N., Woonsocket, R.I., *VSJ* (April 1952); K.B.T., Baltimore, *VSJ* (January 1953); Mrs. T.L., Jennings, Mo., *VSJ* (April 1954).

50. The quotations in this paragraph are from: V.D., Lakemore, Ohio, *VSJ* (October 1949); Mrs. W.H., Crown Point, Ind., *SJJ* (August–September 1963); M.R., Cleveland, *VSJ* (September 1941); and D.P.H., Somerset, Mass., *VSJ* (May 1952). For additional letters about male alcohol abuse see Grateful Client of St. Jude, Chicago, *VSJ* (December 1935); T.B., Chicago, *VSJ* (June 1950); R.D., Jackson, Miss., *VSJ* (December 1951); Mrs. M.G., Brooklyn, N.Y., *VSJ* (July 1953).

3. IMAGINING WOMEN

1. Anna-Margaret Record, "This Side of Sainthood," *AM* 81, nos. 3 (January 15, 1955): 18–21; 4 (January 22, 1955): 18–21; 5 (January 29, 1955): 17–21; 6 (February 5, 1955): 18–21; 7 (February 12, 1955): 17–21; 10 (March 5, 1955): 19–21; 11 (March 12, 1955): 18–21.

2. Gilmore, "Wife, Mother, and Saint"; also Courson, "New Beata." Similar themes are emphasized in the lives of other married women saints; see, for example, Westbrook, "Devotional Classic Revived."

3. M. Scott, "Home," 97; Gilmore, "Failure of the Family," 434; "Discipline of Girls"; and William Ward, "In Defense of American Womanhood," *VSJ* (November 1949): 4–5, 26. For women's accountability for world crisis, see, for example, G. Sanderlin, "Child of Her Tears"; "Twin Devotions"; C. Ryan, "Wanted: Mothers"; Sheerin, "Woman." This was one of Huesman's themes as well, in *Saints in Aprons*.

4. See, for example, Sherwood, "Coffee Pot"; D. Phillips, "Diplomat's Dinner."

5. For criticism of modern Catholic women's hopes for good marriages, see, for example, P. Carroll, "Mating of Tess O'Kennedy"; and P.J.C., "Contentment." The importance of a spiritual approach to marriage was the central message of the domestic hagiographies, too. Patrick J. Carroll, C.S.C., was editor of *Ave Maria* from 1934 until 1952, and the byline P.J.C. in *Ave Maria* always refers to him. The advice about bad husbands is from Macelwane, "Make Your Marriage Happy," 54. The comment on "unsexing" is from C. Phillips, "On Women's Poetry"; for a later example of worry about gender ambiguity see Sheehan, "When You Marry." For other examples of the threat of young women's desires see Hurst, "Sibyl's Awakening"; Tansey, "Going Home." The tale of the girl and the simple shepherd is told in Edgerton, "Desert Love," 18.

6. Moriarty, "Jim Graney's Wife"; see also Cloton, "Larry's Wife"; Carney, "Return of Norah"; Carroll, "Mating of Tess O'Kennedy"; Gilmore, "Failure of the Family"; Moriarty, "Jane Comes Home"; Tracy, "December Drama"; Edgerton, "Desert Love." On the recent history of American popular romance, see Radway, *Reading the Romance*. Barbara's story is told in Tansey, "Receive This Word"; the final quotation in the paragraph is from E. Walker, "East End Granny," 783.

7. Taves discusses the Ligourian turn in modern American Catholic spirituality in *Household of Faith*, 74–82; see also White, *Diocescan Seminary*, 139. Kane, *Separatism and Subculture*, 170. The best discussion I know of the shaping of the modern American seminary ethos is in Tentler, *Seasons of Grace*, 367–368. Tentler carefully analyzes the evolution of the American seminary in Detroit toward this ever more exclusive male ideal. The adjective "unscrupulous" in the text above comes from Sheerin, "Woman," 695.

8. Stehle, "Women and the Clergy," 326–328. On Cardinal Mooney see Tentler, *Seasons of Grace*, 368.

9. Grey, "Devout Female Sex," 609–610; Joachim DePrada, C.M.F., "To Whom Shall We Turn?" *VSJ* (December 1958), 34; Huels, *Friday Night Novena*, 21–23; McCarthy, "Rosary is Power," 529–530. I have heard it drily observed by the clergy at several different shrines around the United States that the real problem with ordaining women is that it would leave their pews empty. Tentler discusses the hostility of some of Detroit's clergy to female piety in *Seasons of Grace*, 402–408. Huesman quotes an altar boy's cute observation that women must be holier than men since he sees so many of them in church all the time, a perception Huesman herself confirms, *Saints in Aprons*, xi; see also 18–19; 31.

10. Ivancovich, "Motherhood," 339.

11. Tansey, "Will-o-the-Wisps"; Sister M. Marguerite, "Barter and Exchange," 4.

12. For a brief discussion of this concept see Laplanche and Pontalis, *Language of Psychoanalysis*, 160–161.

13. The expression of pity for children who have lost their mother is from "Twin Devotions," 740. For another statement of this exclusion of the father, which roots it in natural law, see Sweeney, "When Ignorance Is Bliss." The image of the "sweet-faced" victim comes from T.E.B., "Sacrifice and Happiness," 180; see also J. Murphy, "Human Suffering"; and G. Sanderlin, "Child of Her Tears." See also McShane, "Mirrors and Teachers."

14. Huesman, *Saints in Aprons*, 38. See also, for example, Macelwane, "Make Your Marriage Happy"; and Simeon, "Episode for Women." Sheen quotation from "How to Stay Married."

15. Tentler has excellent discussions of the CYO in the broader context of social anxieties about young people in *Seasons of Grace*, 203–204, 428–429.

16. Tansey, "Receive This Word," 14; "Word to the Wise."

17. "Union of Jesus and Mary," 820; "Twin Devotions," 738; Sharkey, *Woman Shall Conquer*, 191–192. For another expression of this very widely shared Marian theology see Mullaney, "Rosary."

18. Kelly, "Our Lady of Fatima"; see also Williams, "Mary's Toy."

19. Tonne, "Swords of Sorrow," *SAM* 48, no. 8: 47. The devotion to the pierced heart of Mary offered ample occasion for this kind of spiritual imagining. See also, for example, McNamara, "Mary, Mother of Sorrows." The statement about the special intimacy of mothers (*not* fathers) and children is from Sweeney, "When Ignorance Is Bliss," 39. Note in the text the absence of an article before "father," which almost makes it seem as though Sweeney were talking suddenly of his own. Sheen's comment is from "Mother Means Love," 2–3.

20. Bodnar, *Transplanted,* 81–82.

21. Reedy, "Mothers of Our Day"; and "If You're So Well Educated."

22. Bishop, "Your First Girl," 7.

23. Moriarty, "Jim Graney's Wife," 495–496.

24. Frier, "Saints' Ways," 110–111; Bishop, "Your First Girl," 8.

25. Simeon, "Episode for Women," 18; see also Aaron, "These Saturday's Children."

26. Mary's conversation with the children at LaSalette is quoted and discussed in Zimdars-Swartz, *Encountering Mary,* 27–43.

27. Gilmore, "Wife, Mother, and Saint," 242. For women's sacrifice of their pain for men's well-being see Westbrook, "A Devotional Classic Revived"; Cloton, "Paid Back"; Cloton, "Larry's Wife." Domestic hagiographies generally urged women to suffer patiently their husbands' cruelties in order eventually to redeem them; see, for example, T.E.B., "Sacrifice and Happiness," 180; Hasley, "I Like Married Life"; Simeon, "Episode for Women," 18. *Integrity* is quoted in Fisher, *Catholic Counterculture,* 118.

28. "For the Ladies," *VSJ* (October 1942): 16; Gilmore, "Wife, Mother, and Saint," 242.

29. Advice for female parishioners is from Sheerin, "Woman," 696. "Wives can conquer fiery, untamed husbands by silence," P.J.C. wrote, "when a tempest would be impotent" ("Significance of Silence"). The story about the sick woman is from Gardner, "Undaunted Christmas Spirit." The dangers of women's complaining are discussed in Sister M. Adelaide, R.S.M., "Short Wave to Saint Jude," *VSJ* (April 1950): 4. St. Jude's warning is from Hasley, "I Like Married Life," 16.

30. Quotations from, respectively, Tonne, "Swords of Sorrow," *SAM* 48, no. 11: 31; A. Clark, "Silent Saint"; and Huesman, *Saints in Aprons,* 116–117. "We can only pray," Huesman concludes, "that our sorrow will be, as it was for our Sorrowful Mother, the cause of our joy."

31. Sheehan, "When You Marry," 10–11; Aaron, "These Saturday's Children," 20. Advice to women on encouraging their men to speak is from 63. Macelwane, "Make Your Marriage Happy," 9.

32. Minogue, "Gran," 397. See Dolan, *American Catholic Experience,* 394, for a discussion of American Catholic fears for the family and for the quotation from the bishops' letter. George Sanderlin, "Who Crucifies Christ?" *VSJ* (March 1949): 26, 31. The allusion to the Communist threat against the Catholic family, a fear that had been widespread among American Catholics since the 1920s, comes from Cotter, "Greater Menace?"

33. Peyton is quoted in Huesman, *Saints in Aprons,* 208. Macelwane, "Make Your Marriage Happy," 7. Halsey discusses the aggressively naive ethos of Catholic literary and film criticism after the First World War in *Survival of American Innocence,* 99–123. The National Legion of Decency regularly posted objections to films on grounds such as "light treatment of marriage; reflects the acceptability of divorce; suggestive situations and costuming" (for the film "The Captain's Paradise," which received a B rating—"morally objectionable" for all audiences—from the Legion); "reflects the acceptability of divorce" ("Deadline," rated B); and "tends to justify divorce and remarriage" ("The Desperate Search," rated B). See *Motion Pictures Classified,* 31, 46–47 et passim.

34. G. Sanderlin, "Pioneering in the Twentieth Century."

35. I am borrowing from Therborn's taxonomy of ideology. Therborn writes that there are "three fundamental modes of ideological interpellation," through which ideologies "subject and qualify subjects by telling them, relating them to, and making them recognize" what is, what is good, and what is possible. Each of these has what Therborn calls "temporal and spatial dimensions," meaning that each includes some account of what has existed and was good in the past, as well as what is possible in the future, and of *where* in culture there is being, goodness, and potential. See *Ideology of Power*, 18, et passim.

4. "I RECOGNIZE HIM WHEN HE TURNS"

1. 800: SM-F-65+-Springfield, Mo.-D; 800: IG-F-50+-Chicago-M. SM told me that she sees the "face" of "a very real man, a very real person" when she prays to Jude.

Many Americans felt strongly about Eleanor Roosevelt's eyes during the Depression: McElvaine quotes an unnamed contemporary who wrote that the First Lady's eyes "caressed one with sympathy and studied one with intelligence" (*Great Depression*, 108). Communication with the sacred through a meeting of eyes is a feature of many religious traditions; see, for example, Eck, *Darsan*.

2. ?E.F.H., St. Louis, *VSJ*, September, 1954; ?O.J.B., Forest Park, Ga., *SJJ*, April, 1967; Per.comm.: FD-F-59-Evanston, Ill.-M.

3. The quotation in the text is from Mrs. A.C., Detroit, *SJJ* (October 1968). Note the shift in her sentence from "Prayer Card" to "him." The belief that statues and icons of the saints responded directly to human events and crises has been a constant feature of Catholic popular piety. This paragraph is also based on Mrs. R.D., Hazelton, Pa., *VSJ* (November 1955); 800: KL-F-65+-Hernando, Fla.-M; 800: SM-F-65+-Springfield, Mo.-D; Mr. and Mrs. A.C.B., Detroit, *VSJ* (July 1952); J.H., Washington, D.C., *VSJ* (May 1950); and 800: BP-F-50+-Bronx, N.Y.-M. SM said that Jude has "just become such an essential friend that . . . I can kind of talk to him every day." Mrs. A.C.B., who wrote the letter also signed by her husband, says she put "St. Jude Seals" on all her bills in response to Jude's helping with the family's financial crisis.

4. Another woman told me that "when [St. Jude] is smiling I know everything will be o.k." Per.comm.: FE-F-53-Chicago-M. The comment about Jude's "penetrating" eyes is from Per.comm. BF-F-75-South Chicago-W. The only account I have ever seen of a vision Jude came from a Protestant woman, 800: TF-F-40+-Tampa, Fla.-M. When I asked whether St. Jude ever spoke to her directly so that she could hear him with her ears, Clara, whose devotion to the saint is obviously very strong, joked, "If he ever does, then we have a miracle."

5. Eugene Sugranes, C.M.F., "Christ Child and Saint Jude Chum Together," *VSJ* (December 1935): 5; "St Jude: The Saint of the Impossible," *SJJ* (October–November, 1962): 2–3; the devout enjoyed imagining Jude and Jesus playing together, too, for example, Per.comm.: IA-F-58-Chicago-S. Descriptions of Jude as sturdy yet royal are from Eugene Sugranes, C.M.F., "Saint Jude the Wonder-Worker: His First Miracle," *VSJ* (May

1935): 7; Puigvi, "Jottings on Devotion"; see also the letter addressed to the devout, *VSJ* (February 1947): 7. Jude's concern for Gentiles is mentioned in "From the Shrine," *VSJ* (February 1942): 14; "St. Jude: The Saint of the Impossible," *SJJ* (June 1962): 3.

6. The Shrine presented this story in imaginative detail in the comic book, "Jude: The Forgotten Saint."

7. On Jude's relationship with Jesus as one of the sources of his power see, for example, James Tort, C.M.F., "Dedication Anniversary of the National Shrine of Saint Jude," *VSJ* (February 1935): 12; Sugranes, "St. Jude's Pilgrimage"; and "Why Appeal to Saint Jude?" *VSJ* (May 1948): 7. The recognition of Jude's power by other saints is mentioned in "From the Shrine," *VSJ* (April 1942): 5. On Jude's loss of identity see "Jude: The Forgotten Saint."

8. "Director's Column," *SJJ* (January 1967): 2; this theme is first introduced in "St. Jude and Judas," *SJJ* (June–July 1961): 2. The image cited is in "Jude: The Forgotten Saint."

9. Miss E.N., Sugar Land, Texas, *VSJ* (February 1954); on this theme of inversion see also, for example, ?M.C., Chicago, *VSJ* (May 1935); E.D., St. Paul, Minn., *VSJ* (May 1937); ?L.E., Houston, *VSJ* (April 1941); ?G.D., Outremont [Quebec?], *VSJ* (August 1951); ?P.I.H., Belmont, Mass., *VSJ* (July 1958). This paragraph is also based on the following articles by Joachim DePrada, C.M.F.: "The Persian Story," *VSJ* (January 1958): 33–34; "The Tables Turned," *VSJ* (February 1958): 31–33; and "The Apostolic Letter," *VSJ* (April 1958): 33–34. The remark about purity is by Donald J. Thorman, quoted in "St. Jude: The Saint of the Impossible," *SJJ* (June 1962): 2–3.

10. "God's right-hand man" is from ?C.L., Chicago, *VSJ* (June 1951). On Jude's modesty, "From the Shrine," *VSJ* (January 1942): 17. On Jude's other virtues, Sugranes, "Who Is Saint Jude?" Sugranes says that Jude has been so busy "in doing good, in granting favors, in making history, that he has forgotten to write it. As usual, he has remained speechless and silent, voiceless and inarticulate."

11. The reference to Long is from Brinkley, *Voices of Protest,* 29. Brinkley notes that people talked about Long "as if he were a relative or a close friend," and quotes a St. Louis reporter who wrote in 1935 that the governor's followers "worship the ground he walks on. He is part of their religion." Father Coughlin was also viewed by his more ardent followers as an angel; see ibid., 260. On Father Divine see Weisbrot, *Father Divine,* and Watts, *God, Harlem U.S.A.* The figure on the Lone Ranger is from Ware, *Holding Their Own,* xvi. "Many such heroes," Susman comments on Depression-era saviors, "when not in their heroic disguises and [when] regarded as ordinary citizens found themselves either humiliated or treated with some contempt by their fellows. Only in their hidden identities did they find praise and admiration" (*Culture as History,* 204–205). Susman discussed Frank Capra's movies in ibid., 196. McElvaine cites Fillmore Sanford's 1949 study of Roosevelt's popularity in Philadelphia (*Great Depression,* 115).

12. DePrada, "Tables Turned," 32.

13. A good example of this style of Catholic Hollywood reporting is Tom Rogers, "Meet Your Own Harry Lillis Crosby," *VSJ* 11, no. 10 (February 1946): 10–11, 20; for a critical

reflection on this tendency of the Catholic press to canonize Hollywood stars see the editorial, "Jennifer Jones and Too Much Publicity," *VSJ* 10, no. 1 (May 1944): 3.

14. For other illustrations of this principle see Rice, *Saint Jerome in the Renaissance*, 82–83, 198–199; J. Brown, *Immodest Acts*, 106; Atkinson, " 'Your Servant, My Mother' "; and Molinari, *Saints*, 101, and 211, n.110.

15. Puigvi, "Jottings on Devotion."

16. 800: KJ-F-50+-Portsmouth, N.H.-D/R; Per.corr.: SM-F-65+-Springfield, Mo.-D. I also spoke with SM on the telephone, so she appears under the 800 classification, too (as in n. 1 above). For another example of devotionalism as a realm in which women used (and displayed) crafts skills for religious ends, see the description of the practice of making and investing statues of the Infant of Prague with sequined copes in Freshman, "Star-Light of Faith."

17. Per.comm.: DA-F-Chicago-54-W; another woman wrote me: "I think Saint Jude looks like the statue at the National Shrine of Saint Jude. I picture him as he looks in the statue representation and on my holy card of him. I think he is [a] very sympathetic and compassionate person who has a special interest in persons who feel their lives are hopeless. I think he is very sincere and [here the word "feeling" was crossed out] has an awareness of how we feel when we are going through a desperate situation." Per.comm.: BC-F-36-Chicago-S.

18. Per.comm.: BG-F-63-Chicago-M. William Christian notes that the Spanish women he talked to also preferred to make up their own prayers to the saints, *Person and God*, 137.

19. 800: SM-F-65+-Springfield, Mo.-D.

20. Per.corr.: FAF-F-50+-East Haven, Conn.-?; also 800: AM-F-55+-Chicago-?; 800: JL-F-65+-Illinois ["just outside Chicago"]-W; 800: BP-F-Bronx, N.Y.-50+-M; 800: TF-F-40+-Tampa, Fla.-M; 800: SM-F-65+-Springfield, Mo.-D; and Mrs. F.A., St. Paul, Minn., *VSJ* (February 1937); ?D.C., Chicago, *VSJ* (December 1951).

21. Per.comm.: CG-F-65-Chicago-M; CA-F-56-Chicago-M; CD-F-75-Milwaukee-M; EB-F-53-Chicago-M.

22. For example, ?M.W., Kentucky, *SJJ* (August 1969); Mrs. G.S., Louisville, Ky., *VSJ* (March 1941); ?L.C., Chicago, *VSJ* (April 1941); ?T.K., Massapequa, N.Y., *SJJ* (April–May 1961); Mrs. J.L., Bronx, N.Y., *VSJ* (November 1954).

23. Quotations are from, respectively, Per.comm.: FE-F-55-Chicago-M; AB-F-70-Chicago-W; Per.corr.: SMcC-F-89-LaCrosse, Wis.-?; and Mrs. M.L.L., New York, N.Y., *VSJ* (October 1941).

24. ?D.C., Chicago, *VSJ* (December 1951); Mrs. J.C., Conemaugh, Pa., *SJJ* (March 1964); Mrs. J.D., Torrington, Conn., *SJJ* (October 1966). The story about the boy on the swings was told me by 800: KL-F-65+-Hernando, Fla.-M. KL described this quality of her prayers to St. Jude as "automatic."

25. Quotations are from, respectively, Per.comm.: BF-F-75-South Chicago-W; FA-F-68-Indiana-S; and Per.comm.: AN-F-60+-Los Angeles-?. I have noted elsewhere in this study that men's description of Jude tend to be more restrained and abstract; the few men

who responded to my questions at the Shrine said either that Jude "looked like the Statue at the National Shrine" or that "I really don't know" (Per.comm.: CA-M-45-South Holland, Ill.-M; EA-M-69-Chicago-M). One man said that Jude looked "like my grandfather would look if he had a beard" (EC-M-35-Chicago-S).

26. Per.comm.: MF-F-45+-Yarmouth [Mass.?]-M. MF wrote, "I had a boyfriend onces [sic]. I went with him. But left him. He was real mean to me. So I ask St. Jude to help me fine [sic] someone. So he did. I been married for 9 years in Oct. 27." (I should note that the low level of literacy evident here is rare among the many people who wrote to me.) The comment about Jude's capability is from Per.comm.: EF-F-63-Chicago-W; another woman told me that after her husband was paralyzed in a car accident she put an image of Jude in every room in their home, as if the saint were entering the spaces her husband could no longer. Per.comm.: AC-F-66-Chicago-M. The statement about Jude's reliability, "wart or worry," was made by Per.corr.: SMcC-F-89-LaCrosse, Wis.-?

27. The comments in this paragraph are taken from the following personal communications: FA-F-68-Indiana-S; EE-F-65+-Indiana-M (who noted that her responses to my questions reflected her husband's views as well); DA-M-59-Chicago-M; EI-M-64-Chicago-M; AG-F-55-Chicago-S; GA-F-55-Chicago-M; AI-F-55-Chicago-D; BA-F-27-Chicago-M; FB-F-73-Chicago-W; CH-F-69-Chicago-W; ED-F-56-Chicago-M; BE-F-66-Indiana-M; DA-F-54-Chicago-W; CH-F-69-Chicago-W; EG-F-64-Chicago-M; FE-F-53-Chicago-M; AH-F-33-Chicago-S; DG-F-76-Chicago-M. FA's description went on: "He gives the appearance of a very kindly, understanding, and caring person with a Big Heart. He looks to be a very humble and courageous man, with a very Fatherly disposition, and compassion for all mankind[,] particularly those who are desperate for help. His very close resemblance to His Cousin Jesus is simply outstanding and beautiful." DA encountered the novena to St. Jude through his wife and her friends, and visited the Shrine in their company.

28. Quotations are from, respectively, Mrs.C.B., Niagara Falls, N.Y., SJJ (April 1969); Per.comm.: BC-F-36-Chicago-S; and Per.comm.: EA-F-59-Chicago-M.

29. On the theme of Jude giving abundantly see, for example, Miss F.C.E., Green Bay, Wis., VSJ (August 1941); [Mr.] A.D., Baltimore, VSJ (February 1952); Miss J.Z.T., Detroit, VSJ (May 1954); Mr. and Mrs. W.A., no loc. cited, SJJ (March 1962).

30. Mrs. H.R.W., Bridgeville, Pa., VSJ (December 1953); 800: SM-F-65+-Springfield, Mo.-D; Per.corr.: AS-F-60?-Carol Stream, Ill.-M; see also, for additional examples, Miss S.P., Chicago, VSJ (April 1935); Mrs. E.H.D., Peoria, Ill., VSJ (July 1935); ?C.L.C., Wausau, Wis., VSJ (October 1937); ?C.T., New York, N.Y., VSJ (January 1940); Miss C.A., Chicago, VSJ (October 1941); Mrs. E.C., Altoona, Pa., VSJ (December 1941); ?F.N., Clementon, N.J., VSJ (July 1950); ?J.D., Clinton, Neb., VSJ (October 1950); Miss E.N., Sugar Land, Texas, VSJ (February 1954); ?H.M.H., Pennsylvania, VSJ (January 1955); Miss J.W., New York, N.Y., SJJ (October 1969).

31. 800: KL-F-70+-Milton, Mass.-W.

32. Pat said the same thing: Jude stands in her dining room because "I want him to be part of the gatherings" there.

33. For example, Per.comm.: AG-F-55-Chicago-S; CI-F-62-Chicago-W; Per.corr.: S.McC.-F-89-LaCrosse, Wis.-?; no name given [internal evidence permits identification as female]-50+? [based on reference to adult children]-Pittsburgh,-?

34. Per.comm.: BE-F-66-Chicago-M.

35. Mrs. A.C., Detroit, *SJJ* (October 1968); Per.comm.: DA-F-54-Chicago-W. Another of my sources told me, "I have a medallion [of St. Jude] around my neck that gets used a lot," and when I asked her to clarify this "use" she said, "when I'm thinking about him I finger it" (800: KJ-F-50+-Portsmouth, N.H.-D/R). Still another mentioned that whenever she gets into her car, she "pats the St. Jude," her term for the statue attached to her dashboard. 800: LN-F-55+-San Bernardino, Calif.-M.

36. Molinari carefully discusses this criticism in *Saints*, 42–3, 109–119; 138–143; 230; a sophisticated psychological and theological critique of devotionalism can be found in Meissner, *Psychoanalysis and Religious Experience*.

37. Per.comm.: CG-F-65-Chicago-M.

38. For some expressions of devotional courtesy see Mr. J.K., Chicago, *VSJ* (January 1935); Mrs. J.M., Belmont, Mass., *VSJ* (October 1937); Mrs. S.G., Chicago, *VSJ* (March 1941); L.S., Pennsylvania, *VSJ* (September 1943); ?F.J., Louisville, Ky., *VSJ* (March 1950); Mr. J.R.Q., South Braintree, Mass., *VSJ* (January 1954); Mrs. R.L.L., Portland, Maine., *VSJ* (September 1954). The statement of gratitude is from ?J.L., Rutland, Vt., *VSJ* (October 1951). Examples of devout worrying about bothering St. Jude with their requests include Anon. Per.corr. cited in note 33 above; also Mrs. J.C., Cincinnati, *VSJ* (December 1958); Per.comm.: BD-F-46-Chicago-M.

39. ?M.S., Brooklyn, N.Y., *VSJ* (April 1937); Mrs. E.O., Chicago, *VSJ* (May 1935); Mrs. K., Chicago, *VSJ* (May 1935); Mrs. J.T., Swissvale, Pa., *VSJ* (September 1936); ?R.F., Fort Wayne, Ind., *VSJ* (July–August 1938).

40. This last comment is by 800: JF-F-55+-Troy, Mich.-D? The remarks about owing Jude in return for his help are from, respectively, ?H.R, Brooklyn, N.Y., *VSJ* (July 1951); and Miss A.C., Chicago, *VSJ* (April 1954).

41. See, for example: ?M.S.M., Santa Ana, Calif., *VSJ* (January 1935); ?M.S., Brooklyn, N.Y., *VSJ* (April 1937); ?E.D., Ohio, *VSJ* (June 1943); ?R.S., Gallup, N.M., *VSJ* (August 1951); Mrs. T.M., Baton Rouge, La., *SJJ* (August 1967).

42. On putting Jude to the test, Per.comm.: DD-F-62-Whiting, Ind.-M. The sentence about Jude's desiring to be known is from Per.corr.: HH-F-65+-Regina, Sask.-?. For examples of devout holding Jude to his titles see Per.comm.: AC-F-66-Chicago-M; Per.corr.: JWM-?-?-Oak Lawn, Ill.-?; ?A.J.Z., no loc. cited, *VSJ* (June 1953); Mrs. H.W., Chicago, *VSJ* (July 1953); ?S.K., Dorchester, Mass., *VSJ* (June 1951).

43. ?A.J.Z., no location specified, *VSJ* (June 1953); for other examples of this bartering, negotiating relationship with Jude, see Mrs. V.R., no loc. cited, *VSJ* (March 1935); Mrs. I.W., Pittsburgh, *VSJ* (December 1935); Mrs. E.H., Milwaukee, *VSJ* (August 1936); ?L.C., Brooklyn, N.Y., *VSJ* (February 1937); Mrs. B.H., Richmond Hill, N.Y., *VSJ* (February 1937); Mrs. H.V., Warren, Ohio, *VSJ* (February 1940); Mrs. Vincent L. Toomey, Washington, D.C., *VSJ* (April 1942); ?M.E.B., Missouri, *VSJ* (November 1942); ?M.W., Pittsburgh, *VSJ*

(October 1949); ?J.H., Philadelphia, *VSJ* (December 1949); ?M.S., Woodward, Iowa, *VSJ* (December 1949); ?M.I.R., Buffalo, N.Y., *VSJ* (August 1951); Mrs. E.N., Chicago, *VSJ* (September 1953).

44. On the danger of Jude's inverting actions see, for example, Mrs. C.E.V., no loc. cited, *VSJ* (February 1958); Mrs. P.A., Pittsburgh, *VSJ* (July 1958); ?M.G., Pawtucket, R.I., *VSJ* (September 1958); Mrs. G.S., Lonton, Va., *SJJ* (May 1963). The fear that a successful outcome for oneself could represent disaster for someone else is evident in Mrs. C.E.V., no address, *VSJ* (February 1958). The devout quoted in the text is Miss E.N., Sugar Land, Texas, *VSJ* (February 1954); a similar sentiment was expressed by 800: SM-F-65+-Spring-field, Mo.-D. On Jude's freedom and the resulting unexpectedness of some of his actions, see, for example, ?A Perpetual Member of the St. Jude League, Chicago, *VSJ* (January 1935); Mr. W.Q., Chicago, in the same issue; Mrs. B.M., Chicago, *VSJ* (January 1937); Mrs. V.V., Los Angeles, *VSJ* (April 1937); ?F.S., Los Angeles, *VSJ* (October 1941); ?M.R., Media, Pa., *VSJ* (February 1942); ?P.F., Pennsylvania, *VSJ* (August 1943); ?G.D., Arizona, *VSJ* (September 1943); ?M.M.K., Chicago, *VSJ* (April 1954); Miss J.T.Z., Detroit, *VSJ* (May 1954).

45. 800: SG-F-55?-Toledo, Ohio-M. S.G. wept during our conversation and concluded with this sad reflection on Jude's "forgetting" her: "I think that . . . you, you know, you get to the point where you lose all faith. And even though I do believe that there is a force stronger than [us], I just sometimes think that what happens is inevitable. It's almost like we're little puppets, that things are just meant to be." This issue also came up prominently in my conversation with 800: BP-F-50+-Bronx, N.Y.-M. BP said, "I put [a 'Thank You, St. Jude' notice] in one of the newspapers and then I said, 'Is this going to be like every month that I'm going to have to publicize this?' I discussed it with a friend, another friend who has a devotion to St. Jude, whose brother is a priest. And I said, 'Do I have to do something like this, or am I going to be jinxed if I don't?' And she said, 'No, you don't have to do anything like that.' " The subject was addressed by the Shrine, too, which sought to allay people's fears; see, for example, "Director's Column," *SJJ* (October 1967): 2. On chain letters see, for example, "Director's Column," *SJJ* (October 1967): 2. Several of my sources mentioned their discomfort with these letters. The Shrine clergy actively discouraged the practice, although the letters continued to circulate, and still do.

46. Joachim DePrada, C.M.F., "The Meaning of Saint Jude," *VSJ* (October 1954): 8; "Personal Devotion to a Saint," *SJJ* (March–April 1963): 2–3; "Director's Column," *SJJ* (October 1967): 2. Stephen Wilson identifies this concern as an ancient feature of the Catholic cult of saints, in his introduction to *Saints and Their Cults*, 19, 22.

5. "SHE WOULD TELL ME HER TROUBLES, AND I MINE"

1. Sister M. Marguerite, "If You Had Gone to Mary," 4, 20, 25.

2. This chapter is based on my reading of all of the letters written to the Shrine, as well as on the stories women told me directly about St. Jude. Specific sources will be cited below, but readers interested in studying the narrative practices of this devotion might

consult the following selection of examples from the *Voice of St. Jude* and *St. Jude's Journal:* Miss H.B., Hornell, N.Y. (January 1935); Mrs. M.S., Chicago (January 1935); ?Friends of Saint Jude, Chicago (March 1935); Mrs. H., Chicago (April 1935), and in the same issue also M.G.C., Chicago, and A Devoted Client of Saint Jude, Chicago; ?H.M.S., Cleveland (May 1935), and in the same issue also Mrs. M.K., Chicago; Mrs. J.C., Chicago (June 1935); in the July, 1935, issue see Mrs. W.F.K., Kankakee, Ill.; ?M.V.Z., Melrose Park, Ill.; M.E.M., Astoria, N.Y.; and ?M.O., Chicago; Miss M.E.A., Baltic, Conn. (December 1935); Mr. and Mrs. B.C. [written by Mrs. B.C.], Detroit (August 1936); Mr. and Mrs. M.J.B. [written by Mrs. M.J.B.], Chicago (October 1936); A.K., Chicago (November 1936); ?A.K., Jersey City, N.J. (January 1937); in the February 1937 issue see ?P.N., Siloam Springs, Ark., and Mrs. J.V., Berkeley, Calif.; ?E.A., Brooklyn, N.Y. (May 1937); Mrs. J.M., Belmont, Mass. (October 1937); in December 1937 see ?E.S.S., New York, N.Y., and Mrs. V.F., Sayreville, N.J.; ?M.R., Pittsburgh (January 1938); in March 1938 see Mrs. F.M., Bronx, N.Y.; Mrs. M.L., Chicago; and Mrs. A.M., Pittsburgh; Mrs. M.C., Bronx, N.Y. (July–August 1938); A.M., Chicago (January 1940); Mrs. W.B., Mark Center, Ohio (February 1940); M.H., Toledo, Ohio (October 1940); A New Patron, Louisville, Ky. (November 1940); in December 1940 see Mrs. H.W., Minneapolis; Mrs. A.L., Louisville, Ky.; and Mrs. J.R., Chicago; ?M.K.L., Shreveport, La. (January 1941); in March 1941 see Mrs. E.R., Wyandotte, Mich.; Mrs. W.H., Joliet, Ill.; and Mrs. O.F.K., St. Paul, Minn.; in April 1941 A Happy Mother, St. Louis; Mrs. A.G., Chicago; and Mrs. J.S., Brooklyn, N.Y.; Mrs. J.B., Portland, Ore. (June 1941); in August 1941 see Mrs. W.H., Chicago; Mrs. G.S., Dayton, Ohio; and ?A.M.B., Reno, Nev.; Mrs. T. Schodroski, St. Louis (February 1942); Mrs. E.G., no loc. (August 1942); ?M.O., Ohio (September 1942); ?M.E.B., Missouri (November 1942); ?C.G., Illinois (December 1942); in March 1943 see ?M.D., Illinois; ?M.B., Michigan; and ?M.M., Illinois; ?A.H., Delaware (July 1943); ?J.C., Ohio (August 1943); L.S., Pennsylvania (September 1943); [Mr.] J.F., New York, N.Y. (October 1943); [Mr.] J.F., Bethlehem, Pa. (November 1943); W.G., Dundalk, Md. (January 1944); Mrs. Gertrude Esser, Milwaukee (April 1948); in April 1949 see ?A.C., New York, N.Y.; ?F.L., Compton Plains, N.J.; and ?E.G., Ipswich, Mass.; in May 1949 see ?M.K., Pueblo, Colo.; ?L.L., Baltimore; ?A.A., San Francisco; ?B.B., Yonkers, N.Y.; C.M., Alice, Texas; and ?F.McG., Sheridan, Mont.; M.McD., Lexington, Mass. (June 1949), and in the same issue, M.B., Vergennes, Vt.; in July 1949 ?P.B., Gallitzin, Pa., and R.W., Newton, Mass.; J.G., Chicago (September 1949); in October 1949 V.D., Lakemore, Ohio, and L.N., Madison, Neb.; F.K., Pittsburgh (November 1949); in January 1950 see ?T.H., New York, N.Y., and ?G.R., Lakepost, Calif.; ?J.H., Akron, Ohio (April 1950); R.M., Crawley, La. (May 1950); in June 1950 see ?A.S., Rochester, N.Y.; ?I.V., San Antonio, Texas; and ?L.P., Eunice, La.; B.M., Cleveland (September 1950); J.McC, Fort Wayne, Ind. (October 1950), also in the same issue, ?M.P., Champaign, Ill., and ?V.G., Milwaukee; in December 1950, M.C., Chicago; I.B., Kent, Conn.; and P.F., South Bend, Ind.; ?C.S., St. Louis (March 1951), and in the same issue, ?J.C., Chicago, and D.R., Santa Clara, Calif.; in April 1951, D.G., Bourbonnais, Ill., and ?F.F., Rochester, N.Y.; in May 1951, E.R., Bronx, N.Y.; D.R., Flushing, N.Y.; L.L., San Gabriel, Calif.; S.J., North Tonawanda, N.J.; and ?V.B., Baton Rouge, La.; A.P., Detroit (June 1951); S.K., Chicago (July 1951); in

Note to page 122

August 1951 see F.J.G., Port Allen, La.; E.M., Baltimore; M.R.S., Santa Monica, Calif.; and ?J.R.W., Chicago; L.E.S., San Pedro, Calif. (September 1951); in October 1951 see ?G.N., Waverly, Iowa; ?R.K., Berkley, Mich.; and ?A.G.G., Edinburgh, Texas; M.C., Plaistow, N.H. (November 1951), and in the same issue ?C.E., Lambertville, Mich.; ?R.D., Jackson, Mich. (December 1951); ?W.B.T., Owensboro, Ky. (January 1952), and in the same issue, ?A.M., Lincoln Park, Mich.; ?E.M., Pittsburgh (February 1952), also in this issue [Mr.] A.D., Baltimore; ?L.M., St. Louis (March 1952); [Mr.] W.L.B., Waukesha, Wis. (April 1952), and in this issue, too, ?W.F., Jasper, Ind., and N.N., Woonsocket, R.I.; in May 1952, D.P.H., Somerset, Mass., and ?E.P., no loc.; in June 1952, ?H.R., Detroit; R.MacP., South Peabody, Mass.; and ?L.C., Blue Island, Ill.; Mr. and Mrs. A.C.B. [written by Mrs. A.C.B.], Detroit (July 1952); [Mr.] J.F.H., Philadelphia (August 1952); A.C., Lafayette, Ind. (November 1952); ?M.F., Columbia, Ill. (December 1952); in January 1953 see Mrs. M.D., Waco, Texas; A.J., Marathon, Wis.; Mrs. H.C.F., Baton Rouge, La.; and K.B.T., Baltimore; in March of the same year, Mrs. A.S., Anthony, N.M.; Mrs. F.S., Chicago; Mrs. M.H., Philadelphia; Mrs. J.K.W., Toledo, Ohio; and Mrs. F.T.K., Finksburg, Md.; in April 1953, Mrs. M.E.G., San Antonio, Texas; Mr. J.F., Staten Island, N.Y.; and Mrs. A.P., Perryville, Mo.; Mrs. E.M.B., Detroit (June 1953); in July 1953, Mrs. G.H., Chicago; ?M.Z., Jackson Heights, N.Y., and Miss L.M., Baltimore; in August 1953, Mrs. L.V.D., Buda, Ill.; Miss E.M.L., Bellevue, Ky., and Mrs. H.S., Lyle, Minn.; in September of that year, Mrs. M.M.M., Tampico, Ill.; Mrs. E.N., Chicago; and Mrs. A.B.A., Baltimore; Mrs. A.S., Baltimore (October 1953), and in this issue, too, Mrs. A.L.P., Cincinnati, and Mrs. G.J.Q., Ogden, Utah; Miss J.Y., Scranton, Pa. (November 1953); in December 1953, Mrs. P.K., Chicago; Mrs. D.M., Hicksville, N.Y., and Mrs. J.C., Brooklyn, N.Y.; in February 1954, Mrs. R.O., St. Louis, and Mrs. M.C., Pittsburgh; Mrs. A.M., Somerset, Ohio (March 1954); Mrs. T.L., Jennings, Mo. (April 1954); Mrs. J.L.P., Dorchester, Mass. (May 1954); Mrs. M.V., no loc. (June 1954); in July 1954, Mrs. D.C., Worcester, Mass.; Mrs. N.P.LaR., no loc.; [Mr.] L.J.W., Wyandotte, Mich.; and M.T.B., Worcester, Mass.; Mrs. I.T.B., Chicago (August 1954), and in the same issue, B.A.B., Beverly Hills, Calif.; Mrs. W.B., Reading, Ohio (September 1954); in October 1954 see Miss M.P., Detroit; Mrs. F.W., Beldenville, Wis.; and Mrs. D.C.S., Staten Island, N.Y.; Mrs. R.E., Windsor, Vt. (November 1954), and in this issue Mrs. G.F.C., Chicago; Miss M.J.D., Lowell, Mass. (December 1954); in February 1955 see M.C.W., Louisville, Ky., and Mrs. A.M., Cincinnati, Ohio; Mrs. S.K., Cleveland, Ohio (March 1955), and also Mrs. M.H., Evansville, Ind., and Mrs. A.L.D., Springfield, Mass.; in April 1955 see Mr. and Mrs. F.L. and Family [written by Mrs. F.L.], Edinburgh, Texas; Mrs. J.W.W., Louisville, Ky.; Mr. and Mrs. J.A.C. [written by Mrs. J.A.C.], Independence, La.; and Mrs. W.B., Brewster, N.Y.; Mr. J.F., St. Paul, Minn. (May 1955); Mrs. E.J.McC., no loc. (July 1955), and also in this issue Mrs. C.W.L., Oklahoma; in September 1955, Mrs. M.A.K., Pickering, Ont.; ?M.E.G., South Coventry, Conn., and ?E.C.S., Lafayette, Calif.; C.R., New Milford, N.J. (October 1955), and in this issue, too, Mrs. C.W.F., Newport, Ky.; Mrs. M.V.J., Dallas (November 1955); Mrs. M.D.S., Centerline, Mich. (February 1958); in March 1958, Mrs. A.B., Methuen, Mass.; Mrs. R.H., New Castle, Del.; and Mrs. E.R.P., Lawrence, Mass.; Mrs. F.H., Baltimore (May 1958); ?R.O., West Chicago (August 1958); Mrs. C.A.B., Brookline, Mass. (October

1958); Mrs. W.J.H., Boise, Idaho (November 1958); Mrs. L.B., Buffalo, N.Y. (December 1958).

3. Per.comm. B.D.-F-46-Chicago-M; for some expressions of women's eagerness to publish their stories of Jude's interventions see also in the *Voice of St. Jude* Mrs. V.B., Bronx, N.Y. (August 1936); ?M.R., Pittsburgh (January 1938); Mrs. M.R., Jamaica, N.Y. (June 1938); Mrs. P.K., Louisville, Ky. (May 1953); Mrs. J.R.H., Henderson, Ky. (September 1953); Mrs. Anne Mc., Cincinnati (October 1953); Mrs. G.N., Long Island, N.Y. (December 1953); Miss E.N., Sugar Land, Texas (February 1954); Mrs. J.B.M., Lake Charles, La. (March 1954); Mrs. S.R., Woodland, Calif. (November 1955). For the devout's articulation of why they undertook to write letters see Miss H.M., Chicago (April 1935); ?M.C., Chicago (May 1935); Mr. and Mrs. M.J.B. [written by Mrs. M.J.B.], Chicago (October 1936); Mrs. J.V., Berkeley, Calif. (February 1937); Mrs. W.T., Swissvale, Pa. (July–August 1938); Mrs. P.L., Chicago (January 1941); ?C.K., Chicago (August 1941); ?D.J., New York, N.Y. (September 1941); ?L.A., New York, N.Y. (August 1942); ?M.M., Connecticut (January 1943); F.K., Pittsburgh (November 1949); ?L.K., Chicago (March 1950); ?F.N., Clementon, N.J. (July 1950); ?A.M., Lincoln Park, Mich. (January 1952); Mr. A.D., Baltimore, Md. (February 1952); S.A., Hatboro, Pa. (May 1952); ?C.A., Olean, N.Y. (June 1952); ?L.C., Blue Island, Ill. (June 1952); K.B.T., Baltimore (January 1953); Mrs. T.F., Brooklyn, N.Y. (February 1953); Mrs. F.S., Chicago (March 1953); Mrs. E.M.B., Detroit (June 1953); Mr. L.M., Ozone Park, N.Y. (May 1953); Mrs. P.E.McN., Springboro, Pa. (July 1953); Mrs. B.O., Springfield, Mass. (September 1953); Mrs. L.F.C., Buffalo, N.Y. (September 1953); Mrs. P.K., Chicago (December 1953); Mrs. H.J.L., St. Paul, Minn. (June 1954); Mrs. A.L.D., Springfield, Mass. (March 1955); Mrs. M.J., Whitestone, Long Island, N.Y. (April 1955); C.R., New Milford, N.J. (October 1955).

4. The assurance about how to fulfill the vow comes from the "Editor's Note" appended to the angry communication from Mrs. G.M.W., Braddock, Pa., *VSJ* (September 1953); the angry admonition is from "St. Jude's Mail," *VSJ* (June 1943): 11. A gentler caution superseded this in April 1952, explaining that the huge volume of mail received in Chicago made it impossible for the Shrine to print every thanksgiving, in "To Our Readers," *VSJ* (April 1952): 32. The letter from Mrs. G.M.W. began, "I am writing this letter to you and meaning to get an answer to the question why was my letter of thanksgiving not published in your magazine yet, as I had requested" (Mrs. G.M.W., Braddock, Pa., *VSJ* [September 1953]). A milder note of reproach is evident in a communication from Mrs. J.O., Bridgeport, Conn., *VSJ* (April 1938). For the devout's insistence that full letters be printed see the "Editor's Note," *VSJ* (September 1953): 41. For an example of the devout's writing despite disabilities see Mrs. P.K., Louisville, Ky., *VSJ* (May 1953); my own sources made similar comments, telling me that they were writing even though "my eyes are very frail" (Per.corr. KG-F-80+?-Smithtown, N.Y.-W?) or "I am so crippled with arthritis and two weeks ago had a cataract operation" (Per.comm. AB-F-70-Aurora, Colo.-W?).

5. The correspondent quoted here is H.R., Detroit, *VSJ* (June 1952); textual evidence suggests that the writer is female. For examples of the urgency of the devout's impulse to

narrative see ?A.F., Chicago, *VSJ* (May 1952); Mrs. Y.M., Littleton, N.H., *VSJ* (July 1953); Mrs. J.C., Brooklyn, N.Y., *VSJ* (December 1953). The last communication begins, "I must write these few lines to let you know that Saint Jude has again come to my aid."

6. George Hull makes this point explicitly in his discussion of the founding of the periodical in "Life Begins at Forty," *VSJ* (June 1935): 9.

7. Mrs. G.H., Chicago, *VSJ* (July 1953). The gender of the stranger is clearly indicated in the text.

8. Mrs. P.K., Louisville, Ky., *VSJ* (May 1953).

9. The phrases quoted in the text are from Mrs. W.B., Reading, Ohio, *VSJ* (September 1954); Mrs. F.M., Bronx, New York, *VSJ* (March 1938); Mrs. M.D., Waco, Texas, *VSJ* (January 1953). For some additional examples of women building a network of support through the devotion see: Mrs. W.F.K., Kankakee, Ill., *VSJ* (July 1935); Mrs. M.Z., San Antonio, Texas, *VSJ* (February 1937); ?L.A., Seattle, *VSJ* (June 1949); R.W., Newton, Mass., *VSJ* (July 1949); ?M.McC., St. Cloud, Minn., *VSJ* (November 1950); M.C., Chicago, *VSJ* (December 1950); R.M., St. Louis, *VSJ* (June 1951); ?A.T., Detroit, *VSJ* (October 1951); S.A., Hatboro, Pa., *VSJ* (May 1952); P.L.W., Indianola, Neb., *VSJ* (July 1952); A.J., Marathon, Wis., *VSJ* (January 1953); Mrs. A.P., Perryville, Mo., *VSJ* (April 1953); Miss M.A., Pittsburgh, *VSJ* (June 1953); Mrs. J.M., Jr., Wyandotte, Mich., *VSJ* (August 1953); Mrs. M.M.M., Tampico, Ill., *VSJ* (September 1953); Mrs. G.J.F., St. Louis, *VSJ* (October 1953). Note that although the gender of the correspondent is uncertain in many of these cases, each letter clearly documents women's networks of prayer.

10. 800: TF-F-40+-Tampa, Fla.-M; 800: KL-F-70+-Milton, Mass.-W.

11. E.M., Pittsburgh, *VSJ* (February 1952). The text does not permit certain identification of the correspondent's gender in this case. I base my assumption that E.M. is a woman on two phrases: the reference to "my baby girl" and the identification of the stranger as "this girl too."

12. This last remark about growing up with other women who prayed to the saints is from Per.comm. D.G.-F-76-Chicago-M?. For examples of women praying together or for each other see R.G., Greene, R.I., *VSJ* (September 1951); Miss A.C., Chicago, *VSJ* (April 1954). I could find no definite example of a man praying for another man, although there are many cases of women praying for their husbands' male friends. The woman who mentions praying with her sister-in-law is A.C., Lafayette, Ind., *VSJ* (November 1952); on this devotional solidarity see also R.W., Newton, Mass., *VSJ* (July 1949); Mrs. A.P., Perryville, Mo., *VSJ* (April 1953); and Per.comm. A.H.-F-33-Chicago-S; BI-F-67-Chicago-W; and B.G.-F-63-Chicago-M. The latter wrote me, "Thru the years [we four sisters] have kept Saint Jude quite busy with our causes but we've also tried to spread devotion to Saint Jude whenever and wherever we can. He has become a close friend and confident [*sic*]. We praise him to the high heavens whenever possible."

13. Per.comm. CD-F-Milwaukee-75-M; SMcC-F-89-LaCrosse, Wis.-W?

14. Wrobel, *Our Way,* 56–57; see also Komarovsky, *Blue-Collar Marriage,* 205–219.

15. Mrs. Gertrude Esser, Milwaukee, *VSJ* (April 1948).

16. Mrs. J.M., Jr., Wyandotte, Mich., *VSJ* (August 1953). For other examples of this

exchange see: P.L.W., Indianola, Neb., *VSJ* (July 1952); A.J., Marathon, Wis., *VSJ* (January 1953); Mrs. P.K., Louisville, Ky., *VSJ* (May 1953), and in this issue Mrs. J., Clarendon Hills, Ill.; Mrs. A.M., Elmwood Park, Ill., *VSJ* (October 1953), and in this issue Mrs. G.J.F., St. Louis; Mrs. M.V., no loc., *VSJ* (June 1954); Mrs. W.B., Reading, Ohio, *VSJ* (September 1954); Mrs. G.F.C., Chicago, *VSJ* (November 1954).

17. Per.comm.: FA-F-68-Indiana [no other location specified]-68-S; for some other examples see R.W., Newton, Mass., *VSJ* (February 1951); Mrs. L.L.M., Springfield, Mass., *VSJ* (June 1953); B.A.B., Beverly Hills, Calif., *VSJ* (August 1954).

18. "Readers," a distraught woman addressed subscribers to the *Voice of Saint Jude* in 1958, "please pray with me so that St. Jude will help reunite me with my baby whom I haven't seen for many, many long months." Mrs. E.W., Pittsburgh, *VSJ* (February 1958).

19. Quotations from, respectively, Mrs. H., [no location cited], *SJJ* (October 1968); and Untitled notice, *SJJ* (January 1967), n.p. Examples of the logistics of introduction to Jude can be found in Per.corr. AG-F-65-[Michigan postmark]-?; and Mrs. M.K., Chicago, *VSJ* (May 1935).

20. "After not speaking to a neighbor for six years," a client wrote the Shrine in 1967, "I prayed to St. Jude and told the neighbor I was sorry for the way I acted. St. Jude answered my prayer and I'll be forever grateful." Mrs. C.T., Chester, Pa., *SJJ* (August 1967).

21. Per.corr. HH-F-65+-Regina, Sask.-?. For stories of women spreading devotion to St. Jude see, for example, Mrs. M.L., Chicago, *VSJ* (December 1935); No initials, Moultrieville, S.C., *VSJ* (August 1937); Mrs. F.M., Bronx, N.Y., *VSJ* (March 1938); Mrs. J.O., Bridgeport, Conn., *VSJ* (April 1938), and in this issue as well Miss A.H., Somerville, Mass.; Mrs. M.C., Bronx, N.Y., *VSJ* (July–August 1938); R.W., Newton, Mass., *VSJ* (July 1949); L.K., Detroit, *VSJ* (September 1950); ?R.C., Beaumont, Calif., *VSJ* (March 1951); ?F.F., Rochester, N.Y., *VSJ* (April 1951); R.M., St. Louis, *VSJ* (June 1951); ?A.T., Detroit, *VSJ* (October 1951); D.P.H., Somerset, Mass., *VSJ* (May 1952); ?M.L.G., Detroit, *VSJ* (November 1952); Mrs. M.D., Waco, Texas, *VSJ* (January 1953), and in this issue, too, A.J., Marathon, Wis.; Mrs. J.I.H., New Iberia, La., *VSJ* (April 1953); Mrs. G.H., Chicago, *VSJ* (July 1953); Mrs. J.M., Jr., Wyandotte, Mich., *VSJ* (August 1953); Mrs. H.P.S., South Gate, Calif., *VSJ* (February 1954).

22. Mrs. J.B.M., Lake Charles, La., *VSJ* (March 1954).

23. D.P.H., Somerset, Mass., *VSJ* (May 1952).

24. This story of a woman on the verge of a nervous breakdown is from Mrs. P.K., Chicago, *VSJ* (December 1953); the earlier quotation in the paragraph is from B.Z., Detroit, *VSJ* (November 1950). I was also told about the powerful effect of reading others' letters to the Shrine by 800: KL-F-70+-Milton, Mass.-W.

25. Quotations from, respectively, Per.corr. AG-F-65-[Michigan postmark]-?; and Per.corr. HH-F-65+-Regina, Sask.-?

26. 800: JF-F-55+-Troy, Mich.-D?.

27. See ?R.M.C., Kansas City, *VSJ* (May 1940), for example, and ?F.S., Los Angeles, *VSJ* (October 1941).

28. Quotations from, respectively, ? "A Friend," Chicago, *VSJ* (June 1935); and J.H., Dayton, Ohio, *VSJ* (May 1949).

29. At the beginning of their prayers to St. Jude the devout write something like, "Please place a light in front of the statue of Saint Jude at the National Shrine for my special intention as I wish very much to have this request answered"; at the end they say, "in gratitude I want another vigil light burned in his honor in his national shrine." These particular sentences are from ?J.H., Philadelphia, *VSJ* (December 1949), and ?E.K., Maryland, *VSJ* (July 1943), but they are typical of thousands of such requests.

30. Scarry, *Body in Pain*, 11.

31. See, for example, Mrs. H., Chicago, *VSJ* (April 1935); Mrs. W.T.H., Raleigh, N.C., *VSJ* (June 1935); Mr. and Mrs. B.C. [written by Mrs. B.C.], Detroit, *VSJ* (August 1936); ?G.G., South Boston, Mass., *VSJ* (May 1937); Mrs. J.C., Chicago, *VSJ* (April 1940); Mrs. F.S., Chicago, *VSJ* (June 1940); Mrs. E.K., Louisville, Ky., *VSJ* (January 1941); ?L.H., New York, N.Y., *VSJ* (June 1941); ?A.G., no loc. cited, *VSJ* (August 1942); ?M.M., Illinois, *VSJ* (January 1943); ?N.B., Mishawauka, Ind., *VSJ* (March 1950); ?E.M., Baltimore, *VSJ* (August 1951); S.A., Hatboro, Pa., *VSJ* (May 1952); Miss B.J., Cleveland, *VSJ* (January 1954); Miss M.P., Detroit, *VSJ* (October 1954); Mrs. H. LeC., Westbrook, Minn., *VSJ* (November 1954).

32. Per.comm.: CH-F-69-Chicago-W.

33. Per.corr.: RA-F-62-[because of the specificity of the account, I will not give a location here]-M.

34. I am borrowing this phrase from Crapanzano, *Tuhami*, 140. Crapanzano is describing his own role as the necessary other in his friend Tuhami's narrative construction of himself. As Crapanzano says, "I became, I imagine, an articulatory pivot about which [Tuhami] could spin out his fantasies in order to create himself as he desired. I was created to create him."

35. Other examples of practices seemingly intended to offer closure include naming children born in difficult circumstances after the saint (see, for example, Mrs. R.W., St. Paul, Minn., *VSJ* [July 1937]; Mrs. R.A.M., Washington, Ind., *VSJ* [January 1941]; ?L.B., Spokane, Wash., *VSJ* [December 1950]; Mr. and Mrs. I.E., Chicago, *VSJ* [December 1954]; Mrs. R.M.S., Chicago, *VSJ* [January 1955]); enrolling the once-afflicted person in the League of St. Jude after the crisis (see, for example, Mrs. M.M., Joliet, Ill., *VSJ* [August 1936]; Mrs. A., Chicago, *VSJ* [September 1936]; Mrs. R.R., Chicago, *VSJ* [April 1937]); subscribing to the *Voice of St. Jude* in thanksgiving for the saint's intervention (see, for example, Mrs. W.B., Pottsville, Pa., *VSJ* [July 1937]; Mrs. F.J.J., Trumbull, Conn., *VSJ* [March 1954]); and requesting medals, as in ?H.J., Louisiana, *VSJ* (February 1943). Simple declarative thank you notices with little or no narrative elaboration, sent either to the Shrine or to a client's local newspaper, may also be construed as gestures of closure. Crapanzano emphasizes closure in his account of Tuhami's religious practice; the saints, he writes, "enable the articulation—and ritual fixation—of the individual's personal experience" (*Tuhami*, 96).

36. Mrs. C.V., Centerville, Ind., *SJJ* (October 1967).

37. This is how I understand the dynamic between structure and antistructure, or structure and communitas, discussed in reference to pilgrimage by Turner in "Pilgrimages as Social Processes," in *Dramas, Fields, and Metaphors: Symbolic Action in Human*

Society, 166–230. This paragraph represents an elaboration of some ideas first presented in "Center Out There," 223–224.

6. HEALINGS

1. On the Shrine's use of healing language see, for example, advertisements for "Dr. O'Connell Dentists," *VSJ* (April 1935): 18; "Wanted! Men and Women Who Are Hard of Hearing," and "Suffer Varicose Leg Sores?" in *VSJ* (July 1944): 18; "Gas Pain Relief," *VSJ* (September 1950): 27; and "No Time Limit Hospital Plan," *VSJ* (October 1953): 5. This paragraph also draws from Interview at the National Shrine, January 1989; Per.comm. BG-F-63-Chicago-M; BF-F-75-Chicago-W; and James Tort, C.M.F., "Dedication Anniversary of the National Shrine of Saint Jude," *VSJ* (February 1935): 12–13. See Christian, *Local Religion,* chapter 2, on the intersection of medical history and popular devotions as well.

2. I borrow the distinction between psychogenic and somatogenic from Shorter, *From Paralysis to Fatigue,* 2. Shorter warns historians not to be too quick in deciding whether diseases are psychogenic or somatogenic because doctors themselves, in the actual presence of distressed persons, have found the distinction vexing and because the interactions of body and mind are so complex, subtle, and difficult to track. My comment in the text is not meant to be definitive; in the examples cited I base my (modest and tentative) diagnosis of psychogenic illness on the two factors cited by Shorter as helpful indicators: doctors could find no organic basis for the complaint, and symptoms disappeared on their own. The specific complaints cited in the text here are from Mrs. M.L., Chicago, *VSJ* (March 1938); M.E.M., Astoria, New York, *VSJ* (July 1935); ?A.G., Chicago, *VSJ* (September 1936); ?O.S., Texas, *VSJ* (August 1937); Mrs. E.L.B., Torrance, Calif., *VSJ* (April 1958).

3. The next two paragraphs reflect my reading of a number of powerful studies of the phenomenology of sickness and pain, in particular Scarry, *Body in Pain;* Buytendijk, *Pain;* Bakan, *Disease, Pain, and Sacrifice;* Sontag, *Illness as Metaphor;* Register, *Living with Chronic Illness;* Frank, *At the Will of the Body;* Broyard, *Intoxicated by My Illness;* and esp. Panichas, *Simone Weil Reader.* I am also grateful for the illuminating conversations I had with students and graduate teaching assistants in a course on religion and pain that I taught first at Fordham University and then Indiana, especially Jan Tarlin, Jeff Fry, Sarah Pike, Jenny Girod, Michael Nicklas, Ona Kiser, Robert Kapitske, Patricia Lennon, Deborah Reichler, Dawn Bakken, Jeff Edminister, Anne Barnhart, Kristy Nabhan, and Jason Bivins.

4. This distinction comes from Kleinman, *Illness Narratives,* passim. I have learned a great deal from Dr. Kleinman's work about how to think about "illness" and medical care.

5. This account of medical history in the first three decades of the century relies on Starr, *Social Transformation,* esp. 79–232; and Shorter, *Bedside Manners,* 75–139.

6. Starr, *Social Transformation,* 150; for this paragraph and the next I also relied on pp. 24, 73, 133, 145–179, and 261–263 of this work.

7. On this last point see Macklin, *Mortal Choices,* 43.

8. Kleinman has some especially trenchant observations about this process in *Illness*

Narratives, 127, 135, 180–182; see also Reiser, *Medicine*. My understanding of the place of diagnosis in medical history was also shaped by Shorter, *Bedside Manners*, 75, 91; and Starr, *Social Transformation*, 136–137.

9. Shorter, *Bedside Manners*, 195–196.

10. I first discussed this idea of the future orientation of time in modern medicine in "Center Out There," 222–223.

11. I am following Shorter here in this analysis of the limits of modern medicine's power to heal. On the expectations raised by diagnosis, see *Bedside Manners*, 98.

12. Shorter, *Bedside Manners*, 196. Shorter also comments on the narrowness of modern medical pedagogy (ibid., 185), and this interpretation of medical education since the war is confirmed by many autobiographical accounts of medical training. One of the best is Konner, *Becoming A Doctor*. The physician quoted is Michael J. Lepore, *Death of the Clinician* (Springfield, Ill.: Charles C. Thomas, 1982): 3, cited in Shorter, *Bedside Manners*, 195. Kleinman also discusses how the biomedical model of healing "disempowers" the patient, *Illness Narratives*, 9.

13. Shorter, *Bedside Manners*, 110–113, 151–153. Kselman also makes the point about women outnumbering men at healing shrines, in *Miracles and Prophecies*, 54–55.

14. My thinking about women and medicine has been helped by Doane's discussions of the subject in the context of her work on film history. The phrase quoted in this sentence is from "Clinical Eye," 205; see also *The Desire to Desire*. Doane says that women's bodies were "*over*-present" to them in the new medical culture ("Clinical Eye," 206). For a careful examination of the medicalization of women over the last century and a half see Shorter, *From Paralysis to Fatigue*, passim.

15. Kleinman, *Illness Narratives*, 159.

16. Doane, "Clinical Eye," 210, 218.

17. Starr, *Social Transformation*, 22. Starr writes that the shift from "the household to the market" in health care involved "a shift from women to men as the dominant figures in the management of health and illness." Shorter says that "this women's culture of medicine once embraced millions of women patients," *Bedside Manners*, 71.

18. Frederick B. Balmer, M.D., "Health and Thanksgiving: A Tribute to Your Family Doctor," *VSJ* (November 1936): 5. Other articles in this series included "Your Health in the New Year," *VSJ* (January 1937): 12, 18; "Safeguarding Health," *VSJ* (February 1937): 9–10; "Be Prepared to Help in Emergencies," *VSJ* (March 1937): 11–12; and "First Aid in Emergencies," *VSJ* (May 1937): 5–6.

19. For this theology of sanctification through suffering, as it was elaborated in American Catholic devotional journals in this century, see, for example, Sister Marcella Murray, "Magazines"; Sister M. Teresita, "Opportunities"; T. Fox, "Drama with a Happy Ending"; Joachim DePrada, C.M.F., "To Whom Shall We Turn?" *VSJ* 24 (December 1958): 34; Garesché, S.J., "Catholic Hospital Apostolate"; Wilkerson, "Patient Care." The ethos was pervasive, and virtually any issue of any devotional periodical contained some expression of it. The ambivalent ethos of suffering and pain in modern American Catholicism is

evident in the following examples, among many others: "Our Foolish Discontent"; "Sympathy for the Sick"; "Virtue More Admired"; "Best of All Devotions"; "Relief of the Holy Souls"; Sprenger, "Do It for Mom, Patty"; Willock, "Suffering and Spiritual Growth"; and Dukette, "Salvation in Suffering."

20. For examples of such advice to nurses see Morrison, "Religion in the Curriculum of the Catholic School of Nursing"; and "Nurses' Apostolate." The chaplain quoted is Healy, "Opportunities for Religious Education," 261.

21. Haffner, "One Day at a Time," 343. On Dooley's cancer in American Catholic popular culture see Fisher, *Catholic Counterculture*, 187.

22. Healy, "Opportunities for Religious Education," 261.

23. In "Sick Room Study" the author imagines the sick person ministering to the priest who comes to call on him or her. The metaphor of the beauty shop is from Whelan, "Sick and Aged," 984. The description of the dying girl comes from Tracy, "After Dark," 136.

24. Rogers, "Letters to the Needy," 616; the quotation about Lourdes is from Small, "Vignettes of Lourdes," 771.

25. Sister Celestine, "Sister's Role," 75. The story about the young woman from Dallas is told by Ward, "How and Why of Suffering," 498.

26. American Catholics were articulating an ancient ambivalence; for a useful overview of the complex understandings of sickness, pain, health, and healing in Catholic cultures, see Amundsen, "Medieval Catholic Tradition"; and O'Connell, "Roman Catholic Tradition." About the Tridentine tradition to which American Catholics were immediately heir, O'Connell notes, "Priests and people were likely moreover to ascribe a specific suffering to a specific moral lapse, their own or others', a habit they maintained in the face of official ecclesiastical and theological disapproval" (122).

27. Buckley, "In Bitter Praise of Pain," 528; see also, for example, J. Murphy, "Human Suffering"; and Martindale, "Making Use of Pain." The equation of pain with hangovers is made by Hart, "Meaning of Pain," 53.

28. Quotations from, respectively, P.J.C., "Error and Disease"; and O'Donnell, "Apostolate of the Sick Room," 267.

29. For an example of a missionary's complaint see Schaeuble, "Lepers and Leprosy"; on the association between Hansen's Disease and immorality see Daws, *Holy Man*, 132–134.

30. The pen-pal system is described in Blair, "Share Your Fun." Each issue of *The Ligourian*, a popular devotional periodical, had a special page "For the Shut-In." On CUSA see Hessel, "Catholic Action"; Brindel, "I Am a Cusan"; Tansey, "Catholic Union of Sick Associates"; Shelley, "Find Happiness in CUSA"; LaMontagne, "I Am a Cusan."

31. Mallett, "Overcoming Handicaps," 106.

32. Heath, "From Evil to Good," 19. The remark about lepers is from Doran, "One Way Ticket," 32. Doran's ticket to Molokai, incidentally, was round-trip.

33. "They Also Serve: A Series of Letters from an Invalid," *VSJ* (September 1950): 16–17. Konner provides a "Glossary of House Officer Slang" in *Becoming a Doctor*, 379–390.

34. See, for example, "One Lesson"; C. Fox, "Voice of God"; Schwitalla, "Influence of

the Catholic Hospital"; O'Boyle, "I Saw the Eyes"; Crock, "Mystery of Suffering"; Jennie Marie Mucker, "Hidden Apostles," *VSJ* (February 1954): 10–12; and O. Sanderlin, "My Operation."

35. O'Connor, "Are You Pain's Puppet?" For similar advice to the sick see, for example, Shuler, "Silver Lining of Convalescence"; O'Donnell, "Apostolate of the Sick Room"; Lahey, "Letter to Shut-Ins"; Waters, "Religious Communities for the Sick"; and Martindale, "Making Use of Pain." The comment about ribbons is from Haffner, "One Day at a Time," 344; the dying woman is described in Hoffman, "Candle's Beams," 18.

36. "A headache compared with His crown of thorns! Possibly this may make us a little less timorous in asking for 'more'!" (Martindale, "Making Use of Pain," 53).

37. "Pain can bring greatness to us. It can make people great. It need not. We have seen it in some of our sick, making them only discontented till they find life terribly wearisome. But this failure to grow great by suffering is not due to suffering but to the soul," wrote Jarrett, in "Problem of Suffering," 263; see also Buckley, "In Bitter Praise of Pain," 527. The quotation about Gemma Galgani is from Hagspiel, "New Hospital Patroness," 98; the comment about the child in an iron lung is from "Heroes."

38. See, for example, the peaceful, productive, and well-organized life of leper colonies portrayed in Renneker, "Gateway to Heaven"; Risley, "Damien's Spirit in America"; and Brussel, "Two-Way Door at Carville."

39. "Suffering and Imagination," 596.

40. McCahill, "Christ in the Wounded," 566–567. On the denial of Jesus' suffering see, for example, Cunningham, "Is One of You Sick?" 8–9. Docetic Christologies "denied [Jesus'] real humanity and His actual death," according to Williston Walker, as a way of resolving the terrible contradiction between Jesus' earthly existence and belief in his glory. "The simplest solution of the Christological problem may well have seemed to some the denial of the reality of His earthly life altogether" (*History of the Christian Church*, 51). The remark about Molokai is from Doran, "One Way Ticket," 35; an example of the notion that sickness brings family members together is Boyle, "Long Journey," 10.

41. Waters, "Religious Communities for the Sick," 241. The CUSA motto is taken from an undated prayer card printed by the organization in Bayonne, N.J.

42. J. Murphy, "Human Suffering," 484. For some examples of the theme that one person's pain can benefit others see Hardesty, "Maintenance of the Individuality"; Farrell, "Why the Suffering?" An especially poignant meditation on this view of pain, written by a woman paralyzed from the waist down since the age of seventeen, is V. Murphy, "Sickbed Voyage of Discovery." The writer tells herself, "You are one of the crosses that have made [your family] good" (76).

43. Boyle, for example, contrasts her own resignation to and acceptance of her incurable cancer with the way her non-Catholic relatives rebel against and get angry with their diseases, in "The Long Journey," 11. Recall that Marcy Balaird made a similar comparison between herself and her Protestant sister-in-law. That non-Catholics do not know how to take life on the chin as Catholics do was a commonplace in the devotional press and may

have been the echo among their children of the pride of working-class Catholics of the ethnic enclaves.

44. See, for example, Hart, "Meaning of Pain"; and Heath, "From Evil to Good." The comment that the problem of pain had been "solved" is from Morrison, "Religion in the Curriculum," 423.

45. Jerry Filan's story is told in Shelley, "Find Happiness in CUSA"; and Tansey, "Catholic Union of Sick Associates."

46. Quotations from, respectively, V. Murphy, "Sickbed Voyage of Discovery," 76; and Dukette, "Salvation in Suffering," 78. The story of the girl with polio is from Sprenger, "Do It for Mom, Patty," 51.

47. See, for example, O'Hara, "Good Life." Dooley is quoted in Fisher, *Catholic Counterculture*, 187.

48. See Fisher, *Catholic Counterculture*, 94–99. Here he is talking specifically about the appeal of Dorothy Day's dark anarchism to college-educated children of the Catholic ghettos, but the point can be generalized, as I argue in the text.

49. "Sick Room Study."

50. Wilkerson, "Patient Care," 80. For a brief history of the National Association of Catholic Chaplains, see Gustin with Murray, *National Association*. This paragraph is also based on "Visitation of the Sick"; Barry, "Sacraments for the Sick"; "On Visiting Hospitals"; "Hospital Chaplain" (*HP*); Kraff, "Difference in the Ministry"; and Hospital Chaplain, "God's Way with Souls."

51. The last comment here is by Healy, "Opportunities for Religious Education," 259. The warning about people watching like hawks is from A Chaplain, "Pointers for Hospital Chaplains." On home visits see, for example, Owenita Sanderlin, "Odds and Ends," *VSJ* (July 1958): 31–33; Whelan, "Sick and Aged," 984; and Danagher, "How to Use the Stations Crucifix." For descriptions of sick call sets see "Sick Call Crucifix"; and "Sick Call Set," *VSJ* (September 1946): 20. The insistence that calling on the sick is to anticipate the need for the sacraments is from Barry, "Sacraments for the Sick," 825; see also "Hospital Chaplain" (*HP*), 262.

52. Barry, "Sacraments for the Sick," 825.

53. Taylor, "Four Years in a Hospital"; Kraff, "Difference in the Ministry," 83.

54. Whelan, "Sick and Aged," 984.

55. See O'Connell, "Roman Catholic Tradition." After the Second Vatican Council, Extreme Unction was renamed the Sacrament of the Sick, and greater emphasis was placed on the consolation (and even possible physical help) it offered ill but not necessarily dying persons.

56. For expressions of this ethos see Hospital Chaplain, "God's Way with Souls"; Healy, "Opportunities for Religious Education"; Sister M. Chrysologa, " 'Apostolate to Aid the Dying' "; Sister Celestine, "Sister's Role." The "cardinal rule" of spiritual care in the hospital, Sister Celestine writes, is to "*call the priest in time.*" For a sense of the drama of the sick call as priests understood it see Moore, "Sick Calls."

57. This is commented on by Cunningham, "Is One of You Sick?" See also O'Connell, "Roman Catholic Tradition," 122–123. The description of the hospital as the "anteroom to eternity" is from Magnier, "Man with the Oils," 399, 402. Magnier, like other chaplains, always represents the sick as the dying.

58. The most useful review of this subject is Kelsey, *Healing and Christianity*.

59. S. Wilson, "Introduction," *Saints and Their Cults*, 18.

60. The explosive convergence of all these interests, worldviews, and pretensions on a little girl who claimed to see the Virgin fundamentally shaped the development of the cult of Our Lady of Lourdes, making it a case study of the vicissitudes of the miraculous in modern Catholic culture.

61. On the nineteenth century see Taves, *Household of Faith*, 60; for a modern case see Odell, *Father Solanus*. Sister Celestine ("Sister's Role," 76) reports the instance of an older hospital sister believed by patients to be a healer. The first positive evaluations of religious healing appeared in the devotional press in the mid-1960s, when the ethos of suffering and pain was being called into question. For an example of both reconsiderations, of pain and healing, see Heath, "From Evil to Good," 18–19. Some writers in the 1960s sought to transform that ethos into a motivation for political action and social responsibility; see, for example, Luka, "Way of the Cross." For a discussion of the revival of faith healing among Catholic charismatics in the 1970s by a participant in the movement, see O'Connor, *Pentecostal Movement*. O'Connor's discussion of healing is not completely free of ambivalence; he is uneasy at times with this manifestation of the Spirit's presence (see, for example, 162–164). Although this ambivalence was widely felt in the movement, Mc-Guire's work on the Catholic charismatics indicates that they had broken from the ever weakening ethos of suffering and pain (*Ritual Healing in Suburban America*, 45–46).

62. My sense of this is impressionistic. The subject of immigrant vernacular healing awaits a study of its own.

63. Dukette, "Salvation in Suffering," 78. The warning about losing "the shining thread of Him" is from Tracy, "After Dark," 138.

64. Jarrett, "Problem of Suffering," 264. Ward criticizes the idea, which he says is shared by "some Catholics," that sedation is spiritually wrong ("How and Why of Suffering," 499). Vann approved what he considered the heroic Christian refusal of "anesthetic drugs, twilight sleep, psychotherapy, and so forth," a resistance that he proudly claimed had its "roots in a feeling that the naked will should be left to conquer the rebellions and repulsions of the instincts, so that the reward due to fighting the good fight may not be forfeit" ("True Balance," 486). Vann went on to caution his readers against the "glorification of pain" that he has just urged upon them.

65. The simile of turning off Niagara Falls is from Chiappetta, "Prayers of the Sick," 526. The Catholic Union of the Sick in America was specifically conceived as a means of preventing the "terrific wastage of suffering which takes place when the sick are unaware [of] or indifferent to the truly marvelous opportunities they providentially have at hand," according to Bishop John C. Cody of London, Ontario, quoted in Brindel, "I Am a Cusan," 173.

66. Barry, "Sacraments for the Sick," 825. The discussion of "thought germs" is from P.J.C., "Error and Disease." On the seductiveness of the sick see "Sick Room Study," which urges sick people to "gratify and capture the attention of all those around you."

67. Garesché, "Shall I Be a Nurse?" 712. Garesché was careful to point out that "at least in our form of civilization" nurses come under the "direction and authority of the physician." This discussion of Catholic nurses is also based on Goebel, "Course in Religion"; Sister M. Andrew, "Integrative Process"; Sister St. Stanislaus, "Phases of the Individuality"; Morrison, "Religion in the Curriculum"; Sister Mary Agnes, "Sociology in the Curriculum"; Schwitalla, "Another Sister's Life"; "Belleville Diocesan Association"; "Cardinal's Letter on Nursing"; J. Griffin, "Sermon, Pontifical Mass"; Sister M. Teresita, "Opportunities"; "Nurses' Apostolate"; and "Messages to the Convention."

68. The nursing educator quoted is Sister Celestine, "Sister's Role," 75. Sister Celestine was not herself free from the statistical ethos of pastoral care, however, or from the emphasis on the dying. The distinction between visiting women and sacramentally hasty men was explicit in the literature, as, for example, in Wilkerson, "Patient Care," 79–80. For examples of women's criticism of priests and doctors see Morgan, "Challenge to the Apostolate"; and Magnier, "Man with the Oils," 401. Magnier quotes a non-Catholic nurse who criticized his "jack-in-the-box" way of taking care of patients, a challenge he brushes off by accusing her of not understanding Catholic sacramental theology: "*Ex opere operato* was not part of her vocabulary nor the Body of Christ her daily bread."

69. This description is from Sister Xavier Miriam, "Caring for Souls"; Sister Celestine also emphasizes the importance of devotional practice in the pastoral work of hospital sisters, "Sister's Role," 76. *HP* routinely reported on devotional activities in Catholic hospitals, offering an extensive source for a history of these practices.

70. ?A.C., N.Y., *VSJ* (December 1940); P.R., St. Louis, *VSJ* (July 1950); ?A.B., Minneapolis, *VSJ* (August 1952). For other examples of the use of devotional objects in the hospital setting see Mrs. H., Chicago, *VSJ* (April 1935); ?I.V., San Antonio, Texas, *VSJ* (June 1950); ?M.L., Los Angeles, *VSJ* (September 1950); ?M.P., Champaign, Ill., *VSJ* (October 1950); ?A.T., Detroit, *VSJ* (October 1951); A.J., Marathon, Wis., *VSJ* (January 1953); Mrs. N.P.LaR., no loc., *VSJ* (July 1954); Mrs. F.W., Beldenville, Wis., *VSJ* (October 1954); ?E.L.A., Santa Barbara, Calif., *VSJ* (August 1958).

71. Mr. L.M., Ozone Park, New York, *VSJ* (May 1953). L.M. reports his daughter's pinning a medal on his pajamas. The specific applications of oil cited are from Mrs. E.R., Wyandotte, Mich., *VSJ* (March 1941); ?M.K., Pueblo, Colo., *VSJ* (May 1949); ?F.R., Gulfport, Miss., *VSJ* (September 1950); and Mrs. R.J.S., Allen Park, Mich., *SJJ* (August–September 1962). For other examples of the use of St. Jude's Holy Oil see ?M.M., Connecticut, *VSJ* (January 1943); ?J.M., Aksby, Minn., *VSJ* (November 1943); J.H., Washington, D.C., *VSJ* (April 1949); ?W.B., Stamford, Conn., *VSJ* (October 1949); ?T.K., Denver, *VSJ* (September 1950); ?T.L., Cheyenne, Wyo., *VSJ* (July 1951); ?A.T., Detroit, *VSJ* (October 1951); ?W.F., Jasper, Ind., *VSJ* (April 1952); Mrs. F.F., Gaylord, Mich., *VSJ* (June 1953); Sister Mary Lelia Sherlock, C.S.J., Mount Carmel Hospital, Pittsburg, Kan., *VSJ* (December 1953); Mrs. M.H., Evansville, Ind., *VSJ* (March 1955).

72. Mrs. M.M.M., Tampico, Ill., *VSJ* (September 1953). Scores of healing narratives were published over the years by the *Voice of St. Jude*. My study is based on a close reading of all of them, and many will be cited in the notes that follow. Interested readers might look at the following examples: ?J.J.V., Cicero, Ill. (March 1935), and in the same issue ?M.C., Fort Wayne, Ind.: Mrs. H., Chicago (April 1935); Mrs. E.O., Chicago (May 1935), and in the same issue, Mrs. M.H.F., Chicago; Mrs. B.G., Brooklyn, N.Y. (June 1935), and in this issue too ?T.J.M., Chicago; ?M.J.R., Chicago (July 1935), and in the same issue Mrs. W.F.K., Kankakee, Ill., and ?M.O., Chicago; in December 1935 see Devotee of St. Jude, Chicago; Mrs. A.A., Chicago; and Mrs. J.B., Chicago; ?J.S., Westphalia, Mich. (July 1937); Mrs. O.A., Oak Lawn, Ill. (April 1938); Mrs. M.C., Bronx, N.Y. (July–August 1938); in December 1940 see Mrs. H.W., Minneapolis; Mrs. A.L., Louisville, Ky.; and ?A.C., New York, N.Y.; Mrs. E.G., no loc. (August 1942); ?E.S., New Jersey (January 1943); Mrs. Gertrude Esser, Milwaukee (April 1948); in May 1949 see ?M.K., Pueblo, Colo., and ?A.A., San Francisco; ?A.C., Union City, N.J. (September 1949); ?L.K., Chicago (March 1950); ?L.W., Malden, Mass. (April 1950); ?A.S., Rochester, N.Y. (June 1950); ?V.G., Milwaukee (October 1950), and in the same issue ?M.P., Champaign, Ill.; ?M.McC., St. Cloud, Minn. (November 1950); in September 1951 see L.E.S., San Pedro, Calif., and ?T.F., Chester, Pa.; in May 1952, see D.P.H., Somerset, Mass.; ?E.P., no loc.; S.A., Hatboro, Pa.; R.MacP., South Peabody, Mass. (June 1952); Mrs. J., Clarendon Hills, Ill. (May 1953); in September 1953, see Mrs. L.F.C., Buffalo, N.Y.; Mrs. E.N., Chicago; and Mrs. A.B.A., Baltimore; Mrs. N.P.LaR., no loc. (July 1954), and in the same issue ?M.T.B., Worcester, Mass.; Miss M.J.D., Lowell, Mass. (December 1954); Mrs. J.R.W., Louisville (August 1955); Mrs. V.C., Detroit (November 1955); Mrs. L.B., Buffalo, N.Y. (December 1958). Again, this is not by any means a complete cataloguing of the Shrine's healing stories, only a sample.

73. Mrs. A.S.T., West Shaken, N.Y., *VSJ* (December 1952); for examples of this intimate experience of Jude's presence in prayer see Mrs. F.A., St. Paul, Minn., *VSJ* (February 1937); M.R., Cleveland, *VSJ* (September 1941); ?F.K., Brooklyn, N.Y., *VSJ* (July 1949); ?A.S., Rochester, N.Y., *VSJ* (June 1950); J.McC., Fort Wayne, Ind., *VSJ* (October 1950); T.L.G., St. Louis, *VSJ* (March 1952); ?E.L., New York, N.Y., *VSJ* (September 1952); Per.comm.: CA-F-56-Chicago-M.

74. On Jude's presence in medical settings see, for example, Mrs. A.F.B., Hoopeston, Ill., *VSJ* (November 1940) [the correspondent noted that she was writing on the first anniversary of a stroke that paralyzed her right side]; L.E.S., San Pedro, Calif., *VSJ* (September 1951); Mr. W.F.F., Newark, N.J., *VSJ* (December 1952); Mrs. P.B., Crestline, Ohio, *VSJ* (October 1958); ?Anon., *SJJ* (October 1968); Miss F.H., *SJJ* (June 1969). On the saint's keeping people company in the different periods of waiting characteristic of modern medicine see, for example, Therese Ryan, Boston, *VSJ* (April 1942); ?A.W., Chicago, *VSJ* (June 1951); Mrs. G.B., Sarnia, Ont., *SJJ* (June–July 1961); Mr. and Mrs. D.N., Omaha, Neb., *SJJ* (October 1966). The latter report: "Our five year old son was taken ill and tests were given him as it was feared he had one of two very serious diseases. Though we have implored many favors of Saint Jude, this was the greatest. After two days and nights of prayer and worry, all tests came back negative."

75. 800: KL-F-70+-Milton, Mass.-W.

76. The incubator story is from M.McD, Lexington, Mass., *VSJ* (June 1949); here the phrases "my baby" and "my little daughter" suggest that the correspondent is female. The story about earaches is from ?L.V., Northampton, Mass., *VSJ* (June 1951); this writer spent the day attending to the boy's troubled ears, which again leads me to conclude that this was a woman writing. For other examples of such correspondence see ?H.M.S., Cleveland, *VSJ* (May 1935); Mrs. J.R., Chicago, *VSJ* (December 1940); J.H., Washington, D.C., *VSJ* (May 1950); Mrs. A.L.P., Cincinnati, *VSJ* (October 1953); Mrs. M.A.K., Pickering, Ont., *VSJ* (September 1955); Mrs. P.B., Crestline, Ohio, *VSJ* (October 1958).

77. ?A.S., Rochester, N.Y., *VSJ* (June 1950). It is reasonable to assume that the correspondent in this case is the boy's mother, given that she reports staying home all day to care for her son and teaches him to pray, a duty almost always assumed by women in Catholic culture.

78. This paragraph is based on Mrs. E.K., Louisville, Ky., *VSJ* (January 1941); C.F., Pennsylvania, *VSJ* (October 1942); ?L.M., St. Louis, *VSJ* (March 1952); ?W.F., Jasper, Ind., *VSJ* (April 1952); Mrs. A.B.A., Baltimore, *VSJ* (September 1953); Mrs. R.E., Windsor, Vt., *VSJ* (November 1954); Mrs. G.F.C., Chicago, *VSJ* (November 1954); ?S.M.M., N. Tonawanda, N.Y., *SJJ* (August 1968); 800: TF-F-40+-Tampa, Fla.-M; Per.comm.: CB-F-48-Chicago-M.

79. For examples of women taking charge in sick times see M.E.M., Astoria, N.Y., *VSJ* (July 1935); no initials, Bronx, N.Y., *VSJ* (August 1936); Mrs. M.N., Chicago, *VSJ* (March 1938); Mrs. L.H.M., Fort Madison, Iowa, *VSJ* (December 1940); Mrs. A.W.B., Detroit, *VSJ* (June 1941); A Grateful Client, no loc., *VSJ* (August 1942); M.C., Chicago, *VSJ* (December 1950); D.P.H., Somerset, Mass., *VSJ* (May 1952), and in the same issue S.A., Hatboro, Pa.; Mrs. J.I.H., New Iberia, La., *VSJ* (April 1953); Mr. L.M., Ozone Park, N.Y., *VSJ* (May 1953); Mrs. L.F.C., Buffalo, N.Y., *VSJ* (September 1953); Mrs. A.L.P., Cincinnati, *VSJ* (October 1953); Mrs. G.F.C., Chicago, *VSJ* (November 1954); Miss M.J.D., Lowell, Mass., *VSJ* (December 1954); Mrs. W.B., Brewster, N.Y., *VSJ* (April 1955); Mrs. J.R.W., Louisville, Ky., *VSJ* (August 1955); Mrs. M.A.K., Pickering, Ont., *VSJ* (September 1955); [Mr.]C.E.L., Ashtabula, Ohio, *VSJ* (February 1958). The last correspondent cited here, C.E.L., reported: "I was badly hurt in a railroad accident, had my spleen removed, wasn't expected to live. My wife pinned a St. Jude medal inside my oxygen tent. I made a complete recovery." Note that this is not a complete listing of such stories, but a small, representative selection.

80. One of my sources underlined the pronoun referring to herself in a story about Jude's intervention to help her husband with bleeding ulcers: Per.comm.: CD-F-75-Milwaukee-M. The woman whose child had a skin disease is Mrs. M.J.B., Findlay, Ohio, *VSJ* (November 1941). The story of the boy with a virus was told me by Per.comm.: BA-F-42-Indiana-M.

81. For some examples of such plots see Mrs. J.B.M., Chicago, *VSJ* (August 1936) [this story concerns unemployment, not sickness]; ?D.P., Minnesota, *VSJ* (November 1942); ?M.W., Pittsburgh, *VSJ* (October 1949); Mrs. L.L.M., Springfield, Mass., *VSJ* (June 1953); Mrs. G.H., Niagara Falls, N.Y., *SJJ* (August 1968), and in the same issue Mrs. E.M.C., New

London, Conn. The Shrine itself stressed the healing efficacy of novena time, in, e.g., Novena Announcement, *VSJ* (February 1952): 3.

82. The woman whose daughter had trouble conceiving is 800: SM-F-65+-Springfield, Mo.-D. The subject of Isabel's husband's migraines came up twice in our long conversation, at first briefly, later in a more extended way when we explored explicitly her understanding of her own role in the healing process. The initial sentence quoted in the text comes from her first mention of the situation, the sentence after the elision is taken from her later remarks, made in the context of a reflection on how women get practical things done—like taking care of headaches—more efficiently and effectively than men do.

83. Mrs. R.L.C., writing from San Jose, Calif., in January 1954, for example, told the Shrine that she had prayed to Jude that her brother and sister-in-law would "be blessed with a fine healthy baby of their own." She continued, "As they are not Catholics and do not live near me, but on the East Coast, I had no occasion to mention the Novena to them. However, today, I have learned that they are truly expecting a baby in July—exactly nine months from October, when I made the Novena!"

84. For example M.R., Cleveland, *VSJ* (September 1941); L.K., Detroit, *VSJ* (September 1950); Mrs. R.E., Windsor, Vt., *VSJ* (November 1954); ?F.H.S., San Antonio, Texas, *SJJ* (October–November 1963); Mrs. M.D., no loc. cited, *SJJ* (August 1966).

85. S.A., Hatboro, Pa., *VSJ* (May 1952). Other clear examples of this notion (although written by correspondents whose gender cannot be definitively identified from the evidence of their letters) are ?M.Mc., St. Cloud, Minn., *VSJ* (November 1950) and ?R.G., Greene, R.I., *VSJ* (September 1951).

86. See, for example, Mrs. M.N, Chicago, *VSJ* (March 1938); ?M.L., Los Angeles, *VSJ* (September 1950); Mrs. G.F.C., Chicago, *VSJ* (November 1954). The woman whose husband gave up drinking is 800: JK-F-65+-Worcester, Mass.-W; the quotation about the little girl is from Mrs. P.B., Crestline, Ohio, *VSJ* (October 1958).

87. Mrs. L.H.M., Fort Madison, Iowa, *VSJ* (December 1940), is the source of the story about the girl exposed to infantile paralysis. The story about the boy with nosebleeds is from Mrs. R.J.S., Allen Park, Mich., *SJJ* (August–September 1962). The woman who obtains her healing oil from Baltimore is Per.corr.: SMcC-F-89-LaCrosse, Wis.-? For an example of a devout recognized as being especially efficacious with healing oil see ?A.deL., New York, N.Y., *SJJ* (October–November 1963).

88. This notice appeared in April 1954 on the letters page of the *Voice of Saint Jude:* "St. Jude's Holy Oil is pure olive oil that has been blessed and touched with the sacred relic of St. Jude. The oil itself has no medicinal or curative powers. It is intended for EXTERNAL use as an outward sign of devotion to St. Jude, the patron of desperate or hopeless cases" ("St. Jude Holy Oil," *VSJ* [April 1954]: 33). Because this was its most popular devotional item, however, it was impossible completely to deny its efficacy, and the same notice continues: "Many faithful friends of Saint Jude use St. Jude's Holy Oil in this way and some of them attribute cures and improved health to the use of this oil as a sign of their faith in St. Jude." This does not mean that the clergy were cynical in their treatment of the

oil. As believing men themselves, responsible for the supervision of an important cult, they undoubtedly shared the devout's belief that the oil did have supernatural healing properties, although as educated, modern men they may not have wanted to say as much aloud. Furthermore, federal legislation long advocated by medical doctors restricted what could be claimed for home remedies, another reason for caution and restraint in this matter. Read in the broader context of the ethics of the devotion, the notice is an expression of ambivalence and uncertainty, not deceit.

89. This paragraph is based specifically on the following (although I should emphasize that these represent absolutely the smallest fraction of healing letters in the Shrine's correspondence): ?M.K., Pueblo, Colo., *VSJ* (May 1949) [using oil to reduce swelling of bruised hand]; ?W.B., Stamford, Conn., *VSJ* (October 1949) [using oil to lessen back pain]; ?I.B., Chicago, *VSJ* (December 1949) [prayed through convalescence]; ?J.R., Chicago, *VSJ* (January 1950) [headaches]; ?T.H., New York, N.Y., *VSJ* (January 1950) [infected fingers]; ?F.R., Gulfport, Miss., *VSJ* (September 1950) [skin rash]; ?W.M., Spokane, Wash., *VSJ* (June 1951) [heart attack]; ?W.F., Jasper, Ind., *VSJ* (April 1952) [swollen ankles]; I.C.T., Detroit, *VSJ* (December 1953) [arthritis].

90. 800: LN-F-55+-San Bernardino, Calif.-M.

91. Per.corr.: SMcC-F-89-LaCrosse, Wis.-?

92. See, for example, Mrs. W.G., Milwaukee, *VSJ* (February 1937); ?V.G., Milwaukee, *VSJ* (October 1950); Mrs. D.J.W., Bonita, La., *VSJ* (April 1953); ?A.S., no loc. cited, *VSJ* (June 1954).

93. Kleinman, *Illness Narratives,* 249, 185; see also Starr, *Social Transformation,* 74–75.

94. ?A.A., San Francisco, *VSJ* (May 1949); see also Mrs. W.F.K., Kankakee, Ill., *VSJ* (July 1935); R.W., Newton, Mass., *VSJ* (July 1949); ?A.K., Boswell, Pa., *VSJ* (September 1949); [Mr.]S.K., Chicago, *VSJ* (July 1951); C.A., Chicago, *VSJ* (November 1951); ?H.K.P., Pittsburgh, *VSJ* (July 1952); Mrs. E.B., Evansville, Ind., *VSJ* (January 1954); Mrs. F.J.J., Trumbull, Conn., *VSJ* (March 1954); Mrs. S.K., Cleveland, *VSJ* (March 1955).

95. 800: JL-F-65+-Illinois-W described praying in her hospital room with other family members. For examples of married couples calling on Jude see J.H., Washington, D.C., *VSJ* (May 1950); and A.P., Detroit, *VSJ* (June 1951). For examples of Jude's restoring sick people to their families see Mrs. M.E., Yonkers, N.Y., *VSJ* (June 1941); and Mrs. G.E.L., Detroit, *VSJ* (February 1954).

96. Macklin, *Mortal Choices,* 58–59.

97. Register, *Living with Chronic Illness,* 219. The phrase "bombarding heaven" is from 800: SM-F-65+-Springfield, Mo.-D.

98. For example, Mrs. L.L., no loc. cited, *SJJ* (February–March 1961). She writes: "I became worried about my health and so my husband and I began to pray to St. Jude. Our prayer was answered and we are sure St. Jude interceded for us. We will always be grateful to him."

99. Mrs. M.H., Evansville, Ind., *VSJ* (March 1955).

100. 800: JK-F-65+-Worcester, Mass.-W. For examples of prayers for men's deathbed

reconciliations with the church see ?F.R., Texas, *VSJ* (January 1943); ?A.W., Brooklyn, N.Y., *VSJ* (June 1949); ?P.McD., Gary, Ind., *VSJ* (November 1949); and ?L.M., Middleford, Pa., *VSJ* (December 1949). The only case of prayers for a woman's deathbed reconciliation with the church I noted was Mrs. M.J., Dayton, Ohio, *VSJ* (December 1958).

101. For the image of doctors in the devout's illness narratives, see the following examples: ?J.J.V., Cicero, Ill., *VSJ* (March 1935); Mrs. W.A.D., Detroit, *VSJ* (April 1940); A Grateful Client, no loc., *VSJ* (August 1942); ?F.McG., Sheridan, Mont., *VSJ* (May 1949); M.McD., Lexington, Mass., *VSJ* (June 1949); ?A.C., Union City, N.J., *VSJ* (September 1949); ?J.R., Chicago, *VSJ* (January 1950); L.K., Detroit, *VSJ* (September 1950); ?R.G., Greene, R.I., *VSJ* (September 1951); H.S., Larimore, N.D., *VSJ* (April 1952); R.MacP., South Peabody, Mass., *VSJ* (June 1952); Miss C.S., Many, La., *VSJ* (May 1953); Mrs. E.N., Chicago, *VSJ* (September 1953); Mrs. L.M.L., Minneapolis, *VSJ* (January 1955); Mrs. J.R.W., Louisville, Ky., *VSJ* (August 1955).

102. See, for example, Miss H.B., Hornell, N.Y., *VSJ* (January 1935); Miss E.E., Pottsville, Pa., *VSJ* (July–August 1938); A New Patron [who prays for her husband], Louisville, Ky., *VSJ* (November 1940); ?R.W., Newton, Mass., *VSJ* (July 1949); C.M., East St. Louis, Ill., *VSJ* (February 1952).

103. I have selected the following examples of such narratives among many others: ?M.R., Pittsburgh, *VSJ* (January 1938); A New Patron, Louisville, Ky., *VSJ* (November 1940); ?B.H., Youngstown, Ohio, *VSJ* (February 1941); Mrs. A.B., Phoenix, Ariz., *VSJ* (October 1941); Mrs. E.G., [loc. unintellig.], *VSJ* (August 1942); ?A.A., San Francisco, *VSJ* (May 1949), and in the same issue C.M., Alice, Texas; ?A.C., Union City, N.J., *VSJ* (September 1949); ?L.K., Chicago, *VSJ* (March 1950); Mrs. J., Clarendon Hills, Ill., *VSJ* (May 1953); ?F.F., Rochester, N.Y., *VSJ* (April 1951); A.P., Detroit, *VSJ* (June 1951); E.M., Pittsburgh, *VSJ* (February 1952); Mrs. F.T.K., Finksburg, Md., *VSJ* (March 1953); Mrs. L.F.C., Buffalo, N.Y., *VSJ* (September 1953), and in the same issue Mrs. E.N., Chicago; Mrs. G.E.L., Detroit, *VSJ* (February 1954); Mrs. R.U., Jr., Culver City, Calif., *VSJ* (May 1954); Mrs. M.J.D., Lowell, Mass., *VSJ* (December 1954); Mrs. S.K., Cleveland, *VSJ* (March 1955); Mrs. M.A.K., Pickering, Ont., *VSJ* (September 1955); Mrs. C.A.B., Brookline, Mass., *VSJ* (October 1958), and in the same issue Mrs. T.B., Kingsford, Mich.

104. This last statement is from Mrs. A.M., Arlington, Mass., *VSJ* (December 1958). The story about the man with the boil is from No signature, Bronx, New York, *VSJ* (August 1936). The woman with the growth on her eye is Mrs. O.A., Oak Lawn, Ill., *VSJ* (April 1938); for another example of this phenomenon see Mrs. J.R., Chicago, *VSJ* (December 1940). I also learned about avoiding medical care from Per.corr.: CVG-F-75+-Richmond, Va.-W.

105. For example, Mrs. H.H.N., Chicago, *VSJ* (August 1941); ?R.H.Hummert, Dayton, Ohio, *VSJ* (January 1942); M.D., Illinois, *VSJ* (March 1943); ?A.A., San Francisco, *VSJ* (May 1949); M.McD., Lexington, Mass., *VSJ* (June 1949); ?L.W., Malden, Mass., *VSJ* (April 1950); Mrs. S.K., Cleveland, *VSJ* (March 1955); Mrs. T.H., Ashland, Mass., *VSJ* (September 1958); ?A.N., Saginaw, Mich., *SJJ* (February 1969); Mrs. B.B., Mt. Clemens, Mich., *SJJ* (April 1969).

106. For example, Mrs. H., Chicago, *VSJ* (April 1935); ?M.S., Brooklyn, N.Y., *VSJ* (April 1937); ?A.A., San Francisco, *VSJ* (May 1949); ?I.D., Titusville, Pa., *VSJ* (September 1949); C.M., East St. Louis, Ill., *VSJ* (February 1952); Mr. L.M., Ozone Park, N.Y., *VSJ* (May 1953); ?S.M.M., North Tonawanda, N.Y., *SJJ* (August 1968). One of my sources wrote me: "I have received my answers to my prayers asking St. Jude to have my husband give up drinking. He has had hip surgery and I have had a triple bypass heart surgery. Also I had an infected toe from an ingrown toenail. This just would not heal. I prayed to St. Jude to save my toe and after 2 years it finally healed. The Doctor cannot believe, and said he was sure I would loose [*sic*] the toe and the foot. He asked me who I had up there[.] So I told him it was Saint Jude and gave him a prayer [card] with a relic. He was very please[d] to think I gave him a prayer card, and more information about St. Jude [illeg.]." Per.comm: AE-F-75-Chicago-M.

107. For some examples of devout proclaiming that a miracle had occurred for them see: Miss E.L., Long Beach, Calif., *VSJ* (April 1935); Mrs. J.A.D., Saginaw, Mich., *VSJ* (June 1935); ?M.O., Chicago, *VSJ* (July 1935), and in the same issue Mrs. E.H.D., Peoria, Ill.; ?J.F., Chicago, *VSJ* (January 1937); ?M.S., Brooklyn, N.Y., *VSJ* (April 1937); Mrs. M.S., Jamestown, N.D., *VSJ* (May 1937); Mrs. T.K., Waterbury, Conn., *VSJ* (June 1938), and in the same issue Mrs. O.K., New York, N.Y., and ?G.K., Avoca, Pa.; Mrs. W.B., Mark Center, Ohio, *VSJ* (February 1940); Mrs. H.W., Minneapolis, *VSJ* (December 1940); Mrs. G.J.H., Toledo, Ohio, *VSJ* (January 1941); Mrs. A.B., Phoenix, Ariz., *VSJ* (October 1941); ?J.C., Kent, Ohio, *VSJ* (March 1942); ?C.G., Illinois, *VSJ* (December 1942); M.D., Maryland, *VSJ* (March 1943); ?A.W., Middle Village, N.Y., *VSJ* (December 1949); ?J.R., Chicago, *VSJ* (January 1950); ?M.L., Los Angeles, *VSJ* (September 1950); A.P., Detroit, *VSJ* (June 1951); ?M.I.R., Buffalo, N.Y., *VSJ* (August 1951); ?G.N., Waverly, Iowa, *VSJ* (October 1951); ?C.E., Lambertville, Mich., *VSJ* (November 1951); ?M.C., Brownsville, Texas, *VSJ* (January 1952); C.M., East St. Louis, Ill., *VSJ* (February 1952); ?L.M., St. Louis, *VSJ* (March 1952); S.A., Hatboro, Pa., *VSJ* (May 1952); Mrs. J.K.W., Toledo, Ohio, *VSJ* (March 1953); Mrs. M.M.M., Tampico, Ill., *VSJ* (September 1953); J.F.S., New York, N.Y., *VSJ* (October 1953); ?E.F.H., St. Louis, *VSJ* (September 1954); Mr. J.F., St. Paul, Minn., *VSJ* (May 1955) [note that it was the correspondent's fiancée who suggested he pray to St. Jude].

108. For other examples of this process of assessing, see Mrs. M.J.B., Findlay, Ohio, *VSJ* (November 1941); Mrs. R.J., [Milwaukee?], *VSJ* (August 1942); C.A., Chicago, *VSJ* (November 1951); C.M., East St. Louis, Ill., *VSJ* (February 1952). Two letters, both written by men, attempt to figure out what could be attributed to Jude's intervention and what to luck: J.M., Texas, *VSJ* (August 1943), and Mr. W.D., Berkeley, Calif., *VSJ* (October 1954). Luck does not seem to have been a useful explanatory category for women.

109. ?J.J.V., Cicero, Ill., *VSJ* (March 1935); see also ?T.J.M., Chicago, *VSJ* (June 1935). The comment about X ray treatments is from L.E.S., San Pedro, Calif., *VSJ* (September 1951).

110. See, for example, Mrs. H., Chicago, *VSJ* (April 1935); M.H., Toledo, Ohio, *VSJ* (October 1940); A New Patron, Louisville, Ky., *VSJ* (November 1940); Mrs. T. Schodroski, St. Louis, *VSJ* (February 1942).

111. Quotations from, respectively, Miss H.B., Hornell, N.Y., *VSJ* (January 1935); Mrs. A.B., Phoenix, Ariz., *VSJ* (October 1941); and J.C.V., Chicago, *VSJ* (January 1942).

112. Mrs. H.W., Minneapolis, *VSJ* (December 1940).

113. Mrs. M.C., Bronx, N.Y., *VSJ* (July–August 1938). For an excellent discussion of devotion to Blessed Kateri Tekakwitha see Preston, "Necessary Fictions."

114. For a powerful expression of this response see Mrs. D.B., Chardon, Ohio, *SJJ* (October–November 1962).

115. ?L.D., Salt Lake City, *VSJ* (October 1943); Mrs. Gertrude Esser, Milwaukee, *VSJ* (April 1948); ?R.B., Ellenson Park, Pa., *VSJ* (April 1949); ?C.S., St. Louis, *VSJ* (March 1951); Mrs. M.C., Pittsburgh, *VSJ* (February 1954). ?L.K., Chicago, *VSJ* (March 1950) is a particularly good example of this discrepancy, although the gender of the correspondent is not clear.

116. I first discussed these issues in "Cult of Saints."

117. For example, Mrs. M.C., Bronx, N.Y., *VSJ* (July–August 1938), E.M., Pittsburgh, *VSJ* (February 1952).

118. See ?L.W., Malden, Mass., *VSJ* (April 1950); P.R., St. Louis, *VSJ* (July 1950); ?M.P., Champaign, Ill., *VSJ* (October 1950); I.C.T., Detroit, *VSJ* (December 1953); ?A.S., no loc. cited, *VSJ* (June 1954); ?H.W., Victoria, Texas, *VSJ* (November 1954); Mrs. A.L.D., Springfield, Mass., *VSJ* (March 1955); ?R.M.S., Norwood, Mass., *SJJ* (January–February 1963).

119. For example, M.McD., Lexington, Mass., *VSJ* (June 1949); [Mr.]C.E.L., Ashtabula, Ohio, *VSJ* (February 1958); Mrs. B.C., Pasadena, Texas, *SJJ* (February–March 1961); Mrs. M.V.W., Oakhurst, N.Y., *SJJ* (October–November 1961); Mrs. M.G., no loc. cited, *SJJ* (August 1969).

120. Perhaps this is why so many female hospital professionals seem to have participated in the cult inside medical precincts. See, for example, Mrs. P.K., Louisville, Ky., *VSJ* (May 1953); Mrs. M.M.M., Tampico, Ill., *VSJ* (September 1953); and Mrs. H.P.S., South Gate, Calif., *VSJ* (February 1954). One woman who has been "in the medical profession" for twenty years wrote me that she distributes prayer cards so "others get to know his most powerful intercession also." Per.corr.: FAF-F-50+-East Haven, Conn.-?

121. 800: KL-F-70+-Milton, Mass.-W.

122. See, for example, ?H.H., Texas, *VSJ* (August 1943); ?M.B., Detroit, *VSJ* (August 1952). The latter writes, "For almost five weeks, I worried secretly, afraid to visit my doctor. One day I received a letter from you, the Claretian Fathers [possibly a routine solicitation], and found inside the prayer to Saint Jude. As I read it, I felt at peace for the first time."

123. Amundsen, "Medieval Catholic Tradition," 81–83; for a popular expression of this theme see Sharkey, *Woman Shall Conquer,* passim.

124. Per.comm. DA-F-54-Chicago-W.

125. Kleinman, *Illness Narratives,* quotations from 185–186,.48, and 22, respectively.

126. Kleinman writes, "the clinician comes to recognize that the narration of the illness, in part, creates the experience because of the special concerns—cognitive, affective, moral—that patients bring to their encounters with the events and career of chronic illness" (ibid., 233).

127. Ibid., 54, 154, 228, 230, 232–33, 244–49. For an example of this ethos in practice, by a hospital chaplain influenced by Dr. Kleinman's writings, see Vanderzee, *Ministry.*

128. See Shorter, *Bedside Manners,* 157, 169.

7. "THERE'S MIRACLES, AND MIRACLES, AND MIRACLES"

1. Per.corr.: AS-F-60?-Carol Stream, Ill.-M; Mrs. J.C., Yuma, Ariz., *SJJ* (August 1967); "different person" appears in Mrs. E.F., Detroit, *VSJ* (February, 1941).

2. S.M.T., Chicago, *VSJ* (June 1935).

3. Mrs. M.E., Chicago, *VSJ* (January 1935).

4. Quotations are from, respectively, R.M., Crawley, La., *VSJ* (May 1950); Mrs. J.K.W., Toledo, Ohio, *VSJ* (March 1953); Miss B.J., Cleveland, *VSJ* (January 1954); J.H., Washington, D.C., *VSJ* (May 1950); 800: LN-F-55+-San Bernardino, Calif.-M; and Per.corr.: SMcC-F-89-LaCrosse, Wis.-W? For some other examples of this deus-ex-machina quality of devotional narratives see: Mrs. V.V., Los Angeles, *VSJ* (April 1937); Mrs. [no initials cited; gender identifiable from text], Moultrieville, S.C., *VSJ* (August 1937); M.R., Jamaica, N.Y., *VSJ* (June 1938); Mrs. W.B., Mark Center, Ohio, *VSJ* (February 1940); ?E.S., New Jersey, *VSJ* (January 1943); ?B.B., Yonkers, N.Y., *VSJ* (May 1949); B.M., Cleveland, *VSJ* (September 1950); R.W., Newton, Mass., *VSJ* (February 1951); S.J., North Tonawanda, N.J., *VSJ* (May 1951); M.C., Plaistow, N.H., *VSJ* (November 1951); S.C., LaGrange Park, Ill., *VSJ* (September 1952); Miss L.M., Baltimore, *VSJ* (July 1953); Mrs. E.N., Chicago, *VSJ* (September 1953); Miss J.C., Detroit, *VSJ* (April 1954); Mr. and Mrs. F.L. and family, Edinburg, Texas, *VSJ* (April 1955).

5. 800: KJ-F-50+-Portsmouth, N.H.-D/R.

6. M.C., Chicago, *VSJ* (December 1950). Another female correspondent reported that she made a fifty-four-day "rosary novena" while she and her husband were looking for a home. A.R.S., Chicago, *VSJ* (September 1958).

7. Mrs. E.C., Brooklyn, N.Y., *SJJ* (April–May 1964). A woman wrote me that when her husband was diagnosed as having cancer "I prayed so hard . . . everyday so my husband would get well and after praying to St. Jude my husband is now in remission." Per.corr.: AG-F-65+-[Michigan postmark]-? For other examples of this equation of the intensity of a woman's prayers with a successful outcome for someone else see R.M., St. Louis, *VSJ* (June 1951); W.M., Lake Villa, Ill. *VSJ* (September 1951).

8. The two devout quoted are, respectively, Mrs. B.Z., Sun Prairie, Wis., *VSJ* (May 1954); and Mrs. C.R.D., no loc. cited, *SJJ* (October–November 1963).

9. Quotations are from, respectively, F.J.G., Port Allen, La., *VSJ* (August 1951); H.W., Chicago, *VSJ* (July 1953); and P.F., South Bend, Ind., *VSJ* (December 1950).

10. Quotation is from M.S., Spokane, Wash., *VSJ* (April 1951). The woman who spoke to St. Jude in the bathroom at work is 800: TF-F-40+-Tampa, Fla.-F-M.

11. Quotations are from, respectively, F.K., Pittsburgh, *VSJ* (November 1949); Mrs. J.M., no loc. cited, *SJJ* (June 1969); and Mrs. K.M., Chicago, *SJJ* (October–November 1963). Ellipsis in F.K.'s quotation is in the printed text. For some other examples of this

theme see Mrs. R.P.S., no loc. cited, *SJJ* (August–September, 1963); Mrs. M.B.M., Orlando, Fla., *SJJ* (June 1967); Mrs. V.N., Indio, Calif., *SJJ* (October 1967); Mrs. W.H., no loc. cited, *SJJ* (February, 1969), and in the same issue, B.L.I., Cortland, N.Y.; Mrs. R.S., Seattle, *SJJ* (October 1969).

12. For a sympathetic portrait of Father Molinari's work as Jesuit postulator general see Woodward, *Making Saints,* 93, 101, 106–107.

13. Molinari, *Saints,* 42, 109, 141–142.

14. Meissner, *Psychoanalysis and Religious Experience,* 138, 142, 144, 150, 159.

15. The stories cited in this paragraph are from, respectively, Mrs. A.S., Middle River, Md., *VSJ* (March 1941); 800: SM-F-65+-Springfield, Mo.-D; Mrs. M.J.G., Hollywood, Calif., *SJJ* (June 1962); Mrs. G.J.Q., Ogden, Utah, *VSJ* (October 1953); and Mrs. M.V.J., Dallas, *VSJ* (November 1955).

16. 800: TF-F-40+-Tampa, Fla.-M.

17. The last two quotations are from, respectively, Mrs. B.W., New York, N.Y., *SJJ* (April 1969); and Miss M.P., no loc. cited, *SJJ* (August 1967).

18. Leavitt, " 'Science' Enters the Birthing Room," 302.

19. Mrs. P.K., Louisville, Ky., *VSJ* (May 1953).

20. C.M., Alice, Texas, *VSJ* (May 1949).

21. Per.comm.: BC-F-39-Joliet, Ill.-S. The woman who left her prayer card in her desk is Mrs. C.W.F., Jr., Newport, Ky., *VSJ* (October 1955).

22. This last comment is from Mrs. M.F., Cincinnati, *VSJ* (July 1955). This paragraph is also based on Miss S.M., Pittsburgh, *VSJ* (March 1940); Miss L.G., Coalton, W.Va., *VSJ* (April 1953); Miss M.D., Cincinnati, *VSJ* (May 1953); Mrs. M.B., Bristol, Conn., *VSJ* (May 1953); Mrs. J.T., San Francisco, *VSJ* (June 1935); Mrs. G.H., Chicago, *VSJ* (July 1953). ?R.S., Toledo, Ohio, *VSJ* (December, 1949); Miss A.C.T., Lewiston, Idaho, *VSJ* (June 1941); and Mrs. W.C., Chicago, *VSJ* (May 1958).

23. My understanding of the saint as a figure in between has been profoundly inspired by Winnicott, who offers what the psychologist of religion James W. Jones calls a "relational model of the origin of culture and social institutions" (*Contemporary Psychoanalysis and Religion,* 58). Winnicott is an influential thinker of the object relations school of analytic theory, which focuses on how the self comes to be in an ongoing process in specific relationships with others. Because of this emphasis on real relationships in distinct cultural formations, object relations thought is the most available of all analytic theories (I believe) for use by historians and anthropologists. Winnicott's concern was to describe how the human imagination took hold of the world as persons grew, changed, and developed, meeting (as best they could) life's challenges and possibilities. He mapped out a process he called "transitional," by means of which a child, separating from his or her caregivers, "played" him- or herself into the world, using relationships (real and imaginary) as a way of making the way outward. Winnicott thus pointed past the sterile dichotomy in much analytic thought between separated/individuated persons and persons-in-relationship. Winnicott and others understood that humans would face the challenge of engaging and reengaging the world throughout their lives, and so assumed that

the kind of creativity characteristic of the transitional moment was possible throughout life, in art and religion.

Although Winnicott and analysts influenced by him exquisitely limned the protean nature of the self-encountering-the-world, fluidly, dialectically, they often either overlooked or only briefly alluded to the way the world itself, "reality," dissolved in the transitional space. For obvious clinical reasons, these theorists focused on how the transitional process enabled children (and later adults) to cope with or accommodate themselves to the world, not necessarily how it challenged the world or the self's place in it. They tended to take something called "reality" for granted, leaving unexamined the ways in which the transitional imagination—the imagination that moves relationally, that draws on the full history, real and imaginary, of a person's relationships, combines primary and secondary process thinking—can bring people into creative confrontation with the apparent givenness of their everyday world. This last chapter is concerned explicitly with this dialectic. The key text of Winnicott's work for me was *Playing and Reality*; I studied him with the help of Hughes, *Reshaping the Psychoanalytic Domain*; Phillips, *Winnicott*; and especially Greenberg and Mitchell, *Object Relations in Psychoanalytic Theory*. The idea of persons using literary and Biblical characters as life-changing relationships comes from Shengold, *"The Boy Will Come to Nothing!"*

Historians come uneasily to psychological theory, in part because psychological theorists so often blithely ignore the cultural and historical in favor of a naturalized and falsely universalized account of human experience. This chapter is not proposing a "psychohistory" along the old lines; I am not "psychoanalyzing" Jude's devout. Rather, I am trying to explore some of the specific qualities of their imagining of Jude in its actual relationship with the real events of their lives and against the background of their encounters with this religious idiom in the enclaves they were leaving in these years. Winnicott and others offered me some tools for this work, which I used along with other, social-historical and anthropological, instruments. I was led into this psychological reading by two factors: women's own accounts of their connection to Jude and the widely accepted idea among critics of devotionalism that such practices are "regressive." I wanted to figure out what "regressive" might mean as something other than a term of abuse. The text proposes what amounts to a theory of hagiological regression, not along Freudian lines (as Crapanzano does in his study of a Moroccan saint's cult, *Tuhami*), but as provoked by post-Freudians like Winnicott. A helpful, politically inflected reading of object relations theory may be found in Flax, *Thinking Fragments*. My thinking about "regression," a word that really should not be used casually, was shaped by Loewald in his *Psychoanalysis* and *Sublimation*. My concerns that psychological theory tended to float above the observable facts of culture and society, indulging a dangerous, antiempirical tendency to make things up about infants and children by the dubious process of working backward from adult experience, were addressed by the extraordinary work of Stern, *Interpersonal World*. Stern challenges theorists to ground themselves in the (beautifully crafted) studies of empirically oriented research psychologists (whom he challenges in turn to attend to the human insights of the theorists). Also useful was Ricoeur, "Question of Proof."

24. See, for example, Mr. and Mrs. E.C., Dalton, Ill., *SJJ* (August–September, 1962). 800: KL-F-65+-Hernando, Fla.-M described her reactions to her children's divorces. Helen's story is from Per.corr.: RA-F-62-[loc. withheld]-M. One woman wrote me a very revealing and touching reflection on the subject of finding peace through Jude amid one's many responsibilities. "I guess you might describe me as a worrier," she began. "I worry about things before they happen. I realize it is a terrible trait, however, this is the way God made me and I just had to learn to live with it. To someone else this may seem funny, but to me it's a terrible burden, so in order to learn to live with this I turned to St. Jude to help me. Whenever I go off on one of my worry streaks I pray to *Jesus, Mary, Joseph, St. Jude and St. Anne* to help me with this particular problem" (emphasis in original). This is the same woman who commented that she would not be "as good a person" without Jude's help, AS-F-60?+-Carol Stream, Ill.-M.

25. 800: KJ-F-50+-Portsmouth, N.H.-D/R.

26. See, for example, J.F., East McKeesport, Pa., *VSJ* (November 1943); T.B., Chicago, *VSJ* (June 1950); ?L.L., Baltimore, *VSJ* (May 1949); Mrs. E.W., no loc. cited, *SJJ* (February–March 1961).

27. 800: TF-F-40+-Tampa, Fla.-M. T.F. told me that she distributed St. Jude prayer cards at Al-Anon meetings. The woman who keeps Jude's statue in her living room is Per.comm.: AE-F-75-Chicago-M.

28. Per.comm.: EG-F-64-?[26 miles from the Shrine]-M.

29. Per.corr.: ACC-F-?-[loc. withheld]-M. I have changed the son's name. The profanity was elided in the original.

30. Miss H.M., Chicago, *VSJ* (April 1935); Mrs. A.F.B., Hoopeston, Ill., *VSJ* (November 1940); ?J.S., Fort Smith, Ark., *VSJ* (March 1949); ?V.B., Baton Rouge, La., *VSJ* (May 1950); Mrs. E.M., Elmhurst, N.Y., *VSJ* (February 1958).

31. The stories told in this paragraph are from, respectively, Mrs. I.L., Detroit, *VSJ* (February 1941); K.K., Hyde Park, Mass., *SJJ* (March–April 1963); and Mrs. M.J.G., Hollywood, Calif., *SJJ* (June 1962).

32. "I don't think that all the things we want are good for us," one woman told me, and Jude enabled her to know what was not and to accept it. 800: SM-F-65+-Springfield, Mo.-D.

33. The comment about praying for what is best is from 800: NJ-F-65+-St.Peter's, Mo.-M. [Mr.]W.L.B., Waukesha, Wis., *VSJ* (April 1952) alludes to "breaks." For examples of people praying for the grace of endurance see ?C.W., El Monte, Calif., *SJJ* (June 1966); and Mrs. A.A., Hacienda Heights, Calif., *SJJ* (August 1967).

34. See, for example, Mrs. R.F.M., Brooklyn, N.Y., *VSJ* (February 1954). For some examples of the devout's relief at simply making the movement from private to public in their experiences of hopelessness see Miss J.Y., Scranton, Pa., *VSJ* (November 1953); Mrs. M.D., Chicago, *VSJ* (May 1954); Mrs. P.A.S., Columbus, Ohio, *VSJ* (October 1958).

35. Per.comm.:CB-F-48-[I will not cite location here because the detail about the Ronald McDonald House could make this correspondent identifiable]-M. On people struggling to accept God's will with Jude's help see also: ?H.L., Spokane, Wash., *VSJ*

(March 1949); ?F.N., Clementon, N.J. *VSJ* (July 1950); Mrs. H.W.S., Niagara Falls, N.Y., *VSJ* (December 1955).

36. Clara made the same point: it's not that Jude says "no," she told me. "It's not 'yes,' it's not 'no,' it's not 'maybe.' It's just that things happen that are best. It might not look that way at the time, but time is the essence. Something else will happen that proves to you that [what you wanted] was not the best thing to happen at that time."

37. Therborn, *Ideology of Power*, 16–17.

38. Kovel, *Age of Desire*.

39. Miss E.M., no loc. cited, *SJJ* (August–September 1961).

Bibliography

Members of religious orders who have retained their family names are alphabetized accordingly. Otherwise such authors are alphabetized according to their saints' names, except that the "Mary" (often abbreviated as "M."), which is a common element of the names of nuns and sisters, is ignored in alphabetizing their works. Short articles, messages from Shrine clergy, notices of Shrine events, and devotional promotions from the *Voice of St. Jude* and *St. Jude's Journal* are cited only in the notes.

PRIMARY SOURCES

Aaron, Sister Germaine, O.S.B. "These Saturday's Children." *Ave Maria* 102, no. 9 (August 28, 1965): 18–20.

Sister Mary Agnes, C.S.C. "Sociology in the Curriculum of the School of Nursing." *Homiletic and Pastoral Review* 21, no. 2 (February 1940): 45–47.

Sister M. Andrew, R.N., B.S. "The Integrative Process in the Curriculum with Reference to the School's Objectives." *Homiletic and Pastoral Review* 20, no. 10 (October 1939): 342–345.

Armstrong, April Oursler. "The Strange Truth About Novenas." *Messenger of the Sacred Heart* 93, no. 8 (August 1958): 34–37, 66.

"The 'Ask Father' Complex." *Ave Maria* 96, no. 17 (October 27, 1962): 17.

Aubuchon, Marie. "Partnership with a Saint." *Hospital Progress* 39, no. 4 (April 1958): 84–85.

Barry, Donald L. "Sacraments for the Sick." *Homiletic and Pastoral Review* 48, no. 11 (August 1948): 824–827.

Beckman, Rev. Joseph F. "Winning Converts Through Suffering." *Homiletic and Pastoral Review* 58, no. 8 (May 1958): 790–791.

"Belleville Diocesan Catholic Association of Nurses." *Hospital Progress* 21, no. 5 (May 1940): 173–174.

Benedict, Martin. "The Liturgy vs. Private Devotions." *Ave Maria* 65, no. 9 (February 1958): 23–25.

"The Best of All Devotions." *Ave Maria* 26, no. 3 (July 16, 1927): 84–85.

Bishop, Jim. "Your First Girl." *Sign* 32, no. 10 (May 1953): 7–8.

Blair, Alice. "Share Your Fun." *Catholic Women's World* 1, no. 4 (October 1939): 37.

Blakely, Paul L. "Men and Women." *Catholic Mind* 41, no. 964 (April 1943): 15–17.

Blanshard, Paul. *American Freedom and Catholic Power.* Boston: Beacon, 1949.

——. *Communism, Democracy, and Catholic Power.* Boston: Beacon, 1951.

Boyle, Mary Agnes. "The Long Journey." *Ave Maria* 78, no. 12 (September 19, 1953): 10–13.

Breig, Joe. "The Hell of the Forgotten." *Ave Maria* 86, no. 22 (November 30, 1957): 7.

Brindel, Paul, O.S.B., Oblate. "I Am a Cusan." *Hospital Progress* 38, no. 9 (September 1957): 32, 34, 173.

Brown, Beatrice Bradshaw. "Obedience and Sanctity: A Note on Saint Bernadette." *Catholic World* 152, no. 1,031 (February 1941): 559–562.

Bruce, William George. "The Story of Hospital Progress." *Hospital Progress* 21, no. 4 (April 1940): 103–104.

Brussel, James A. "Two-Way Door at Carville." *Catholic Digest* 13, no. 8 (June 1949): 52–54.

Buckley, Boniface, C.P. "In Bitter Praise of Pain." *Sign* 24, no. 10 (May 1945): 527–528.

Buechel, William W. "My Catholic Keepsakes." *Voice of St. Jude* (August 1944): 12, 18.

Calkins, Frank, O.S.M. "Our Lady of Childbirth." *Ave Maria* 96, no. 14 (October 6, 1962): 23–25.

Canavan, Francis P., S.J. "The Finality of Sex." *Catholic World* 178, no. 1,066 (January 1954): 278–283.

"Cardinal's Letter on Nursing." *Hospital Progress* 21, no. 5 (May 1940): 174.

Carney, S. Waldron. "The Return of Norah." *Ave Maria* 15, no. 9 (March 4, 1922): 268–272.

Carroll, Lelia. "The Legion of Mary." *Ave Maria* 36, no. 3 (July 16, 1932): 65–69.

Carroll, P. J., C.S.C. "The Mating of Tess O'Kennedy." *Ave Maria* 25, no. 3 (January 15, 1927): 77–84.

———. "The Editor's Page." *Ave Maria* 63, no. 11 (March 16, 1946): 326.

"Catholic Nurses Observe Hospital Day." *Hospital Progress* 21, no. 6 (June 1940): 32A.

Sister Celestine. "A Sister's Role in Spiritual Care." *Hospital Progress* 33, no. 10 (October 1952): 75–77.

"Center Capping Exercises About Our Lady." *Hospital Progress* 21, no. 6 (June 1940): 38A.

A Chaplain. "Pointers for Hospital Chaplains." *Homiletic and Pastoral Review* 65, no. 3 (December 1964): 193–194.

"The Chaplain's Conference of the Twenty-Third Annual Convention of the Catholic Hospital Association." *Hospital Progress* 19, no. 11 (November 1938): 384–385, 390.

Chiappetta, Timothy, O.F.M., Cap. "Prayers of the Sick." *The Priest* 11, no. 6 (June 1956): 526–527.

Sister Mary Chrysologa, S.P.S.T. " 'The Apostolate to Aid the Dying' Marks Its Silver Anniversary." *Hospital Progress* 37, no. 6 (June 1956): 65.

Clark, Alice Pauline. "The Silent Saint." *Ave Maria* 35, no. 12 (March 19, 1932): 353.

Cloton, Pauline Marie. "Paid Back." *Messenger of the Sacred Heart* 55, no. 2 (February 1921): 94–102.

———. "Larry's Wife." *Messenger of the Sacred Heart* 55, no. 6 (June 1921): 325–332.

"The Common Sense of the Saints." *Ave Maria* 12, no. 19 (November 6, 1920): 598–599.

Connolly, Myles. *Mr. Blue.* Garden City, N.Y.: Image, 1954 [orig. pub. 1928].

Cotter, Jerry. "The Greater Menace?" *Voice of St. Jude* (March 1948): 9, 22.

"County Hospital Has May Procession." *Hospital Progress* 21, no. 6 (June 1940): 20A.

Countess de Courson, "A New Beata. Anna Maria Taigi." *Ave Maria* 11, no. 25 (June 19, 1920): 782–787.

Creel, Clyde S. "The Glory of Motherhood." *Ave Maria* 77, no. 7 (February 14, 1953): 215–216.

Crock, Clement H. "Mystery of Suffering." *Homiletic and Pastoral Review* 50, no. 6 (March 1950): 549–551.

Cross, Mary. "Charlie: A Failure." *Ave Maria* 25, no. 23 (June 4, 1927): 719–722.

Cunningham, B. J., C.M. "Is One of You Sick?" *Ave Maria* 81, no. 21 (May 21, 1955): 8–11.

Cushing, Richard J. "A Patient's Prayer." *Hospital Progress* 38, no. 4 (April 1957): 104.

Father Cuthbert. "The Halo of Sanctity." *Ave Maria* 26, no. 2 (July 9, 1927): 48–49.

Daly, Mary Tinley. "Block Rosary." *Catholic Digest* 13, no. 3 (January 1949): 36–38.

Danagher, John J., C.M. "Indulgences Lost by Lending Beads?" *Homiletic and Pastoral Review* 53, no. 4 (January 1953): 382–383.

——. "How to Use the Stations Crucifix." *Homiletic and Pastoral Review* 53, no. 10 (July 1953): 943–944.

"Dedicate Hospital Shrine." *Hospital Progress* 21, no. 1 (January 1940): 23A.

Deedy, John, Jr. "Operation Crossroads." *Ave Maria* 84, no. 4 (July 28, 1956): 11–13.

Delaney, Frances M. "Tuesday Night Novena." *Ave Maria* 52, no. 21 (November 23, 1940): 727–728.

deLeeuw, Adele. "Bookcases and Broccoli." *Catholic Women's World* 1, no. 5 (November 1939): 12–13, 39, 43.

"Dignity of Nursing Stressed." *Hospital Progress* 21, no. 6 (June 1940): 20A.

"The Discipline of Girls." *Ave Maria* 25, no. 26 (June 25, 1927): 821.

Donovan, Joseph P., C.M., J.C.D. "Novenas and Devotional Tastes," *Homiletic and Pastoral Review* 43 (April 1943): 643–644.

——. "Is the Perpetual Novena a Parish Need?" *Homiletic and Pastoral Review* 46 (January 1946): 252, 254.

——. "Perpetual Help Wafers." *Homiletic and Pastoral Review* 50 (July 1950): 969–970.

Doran, John B. "One Way Ticket: A Visit to Molokai." *Catholic World* 171, no. 1,021 (April 1950): 30–35.

"The Doyle's Family Rosary." *Ave Maria* 71, no. 18 (May 6, 1950): 549.

Duesing, David, O.S.B. "I Can't Be a Saint." *Voice of St. Jude* (August 1940): 13–16.

Dukette, Jerome, O.F.M., Conv. "Salvation in Suffering." *Homiletic and Pastoral Review* 58, no. 1 (October 1957): 77–79.

Dunn, James A. "The Picture." *Sign* 28, no. 8 (March 1949): 20–23.

Dutton, Joseph. *Joseph Dutton: His Memoirs.* Ed. Howard D. Case. Honolulu: Press of the Honolulu Star-Bulletin, 1931.

Earls, Michael, S.J. "Greater Than Blood." *Ave Maria* 11, no. 11 (March 13, 1920): 333–336.

Edgerton, Constance. "Desert Love." *Voice of St. Jude* (April 1938): 17–18.

Ernst, A. L., M.S.C., "The Pentecost Novena: A Dead Letter?" *The Priest* 11, no. 7 (July 1956): 576–577.

Farrell, Bertin, C.P. "Why the Suffering?" *Sign* 45, no. 10 (May 1966): 55.

Sister M. Fidelise. "Vigilance in the Selection of the Holdings for the Catholic Hospital Library." *Hospital Progress* 21, no. 2 (February 1940): 49.

——. "A Child Is Special and a Sick Child Is Extra Special." *Hospital Progress* 37, no. 12 (December 1956): 50–53.

"Form Federation of Nurses." *Hospital Progress* 21, no. 3 (March 1940): 26A.

Fox, Charlotte Wilma. "The Voice of God." *Ave Maria* 35, no. 18 (April 30, 1932): 557–561.

Fox, Thomas A., C.S.P. "Drama with a Happy Ending." *Homiletic and Pastoral Review* 49, no. 7 (April 1949): 565–567.

Freshman, Esther. "The Star-Light of Faith." *Ave Maria* 81, no. 25 (June 18, 1955): 8–13.

"A Friendship of Saints." *Ave Maria* 25, no. 4 (January 22, 1927): 111–113.

Frier, Catherine Jones. "Saints' Ways." *Ave Maria* 35, no. 4 (January 23, 1932): 110–115.

Fritsch, Alma M. "Her Symphony." *Voice of St. Jude* (June 1938): 12–13.

Gamble, James D. "No Place for A Woman." *Catholic Women's World* 1, no. 4 (October 1939): 3, 22, 32, 42.

———. "Working Wife." *Catholic Women's World* 2, no. 2 (February 1940): 4–5, 16, 20.

Gardner, Maude. "The Undaunted Christmas Spirit." *Voice of St. Jude* (December 1937): 15–17.

Garesché, E. F., S.J. "Catholic Hospital Apostolate." *Ave Maria* 73, no. 18 (May 5, 1951): 551–555.

———. "Shall I Be a Nurse?" *Ave Maria* 75, no. 23 (June 7, 1952): 711–714.

Gillis, J. R., O.P. "Are Medals Superstitious?" *Catholic Digest* 9, no. 4 (February 1945): 12–15.

Gilmore, Florence. "The Little Ring." *Ave Maria* 25, no. 6 (February 5, 1927): 206–209.

———. "Wife, Mother, and Saint." *Ave Maria* 35, no. 8 (February 20, 1932): 240–243.

———. "The Failure of the Family." *Ave Maria* 35, no. 14 (April 2, 1932): 431–436.

Gluckert, Eugenie. "A Slice of Heaven." *Ave Maria* 48, no. 12 (May 1941): 9–11, 36.

Goebel, Rev. Edmund J. "The Course in Religion as an Aid in Achieving the Objectives of a School of Nursing." *Hospital Progress* 20, no. 10 (October 1939): 338–339.

Grey, Francis W., O.S.B. "The Devout Female Sex." *Ave Maria* 26, no. 20 (November 12, 1927): 609–612.

Griffin, James A. "Sermon, Pontifical Mass, June 17, 1940." *Hospital Progress* 21, no. 6 (June 1940): 181–184.

Griffin, Robert F. "De Senectute." *Ave Maria* 96, no. 16 (October 20, 1962): 20–22, 28.

Gumbinger, Cuthbert, O.F.M., Cap. "Leprosy." *Catholic Digest* 4, no. 10 (August 1940): 77–81.

Haffner, Katherine Neuhaus. "One Day at a Time." *Ave Maria* 72, no. 11 (September 9, 1950): 343–344.

Hagspiel, Bruno, S.V.D. "A New Hospital Patronness: St. Gemma Galgani." *Hospital Progress* 21, no. 3 (March 1940): 97–98.

"Hansenotic Heroine." *America* 79, no. 16 (July 24, 1948): 360.

Hardesty, Rev. G. "The Maintenance of the Individuality of the Catholic Hospital." *Hospital Progress* 20, no. 10 (October 1939): 345–347.

Hart, Hubert N. "Notes on the Meaning of Pain." *Catholic World* 177, no. 1,057 (April 1953): 50–53.

Hasley, Lucille. "I Like Married Life." *Sign* 28, no. 8 (March 1949): 14–17.

———. "Catholicism and Suffering." *Ave Maria* 76, no. 22 (November 29, 1952): 704.

Hayes, Mary Ellen. "My Collection of Saints." *Ave Maria* 52, no. 18 (November 2, 1940): 563–565.

Healy, Joseph L., S.J. "Opportunities for Religious Education in the Hospital." *Hospital Progress* 18, no. 8 (August 1937): 259–261.

Heath, Thomas, O.P. "From Evil to Good." *Ave Maria* 101, no. 11 (March 13, 1965): 16–19.

"Heroes." *Ave Maria* 46, no. 11 (September 11, 1937): 341.

Hermann, Alfred, O.F.M. "If Miracles Thou Fain Wouldst See." *St. Anthony's Messenger* 40 (September 1932): 171–172.

Hessel, Mary S. "Catholic Action for the Sick by the Sick." *Catholic World* 167, no. 998 (May 1948): 163–166.

Heuer, Marie G. "When You Buy Towels." *Catholic Women's World* 2, no. 2 (February 1939): 15.

Hoffman, Mary E. "The Candle's Beams." *Ave Maria* 81, no. 16 (April 16, 1955): 16–18.

Hood, Margaret McManus. "The Shrines in the Home Movement." *Catholic Women's World* 2, no. 10 (October 1940): 35, 38, 40.

A Hospital Chaplain. "God's Way with Souls." *Hospital Progress* 11, no. 4 (April 1930): 172–174.

"The Hospital Chaplain." *America* 55, no. 12 (June 27, 1936): 269.

"The Hospital Chaplain." *Hospital Progress* 18, no. 8 (August 1937): 262–263.

"How the Chinese Pray the Rosary." *Catholic Digest* 18, no. 7 (May 1954): 101–105.

Huesman, Rose M. *Saints in Aprons.* Milwaukee: Bruce, 1962.

Hurst, Ben. "Sibyl's Awakening." *Ave Maria* 26, no. 22 (November 26, 1927): 688–691.

Ivancovich, Nellie R. "Motherhood." *Ave Maria* 35, no. 11 (March 12, 1932): 338–340.

James, Stanley B. "The Saint as Controversialist." *Ave Maria* 34, no. 1 (July 4, 1931): 12–15.

Jarrett, Bede, O.P. "The Problem of Suffering." *Homiletic and Pastoral Review* 34, no. 3 (December 1933): 260–265.

Jenks, William, C.SS.R. "We Will Meet the Challenge!" *Homiletic and Pastoral Review* 50, no. 5 (February 1950): 440–442.

Jensen, Lyda A. "Our Handicapped: A National Asset." *America* 72, no. 11 (December 16, 1944): 207–208.

"Join the League of Saint Dymphna." *Ave Maria* 48, no. 2 (July 1940): 53.

Kelly, Rev. John Bernard. "Our Lady of Fatima, Parish Hostess." *Homiletic and Pastoral Review* 46, no. 4 (January 1946): 295–297.

Kenny, Virginia. "Please Father, Tell Us About Eternity!" *Voice of St. Jude* (January 1946): 10, 16.

——. "Dear Saint Joseph." *Voice of St. Jude* (March 1946): 9.

——. "Dormitio." *Voice of St. Jude* (September 1946): 10, 21–22.

——. "Dear Saint Joseph." *Voice of St. Jude* (March 1947): 17, 4.

Kent, Eugene. "Il Santuario de Chimayo." *Ave Maria* 11, no. 3 (January 17, 1920): 65–68.

Kraff, Rev. Anthony, C.PP.S. "The Difference in the Ministry Between Hospital and Parish." *Hospital Progress* 38, no. 11 (November 1957): 82–84.

L.R. "For the Sake of a Rosary." *Ave Maria* 26, no. 14 (October 1, 1927): 425–428.

Lahey, Thomas A., C.S.C. "A Letter to Shut-Ins." *Ave Maria* 71, no. 8 (February 25, 1950): 245–249.

LaMontagne, Joseph, S.S.S. "I Am a Cusan." *The Priest* 11, no. 9 (September 1956): 776–780.

Lawlor, R.V. "Catholics and Hansen's Disease." *America* 86, no. 17 (January 26, 1952): 436.

"Law of Faith and the Law of Prayer." *Ave Maria* 87, no. 21 (May 24, 1958): 16–17.

"League General Communion Day." *Hospital Progress* 21, no. 5 (May 1940): 64A.

Lehr, Margaret. "The Advantages of a Handicap." *Ave Maria* 69, no. 23 (June 4, 1949): 728.

"Lepers and the Church." *Catholic Mind* 40, no. 941 (March 8, 1942): 30–31.

Livingston, Patricia. "Sermons for a Housewife." *Ave Maria* 101, no. 5 (January 30, 1965): 10–12.

Longley, A. "Make Christian Burial Christian." *Ave Maria* 99 (June 20, 1964): 289–297.

Luka, Father Ronald. "The Way of the Cross Today: Through the Streets of Selma, and the Trails of Vietnam." *Ave Maria* 101, no. 15 (April 10, 1965): 6–9.

McCahill, William P. "Christ in the Wounded and the Maimed." *Catholic Mind* 49, no. 1,065 (September 1951): 563–569.

McCarthy, John J. "The Rosary is Power." *Ave Maria* 76, no. 17 (October 25, 1952): 529–531.

Macelwane, Geraldine F. "Make Your Marriage Happy." *Sign* 31, no 11 (June 1952): 7–9, 54.

MacEoin, Gary. "Has the Rosary Survived the Council?" *Ave Maria* 104, no. 2 (July 9, 1966): 12–14, 28.

McInnes, Valentine A., O.P. "The Liturgy of the Word and the Rosary." *Homiletic and Pastoral Review* 65, no. 8 (May 1965): 648–654.

McLellan, Joseph. "Everyman's Nagging Wife." *Ave Maria* 90, no. 13 (September 26, 1959): 5–9.

McNamara, Patrick, O.S.M. "Mary, Mother of Sorrows." *Ave Maria* 87, no. 14 (April 5, 1958): 12–14.

McNaspy, C. J., S.J. "The Fracas About Saints." *America* 120, no. 21 (May 24, 1969): 608.

Madden, Mrs. E. R. "The Army Gets a Mother." *Voice of St. Jude* (September 1942): 6–7, 15, 17.

Magnier, Patrick A., C.SS.R., "The Man with the Oils." *American Ecclesiastical Review* 155, no. 6 (December 1966): 399–402.

Mahony, George A. "Our Friend, the Hospital Chaplain." *Homiletic and Pastoral Review* 37, no. 12 (September 1937): 1260–1264.

Mallett, Frank J. "Overcoming Handicaps." *Ave Maria* 46, no. 4 (July 24, 1937): 105–107.

Marbach, Ethel. "Liturgical Customs from Many Lands for the Family Through the Year We Have Tried at Our House." *AM* 102 (July 24, 1965): 14–15.

Sister M. Marguerite, R.S.M. "Mary's Way of the Cross." *Voice of St. Jude* (June 1945): 5, 30–31.

———. "This is the Way." *Voice of St. Jude* (August 1946): 4, 13.

———. "How Holy Shall We Be?" *Voice of St. Jude* (November 1946): 12, 21–22.

———. "Sylvia Said No." *Voice of St. Jude* (December 1946): 4–5, 17.

———. "Sylvia Said Yes." *Voice of St. Jude* (January 1947): 4, 21.

———. "Barter and Exchange: For Fathers Only." *Voice of St. Jude* (May 1947): 4, 19, 24.

———. "Pain Is a Teacher." *Voice of St. Jude* (July 1947): 4, 17.

———. "If You Had Gone to Mary." *Voice of St. Jude* (July 1948): 4, 20, 25.

Father Marrison, O.C.D. "The Woman in Social Life." *Little Flower Magazine* 15, no. 9 (December 1934): 5.

Martindale, C. C., S.J. "The Return of the Saints." *Catholic World* 159, no. 996 (March 1948): 510–516.

———. "Making Use of Pain." *The Priest* 13, no. 1 (January 1957): 51–54.

"A Matter of Taste." *Sign* 45, no. 3 (October 1965): 43.

May, Rev. John L. "Page Ye the Lord?" *Hospital Progress* 38, no. 10 (October 1957): 58–59.

"Messages to the Twenty-Fifth Annual Convention of the Catholic Hospital Association." *Hospital Progress* 21, no. 7 (July 1940): 214–226.

Miller, R. DeWitt. "Lourdes of the West." *Ave Maria* 48, no. 1 (June 1940): 14–16.

Minogue, Anna C. "Gran." *Ave Maria* 35, no. 13 (March 26, 1932): 397–402.

"Miracles Wrought by Relics." *Ave Maria* 12, no. 25 (June 17, 1876): 391–393.

"The Miraculous Infant Jesus of Prague." *Little Flower Magazine* 14, no. 10 (January 1934): 3, 30.

Mohler, Edward F. "The Man the Whole World Loves." *Voice of St. Jude* (March 1947): 8–9.

———. "Danny Thomas Votes for Saint Jude." *Voice of St. Jude* (February 1948): 26–27.

Sister Mary Monica. "Beautiful Customs." *Ave Maria* 67, no. 3 (January 17, 1948): 88.

Moore, E. Roberts. "Sick Calls Come at 2:00 A.M." *Catholic Digest* 15, no. 4 (February 1951): 91–96.

Morgan, Sister Justina. "Challenge to the Apostolate of Care." *Hospital Progress* 39, no. 11 (November 1958): 68–70, 154, 162.

Moriarty, Helen. "Jim Graney's Wife." *Ave Maria* 12, nos. 15 (October 9, 1920): 463–466; 16 (October 16, 1920): 494–498.

———. "Jane Comes Home." *Ave Maria* 35, no. 12 (March 19, 1932): 366–372.

Morrison, Bakewell, S.J. "Religion in the Curriculum of the Catholic School of Nursing." *Hospital Progress* 20, no. 12 (December 1939): 419–427.

Motion Pictures Classified by National Legion of Decency. 1955 ed. New York: Executive Staff of the National Legion of Decency, 1955.

Mullaney, Rev. Thomas U., O.P. "The Rosary: Our Secret Weapon." *Ave Maria* 88, no. 14 (October 4, 1958): 5–7, 23.

Murphy, Rev. James J. "Human Suffering." *Homiletic and Pastoral Review* 49, no. 6 (March 1949): 482–486.

Murphy, Vivian T. "Sickbed Voyage of Discovery." *Catholic Digest* 14, no. 7 (May 1950): 74–76.

Murray, Edmund J., C.S.C. "Patron Saints and Their Assignments." *Ave Maria* 68, no. 18 (October 30, 1948): 551–557.

Murray, Sister Marcella, O.S.B. "Magazines in the Catholic Hospital Library." *Hospital Progress* 21, no. 2 (February 1940): 50–51.

"Nail-Pierced Hands." *America* 60, no. 15 (January 14, 1939): 374.

Neill, Isabel. "The Call of the Mother." *Ave Maria* 25, no. 20 (May 14, 1927): 609.

Nesbitt, Marian. "The Saints and Friendship." *Ave Maria* 31, nos. 19 (May 10, 1930): 584–589; 20 (May 17, 1930): 618–622; 21 (May 24, 1930): 650–654; 22 (May 31, 1930): 690–692.

"New Council of Catholic Nurses Formed." *Hospital Progress* 21, no. 6 (June 1940): 43A.

Nixon, Joan Lowery. "Retreat for Mothers." *Voice of St. Jude* (September 1955): 16–17.

"The Nurses' Apostolate." *Catholic Women's World* 2, no. 2 (February 1940): 30.

"Nurses' Apostolate Spreads." *Hospital Progress* 21, no. 3 (March 1940): 24A.

O'Boyle, Msgr. Patrick. "I Saw the Eyes of Suffering Children." *Voice of St. Jude* (June 1947): 7, 13, 24.

O'Brien, Mrs. William. "How to Face Sorrow." *Ave Maria* 43, no. 2 (January 11, 1936): 50–52.

O'Conner, Mary. "Are You Pain's Puppet?" *Ave Maria* 73, no. 7 (February 17, 1951): 216.

O'Donnell, Dean H. "Apostolate of the Sick Room." *Ave Maria* 63, no. 9 (March 2, 1946): 263–267.

O'Flynn, Thomas, C.M. "The Rosary and the Liturgy." *American Ecclesiastical Review* 155, no. 4 (October 1966): 234–241.

O'Hara, Robert, C.P. "The Good Life." *Sign* 29, no. 1 (August 1949): 52–53.

O'Neill, Teresa. "Ann's Conversion." *Voice of St. Jude* (April 1945): 19.

"One Lesson Taught by the War." *Ave Maria* 15, no. 9 (March 4, 1922): 275–276.

"On Visiting Hospitals." *Homiletic and Pastoral Review* 65, no. 6 (March 1965): 449–454.

O'Reilly, Bryan M. "Catholic America Comes of Age." *Catholic World* 166, no. 994 (January 1948): 340–347.

Oswald, Ruth. "Orchid for Our Lady." *Voice of St. Jude* (January 1947): 13, 15.

——. "Lost: A Singing Voice." *Voice of St. Jude* (September 1947): 8.

——. "A Better Approach." *Voice of St. Jude* (February 1948): 14, 22.

"Our Foolish Discontent." *Ave Maria* 11, no. 15 (April 10, 1920): 469.

"Our Mother." *Ave Maria* 15, no. 5 (February 4, 1922): 147.

P[atrick]. J. C[arroll, C.S.C.]. "Error and Disease." *Ave Maria* 35, no. 2 (January 9, 1932): 53.

——. "Contentment." *Ave Maria* 35, no. 14 (April 2, 1932): 437.

——. "Intolerance Towards God's Mother." *Ave Maria* 35, no. 19 (May 7, 1932): 597–598.

——. "Significance of Silence." *Ave Maria* 36, no. 18 (October 29, 1932): 565.

——. "Standard of Living." *Ave Maria* 36, no. 19 (November 5, 1932): 597.

Phillips, Charles. "On Women's Poetry." *Ave Maria* 35, no. 3 (January 16, 1932): 82–84.

Phillips, Delphia. "The Diplomat's Dinner." *Ave Maria* 35, no. 1 (January 2, 1932): 14–16.

Portasik, Richard, O.F.M. "Popular Devotions." *Homiletic and Pastoral Review* 66, no. 12 (September 1966): 1017–1022.

Price, Basil M., S.J. "The Mile Rosary." *America* 88, no. 4 (October 25, 1952): 98–99.

Puigvi, Rev. Joseph M., C.M.F. "Jottings on Devotion to St. Jude." *Voice of St. Jude* (December 1946): 3.

——. "At St. Jude National Shrine." *Voice of St. Jude* (December 1947): 7, 25.

Reedy, John, C.S.C. "The Mothers of Our Day." *Ave Maria* 101, no. 19 (May 8, 1965): 2.

——. "If You're So Well Educated, So Free, So Respected as a Person, How Come You're Not Happy?" *Ave Maria* 103, no. 19 (May 7, 1966): 2.

"Relief of the Holy Souls." *Ave Maria* 36, no. 19 (November 5, 1932): 595–596.

Renneker, George J., S.M. "Gateway to Heaven." *Catholic Digest* 5, no. 5 (March 1941): 11–13.

Reuter, Rev. James B., S.J. "By Post from Culion." *Messenger of the Sacred Heart* 89, no. 4 (April 1954): 30–35, 83.

"Risks Life to Save Boy." *Hospital Progress* 21, no. 4 (April 1940): 18A.

Risley, Marius. "Damien's Spirit in America." *Catholic Digest* 6, no. 3 (January 1942): 40–45.

Rogers, Florence White. "Letters to the Needy." *America* 50, no. 26 (March 31, 1934): 616–617.

"The Rosary Over the Radio." *American Ecclesiastical Review* 129, no. 4 (October 1953): 275–276.

Sister Rose Mary, S.C.L. "The Library of the Catholic Hospital." *Hospital Progress* 21, no. 2 (February 1940): 47–48.

Rosett, Louise Carey. "Religious Orders for the Sick." *Catholic World* 173, no. 1,033 (April 1951): 48–53.

Rush, Alfred C., C.SS.R. "The Rosary and the Christian Wake." *American Ecclesiastical Review* 152, no. 5 (May 1965): 289–297.

Ryan, Calvin T. "Wanted: Mothers." *Voice of St. Jude* (October 1943): 11, 14.

S.T.D. "Only in Sorrow." *Ave Maria* 36, no. 23 (December 3, 1932): 723.

"Saints of the Weather." *Ave Maria* 11, no. 4 (January 24, 1920): 114–115.

Sanderlin, George. "The Mighty Midget." *Voice of St. Jude* (May 1946): 10, 15.

—— "What Are We Afraid Of?" *Voice of St. Jude* (July 1947): 8, 25.

——. "Pioneering in the Twentieth Century." *Voice of St. Jude* (December 1947): 8, 26–27.

——. "The Power of Destruction." *Voice of St. Jude* (March 1949): 28–29.

——. "The Child of Her Tears." *Voice of St. Jude* (August 1949): 5, 20–21, 29.

Sanderlin, Owenita. "We Meet Again." *Voice of St. Jude* (October 1946): 9, 23.

——. "The Masterpiece." *Voice of St. Jude* (February 1947): 11–12.

——. "Empty House: Reminiscences of a Mother Whose Children Have Grown Up." *Voice of St. Jude* (March 1947): 15, 26–27.

——. "A Father for Ronny." *Voice of St. Jude* (December 1947): 16, 20.

——. "Till the Sun Comes Out." *Voice of St. Jude* (January 1948): 15, 23.

——. "My Operation." *Voice of St. Jude* (August 1955): 29–31.

Savage, Alma. "Christina Leonard: Psychiatrist." *Catholic Women's World* 1, no. 5 (November 1939): 22–23, 30.

Schaeuble, Paul, O.S.B. "Lepers and Leprosy." *Homiletic and Pastoral Review* 45, no. 5 (February 1945): 381–382.

Schlarman, Very Rev. Joseph. "Ite, Missa Est." *Hospital Progress* 21, no. 7 (July 1940): 235–237.

Schmitz, Walter J., S.S. "Rosary Devotions." *American Ecclesiastical Review* 126, no. 5 (May 1952): 388.

——. "Marian Devotions." *American Ecclesiastical Review* 127, no. 1 (July 1952): 52–53.

Schneider, John, C.M.F. "Tenth Anniversary." *Voice of St. Jude* (April 1942): 12–17.

Schwitalla, Alphonse M., S.J. "The Influence of the Catholic Hospital in Our Modern Society." *Hospital Progress* 20, no. 9 (September 1939): 311–316.

——. "Convention Call." *Hospital Progress* 21, no. 2 (February 1940): 56–58.

——. "Another Sister's Life." *Hospital Progress* 21, no. 3 (March 1940): 100–101.

——. "From the Editor to the Publisher: An Open Letter to the Bruces." *Hospital Progress* 21, no. 4 (April 1940): 105.

——. "The Silver Jubilee Convention." *Hospital Progress* 21, no. 5 (May 1940): 137–143.

——. "The Silver Jubilee Convention of the Catholic Hospital Association of the U.S. and Canada: The President's Address." *Hospital Progress* 21, no. 6 (June 1940): 185–205.

Scott, Martin, J. "The Home: A Homily to Husbands and Wives, Fathers and Mothers." *Ave Maria* 12, no. 4 (July 24, 1920): 97–100.

Sharkey, Don. *The Woman Shall Conquer.* New York: All Saints, 1961 [orig. pub. 1954].

——. "This Is Your Mother." *Ave Maria* 78, no. 17 (October 24, 1953): 16; 81, nos. 9 (February 26, 1955): 55; 10 (March 5, 1955): 25; 19 (May 7, 1955): 25; 20 (May 14, 1955): 25.

Sheehan, Robert J., C.S.C. "When You Marry." *Ave Maria* 79, no. 5 (January 30, 1954): 8–11.

Sheen, Fulton J. "How to Stay Married Though Unhappy." *Catholic Digest* 17, no. 7 (May 1953): 4–7.

——. "Mother Means Love." *Catholic Digest* 18, no. 2 (December 1953): 1–3.

Sheerin, John B., C.S.P. "Woman: Lead Role or Extra?" *Homiletic and Pastoral Review* 53, no. 8 (May 1953): 693–697.

Shelley, Thomas. "Find Happiness in CUSA." *Catholic Digest* 22, no. 5 (March 1958): 24–26.

Sherwood, Grace H. "The Coffee Pot." *Ave Maria* 35, no. 20 (May 14, 1932): 621–627.

"Shower of Roses." *Little Flower Magazine* 14, no. 10 (January 1934): 22.

Shuler, Mary Catherine. "Silver Lining of Convalescence." *Ave Maria* 59, no. 15 (April 8, 1944): 494–496.

"Sick Call Crucifix." *Ave Maria* 48, no. 1 (June 1940): 47.

"Sick Room Study." *Ave Maria* 54, no. 10 (September 6, 1941): 294.

Sister Mary Simeon, O.P. "An Episode for Women." *Ave Maria* 101, no. 4 (January 23, 1965): 18–19.

Small, James Louis. "Vignettes of Lourdes." *Ave Maria* 11, no. 25 (June 19, 1920): 769–771.

Smith, F. C., S.J. "Spurious Piety." *Catholic Digest* 3, no. 5 (March 1939): 15–17.

Smith, Frank. "Load of Bricks Stumps Priest Who Fled Bullets." *Voice of Saint Jude* (February 1935): 18 [orig. pub. *Chicago Sunday Times,* February 24, 1935].

"Soldier Saints." *Ave Maria* 58, no. 8 (August 21, 1943): 260–261.

"The Soldier's Hail Mary." *Ave Maria* 35, no. 8 (February 20, 1932): 244.

Sprenger, Jane. "Do It for Mom, Patty." *Sign* 32, no. 12 (July 1953): 51–52.

Sister St. Stanislaus, "Phases of the Individuality of the Catholic School of Nursing." *Hospital Progress* 20, no. 10 (October 1939): 347–349.

"Star of Prison Movie Won Role Through Prayer to St. Jude." *Voice of St. Jude* (August 1948): 12.

Stehle, Walter, O.S.B. "Women and the Clergy." *Homiletic and Pastoral Review* 54, no. 4 (January 1954): 326–330.

"Suffering and Imagination." *Ave Maria* 15, no. 19 (May 13, 1922): 595–596.

Sugranes, Rev. Eugene, C.M.F. "Who Is Saint Jude?" *Voice of St. Jude* (January 1935): 5.

———. "St. Jude's Pilgrimage." *Voice of St. Jude* (November 1935): 14.

Sweeney, Hilary, C.P. "When Ignorance Is Bliss." *Sign* 28, no. 11 (June 1949): 39–40.

"Sympathy for the Sick." *Ave Maria* 12, no. 24 (June 12, 1920): 757–758.

Syrianey, Francis. "St. Jude and Robert Vogeler." *Catholic Digest* 15, no. 11 (September 1951): 26–29.

T.A.L. "The Glory of Motherhood." *Ave Maria* 36, no. 5 (July 30, 1932): 149–150.

T.E.B. "Sacrifice and Happiness." *Ave Maria* 36, no. 6 (August 6, 1932): 180–181.

———. "Do You Know the Type?" *Ave Maria* 36, no. 15 (October 8, 1932): 469.

Tansey, Anne. "Sense of Betrayal." *Voice of St. Jude* (May 1944): 12, 17.

———. "Receive This Word." *Voice of St. Jude* (June 1944): 14, 16–17.

———. "Will-o-the-Wisps." *Voice of St. Jude* (July 1944): 10, 17.

———. "Going Home." *Voice of St. Jude* (September 1944): 10, 16.

———. "Purple Heart." *Voice of St. Jude* (November 1944): 10, 16.

———. "Ultimate Victory." *Voice of St. Jude* (February 1945): 12.

———. "The Subject and the Saint." *Voice of St. Jude* (April 1945): 14, 17.

———. "The Girl At the Well." *Voice of St. Jude* (January 1946): 9.

———. "We Must Have Faith." *Voice of St. Jude* (June 1946): 14, 21.

———. "Week-End." *Voice of St. Jude* (November 1948): 8, 26.

———. "Catholic Union of Sick Associates." *Ave Maria* 72, no. 20 (November 11, 1950): 622–625.

———. "Crossbearers with a Purpose." *Voice of St. Jude* (October 1953): 11–13.

Taylor, Charles, O.M.I. "Four Years in a Hospital." *Homiletic and Pastoral Review* 42, no. 9 (June 1942): 809–815.

Sister M. Teresita. "Opportunities for the Promotion of Catholic Action in the Teaching of Professional Adjustments in the Catholic Schools of Nursing." *Hospital Progress* 21, no. 6 (June 1940): 206–212.

"They Are All Stigmatics." *Messenger of the Sacred Heart* 89, no. 2 (February 1954): 19–21, 76.

Thoma, George A. "The Provider." *Voice of St. Jude* (April 1941): 15–16.

Thompson, Blanche Jennings. "Some Valiant Women Saints." *Ave Maria* 70, no. 2 (July 9, 1949): 53–55.

Thompson, Thelma, and Father Joseph Voelker, C.S.C., "The Sisters Who Serve at Carville." *Catholic Digest* 21, no. 10 (August 1957): 103–109.

Tonne, Arthur, O.F.M. "Swords of Sorrow." *St. Anthony's Messenger* 48, nos. 8 (January 1941): 25, 47; 11 (April 1941): 31.

Tracy, Vera Marie. "After Dark: A Hospital Sketch." *Catholic World* 130, no. 776 (November 1929): 134–139.

——. "December Drama." *Ave Maria* 36, no. 24 (December 10, 1932): 750–754.

Trese, Rev. Leo J. "Hold Onto Your Beads." *Sign* 44, no. 10 (May 1965): 36.

"Twin Devotions." *Ave Maria* 26, no. 24 (December 10, 1927): 737–741.

"The Union of Jesus and Mary," *Ave Maria* 12, no. 26 (December 25, 1920): 820–821.

Vann, Gerald, O.P. "True Balance." *Catholic World* 151, no 904 (July 1940): 485–486.

Vaughn, Mary. "I Love Hospitals." *Ave Maria* 79, no. 19 (May 8, 1954): 17–19.

Vega, Pancho. "Lepers See a Movie." *Catholic Digest* 14, no. 5 (March 1950): 30–33.

"A Virtue More Admired Than Cultivated." *Ave Maria* 15, no. 3 (January 21, 1922): 84–85.

"Visitation of the Sick." *Homiletic and Pastoral Review* 48, no. 11 (August 1948): 854.

Walker, E. M. "East End Granny." *Ave Maria* 25, no. 25 (June 18, 1927): 781–783.

Walsh, William Thomas. "What Are Saints?" *Catholic World* 166, no. 1,000 (July 1948): 330–336.

Ward, Ferdinand J., C.M. "How and Why of Suffering." *Homiletic and Pastoral Review* 58, no. 5 (February 1958): 498–499.

Waters, Florence A. "Religious Communities for the Sick." *Ave Maria* 77, no. 7 (February 21, 1953): 241–243.

Wendell, Norbert, O.P. "The World's Perfect Lovers." *Ave Maria* 49, no. 7 (February 18, 1939): 202–205.

Westbrook, T. S. "A Devotional Classic Revived." *Ave Maria* 26, no. 7 (August 13, 1927): 199–202.

Whelan, Rev. Lincoln F. "The Sick and the Aged at Your House." *Homiletic and Pastoral Review* 58, no. 10 (July 1958): 983–984.

Whitbread, Jane, and Vivian Cadden. "Why Men Don't Talk and Women Do." *Catholic Digest* 17, no. 12 (October 1953): 21–24.

Wilkerson, Rev. Jerome F. "Patient Care: Spiritual Needs." *Hospital Progress* 46, no. 7 (December 1965): 76–80.

Williams, Mitchell. "Mary's Toy." *Ave Maria* 69, no. 5 (January 29, 1949): 149–151.

Williamson, Claude C. H., O.S.C. "Saints and Sanctity." *Homiletic and Pastoral Review* 34, no. 11 (August 1934): 1167–1176.

Willock, Ed. "Suffering and Spiritual Growth." *Ave Maria* 88, no. 1 (July 12, 1958): 23–26.

Wilson, John, C.S.C. "Suffering That Sanctifies." *Ave Maria* 62, no. 11 (September 15, 1945): 184–185.

"Wives' 'Equality' with Their Husbands." *America* 90, no. 14 (January 2, 1954): 350.

"A Word to the Wise." *Ave Maria* 26, no. 16 (October 15, 1927): 501.

Woywod, Stanislaus, O.F.M., "A Peculiar Use of Images of the Blessed Virgin and Other Saints." *Homiletic and Pastoral Review* 39, no. 11 (August 1939): 1216–1217.

Sr. Xavier Miriam. "Caring for Souls in a Catholic Hospital." *Hospital Progress* 34, no. 2 (February 1953): 60–61.

SECONDARY SOURCES

Amundsen, Darrell W. "The Medieval Catholic Tradition." In *Caring and Curing: Health and Medicine in the Western Religious Traditions,* ed. Ronald L. Numbers and Darrell W. Amundsen, 65–107. New York: Macmillan, 1986.

Año Nuevo de Kerr, Louise. "Chicano Settlements in Chicago: A Brief History." *Journal of Ethnic Studies* 2 (Winter 1975): 22–32.

Athans, Mary Christine, B.V.M. "A New Perspective on Father Charles E. Coughlin." *Church History* 56 (June 1987): 224–235.

Atkinson, Clarissa W. " 'Your Servant, My Mother': The Figure of Saint Monica in the Ideology of Christian Motherhood." In *Immaculate and Powerful: The Female in Sacred Image and Social Reality,* ed. Clarissa W. Atkinson, Constance H. Buchanan, and Margaret R. Miles, 139–172. (Boston: Beacon, 1985).

Badone, Ellen, ed. *Religious Orthodoxy and Popular Faith in European Society.* Princeton: Princeton University Press, 1990.

Baily, Samuel L. "The Adjustment of Italian Immigrants in Buenos Aires and New York, 1870–1914." *American Historical Review* 88 (April 1983): 281–305.

Bakan, David. *Disease, Pain, and Sacrifice: Toward a Psychology of Suffering.* Chicago: University of Chicago Press, 1968.

Baumgartner, Apollinaris W. *Catholic Journalism: A Study of Its Development in the United States, 1789–1930.* New York: AMS Press, 1967.

Bennett, Sheila Kishler, and Glen H. Elder, Jr. "Women's Work in the Family Economy: A Study of Depression Hardship and Women's Lives." *Journal of Family History* 4 (Summer 1979): 153–176.

Bodnar, John. *Workers' World: Kinship, Community, and Protest in an Industrial Society, 1900–1940.* Baltimore: Johns Hopkins University Press, 1982.

——. *The Transplanted: A History of Immigrants in Urban America.* Bloomington: Indiana University Press, 1985.

Brinkley, Alan. *Voices of Protest: Huey Long, Father Coughlin, and the Great Depression.* New York: Knopf, 1982.

Brown, Judith C. *Immodest Acts: The Life of a Lesbian Nun in Renaissance Italy.* New York: Oxford University Press, 1986.

Broyard, Anatole. *Intoxicated by My Illness and Other Writings on Life and Death.* New York: Clarkson Potter, 1992.

Bukowczyk, John J. *And My Children Did Not Know Me: A History of the Polish-Americans.* Bloomington: Indiana University Press, 1987.

Burns, Jeffrey M. *American Catholics and the Family Crisis, 1930–1962: An Ideological and Organizational Response.* New York: Garland, 1988.

Buytendijk, F. J. J. *Pain: Its Modes and Functions.* Trans. Eda O'Shiel. Chicago: University of Chicago Press, 1962.

Chafe, William H. *The American Woman: Her Changing Social, Economic, and Political Roles, 1920–1970.* Oxford: Oxford University Press, 1972.

Chinnici, Joseph P., O.F.M. *Living Stones: The History and Structure of Catholic Spiritual Life in the United States.* New York: Macmillan, 1989.

Chodorow, Nancy. *The Reproduction of Mothering: Psychoanalysis and the Sociology of Gender.* Berkeley: University of California Press, 1978.

Christian, William A., Jr. *Local Religion in Sixteenth-Century Spain.* Princeton: Princeton University Press, 1981.

——. *Person and God in a Spanish Valley.* Princeton: Princeton University Press, 1989.

——. *Moving Crucifixes in Modern Spain.* Princeton: Princeton University Press, 1992.

Cinel, Dino. *From Italy to San Francisco: The Immigrant Experience.* Stanford: Stanford University Press, 1982.

Clark, Dennis. *The Irish in Philadelphia: Ten Generations of Urban Experience.* Philadelphia: Temple University Press, 1973.

Cohen, Miriam. *Workshop to Office: Two Generations of Italian Women in New York City, 1900–1950.* Ithaca, N.Y.: Cornell University Press, 1993.

Cookingham, Mary E. "Working After Childbearing in Modern America." *Journal of Interdisciplinary History* 14, no. 4 (Spring 1984): 773–792.

Cooney, John. *The American Pope: The Life and Times of Francis Cardinal Spellman.* New York: Times Books, 1984.

Coontz, Stephanie. *The Way We Never Were: American Families and the Nostalgia Trap.* New York: Basic, 1992.

Cowan, Ruth Schwartz. "Two Washes in the Morning and a Bridge Party at Night: The American Housewife Between the Wars." *Women's Studies* 3 (1976): 147–172.

Crapanzano, Vincent. *Tuhami: Portrait of a Moroccan.* Chicago: University of Chicago Press, 1980.

Daws, Gavin. *Holy Man: Father Damien of Molokai.* Honolulu: University of Hawaii Press, 1973.

Diner, Hasia R. *Erin's Daughters in America: Irish Immigrant Women in the Nineteenth Century.* Baltimore: Johns Hopkins University Press, 1983.

Doane, Mary Ann. "The Clinical Eye: Medical Discourses in the 'Woman's Film' of the 1940s." *Poetics Today* 6, no. 1–2 (1985): 205–227.

——. *The Desire to Desire: The Woman's Film of the 1940s.* Bloomington: Indiana University Press, 1987.

Dolan, Jay P. *The American Catholic Experience: A History from the Colonial Times to the Present.* Garden City, N.Y.: Doubleday, 1985.

Dubois, Ellen, Mari Jo Buhle, Temma Kaplan, Gerda Lerner, and Carroll Smith-Rosenberg. "Politics and Culture in Women's History: A Symposium." *Feminist Studies* 6, no. 1 (Spring 1980): 26–64.

Ducharme, Jacques. *The Shadows of the Trees: The Story of French-Canadians in New England.* New York: Harper & Brothers, 1943.

Eck, Diana L. *Darsan: Seeing the Divine Image in India.* Chambersburg, Pa.: Anima, 1981.

Elder, Glen H., Jr., and Jeffrey K. Liker. "Hard Times in Women's Lives: Historical Influences Across Forty Years." *American Journal of Sociology* 88 (September 1982): 241–269.

Evans, Sara M. *Born for Liberty: A History of Women in America.* New York: Free Press, 1989.

Fisher, James Terence. *The Catholic Counterculture in America, 1933–1962.* Chapel Hill: University of North Carolina Press, 1989.

Flax, Jane. *Thinking Fragments: Psychoanalysis, Feminism, and Postmodernism in the Contemporary West.* Berkeley: University of California Press, 1990.

Frank, Arthur W. *At the Will of the Body: Reflections on Illness.* Boston: Houghton Mifflin, 1991.

Gamio, Manuel. *Mexican Immigration to the United States.* New York: Arno, 1969 (orig. pub. 1930).

Geary, Patrick J. *Furta Sacra: Thefts of Relics in the Central Middle Ages.* Princeton: Princeton University Press, 1978.

Giddens, Anthony. *The Constitution of Society: Outline of the Theory of Structuration.* Berkeley: University of California Press, 1984.

Gordon, Linda. *Heroes of Their Own Lives: The Politics and History of Family Violence, Boston, 1880–1960.* New York: Viking, 1988.

Greeley, Andrew M. *The Church and the Suburbs.* New York: Sheed and Ward, 1959.

——. *Ethnicity, Denomination, and Inequality.* Beverly Hills, Calif.: Sage, 1976.

——. *The American Catholic: A Social Portrait.* New York: Basic, 1977.

Greenberg, Jay R., and Stephen A. Mitchell. *Object Relations in Psychoanalytic Theory.* Cambridge: Harvard University Press, 1983.

Gustin, Marilyn N., with Rev. Msgr. Harrold A. Murray. *The National Association of Catholic Chaplains: A Twenty-Year History, 1965–1985.* Milwaukee: National Association of Catholic Chaplains, Special Publications, 1985.

Halsey, William H. *The Survival of American Innocence: Catholicism in an Era of Disillusionment.* Notre Dame, Ind.: University of Notre Dame Press, 1980.

Harrell, David Edwin, Jr. *All Things Are Possible: The Healing and Charismatic Revivals in Modern America.* Bloomington: Indiana University Press, 1975.

Hedges, Elaine. "The 19th Century Diarist and Her Quilts." *Feminist Studies* 8, no. 2 (Summer 1982): 293–299.

Helmbold, Lois Rita. "Beyond the Family Economy: Black and White Working-Class Women During the Great Depression." *Feminist Studies* 13, no. 3 (Fall 1987): 629–655.

Hendrickson, Paul. *Seminary: A Search.* New York: Summit, 1983.

Hennesey, James, S.J. *American Catholics: A History of the Roman Catholic Community in the United States.* New York: Oxford University Press, 1981.

Holifield, E. Brooks. *A History of Pastoral Care in America: From Salvation to Self-Realization.* Nashville: Abingdon, 1983.

Huels, John M., O.S.M. *The Friday Night Novena: The Growth and Decline of the Sorrowful Mother Novena.* Berwyn, Ill.: Eastern Province of Servites, 1977.

Hughes, Judith M. *Reshaping the Psychoanalytic Domain: The Work of Melanie Klein, W. R. D. Fairbairn, and D. W. Winnicott.* Berkeley: University of California Press, 1989.

Jeansonne, Glen. *Gerald L. K. Smith: Minister of Hate.* New Haven: Yale University Press, 1988.

Jones, Anita Edgar. "Mexican Colonies in Chicago." *Social Services Review* 2, no. 4 (December 1928): 579–597.

Jones, James W. *Contemporary Psychoanalysis and Religion: Transference and Transcendence.* New Haven: Yale University Press, 1991.

Jones, Peter d'A., and Melvin G. Holli, eds. *The Ethnic Frontier: Essays in the History of Group Survival in Chicago and the Midwest.* Grand Rapids, Mich.: William B. Eerdmans, 1977.

Jones, Robert, and Louis R. Wilson. *The Mexican in Chicago.* Chicago: Chicago Congregational Union, 1931.

Kane, Paula M. *Separatism and Subculture: Boston Catholicism, 1900–1920.* Chapel Hill: University of North Carolina Press, 1994.

Kantowicz, Edward R. *Corporation Sole: Cardinal Mundelein and Chicago Catholicism.* Notre Dame, Ind.: University of Notre Dame Press, 1983.

Kaplan, Temma. "Female Consciousness and Collective Action: The Case of Barcelona, 1910–1918." *Signs* 7 (1982): 545–566.

Kelsey, Morton T. *Healing and Christianity in Ancient Thought and Modern Times.* New York: Harper & Row, 1973.

Kenneally, James K. *The History of American Catholic Women.* New York: Crossroad, 1990.

Kleinman, Arthur, M.D. *The Illness Narratives: Suffering, Healing, and the Human Condition*. New York: Basic, 1988.

Komarovsky, Mirra. *The Unemployed Man and His Family: The Effect of Unemployment Upon the Status of the Man in Fifty-Nine Families*. New York: Dryden, 1940.

——. *Blue-Collar Marriage*. New Haven: Yale University Press, 1987 (orig. pub. 1962).

Konner, Melvin, M.D. *Becoming a Doctor: A Journey of Initiation in Medical School*. New York: Viking, 1987.

Kovel, Joel. *The Age of Desire: Case Histories of a Radical Psychoanalyst*. New York: Pantheon, 1981.

Kselman, Thomas A. "Our Lady of Necedah: Marian Piety and the Cold War." *Working Papers Series*. South Bend, Ind.: Charles and Margaret Cushwa Center for the Study of American Catholicism, University of Notre Dame. Series 12, no. 2 (Fall 1982).

——. *Miracles and Prophecies in Nineteenth Century France*. New Brunswick, N.J.: Rutgers University Press, 1983.

Laplanche, J., and J.-B. Pontalis, *The Language of Psycho-Analysis*. Trans. Donald Nicholson-Smith. New York: W. W. Norton, 1973.

Lears, Jackson. *Fables of Abundance: A Cultural History of Advertising in America*. New York: Basic, 1994.

Leavitt, Judith Walzer. " 'Science' Enters the Birthing Room: Obstetrics in America Since the Eighteenth Century." *The Journal of American History* 70, no. 2 (September 1983): 281–304.

Loewald, Hans, M.D. *Psychoanalysis and the History of the Individual*. New Haven: Yale University Press, 1978.

——. *Sublimation: Inquiries into Theoretical Psychoanalysis*. New Haven: Yale University Press, 1988.

McCaffrey, Lawrence, J. *The Irish Diaspora in America*. Bloomington: Indiana University Press, 1976.

McCaffrey, Lawrence, J., Ellen Skerrett, Michael F. Funchion, and Charles Fanning. *The Irish in Chicago*. Urbana: University of Illinois Press, 1987.

McElvaine, Robert S. *The Great Depression: America, 1929–1941*. New York: Times Books, 1984.

McElvaine, Robert S., ed. *Down and Out in the Depression: Letters from the Forgotten Man*. Chapel Hill: University of North Carolina Press, 1983.

McGuire, Meredith B., with the assistance of Debra Kantor. *Ritual Healing in Suburban America*. New Brunswick, N.J.: Rutgers University Press, 1988.

Macklin, Ruth. *Mortal Choices: Bioethics in Today's World*. New York: Pantheon, 1987.

McShane, Joseph, S.J. "Mirrors and Teachers: A Study of Catholic Periodical Fiction Between 1930 and 1950." *U.S. Catholic Historian* 5 (Spring–Summer, 1987): 181–198.

Marchand, Roland. *Advertising the American Dream: Making Way for Modernity, 1920–1940*. Berkeley: University of California Press, 1985.

Meissner, W. W., S.J., M.D. *Psychoanalysis and Religious Experience*. New Haven: Yale University Press, 1984.

Milkman, Ruth. "Women's Work and Economic Crisis: Some Lessons of the Great Depression." *Review of Radical Political Economics* 8, no. 1 (Spring 1976): 73–97.

Miller, Douglas T., and Marion Nowak. *The Fifties: The Way We Really Were*. Garden City, N.Y.: Doubleday, 1977.

Miller, Kerby A. *Emigrants and Exiles: Ireland and the Irish Exodus to North America*. New York: Oxford University Press, 1985.

Miller, Randall M., and Thomas D. Marzik, eds. *Immigrants and Religion in Urban America*. Philadelphia: Temple University Press, 1977.

Mintz, Steven, and Susan Kellogg. *Domestic Revolutions: A Social History of American Family Life*. New York: Free Press, 1988.

Modleski, Tania. "The Disappearing Act: A Study of Harlequin Romances." *Signs* 5, no. 3 (Spring 1980): 435–448.

Molinari, Paul, S.J. *Saints: Their Place in the Church*. Trans. Dominic Maruca, S.J. New York: Sheed and Ward, 1965.

Mormino, Gary Ross. *Immigrants on the Hill: Italian-Americans in St. Louis, 1882–1982*. Urbana: University of Illinois Press, 1986.

Nelli, Humbert S. *Italians in Chicago, 1880–1930: A Study in Ethnic Mobility*. New York: Oxford University Press, 1970.

Nolan, Janet A. *Ourselves Alone: Women's Emigration from Ireland, 1885–1920*. Lexington: University Press of Kentucky, 1989.

Nolan, Mary Lee, and Sydney Nolan. *Christian Pilgrimage in Modern Western Europe*. Chapel Hill: University of North Carolina Press, 1989.

Obeyesekere, Gananath. *Medusa's Hair: An Essay on Personal Symbols and Religious Experience*. Chicago: University of Chicago Press, 1981.

——. *The Work of Culture: Symbolic Transformation in Psychoanalysis and Anthropology*. Chicago: University of Chicago Press, 1990.

Obidinski, Eugene Edward. "Ethnic to Status Group: A Study of Polish Americans in Buffalo." Ph.D. diss., SUNY-Buffalo, 1968.

O'Connell, Marvin R. "The Roman Catholic Tradition Since 1945," in *Caring and Curing: Health and Medicine in the Western Religious Traditions*, ed. Ronald L. Numbers and Darrel W. Amundsen, 108–145. New York: Macmillan, 1986.

O'Connor, Edward D., C.S.C. *The Pentecostal Movement in the Catholic Church*. Notre Dame, Ind.: Ave Maria Press, 1971.

Odell, Catherine M. *Father Solanus: The Story of Solanus Casey, O.F.M. Cap.* Huntington, Ind.: Our Sunday Visitor Publishing Division, 1988.

Olson, Audrey L. *St. Louis Germans, 1850–1920: The Nature of an Immigrant Community and Its Relation to the Assimilation Process.* New York: Arno, 1980.

Olson, James S. *Catholic Immigrants in America.* Chicago: Nelson-Hall, 1987.

Orsi, Robert A. *The Madonna of 115th Street: Faith and Community in Italian Harlem, 1880–1950.* New Haven: Yale University Press, 1985.

——. "The Cult of the Saints and the Reimagination of the Space and Time of Sickness in Twentieth-Century American Catholicism." In *The Cultures of Medicine,* ed. Kathryn Allen Rabuzzi and Robert W. Daly, 63–77. Baltimore: Johns Hopkins University Press, *Literature and Medicine* 8 (1989).

——. "The Fault of Memory: 'Southern Italy' in the Imagination of Immigrants and the Lives of their Children in Italian Harlem, 1920–1945." *Journal of Family History* 15, no. 2 (1990): 133–147.

——. " 'He Keeps Me Going': Women's Devotion to Saint Jude and the Dialectics of Gender in American Catholicism." In *Belief in History: Innovative Approaches to European and American Religion,* ed. Thomas Kselman, 137–169. Notre Dame, Ind.: University of Notre Dame Press, 1991.

——. "The Center Out There, In Here, and Everywhere Else: The Nature of Pilgrimage to the Shrine of Saint Jude, 1929–1965." *Journal of Social History* 25, no. 2 (Winter 1991): 213–232.

——. " 'Have You Ever Prayed to St. Jude?' Reflections on Fieldwork in Catholic Chicago." In *Reimagining Denominationalism: Interpretive Essays,* ed. Robert Bruce Mullin and Russell E. Richey, 134–161. New York: Oxford University Press, 1994.

Ostafin, Peter A. "The Polish Peasant in Transition: A Study of Group Integration as a Function of Symbiosis and Common Definitions." Ph.D. diss., University of Michigan, 1948.

O'Toole, James M. *Militant and Triumphant: William Henry O'Connell and the Catholic Church in Boston, 1859–1944.* Notre Dame, Ind.: University of Notre Dame Press, 1992.

Panichas, George A., ed. *The Simone Weil Reader.* New York: David McKay, 1977.

Parot, John Joseph. *Polish Catholics in Chicago, 1850–1920: A Religious History.* DeKalb, Ill.: Northern Illinois University Press, 1981.

Phillips, Adam. *Winnicott.* Cambridge: Harvard University Press, 1988.

Polzin, Theresita. *The Polish-Americans: Whence and Whither.* Pulaski, Wis.: Franciscan, 1973.

Pope, Barbara Corrado. "A Heroine Without Heroics: The Little Flower of Jesus and Her Times." *Church History* 57 (March 1986): 46–60.

Preston, James J. "Necessary Fictions: Healing Encounters with a North American Saint." In *The Cultures of Medicine,* ed. Kathryn Allen Rabuzzi and Robert W. Daly, 42–62. Baltimore: Johns Hopkins University Press, *Literature and Medicine* 8 (1989).

Radway, Janice A. *Reading the Romance: Women, Patriarchy, and Popular Literature.* Chapel Hill: University of North Carolina Press, 1984.

Rapp, Rayna, Ellen Ross, and Renate Bridenthal. "Examining Family History." *Feminist Studies* 5 (Spring 1979): 174–200.

Register, Cheri. *Living with Chronic Illness: Days of Patience and Passion.* New York: Free Press, 1987.

Reiser, Stanley Joel. *Medicine and the Reign of Technology.* Cambridge: Cambridge University Press, 1978.

Reisler, Mark. "The Mexican Immigrant in the Chicago Area During the 1920s." *Journal of the Illinois State Historical Society* 66 (Summer 1973): 144–158.

Rice, Eugene F., Jr. *Saint Jerome in the Renaissance.* Baltimore: Johns Hopkins University Press, 1985.

Ricoeur, Paul. "The Question of Proof in Freud's Psychoanalytic Writings." *Journal of the American Psychoanalytic Association* 25 (1977): 835–871.

Rizzuto, Ana-Maria. *The Birth of the Living God: A Psychoanalytic Study.* Chicago: University of Chicago Press, 1979.

Rosenzweig, Roy. *Eight Hours for What We Will: Workers and Leisure in an Industrial City, 1870–1920.* Cambridge: Cambridge University Press, 1983.

Ross, Ellen. "Survival Networks: Women's Neighborhood Sharing in London Before World War I." *History Workshop* 15 (Spring 1983): 4–27.

Rothman, Sheila M. *Woman's Proper Place: A History of Changing Ideals and Practices, 1870 to the Present.* New York: Basic, 1978.

Ryan, Mary P. "The Power of Women's Networks: A Case Study of Female Moral Reform in Antebellum America." *Feminist Studies* 5 (Spring 1979): 66–85.

Sandelowski, Margarete. *Pain, Pleasure, and American Childbirth: From the Twilight Sleep to the Read Method, 1914–1960.* Westport, Conn.: Greenwood, 1984.

Scarry, Elaine. *The Body in Pain: The Making and Unmaking of the World.* New York: Oxford University Press, 1985.

Scharf, Lois. *To Work and to Wed: Female Employment, Feminism, and the Great Depression.* Westport, Conn.: Greenwood, 1980.

Schatz, Ronald W. "Connecticut's Working Class in the 1950s: A Catholic Perspective." *Labor History* 25 (Winter 1984): 83–101.

Scott, Joan Wallace. *Gender and the Politics of History.* New York: Columbia University Press, 1988.

Shanabruch, Charles. *Chicago's Catholics: The Evolution of An American Identity.* Notre Dame, Ind.: University of Notre Dame Press, 1981.

Shengold, Leonard, M.D. *"The Boy Will Come to Nothing!": Freud's Ego Ideal and Freud as Ego Ideal.* New Haven: Yale University Press, 1993.

Shorter, Edward. *Bedside Manners: The Troubled History of Doctors and Patients.* New York: Simon and Schuster, 1985.

———. *From Paralysis to Fatigue: A History of Psychosomatic Illness in the Modern Era.* New York: Free Press, 1992.

Slocum, Flora, and Charlotte Ring. "Industry's Discarded Workers: A Study of 100 St. Louis Relief Families." *Sociology and Social Research* 19 (July–August 1935): 520–526.

Smith, Judith. *Family Connections: A History of Italian and Jewish Immigrant Lives in Providence, Rhode Island, 1900–1940.* Albany: State University of New York Press, 1985.

Smith-Rosenberg, Carroll. "The New Woman and the New History." *Feminist Studies* 3, no. 1–2 (Fall 1975): 5–14.

Sontag, Susan. *Illness as Metaphor.* New York: Vintage, 1979.

Starr, Paul. *The Social Transformation of American Medicine.* New York: Basic, 1982.

Stern, Daniel N. *The Interpersonal World of the Infant: A View from Psychoanalysis and Developmental Psychology.* New York: Basic, 1985.

Susman, Warren I. *Culture as History: The Transformation of American Society in the Twentieth Century.* New York: Pantheon, 1984.

Taves, Ann. *The Household of Faith: Roman Catholic Devotions in Mid-Nineteenth America.* Notre Dame, Ind.: University of Notre Dame Press, 1986.

Tentler, Leslie Woodcock. *Seasons of Grace: A History of the Catholic Archdiocese of Detroit.* Detroit: Wayne State University Press, 1990.

Therborn, Göran. *The Ideology of Power and the Power of Ideology.* London: Verso, 1980.

Thomas, John L., S.J. *The American Catholic Family.* Englewood Cliffs, N.J.: Prentice-Hall, 1956.

Turner, Victor. *Dramas, Fields, and Metaphors: Symbolic Action in Human Society.* Ithaca, N.Y.: Cornell University Press, 1974.

Vanderzee, John T. *Ministry to Persons with Chronic Illnesses: A Guide to Empowerment Through Negotiation.* Minneapolis: Augsburg, 1993.

Walker, Williston. *A History of the Christian Church.* New York: Charles Scribner's Sons, 1970 (orig. pub. 1918).

Ware, Susan. *Holding Their Own: American Women in the 1930s.* Boston: Twayne, 1982.

Watts, Jill. *God, Harlem U.S.A.: The Father Divine Story.* Berkeley: University of California Press, 1992.

Weisbrot, Robert. *Father Divine.* Boston: Beacon, 1983.

Westin, Jeane. *Making Do: How Women Survived the '30s.* Chicago: Follett, 1976.

White, Joseph, M. *The Diocesan Seminary in the United States: A History from the 1780s to the Present.* Notre Dame, Ind.: University of Notre Dame Press, 1989.

Wilson, Stephen, ed. *Saints and Their Cults: Studies in Religious Sociology, Folklore, and History.* Cambridge: Cambridge University Press, 1983.

Winnicott, D. W. *The Maturational Processes and the Facilitating Environment: Studies in the Theory of Emotional Development.* Madison, Conn.: International Universities Press, 1965.

——. *Playing and Reality.* New York: Tavistock, 1971.

——. *Babies and Their Mothers.* Reading, Mass.: Addison- Wesley, 1986.

Woodward, Kenneth L. *Making Saints: How the Catholic Church Determines Who Becomes a Saint, Who Doesn't, and Why.* New York: Simon and Schuster, 1990.

Woolston, Howard B. "Psychology of Unemployment." *Sociology and Social Research* 19 (March–April 1935): 335–340.

Wrobel, Paul. *Our Way: Family, Parish, and Neighborhood in a Polish American Community.* Notre Dame, Ind.: University of Notre Dame Press, 1979.

Yans-McLaughlin, Virgina. *Family and Community: Italian Immigrants in Buffalo, 1880–1930.* Ithaca, N.Y.: Cornell University Press, 1971.

Zimdars-Swartz, Sandra L. *Encountering Mary: From LaSalette to Medjugorje.* Princeton: Princeton University Press, 1991.

Index

American Catholic Hospital Association, 163

American Catholic men: in Great Depression, 51–54; memories of, 84; as object of women's prayers, xi, 53–58, 188, 191–192, 204–206; portrayal of their mothers by, 74, 78–80, 85–87; promotion of devotionalism for, 76; as public promoters of St. Jude devotion, xi, 22, 130, 200; small role of, in devotion of St. Jude, x, xi–xiii, 68–69, 170; women's care for sick, 68, 177; young, 80–81. *See also* fathers; gender differences; immigrants; physicians; priests

American Catholic women: bonding of, through devotion to St. Jude, xi, 44–45, 105, 119, 121–141, 167, 169–170, 181–182, 187, 190–191, 196, 200–203, 208; clerical responses to, 75–76, 106, 148–150, 161–162, 166, 184, 193; empowerment of, through encounters with St. Jude, xii, 44–45, 52, 103, 105–107, 110–111, 138–139, 168–169, 177, 178–184, 186, 187, 195, 197–201, 208; old, 74, 78–83, 86–87, 138, 166, 197–198; passivity of, in devotion to St. Jude, 186–198; pressures on daughters of immigrant, 40–44, 73–94, 102, 125, 128, 148, 186–187, 193; promotions directed toward, 16–17; role of, in devotion of St. Jude, x–xiii, 68–69, 102, 130, 200–207, 210; single, 61; spiritual support of, to sick, 166–167; widows, 47–48, 78; without children, 60; young, 74, 76–77, 80–81, 85–88, 137, 148, 166. *See also* devotionalism; gender differences; hopelessness; mothers; prayers; silence; suffering; work

American Ecclesiastical Review, xvi

Anne, Saint, ix, 136, 174

annulments, 42, 46

Anthony, Saint, ix, 104

Anthony Claret, Saint, 4, 28. *See also* Claretian Missionaries

Apostolate of the Family Rosary, 33, 91

Arizona: discovery of St. Jude in, 6–7, 24, 99

Ave Maria, xvi; on Catholic families, 91; on devotionalism, 33, 76; on sin and illness, 153–155, 166; on suffering, 89, 151, 153–157, 160; on women's apparel, 80–81; on women's roles, 70–74, 77, 84–86

Baker, Father Joseph, 28

"Balaird, Marcy" (fictional woman), 70–73, 88, 93, 193

Bea (Shrine employee), x–xi, xii, 230 n. 13

Bernadette, Saint, 18, 28

Bird Memorial Center (Chicago), 3

birth control, 9, 85

Bishop, Jim, 86, 87

Black Madonna of Czestochowa, 27

Blaise, Saint, 104

Blanshard, Paul, 221 n. 32

Bodnar, John, 83

Bowery Boys, 80

Bridget of Sweden, Saint, ix, 99

Burns, Robert E., 223 n. 41

Cabrini, Mother, 7, 8

Capra, Frank, 101

Carmelites, 8, 15, 29

Catalina, Father Anthony, 21

Catholic culture. *See* American Catholic culture

Catholic Knights of America, 6

Catholic Order of Foresters, 6

Catholic Press Association, xvii

Catholic Union of the Sick in America (CUSA), 153, 156, 158

Catholic Women's World, 153

Catholic World, xvi, 164

Catholic Youth Organization, 80

Chicago: industrialism of, 1; no specific tie to St. Jude in, 28; St. Jude as patron of police in, xi, xii, 9, 22. *See also* immi-

grants; National Shrine of St. Jude;
neighborhoods
childbearing: changes in, 58–60, 66, 199;
post–World War II increase in rate of,
49, 59, 60, 63, 66; use of St. Jude in,
199–200; women's fears about, 59, 62,
138. *See also* pregnancy
child care, 56, 64, 138
Chile, 7
Christian, William, Jr., 31, 224 n. 48
Christopher, Saint, 17, 38
Clara: family of, 176, 204, 206–208; as immigrants' daughter, xiv–xv, 66, 73; on
St. Jude, 95–96, 103, 104, 108, 110, 111,
113, 114, 179, 198, 207–208, 215 n. 7,
269 n. 36
Claretian Missionaries: competition
among, 22–25; and devotion of St.
Jude, x, 8, 19, 21, 37, 187, 214 n. 1; and
Mission of Nuestra Señora de
Guadalupe, 4–7; seminary of (Mo-
mence, Illinois), xii, 9, 19, 28
Cleophas (Jude Thaddeus's father), 98
communism, 9, 90
Coughlin, Father Charles E., 20, 220 n. 29
Council of Trent, 26, 163
courtship, 44–46
Crosby, Bing, 92
cult(s): defined, x; of St. Jude, 19–22, 114–
116, 187–188, gender differences in, x–
xiii, 76, 165, 186–187; of saints, 17–18,
112–114, 193–194. *See also* devotionalism; *names of specific saints*
CUSA (Catholic Union of the Sick in
America), 153, 156, 158

DeLee, Joseph, 60
DePrada, Joachim, 34–35, 76
devotionalism: in Catholic culture, 14–18,
31–32, 76, 92–94, 203–204; and Catholic family romance, 83–86; clerical
fears of popular, 32–38, 94, 163, 209,

211; criticism of, 21, 32–38, 112, 114, 193–
197, 202, 221 n. 32; disciplinary strategies of, against women, 73–78, 84, 86–
88, 92–94, 187; gendered roles in, x–
xiii, 76, 165, 186–187; local *vs.* national,
22–28; material culture of, 26–27, 97;
and medicine, 148–150; as practice of
relationships, 203; as revenue source
for Catholic church, 15–17, 37; Vatican
II and, 32–35, 37, 76, 193. *See also* American Catholic women; cult(s); Jude
Thaddeus, Saint of Hopeless Causes;
prayers; suffering
diagnosis, 146–147, 149. *See also* illness;
physicians
Divine, Father, 101
divorce, xii, xiii, 46, 91, 204
Doane, Mary Ann, 149
Dolan, Jay, 13, 30
domestic abuse, 88–89, 230 n. 13
Dominic, Saint, 76
Donovan, Father Joseph P., 16–18
Dooley, Thomas, 151, 158

ethnicity, changing meanings of in 1920s,
30–31
Extreme Unction (last rites), 162, 163, 181

Family Rosary Crusade, 33, 91
fathers, 83; in Catholic family romance,
79, 82, 85
Filan, Jerry, 157, 165, 183
Fisher, James Terrence, 159

Garcia, Michael, 3
Garesché, Father Edward, 166
Geertz, Clifford, 92
Gemma Galgani, Saint, 155
gender differences: Catholic officials on,
89–90; in culture of consumption, 73;
in experiences of history, 50–51; in
family conflict, 40–41, 80; in medical

advertising of name of, by devout, 32, 121–124, 225 n. 54, 244 n. 45; ambiguities of, 200–201, 209–211; devotion of, ix, 4–9, 19–22, 31–32, 38–39, 114–116, 121–126, 183–184, 187–208; gender differences in, x–xiii, 76, 165, 186–187; ecumenicalism associated with, 29, 98, 171; fear of, 116–118, 209; historical knowledge about, 98–100, 104; as intercessor, 34–35, 136; and Judas, 99–100, 106, 116, 117, 119, 121, 197; as a man, 106–107, 117–118, 187, 197; material culture associated with, 19, 37, 38, 44, 94, 97, 112, 117, 128–130, 143, 167–168, 172–173, 181, 196, 211, 260 n. 88; miracles associated with, 8, 142, 179; national interest in, 28–29, 31; physical appearance of, 96–98, 129, 186, 195; popularity of, in America, ix; refusal of, to help, 207–209; research methods for study of devotion of, xiii–xv; women's corporal experience of, 111–112, 167–168, 177, 196; women's empowerment through encounters with, xii, 44–45, 52, 103, 105–107, 110–111, 138–139, 168–169, 177, 178–184, 186, 187, 195, 197–201, 208; women's imagining of, 94–118, 200, 202; women's storytelling about, xv, 121–126, 134, 168, 187. See also American Catholic men; American Catholic women; hopelessness; League of St. Jude; National Shrine of St. Jude; prayers; statues of St. Jude; Voice of St. Jude

Judy, 207; on church and shrine, 24; on economic depression, 48–49, 189, 198; on prayers to St. Jude, 61; on St. Jude's likeness, 97, 107; on St. Jude's presence, 110–111, 168–169

Kane, Paula, 75
Kathy, xiv–xv, 69, 111, 189

Kleinman, Arthur, 148, 174, 183–184
Knights of Columbus, 5, 67
Knights of St. Gregory, 5, 6
Korean War, 58, 195
Kovel, Joel, 211

Ladies Home Journal, 60
LaGuardia, Fiorello, 30
last rites (Extreme Unction), 162, 163, 181
League of St. Dymphna, 15
League of St. Jude, 9, 16, 19, 21, 22–23, 102, 180; Police Branch of, xi, xii, 9, 22
Leavitt, Judith Walzer, 58–60, 199
leprosy. *See* Hansen's disease
letters. *See* National Shrine of St. Jude: women's letters to
Liguori, Alphonse, 75, 80
Little Flower of Jesus. *See* Thérèse of Lisieux, Saint
Lone Ranger, 101
Long, Huey, 101
Lourdes, 152, 157, 186; grotto, American reproductions of, 15, 27, 28, 225 n. 53
Luke, Saint, 149

McDonald, Rose, 7, 108
McElvaine, Robert, 20, 50
MacEoin, Gary, 33
McShane, Joseph, 79
Madonna of Montevergine, 27
magazines, for Catholic families, x, xvi–xvii, 70–74, 90–92, 102. *See also specific titles*
Maloney, Father James, 35–38, 57
Marguerite, Sister, 119, 121
marriage: choices about partners for, 12–13, 42, 45, 74, 205–206; discord in: after World War II, 57; among children of immigrants, 14, 42; and domestic abuse, 88–89, 230 n. 13; during Great Depression, 52; staying married in spite of, 79, 192; use of St. Jude for help with,

St. Vincent de Paul Society, xii
St. Vincent's Hospital (New York), 167
Sanderlin, George, 79, 90, 91
Scarry, Elaine, 135, 175, 176
Scott, Martin, 73
seminary culture. *See* priests
Sharkey, Don, 81
Sheehan, Father Robert, 89–90
Sheen, Fulton J., xvi, 79, 82, 87
Shorter, Edward, 146, 147, 251 n. 2
Shrine of Our Lady of Victory (Lacka-
wanna, New York), 28
Shrine of St. Anne de Beaupre, 164
Shrine of St. Anthony of Padua (Cincin-
nati), 15–16, 29
Shrine of St. Jude. *See* National Shrine of
St. Jude
Shrine of the North American Martyrs
(Auriesville, New York), 16
"shut-ins," American Catholic cult of, 153,
156, 157
The Sign, 73, 82, 152
silence: as betrayal of St. Jude, 123–124; of
doctors and priests, 150, 160–162; heal-
ing aspects of breaking, 134–141, 173–
177, 184, 204–206, 210; suffering in, 88–
91, 124–125, 150–161, 175. *See also* narra-
tives; prayers
sin: and sickness, 153–155, 166, 183
Smith, Judith, 13
Sorin, Edward, 29
Sorrowful Mother. *See* Mary (mother of
Jesus)
South Chicago. *See* Chicago
Spellman, Francis Cardinal, 30
Starr, Paul, 145, 146, 179
statues of St. Jude, 175; in cars, 61, 95–96,
111; likeness on, 102–103, 107–108; in
Shrine, 7–8, 108; sold by Shrine, 38,
140; symbolism of, 205, 211; in women's
homes, 44, 47, 110–111
Stern, Daniel N., 266 n. 23

suburbs, 12–14, 30, 43, 64, 83, 90
suffering: Catholic attitudes toward, 86–
88, 144, 150–165, 183, 190; in devotional
advertising, 17; gender differences in,
69, 87–92, 165. *See also* childbearing;
illness
Superman, 101
Susman, Warren, 29, 101

Taigi, Anna Maria, 72, 73, 87, 88, 93, 193
Tansey, Anne, 77–78
"Thank you, St. Jude" notices, 32, 121,
225 n. 54, 244 n. 45
theodicy, 207–209
Therborn, Göran, 210, 239 n. 35
Thérèse of Lisieux, Saint (Little Flower of
Jesus), 5, 7–8, 15, 29, 35, 104, 136
Thomas, Danny, x, 25, 62
Thomas, John L., 42, 229 n. 5
Tort, James, 35; as founder of American
devotion to St. Jude, 4–9, 18–19, 24, 28,
99; fund-raising skills of, 17, 18–19, 31;
personal devotion of, to St. Jude, 6–7,
18; resignation of, 21
Turner, Victor, 141

unemployment. *See* Great Depression
U.S. Catholic, 37. See also *Voice of St. Jude*
University of Chicago Settlement House,
3
University of Notre Dame, 28, 29

Vatican II Council (1962–1965): and devotionalism, 32–35, 37, 76, 193; on Mariology, 81
Vietnam War, 57–58, 207
vigil lights, 38, 135; at National Shrine after Vatican II, 35–36, 227 n. 70
Virgin Mary. *See* Mary (mother of Jesus)
Voice of St. Jude, xvi, 19, 22, 79, 119, 125;
advertising in, 16–17, 143; description
of, 9; on illness, 154, 168–169; men por-

trayed in, x; petitionary prayers in, 37;
photos in, 24; physicians in, 149–150;
women's letters to, xii, xiii, 9, 106, 123,
134–135, 192; on women's roles, 73, 74,
77–78, 88–90; on women's work, 63,
64; on World War II, 54

Weil, Simone, 144
widows, 47–48, 78
Wilson, Stephen, 163
Winnicott, D. W., 203, 266 n. 23
The Woman Shall Conquer (Sharkey), 81
women. *See* American Catholic women
work: authorities' opposition to women's,
54, 56, 63, 66, 85; decisions about, 12;
emotional, of women, 53–54, 56, 189–
190; men's, 41, 51, 52, 54, 68; use of St.
Jude for help with women's, 201–202;
women's, 41, 49, 51–52, 54, 56, 58–59,
62–64, 66, 138, 202

World War I, 11–12, 45, 156
World War II: and devotion to St. Jude,
20–21, 49; effects of, on immigrants'
daughters, 43, 54–58; increased birth
rates after, 49, 59, 60, 63, 66; and National Shrine of St. Jude, 21, 54
Wrobel, Paul, 128

Praise for **Thank You, St. Jude**
Women's Devotion to the Patron Saint of Hopeless Causes
Robert A. Orsi

"This book will be of interest to all who are concerned with the influence of religious faith and practice on the lives of 'ordinary' women."
—*Faith and Freedom*

"Jude is still an important figure for a portion of present-day Catholics and surely an essential one for understanding the recent Catholic past. Robert Orsi's splendid book, which is far more complex and subtle in its argument than a brief review can suggest, helps to open that recent past to our understanding and, ultimately, our appreciation."
—Leslie Woodcock Tentler, *Catholic Historical Review*

"[An] engaging social history. . . . Orsi's book takes a fascinating and compelling look at American culture and religious history."
—*Publishers Weekly*

"The voices of Jude's devout female followers ring through in Orsi's narrative, and, together with Orsi's own measured observations, they leave us with a far richer understanding of the relationship between piety and the cultivation of female agency and identities. In this engaging and accessible volume, Orsi has raised questions that will occupy students and scholars in American history, women's history, and religious studies for years to come."
—*Choice*

Related titles available from Yale University Press

The Madonna of 115th Street
Faith and Community in Italian Harlem, 1880–1950
Robert A. Orsi

The Sacred Remains
American Attitudes Toward Death, 1799–1883
Gary Laderman

Material Christianity
Religion and Popular Culture in America
Colleen McDannell

The Democratization of American Christianity
Nathan O. Hatch

A Religious History of the American People
Sydney E. Ahlstrom

The Shaker Experience in America
A History of the United Society of Believers
Stephen J. Stein